ITALIAN
Verbs

Second Edition

Vincent Luciani
Professor Emeritus of Romance Languages
The City College, City University of New York

John Colaneri
Professor of Modern Foreign Languages
Iona College, New Rochelle, New York

BARRON'S

BARRON'S EDUCATIONAL SERIES, INC.

All inquiries should be addressed to:
Barron's Educational Series, Inc.
250 Wireless Boulevard
Hauppauge, New York 11788
http://www.barronseduc.com

International Standard Book Number 0-7641-2063-8

Library of Congress Cataloging-in-Publication Data

Luciani, Vincent, 1906–
     Italian verbs / Vincent Luciani, John Colaneri.
         p.   cm.
     Includes index.
     ISBN 0-7641-2063-8
     1. Italian language—Verb.   I. Colaneri, John,
1930–   II. Title.
PC1271 .L84   2002
458.2′421—dc21   2002016322

PRINTED IN CHINA
9 8 7

Contents

Foreword

Italian Verbs, a handy reference guide for students, businesspeople, and travelers, presents the fully conjugated forms of over 300 commonly used Italian verbs.

The Verbs are arranged alphabetically, one to a page. *On one single page, you will find all verb forms in all tenses.* The subject pronouns have been omitted, as they usually are in conversation, in order to emphasize the verb forms. Feminine forms of verbs conjugated with **èssere** have also been omitted. The first three forms before the semicolon are the first, second, and third persons of the singular. The three forms after the semicolon are the plural forms.

At the bottom of each verb page, you will find sample sentences or idiomatic expressions using forms of the verb.

The introduction includes an explanation of the accents used in the book, general rules regarding irregular verbs, verbs conjugated with avere or essere, models for three regular conjugations, orthographical changes, Italian verb tenses with their English equivalents, a sample English verb conjugation, and an explanation of Italian subject pronouns.

The verb charts are followed by three indexes: an English-Italian verb index, one of irregular verb forms with corresponding infinitives given, and one with over 1,000 verbs conjugated like the model verbs contained in this book.

This book should be helpful to learners of Italian at all levels.

John Colaneri

Accents

Italian has seven vowels, *a*, *i*, *u*, open *e* and *o*, close *e* and *o*. As a rule Italian words bear no accent except on the final vowel. In many contemporary editions an acute accent, (´), is used on final *i*, *u*, and close *e*, and a grave accent, (`), is used on final *a*, *o*, and open *e*. In this text words stressed on the antepenult bear an acute accent on the vowel of that syllable when it is *i*, *u*, close *e*, and close *o*, a grave accent when it is *a*, open *e*, and open *o*. Words stressed on the penult bear a grave accent on the vowel of that syllable if it is an open *e* or open *o* (if there is none, the *e*'s and *o*'s are close). No accent is used in other cases unless the penult is followed by an unstressed *io*. We have adhered to Florentine instead of Roman usage.

General Rules

Except for *dare*, *èssere*, and *stare*, the Past Absolute of irregular verbs is only irregular in the first and third person singular and the third person plural. The other forms are regular, but one must note that *bere*, *condurre*, *dire*, *fare*, *porre*, *trarre* and their compounds are based, except for the Future and the Present Conditional, on the old infinitives *bevere*, *conducere*, *dicere*, *facere*, *ponere*, and *traere*. If one bears this in mind (along with the reservation for *dare*, *èssere*, and *stare*), the Imperfect Indicative and Subjunctive are regular. The endings for the Future and the Present Conditional are always the same, in both regular and irregular verbs. Very often the first person singular and the third person plural of the Present Indicative have the same stem, which forms the first, second, third person singular and the third person plural of the Present Subjunctive.

Verbs Conjugated with Avere or Essere

1. Italian verbs are conjugated with *avere* to form the compound tenses when they are transitive (that is, when they have a direct object).
2. Reflexive verbs, such as *alzarsi*, are conjugated with *èssere*.
3. Impersonal verbs are conjugated with *èssere*, but *fare* is conjugated with *avere*, and the verbs denoting atmospheric conditions may be conjugated with *avere*: for example, *è nevicato*, *ha nevicato*.
4. Some verbs—for instance, *córrere*, *saltare*, and *volare*—are conjugated with *avere* when referring to an action and with *èssere* when referring to the goal of the action.
5. Some verbs, such as *cominciare*, *durare*, and *finire*, take *avere* when an object is expressed or implied and *èssere* when used passively with no object.
6. Some verbs, like *mancare*, have a different meaning according to which auxiliary is used, *avere* or *èssere*. *Ha mancato* means *he failed*, or *he lacked*; *è mancato* means *he missed*, or *he was not present*.
7. Some verbs, like *appartenere*, *dolere*, and *vívere*, are used indifferently with *avere* or *èssere* when they have no object.
8. Some verbs of motion, or limit of motion, as well as others are commonly conjugated with *èssere*. Here is a list of the most common of such verbs:

andare	*to go*
apparire	*to appear*
arrivare	*to arrive*
cadere	*to fall*
capitare	*to happen* (both pers. and impers.)
comparire	*to appear*
costare	*to cost*
créscere	*to grow*
dipèndere	*to depend*
dispiacere	*to displease, to regret*
divenire (diventare)	*to become*
emèrgere	*to emerge*
entrare	*to enter*
esístere	*to exist*
èssere	*to be*
fuggire	*to flee*
giúngere	*to arrive*
montare	*to mount*
morire	*to die*
nàscere	*to be born*
parere	*to appear, to seem*
partire	*to leave*
perire	*to perish*
piacere	*to please, to like*
restare (rimanere)	*to remain, to stay*
rincréscere	*to be sorry, to regret*
ritornare (tornare)	*to go or come back, to return*
riuscire	*to succeed, to go or come out again*
salire	*to go or come up*
scappare	*to escape*
scéndere	*to go or come down*
scomparire	*to disappear*
scoppiare	*to burst, to "croak"*
sórgere	*to rise*
sparire	*to disappear*
stare	*to stay*
succèdere	*to succeed, to come after*
uscire	*to go or come out*
venire (*and most of its compounds*)	*to come*

Regular Conjugations

Regular verbs are divided into three conjugations, according to whether the present infinitive ends in -are, -ere, or -ire. The -ire verbs, moreover, are of two types: those few in which the endings are added directly to the stem (they are *avvertire*, *bollire*, *convertire*, *cucire*, *divertirsi*, *dormire*, *fuggire*, *partire*, *pentirsi*, *seguire*, *sentire*, *servire*, *vestire*, as well as the irregular *aprire*, *coprire*, *offrire*, *scoprire*, *soffrire*) and those (most of them) that insert an -isc between the stem and the ending in the first, second, and third person singular and third person plural forms of the present indicative, imperative, and subjunctive tenses. There are no principal parts in Italian. The verbs of the three conjugations (for the third we use an -isc verb) are inflected in the same way as the following models:

	I	II	III
Infinitive:	portare	crédere	finire
Past Infinitive:	avere portato	avere creduto	avere finito
Present Participle:	portante	credènte	finènte (*rare*)
Past Participle:	portato	creduto	finito
Gerund:	portando	credèndo	finèndo
Past Gerund:	avendo portato	avèndo creduto	avèndo finito
Stem:	port—	cred—	fin—

Indicative Mood

Present:	pòrto	credo	finisco
	pòrti	credi	finisci
	pòrta	crede	finisce
	portiamo	crediamo	finiamo
	portate	credete	finite
	pòrtano	crédono	finíscono
Imperfect:	portavo	credevo	finivo
	portavi	credevi	finivi
	portava	credeva	finiva
	portavamo	credevamo	finivamo
	portavate	credevate	finivate
	poràvano	credévano	finívano
Past Absolute:	portai	credei	finii
	portasti	credesti	finisti

	I	II	III
	portò	credé	finí
	portammo	credemmo	finimmo
	portaste	credeste	finiste
	portàrono	credérono*	finírono
Future:	porterò	crederò	finirò
	porterai	crederai	finirai
	porterà	crederà	finirà
	porteremo	crederemo	finiremo
	porterete	crederete	finirete
	porteranno	crederanno	finiranno
Present Conditional:	porterèi	crederèi	finirèi
	porteresti	crederesti	finiresti
	porterèbbe	crederèbbe	finirèbbe
	porteremmo	crederemmo	finiremmo
	portereste	credereste	finireste
	porterèbbero	crederèbbero	finirèbbero
Imperative Mood:	pòrta	credi	finisci
	(non portare)	(non crédere)	(non finire)
	pòrti	creda	finisca
	portiamo	crediamo	finiamo
	portate	credete	finite
	pòrtino	crédano	finíscano

Subjunctive Mood

Present:	che io pòrti	creda	finisca
	che tu pòrti	creda	finisca
	che egli	creda	finisca
	(lui) pòrti		
	che portiamo	crediamo	finiamo
	che portiate	crediate	finiate
	che pòrtino	crédano	finíscano
Imperfect:	che io portassi	credessi	finissi
	che tu portassi	credessi	finissi
	che portasse	credesse	finisse

* Many regular verbs like *crèdere* may also have the endings *-ètti*, *-esti*, *-ètte*, *-emmo*, *-este*, *-èttero* in the Past Absolute.

	I	II	III
	che portàssimo	credéssimo	finìssimo
	che portaste	credeste	finiste
	che portàssero	credéssero	finìssero

Compound Tenses

Compound tenses are formed from the past participle of the principal verb together with a simple tense of the auxiliary verb *avere* in some cases and of *èssere* in others. They are inflected like the following models:

Present Perfect:

ho portato	**sono** partito (a)
hai portato	**sèi** partito (a)
ha portato	**è** partito (a)
abbiamo portato	**siamo** partiti (e)
avete portato	**sièste** partiti (e)
hanno portato	**sono** partiti (e)

Past Perfect:

avevo portato	**èro** partito (a)
avevi portato	**èri** partito (a)
aveva portato	**èra** partito (a)
avevàmo portato	**eravamo** partiti (e)
avevate portato	**eravate** partiti (e)
avévano portato	**èrano** partiti (e)

Past Anterior:
(2d Past Perfect)

èbbi portato	**fui** partito (a)
avesti portato	**fosti** partito (a)
èbbe portato	**fu** partito (a)
avemmo portato	**fummo** partiti (e)
aveste portato	**foste** partiti (e)
èbbero portato	**fúrono** partito (e)

Future Perfect:
(Future Anterior)

avrò portato	**sarò** partito (a)
avrai portato	**sarai** partito (a)
avrà portato	**sarà** partito (a)
avremo portato	**saremo** partiti (e)
avrete portato	**sarete** partiti (e)
avranno portato	**saranno** partiti (e)

Past Conditional:	avrèi portato	sarèi partito (a)
	avresti portato	saresti partito (a)
	avrèbbe portato	sarèbbe partito (a)
	avremmo portato	saremmo partiti (a)
	avreste portato	sareste partiti (e)
	avrèbbero portato	sarèbbero partiti (e)

Past Subjunctive:	àbbia portato	sia partito (a)
	àbbia portato	sia partito (a)
	àbbia portato	sia partito (a)
	abbiamo portato	siamo partiti (e)
	abbiate portato	siate partiti (e)
	àbbiano portato	síano partiti (e)

Past Perfect Subjunctive:	avessi portato	fossi partito (a)
	avessi portato	fossi partito (a)
	avesse portato	fosse partito (a)
	avéssimo portato	fóssimo partiti (e)
	aveste portato	foste partiti (e)
	avéssero portato	fóssero partiti (e)

NOTE: Due to space limitations, in some cases the past participle has been omitted, as in the following example: avrò, avrai, avrà, avremo, avrete, avranno raccomandato. Remember that the past participle must be added after *each* auxilliary verb.

Orthographical Changes

Verbs in -*care* and -*gare* require the guttural or hard sound of *c* and *g* throughout their conjugation, and hence an *h* is placed after *c* or *g* before an *i* or *e*. Verbs in -*ciare* and -*giare* preserve the palatal or soft sound of *c* and *g* throughout their conjugation and therefore retain the *i* except when it precedes another *i* or an *e*. Verbs in -*sciare* preserve the *sh* sound throughout their conjugation and therefore keep the *i* except when it precedes another *e* or *i*. Other verbs in -*iare* always retain the *i*, but they drop it if it is atonic (there is only one *i*) and keep it if it is stressed (except before -*iamo* and -*iate*). There are no orthographical changes in the second and third conjugations.

Verb Tenses

Italian	English
Presènte Indicativo	Present Indicative
Imperfètto Indicativo	Imperfect Indicative (Past Descriptive)
Passato Remòto	Past Absolute (Simple Past)
Futuro	Future
Condizionale Presènte	Present Conditional
Presènte Congiuntivo	Present Subjunctive
Imperfètto Congiuntivo	Imperfect Subjunctive
Passato Pròssimo	Present Perfect
Trapassato Pròssimo	Past Perfect (1st Past Perfect)
Trapassato Remòto	Past Anterior (2nd Past Perfect)
Futuro Anteriore	Future Perfect (Future Anterior)
Condizionale Passato	Past Conditional
Passato Congiuntivo	Past Subjunctive
Trapassato Congiuntivo	Past Perfect Subjunctive
Imperativo	Imperative

Sample English Verb Conjugation

INFINITIVE	*to see*—vedcre
PRESENT PARTICIPLE	seeing
PAST PARTICIPLE	seen
Present Indicative	I see, you see, he (she, it) sees; we see, you see, they see
	or: (the emphatic form) I do see, you do see, he (she, it) does see; we do see, you do see, they do see
	or: (the progressive form, which also exists in Italian with *stare* and other verbs) I am seeing, you are seeing, he (she, it) is seeing; we are seeing, you are seeing, they are seeing
Past	I saw, you saw, he (she, it) saw; we saw, you saw, they saw
	or: I did see, you did see, he (she, it) did see; we did see, you did see, they did see

	or: I was seeing, you were seeing, he (she, it) was seeing; we were seeing, you were seeing, they were seeing
Future	I shall see, you will see, he (she, it) will see; we shall see, you will see, they will see
Present Perfect	I have seen, you have seen, he (she, it) has seen; we have seen, you have seen, they have seen
Past Perfect	I had seen, you had seen, he (she, it) had seen; we had seen, you had seen, they had seen
Future Perfect	I shall have seen, you will have seen, he (she, it) will have seen; we shall have seen, you will have seen, they will have seen
Imperative	see, let us see, see

The *Imperfect* and the *Conditional* do not exist in English; the first is translated by *I was seeing* (*Past Progressive*) or by *I used to see* or *I would see*; the second by *I should see, you would see, etc.* As for the *Subjunctive*, its tenses are the same as the *Indicative's* (*Present, Past, Future, Present Perfect, Past Perfect, Future Perfect*) and, except for *to be*, are substantially the same. The *Subjunctive* differs from the *Indicative* only in the third person singular of the present tense, where it has no final *s*.

Subject Pronouns

1. The subject pronouns for all verb forms on the following pages have been omitted in order to emphasize the verb forms, which is what this book is all about.

2. The subject pronouns that have been omitted are as follows:

singular	*plural*
io	noi
tu	voi
lui, lei, Lei,	loro, Loro,
egli, ella	essi, esse

3. When you use a verb form in the Imperative (Command) you do not use the subject pronoun with it, as is also done in English. Example: **Parlate!** *Speak!* If you use a reflexive verb in the Imperative, drop the subject pronoun but keep the reflexive pronoun. Example: **Lavatevi!** *Wash yourself!*

to lower, to pull down, to let down

The Seven Simple Tenses		The Seven Compound Tenses	
Singular	Plural	Singular	Plural
1 present indicative		8 present perfect	
abbasso	**abbassiamo**	**ho abbassato**	**abbiamo abbassato**
abbassi	**abbassate**	**hai abbassato**	**avete abbassato**
abbassa	**abbassano**	**ha abbassato**	**hanno abbassato**
2 imperfect indicative		9 past perfect	
abbassavo	**abbassavamo**	**avevo abbassato**	**avevamo abbassato**
abbassavi	**abbassavate**	**avevi abbassato**	**avevate abbassato**
abbassava	**abbassàvano**	**aveva abbassato**	**avévano abbassato**
3 past absolute		10 past anterior	
abbassai	**abbassammo**	**èbbi abbassato**	**avemmo abbassato**
abbassasti	**abbassaste**	**avesti abassato**	**aveste abbassato**
abbassò	**abbassàrono**	**èbbe abbassato**	**èbbero abbassato**
4 future indicative		11 future perfect	
abbasserò	**abbasseremo**	**avrò abbassato**	**avremo abbassato**
abbasserai	**abbasserete**	**avrai abbassato**	**avrete abbassato**
abbasserà	**abbasseranno**	**avrà abbassato**	**avranno abbassato**
5 present conditional		12 past conditional	
abbasserèi	**abbasseremmo**	**avrèi abbassato**	**avremmo abbassato**
abbasseresti	**abbassereste**	**avresti abbassato**	**avreste abbassato**
abbasserèbbe	**abbasserèbbero**	**avrèbbe abbassato**	**avrèbbero abbassato**
6 present subjunctive		13 past subjunctive	
abbassi	**abbassiamo**	**àbbia abbassato**	**abbiamo abbassato**
abbassi	**abbassiate**	**àbbia abbassato**	**abbiate abbassato**
abbassi	**abbàssino**	**àbbia abbassato**	**àbbiano abbassato**
7 imperfect subjunctive		14 past perfect subjunctive	
abbassassi	**abbassàssimo**	**avessi abbassato**	**avéssimo abbassato**
abbassassi	**abbassaste**	**avessi abbassato**	**aveste abbassato**
abbassasse	**abbassàssero**	**avesse abbassato**	**avéssero abbassato**

imperative

—	**abbassiamo**
abbassa (non abbassare)	**abbassate**
abbassi	**abbàssino**

Words related to this verb
abbassare gli occhi   to lower one's eyes
abbassare la voce   to lower one's voice
abbassare i prezzi   to lower one's prices

1

abitare	Ger. **abitando**	Past Part. **abitato**

to live

The Seven Simple Tenses		The Seven Compound Tenses	
Singular	Plural	Singular	Plural
1 present indicative		8 present perfect	
àbito	**abitiamo**	**ho abitato**	**abbiamo abitato**
àbiti	**abitate**	**hai abitato**	**avete abitato**
àbita	**àbitano**	**ha abitato**	**hanno abitato**
2 imperfect indicative		9 past perfect	
abitavo	**abitavamo**	**avevo abitato**	**avevamo abitato**
abitavi	**abitavate**	**avevi abitato**	**avevate abitato**
abitava	**abitàvano**	**aveva abitato**	**avévano abitato**
3 past absolute		10 past anterior	
abitai	**abitammo**	**èbbi abitato**	**avemmo abitato**
abitasti	**abitaste**	**avesti abitato**	**aveste abitato**
abitò	**abitàrono**	**èbbe abitato**	**èbbero abitato**
4 future indicative		11 future perfect	
abiterò	**abiteremo**	**avrò abitato**	**avremo abitato**
abiterai	**abiterete**	**avrai abitato**	**avrete abitato**
abiterà	**abiteranno**	**avrà abitato**	**avranno abitato**
5 present conditional		12 past conditional	
abiterèi	**abiteremmo**	**avrèi abitato**	**avremmo abitato**
abiteresti	**abitereste**	**avresti abitato**	**avreste abitato**
abiterèbbe	**abiterèbbero**	**avrèbbe abitato**	**avrèbbero abitato**
6 present subjunctive		13 past subjunctive	
àbiti	**abitiamo**	**àbbia abitato**	**abbiamo abitato**
àbiti	**abitiate**	**àbbia abitato**	**abbiate abitato**
àbiti	**àbitino**	**àbbia abbitato**	**àbbiano abitato**
7 imperfect subjunctive		14 past perfect subjunctive	
abitassi	**abitàssimo**	**avessi abitato**	**avéssimo abitato**
abitassi	**abitaste**	**avessi abitato**	**aveste abitato**
abitasse	**abitàssero**	**avesse abitato**	**avéssero abitato**

	imperative	
—		**abitiamo**
àbita (non abitare)		**abitate**
àbiti		**àbitino**

Words related to this verb
Io abito a New York.   I live in New York.
Marco abita alla periferia di Torino.   Mark lives in the suburbs of Turin.

Ger. **accadéndo** Past Part. **accaduto** **accadere**

to happen, to occur

The Seven Simple Tenses		The Seven Compound Tenses	
Singular	Plural	Singular	Plural
1 present indicative		8 present perfect	
accade	**accàdono**	**è accaduto**	**sono accaduti**
2 imperfect indicative		9 past perfect	
accadeva	**accadévano**	**èra accaduto**	**èrano accaduti**
3 past absolute		10 past anterior	
accadde	**accàddero**	**fu accaduto**	**fúrono accaduti**
4 future indicative		11 future perfect	
accadrà	**accadranno**	**sarà accaduto**	**saranno accaduti**
5 present conditional		12 past conditional	
accadrèbbe	**accaddrèbbero**	**sarèbbe accaduto**	**sarèbbero accaduti**
6 present subjunctive		13 past subjunctive	
accada	**accàdano**	**sia accaduto**	**síano accaduti**
7 imperfect subjunctive		14 past perfect subjunctive	
accadesse	**accadéssero**	**fosse accaduto**	**fóssero accaduti**
		imperative	

Words related to this verb
È accaduto a casa di Maria. It happened at Mary's house.
É accaduto un incidente. An accident happened.

3

accèndere	Ger. accendéndo	Past Part. acceso

to light, to kindle

The Seven Simple Tenses		The Seven Compound Tenses	
Singular	Plural	Singular	Plural
1 present indicative		**8 present perfect**	
accèndo	accendiamo	ho acceso	abbiamo acceso
accèndi	accendete	hai acceso	avete acceso
accènde	accèndono	ha acceso	hanno acceso
2 imperfect indicative		**9 past perfect**	
accendevo	accendevamo	avevo acceso	avevamo acceso
accendevi	accendevate	avevi acceso	avevate acceso
accendeva	accendévano	aveva acceso	avévano acceso
3 past absolute		**10 past anterior**	
accesi	accendemmo	èbbi acceso	avemmo acceso
accendesti	accendeste	avesti acceso	aveste acceso
accese	accésero	èbbe acceso	èbbero acceso
4 future indicative		**11 future perfect**	
accenderò	accenderemo	avrò acceso	avremo acceso
accenderai	accenderete	avrai acceso	avrete acceso
accenderà	accenderanno	avrà acceso	avranno acceso
5 present conditional		**12 past conditional**	
accenderèi	accenderemmo	avrèi acceso	avremmo acceso
accenderesti	accendereste	avresti acceso	avreste acceso
accenderèbbe	accenderèbbero	avrèbbe acceso	avrèbbero acceso
6 present subjunctive		**13 past subjunctive**	
accènda	accendiamo	àbbia acceso	abbiamo acceso
accènda	accendiate	àbbia acceso	abbiate acceso
accènda	accèndano	àbbia acceso	àbbiano acceso
7 imperfect subjunctive		**14 past perfect subjunctive**	
accendessi	accendéssimo	avessi acceso	avéssimo acceso
accendessi	accendeste	avessi acceso	aveste acceso
accendesse	accendéssero	avesse acceso	avéssero acceso

imperative		
—		accendiamo
accèndi (non accèndere)		accendete
accènda		accèndano

Words related to this verb
Accendi la luce per favore! Please, turn on the light!
Perchè non accendi la radio? Why don't you turn on the radio?

to welcome, to receive

The Seven Simple Tenses		The Seven Compound Tenses	
Singular	Plural	Singular	Plural
1 present indicative		8 present perfect	
accòlgo	accogliamo	ho accòlto	abbiamo accòlto
accògli	accogliete	hai accòlto	avete accòlto
accòglie	accòlgono	ha accòlto	hanno accòlto
2 imperfect indicative		9 past perfect	
accoglievo	accoglievamo	avevo accòlto	avevamo accòlto
accoglievi	accoglievate	avevi accòlto	avevate accòlto
accoglieva	accogliévano	aveva accòlto	avévano accòlto
3 past absolute		10 past anterior	
accòlsi	accogliemmo	èbbi accòlto	avemmo accòlto
accogliesti	accoglieste	avesti accòlto	aveste accòlto
accòlse	accòlsero	èbbe accòlto	èbbero accòlto
4 future indicative		11 future perfect	
accoglierò	accoglieremo	avrò accòlto	avremo accòlto
accoglierai	accoglierete	avrai accòlto	avrete accòlto
accoglierà	accoglieranno	avrà accòlto	avranno accòlto
5 present conditional		12 past conditional	
accoglierèi	accoglieremmo	avrèi accòlto	avremmo accòlto
accoglieresti	accogliereste	avresti accòlto	avreste accòlto
accoglierèbbe	accoglierèbbero	avrèbbe accòlto	avrèbbero accòlto
6 present subjunctive		13 past subjunctive	
accòlga	accogliamo	àbbia accòlto	abbiamo accòlto
accòlga	accogliate	àbbia accòlto	abbiate accòlto
accòlga	accòlgano	àbbia accòlto	àbbiano accòlto
7 imperfect subjunctive		14 past perfect subjunctive	
accogliessi	accogliéssimo	avessi accòlto	avéssimo accòlto
accogliessi	accoglieste	avessi accòlto	aveste accòlto
accogliesse	accogliéssero	avesse accòlto	avéssero accòlto

imperative

—	accogliamo
accògli (non accògliere)	accogliete
accòlga	accòlgano

Words related to this verb
fare buona accoglienza   to welcome someone
È un vero amico. Mi ha accolto a braccia aperte.   He is a true friend. He
welcomed me with open arms.

5

accòrgersi (di)	Ger. accorgèndosi	Past Part. accòrtosi

to notice, to become aware (of)

The Seven Simple Tenses		The Seven Compound Tenses	
Singular	Plural	Singular	Plural
1 present indicative		8 present perfect	
mi accòrgo	ci accorgiamo	mi sono accòrti	ci siamo accòrti
ti accòrgi	vi accorgete	ti sèi accòrto	vi siète accòrti
si accòrge	si accòrgono	si è accorto	si sono accòrti
2 imperfect indicative		9 past perfect	
mi accorgevo	ci accorgevamo	mi èro accòrto	ci eravamo accòrti
ti accorgevi	vi accorgevate	ti èri accòrto	vi eravate accòrti
si accorgeva	si accorgévano	si èra accòrto	si èrano accòrti
3 past absolute		10 past anterior	
mi accòrsi	ci accorgemmo	mi fui accòrto	ci fummo accòrti
ti accorgesti	vi accorgeste	ti fosti accòrto	vi foste accòrti
si accòrse	si accòrsero	si fu accòrto	si furono accòrti
4 future indicative		11 future perfect	
mi accorgerò	ci accorgeremo	mi sarò accòrto	ci saremo accòrti
ti accorgerai	vi accorgerete	ti sarai accòrto	vi sarete accòrti
si accorgerà	si accorgeranno	si sarà accòrto	si saranno accòrti
5 present conditional		12 past conditional	
mi accorgerèi	ci accorgeremmo	mi sarèi accòrto	ci saremmo accòrti
ti accorgeresti	vi accorgereste	ti saresti accòrto	vi sareste accòrti
si accorgerèbbe	si accorgerèbbero	si sarèbbe accòrto	si sarèbbero accòrti
6 present subjunctive		13 past subjunctive	
mi accòrga	ci accorgiamo	mi sia accòrto	ci siamo accòrti
ti accòrga	vi accorgiate	ti sia accòrto	vi siate accòrti
si accòrga	si accòrgano	si sia accòrto	si síano accòrti
7 imperfect subjunctive		14 past perfect subjunctive	
mi accorgessi	ci accorgéssimo	mi fossi accòrto	ci fóssimo accòrti
ti accorgessi	vi accorgeste	ti fossi accòrto	vi foste accòrti
si accorgesse	si accorgéssero	si fosse accòrto	si fòssero accòrti

	imperative	
—		accorgiàmoci
accòrgiti (non ti accòrgere)		accorgétevi
si accòrga		si accòrgano

Words related to this verb

Non si era accorta ohe nevieava. She wasn't aware that it was snowing.
Mi accorsi ohe ero rimasto(a) solo(a). I noticed that I was left alone.

6

to fall asleep, to go to sleep

The Seven Simple Tenses		The Seven Compound Tenses	
Singular	Plural	Singular	Plural
1 present indicative		8 present perfect	
mi addormento	**ci addormentiamo**	**mi sono addormentato**	**ci siamo addormentati**
ti addormenti	**vi addormentate**	**ti sei addormentato**	**vi siete addormentati**
si addormenta	**si addorméntano**	**si è addormentato**	**si sono addormentati**
2 imperfect indicative		9 past perfect	
mi addormentavo	**ci addormentavamo**	**mi èro addormentato**	**ci eravamo addormentati**
ti addormentavi	**vi addormentavate**	**ti èri addormentato**	**vi eravate addormentati**
si addormentava	**si addormentávano**	**si èra addormentato**	**si èrano addormentati**
3 past absolute		10 past anterior	
mi addormentai	**ci addormentammo**	**mi fui addormentato**	**ci fummo addormentati**
ti addormentasti	**vi addormentaste**	**ti fosti addormentato**	**vi foste addormentati**
si addormentò	**si addormentárono**	**si fu addormentato**	**si furono addormentati**
4 future indicative		11 future perfect	
mi addormenterò	**ci addormenteremo**	**mi sarò addormentato**	**ci saremo addormentati**
ti addormenterai	**vi addormenterete**	**ti sarai addormentato**	**vi sarete addormentati**
si addormenterà	**si addormenteranno**	**si sarà addormentato**	**si saranno addormentati**
5 present conditional		12 past conditional	
mi addormenterei	**ci addormenteremmo**	**mi sarèi addormentato**	**ci saremmo addormentati**
ti addormenteresti	**vi addormentereste**	**ti saresti addormentato**	**vi sareste addormentati**
si addormenterèbbe	**si addormenterèbbero**	**si sarèbbe addormentato**	**si sarèbbero addormentati**
6 present subjunctive		13 past subjunctive	
mi addormenti	**ci addormentiamo**	**mi sia addormentato**	**ci siamo addormentati**
ti addormenti	**vi addormentiate**	**ti sia addormentato**	**vi siate addormentati**
si addormenti	**si addorméntino**	**si sia addormentato**	**si síano addormentati**
7 imperfect subjunctive		14 past perfect subjunctive	
mi addormentassi	**ci addormentàssimo**	**mi fossi addormentato**	**ci fóssimo addormentati**
ti addormentassi	**vi addormentaste**	**ti fossi addormentato**	**vi foste addormentati**
si addormentasse	**si addormentàssero**	**si fosse addormentato**	**si fóssero addormentati**

imperative

—	**addormentiamoci**
addormentati (non ti addormentare)	**si addormentatevi**
si addormenti	**si addorméntino**

to seize, to grasp, to hold on to

The Seven Simple Tenses		The Seven Compound Tenses	
Singular	Plural	Singular	Plural
1 present indicative		8 present perfect	
afferro	**afferriamo**	**ho afferrato**	**abbiamo afferrato**
afferri	**afferrate**	**hai afferrato**	**avete afferrato**
afferra	**afferrano**	**ha afferrato**	**hanno afferrato**
2 imperfect indicative		9 past perfect	
afferravo	**afferravamo**	**avevo afferrato**	**avevamo afferrato**
afferravi	**afferravate**	**avevi afferrato**	**avevate afferrato**
afferrava	**afferràvano**	**aveva afferrato**	**avévano afferrato**
3 past absolute		10 past anterior	
afferrai	**afferrammo**	**èbbi afferrato**	**avemmo afferrato**
afferrasti	**afferraste**	**avesti afferrato**	**aveste afferrato**
afferrò	**afferràrono**	**èbbe afferrato**	**èbbero afferrato**
4 future indicative		11 future perfect	
afferrerò	**afferreremo**	**avrò afferrato**	**avremo afferrato**
afferrerai	**afferrerete**	**avrai afferrato**	**avrete afferrato**
afferrerà	**afferreranno**	**avrà afferrato**	**avranno afferrato**
5 present conditional		12 past conditional	
afferrerèi	**afferreremmo**	**avrèi afferrato**	**avremmo afferrato**
afferreresti	**afferrereste**	**avresti afferrato**	**avreste afferrato**
afferrerèbbe	**afferrerèbbero**	**avrèbbe afferrato**	**avrèbbero afferrato**
6 present subjunctive		13 past subjunctive	
afferri	**afferriamo**	**àbbia afferrato**	**abbiamo afferrato**
afferri	**afferriate**	**àbbia afferrato**	**abbiate afferrato**
afferri	**afferrino**	**àbbia afferrato**	**àbbiano afferrato**
7 imperfect subjunctive		14 past perfect subjunctive	
afferrassi	**afferràssimo**	**avessi afferrato**	**avéssimo afferrato**
afferrassi	**afferraste**	**avessi afferrato**	**aveste afferrato**
afferrasse	**afferràssero**	**avesse afferrato**	**avèssero afferrato**

	imperative	
—		**afferriamo**
afferra (non **afferrare**)		**afferrate**
afferri		**afferrino**

Words related to this verb
Afferralo con tutte le tue forze! E' un vaso prezioso.   Hold it firmly. It is a precious vase.
Non so se afferri l'idea.   I don't know if you grasp the idea.

to afflict, to distress

The Seven Simple Tenses		The Seven Compound Tenses	
Singular	Plural	Singular	Plural
1 present indicative		8 present perfect	
affliggo	**affliggiamo**	**ho afflitto**	**abbiamo afflitto**
affliggi	**affliggete**	**hai afflitto**	**avete afflitto**
affligge	**affliggono**	**ha afflitto**	**hanno afflitto**
2 imperfect indicative		9 past perfect	
affliggevo	**affliggevamo**	**avevo afflitto**	**avevamo afflitto**
affliggevi	**affliggevate**	**avevi afflitto**	**avevate afflitto**
affliggeva	**affliggévano**	**aveva afflitto**	**avévano afflitto**
3 past absolute		10 past anterior	
afflissi	**affliggemmo**	**èbbi afflitto**	**avemmo afflitto**
affliggesti	**affliggeste**	**avesti afflitto**	**aveste afflitto**
afflisse	**afflíssero**	**èbbe afflitto**	**èbbero afflitto**
4 future indicative		11 future perfect	
affliggerò	**affliggeremo**	**avrò afflitto**	**avremo afflitto**
affliggerai	**affliggerete**	**avrai afflitto**	**avrete afflitto**
affliggerà	**affliggeranno**	**avrà afflitto**	**avranno afflitto**
5 present conditional		12 past conditional	
affliggerèi	**affliggeremmo**	**avrèi afflitto**	**avremmo afflitto**
affliggeresti	**affliggereste**	**avresti afflitto**	**avreste afflitto**
affliggerèbbe	**affliggerèbbero**	**avrèbbe afflitto**	**avrèbbero afflitto**
6 present subjunctive		13 past subjunctive	
affligga	**affliggiamo**	**àbbia afflitto**	**abbiamo afflitto**
affligga	**affliggiate**	**àbbia afflitto**	**abbiate afflitto**
affligga	**afflíggano**	**àbbia afflitto**	**àbbiano afflitto**
7 imperfect subjunctive		14 past perfect subjunctive	
affliggessi	**affliggéssimo**	**avessi afflitto**	**avéssimo afflitto**
affliggessi	**affliggeste**	**avessi afflitto**	**aveste afflitto**
affliggesse	**affliggéssero**	**avesse afflitto**	**avéssero afflitto**

imperative

—	**affliggiamo**
affliggi (non afflíggere)	**affliggete**
affligga	**affíggano**

Words related to this verb
Lui è afflitto da una grave malattia.   He is afflicted by a serious illness.
Mi hai afflitto con le tue lamentele!   You distressed me with your complaints.

9

affrettarsi Ger. **affrettandosi** Past Part. **affrettatosi**

to hasten, to hurry

The Seven Simple Tenses		The Seven Compound Tenses	
Singular	Plural	Singular	Plural
1 present indicative		8 present perfect	
mi affrètto	**ci affrettiamo**	**mi sono affrettato**	**ci siamo affrettati**
ti affrètti	**vi affrettate**	**ti sèi affrettato**	**vi siète affrettati**
si affrètta	**si affrèttano**	**si è affrettato**	**si sono affrettati**
2 imperfect indicative		9 past perfect	
mi affrettavo	**ci affrettavamo**	**mi èro affrettato**	**ci eravamo affrettati**
ti affrettavi	**vi affrettavate**	**ti èri affrettato**	**vi eravate affrettati**
si affrettava	**si affrettàvano**	**si èra affrettato**	**si èrano affrettati**
3 past absolute		10 past anterior	
mi affrettai	**ci affrettammo**	**mi fui affrettato**	**ci fummo affrettati**
ti affrettasti	**vi affrettaste**	**ti fosti affrettato**	**vi foste affrettati**
si affrettò	**si affrettàrono**	**si fu affrettato**	**si fúrono affrettati**
4 future indicative		11 future perfect	
mi affretterò	**ci affretteremo**	**mi sarò affrettato**	**ci saremo affrettati**
ti affretterai	**vi affrretterete**	**ti sarai affrettato**	**vi sarete affrettati**
si affretterà	**si affretteranno**	**si sarà affrettato**	**si saranno affrettati**
5 present conditional		12 past conditional	
mi affretterèi	**ci affretteremmo**	**mi sarèi affrettato**	**ci saremmo affrettati**
ti affretteresti	**vi affrettereste**	**ti saresti affrettato**	**vi sareste affrettati**
si affretterèbbe	**si affretterèbbero**	**si sarèbbe affrettato**	**si sarèbbero affrettati**
6 present subjunctive		13 past subjunctive	
mi affrètti	**ci affrettiamo**	**mi sia affrettato**	**ci siamo affrettati**
ti affrètti	**vi affrettiate**	**ti sia affrettato**	**vi siate affrettati**
si affrètti	**si affrèttino**	**si sia affrettato**	**si síano affrettati**
7 imperfect subjunctive		14 past perfect subjunctive	
mi affrettassi	**ci affrettàssimo**	**mi fossi affrettato**	**ci fóssimo affrettati**
ti affrettassi	**vi affrettaste**	**ti fossi affrettato**	**vi foste affrettati**
si affrettasse	**si affrettàssero**	**si fosse affrettato**	**si fóssero affrettati**

imperative	
—	**affrettiàmoci**
affrèttati (non ti affrettare)	**affrettàtevi**
si affrètti	**si affrèttino**

Words related to this verb
Maria si affretta a prendere l'autobus. Mary hurries to take the bus.
Affrettati, è tardi! Hurry, it's late!

10

The Seven Simple Tenses		The Seven Compound Tenses	
Singular	Plural	Singular	Plural
1 present indicative		8 present perfect	
aggiungo	aggiungiamo	ho aggiunto	abbiamo aggiunto
aggiungi	aggiungete	hai aggiunto	avete aggiunto
aggiunge	aggiúngono	ha aggiunto	hanno aggiunto
2 imperfect indicative		9 past perfect	
aggiungevo	aggiungevamo	avevo aggiunto	avevamo aggiunto
aggiungevi	aggiungevate	avevi aggiunto	avevate aggiunto
aggiungeva	aggiungévano	aveva aggiunto	avévano aggiunto
3 past absolute		10 past anterior	
aggiunsi	aggiungemmo	èbbi aggiunto	avemmo aggiunto
aggiungesti	aggiungeste	avesti aggiunto	aveste aggiunto
aggiunse	aggiúnsero	èbbe aggiunto	èbbero aggiunto
4 future indicative		11 future perfect	
aggiungerò	aggiungeremo	avrò aggiunto	avremo aggiunto
aggiungerai	aggiungerete	avrai aggiunto	avrete aggiunto
aggiungerà	aggiungeranno	avrà aggiunto	avranno aggiunto
5 present conditional		12 past conditional	
aggiungerèi	aggiungeremmo	avrèi aggiunto	avremmo aggiunto
aggiungeresti	aggiungereste	avresti aggiunto	avreste aggiunto
aggiungerèbbe	aggiungerèbbero	avrèbbe aggiunto	avrèbbero aggiunto
6 present subjunctive		13 past subjunctive	
aggiunga	aggiungiamo	àbbia aggiunto	abbiamo aggiunto
aggiunga	aggiungiate	àbbia aggiunto	abbiate aggiunto
aggiunga	aggiúngano	àbbia aggiunto	àbbiano aggiunto
7 imperfect subjunctive		14 past perfect subjunctive	
aggiungessi	aggiungéssimo	avessi aggiunto	avéssimo aggiunto
aggiungessi	aggiungeste	avessi aggiunto	aveste aggiunto
aggiungesse	aggiungéssero	avesse aggiunto	avéssero aggiunto

	imperative	
—		aggiungiamo
	aggiungi (non aggiúngere)	aggiungete
	aggiunga	aggiúngano

Words related to this verb
Io ho aggiunto molte note al mio memorandum. I have added many notes to my memo.
Mi sorprese quando aggiunse che si sarebbe iscritta in giurisprudenza.
She surprised me when she added that she would have enrolled in a law school.

aiutare	Ger. **aiùtando**	Past Part. **aiùtato**

to help, to aid

The Seven Simple Tenses		The Seven Compound Tenses	
Singular	Plural	Singular	Plural
1 present indicative		8 present perfect	
aiùto	aiutiamo	ho aiutato	abbiamo aiutato
aiùti	aiutate	hai aiutato	avete aiutato
aiùta	aiùtano	ha aiutato	hanno aiutato
2 imperfect indicative		9 past perfect	
aiutavo	aiutavamo	avevo aiutato	avevamo aiutato
aiutavi	aiutavate	avevi aiutato	avevate aiutato
aiutava	aiutàvano	aveva aiutato	avévano aiutato
3 past absolute		10 past anterior	
aiutai	aiutammo	èbbi aiutato	avemmo aiutato
aiutasti	aiutaste	avesti aiutato	aveste aiutato
aiutò	aiutàrono	èbbe aiutato	èbbero aiutato
4 future indicative		11 future perfect	
aiuterò	aiuteremo	avrò aiutato	avremo aiutato
aiuterai	aiuterete	avrai aiutato	avrete aiutato
aiuterà	aiuteranno	avrà aiutato	avranno aiutato
5 present conditional		12 past conditional	
aiuterèi	aiuteremmo	avrèi aiutato	avremmo aiutato
aiuteresti	aiutereste	avresti aiutato	avreste aiutato
aiuterèbbe	aiuterèbbero	avrèbbe aiutato	avrèbbero aiutato
6 present subjunctive		13 past subjunctive	
aiùti	aiutiamo	àbbia aiutato	abbiamo aiutato
aiùti	aiutiate	àbbia aiutato	abbiate aiutato
aiùti	aiùtino	àbbia aiutato	àbbiano aiutato
7 imperfect subjunctive		14 past perfect subjunctive	
aiutassi	aiutàssimo	avessi aiutato	avéssimo aiutato
aiutassi	aiutaste	avessi aiutato	aveste aiutato
aiutasse	aiutàssero	avesse aiutato	avéssero aiutato

	imperative	
—		aiutiamo
aiùta (non aiutare)		aiutate
aiùti		aiùtino

Words related to this verb

Aiuto! Polizia! Help! Police!
Di solito, io chiedo aiuto ai miei fratelli e ai miei cugini. Usually, I ask my brothers and my cousins for help.

Ger. **alludèndo**   Past Part. **allùso**   **alludere***

to allude, to refer, to hint

The Seven Simple Tenses		The Seven Compound Tenses	
Singular	Plural	Singular	Plural
1 present indicative		8 present perfect	
allùdo	**alludiamo**	**ho allùso**	**abbiamo allùso**
allùdi	**alludete**	**hai allùso**	**avete allùso**
allùde	**allùdono**	**ha allùso**	**hanno allùso**
2 imperfect indicative		9 past perfect	
alludevo	**alludevamo**	**avevo allùso**	**avevamo allùso**
alludevi	**alludevate**	**avevi allùso**	**avevate allùso**
alludeva	**alludévano**	**aveva allùso**	**avevano allùso**
3 past absolute		10 past anterior	
allùsi	**alludemmo**	**èbbi allùso**	**avemmo allùso**
alludesti	**alludeste**	**avesti allùso**	**aveste allùso**
allùse	**allùsero**	**èbbe allùso**	**èbbero allùso**
4 future indicative		11 future perfect	
alluderò	**alluderemo**	**avrò allùso**	**avremo allùso**
alluderai	**alluderete**	**avrai allùso**	**avrete allùso**
alluderà	**alluderanno**	**avrà allùso**	**avranno allùso**
5 present conditional		12 past conditional	
alluderèi	**alluderemmo**	**avrèi allùso**	**avremmo allùso**
alluderesti	**alludereste**	**avresti allùso**	**avreste allùso**
alluderèbbe	**alluderèbbero**	**avrèbbe allùso**	**avrèbbero allùso**
6 present subjunctive		13 past subjunctive	
allùda	**alludiamo**	**àbbia allùso**	**abbiamo allùso**
allùda	**alludiate**	**àbbia allùso**	**abbiate allùso**
allùda	**allùdano**	**àbbia allùso**	**àbbiano allùso**
7 imperfect subjunctive		14 past perfect subjunctive	
alludessi	**alludéssimo**	**avessi allùso**	**avéssimo allùso**
alludessi	**alludeste**	**avessi allùso**	**aveste allùso**
alludesse	**alludéssero**	**avesse allùso**	**avéssero allùso**

imperative

—	**alludiamo**
allùdi (non alludere)	**alludete**
allùda	**allùdano**

*Like *alludere*, are *concludere*, *deludere*, *escludere*, and *precludere*.

Words related to this verb

Io non alludevo ai pettegolezzi dei vicini.   I did not refer to the neighbors' gossip.
Non capisco a cosa alludi. Io sono innocente.   I do not understand to what you refer. I am innocent.

alzare	Ger. alzando	Past Part. alzato

to raise, to lift up

The Seven Simple Tenses		The Seven Compound Tenses	
Singular	Plural	Singular	Plural
1 present indicative		8 present perfect	
àlzo	alziamo	ho alzato	abbiamo alzato
àlzi	alzate	hai alzato	avete alzato
àlza	àlzano	ha alzato	hanno alzato
2 imperfect indicative		9 past perfect	
alzavo	alzavamo	avevo alzato	avevamo alzato
alzavi	alzavate	avevi alzato	avevate alzato
alzava	alzàvano	aveva alzato	avévano alzato
3 past absolute		10 past anterior	
alzai	alzammo	èbbi alzato	avemmo alzato
alzasti	alzaste	avesti alzato	aveste alzato
alzò	alzàrono	èbbe alzato	èbbero alzato
4 future indicative		11 future perfect	
alzerò	alzeremo	avrò alzato	avremo alzato
alzerai	alzerete	avrai alzato	avrete alzato
alzerà	alzeranno	avrà alzato	avranno alzato
5 present conditional		12 past conditional	
alzerèi	alzeremmo	avrèi alzato	avremmo alzato
alzeresti	alzereste	avresti alzato	avreste alzato
alzerèbbe	alzerèbbero	avrèbbe alzato	avrèbbero alzato
6 present subjunctive		13 past subjunctive	
àlzi	alziamo	àbbia alzato	abbiamo alzato
àlzi	alziate	àbbia alzato	abbiate alzato
àlzi	àlzino	àbbia alzato	àbbiano alzato
7 imperfect subjunctive		14 past perfect subjunctive	
alzassi	alzàssimo	avessi alzato	avéssimo alzato
alzassi	alzaste	avessi alzato	aveste alzato
alzasse	alzàssero	avesse alzato	avéssero alzato

imperative	
—	alziamo
àlza (non alzare)	alzate
àlzi	àlzino

Words related to this verb

Alza la mano.   Raise your hand.
Non alzare la voce con me! Parliamo con calma.   Don't raise your voice with me!
Let's talk calmly.

to get up, to rise, to stand up

The Seven Simple Tenses		The Seven Compound Tenses	
Singular	Plural	Singular	Plural
1 present indicative		8 present perfect	
mi àlzo	ci alziamo	mi sono alzato	ci siamo alzati
ti àlzi	vi alzate	ti sèi alzato	vi siete alzati
si àlza	si àlzano	si è alzato	si sono alzati
2 imperfect indicative		9 past perfect	
mi alzavo	ci alzavamo	mi èro alzato	ci eravamo alzati
ti alzavi	vi alzavate	ti èri alzato	vi eravate alzati
si alzava	si alzàvano	si èra alzato	si èrano alzati
3 past absolute		10 past anterior	
mi alzai	ci alzammo	mi fui alzato	ci fummo alzati
ti alzasti	vi alzaste	ti fosti alzato	vi foste alzati
si alzò	si alzàrono	si fu alzato	si fúrono alzati
4 future indicative		11 future perfect	
mi alzerò	ci alzeremo	mi sarò alzato	ci saremo alzati
ti alzerai	vi alzerete	ti sarai alzato	vi sarete alzati
si alzerà	si alzeranno	si sarà alzato	si saranno alzati
5 present conditional		12 past conditional	
mi alzerèi	ci alzeremmo	mi sarèi alzato	ci saremmo alzati
ti alzeresti	vi alzereste	ti saresti alzato	vi sareste alzati
si alzerèbbe	si alzerèbbero	si sarèbbe alzato	si sarèbbero alzati
6 present subjunctive		13 past subjunctive	
mi àlzi	ci alziamo	mi sia alzato	ci siamo alzati
ti àlzi	vi alziate	ti sia alzato	vi siate alzati
si àlzi	si àlzino	si sia alzato	si síano alzati
7 imperfect subjunctive		14 past perfect subjunctive	
mi alzassi	ci alzàssimo	mi fossi alzato	ci fóssimo alzati
ti alzassi	vi alzaste	ti fossi alzato	vi foste alzati
si alzasse	si alzàssero	si fosse alzato	si fóssero alzati

imperative

—	alziamoci
àlzati (non ti alzare)	alzatevi
mi àlzi	si àzino

Words related to this verb
Mi sono alzato presto oggi.   I got up early today.
Alzati, è tardi!   Get up, it's late!

15

amméttere	Ger. ammettèndo	Past Part. ammesso

to admit

The Seven Simple Tenses		The Seven Compound Tenses	
Singular	Plural	Singular	Plural
1 present indicative		8 present perfect	
ammetto	ammettiamo	ho ammesso	abbiamo ammesso
ammetti	ammettete	hai ammesso	avete ammesso
ammette	amméttono	ha ammesso	hanno ammesso
2 imperfect indicative		9 past perfect	
ammettevo	ammettevamo	avevo ammesso	avevamo ammesso
ammettevi	ammettevate	avevi ammesso	avevate ammesso
ammetteva	ammettévano	aveva ammesso	avévano ammesso
3 past absolute		10 past anterior	
ammisi	ammettemmo	èbbi ammesso	avemmo ammesso
ammettesti	ammetteste	avesti ammesso	aveste ammesso
ammise	ammísero	èbbe ammesso	èbbero ammesso
4 future indicative		11 future perfect	
ammetterò	ammetteremo	avrò ammesso	avremo ammesso
ammetterai	ammetterete	avrai ammesso	avrete ammesso
ammetterà	ammetteranno	avrà ammesso	avranno ammesso
5 present conditional		12 past conditional	
ammetterèi	ammetteremmo	avrèi ammesso	avremmo ammesso
ammetteresti	ammettereste	avresti ammesso	avreste ammesso
ammetterèbbe	ammetterèbbero	avrèbbe ammesso	avrèbbero ammesso
6 present subjunctive		13 past subjunctive	
ammetta	ammettiamo	àbbia ammesso	abbiamo ammesso
ammetta	ammettiate	àbbia ammesso	abbiate ammesso
ammetta	amméttano	àbbia ammesso	àbbiano ammesso
7 imperfect subjunctive		14 past perfect subjunctive	
ammettessi	ammettéssimo	avessi ammesso	avéssimo ammesso
ammettessi	ammetteste	avessi ammesso	aveste ammesso
ammettesse	ammettéssero	avesse ammesso	avéssero ammesso

imperative	
—	ammettiamo
ammetti (non amméttere)	ammettete
ammetta	amméttano

Words related to this verb

Lui non ammette mai che ha sbagliato.   He never admits that he has made an error.
Lei è stata ammessa all'università.   She was admitted to the university.

The Seven Simple Tenses		The Seven Compound Tenses	
Singular	Plural	Singular	Plural
1 present indicative		8 present perfect	
vado (vo)	andiamo	sono andato	siamo andati
vai	andate	sei andato	siete andati
va	vanno	è andato	sono andati
2 imperfect indicative		9 past perfect	
andavo	andavamo	èro andato	eravamo andati
andavi	andavate	èri andato	eravate andati
andava	andàvano	èra andato	èrano andati
3 past absolute		10 past anterior	
andai	andammo	fui andato	fummo andati
andasti	andaste	fosti andato	foste andati
andò	andàrono	fu andato	fúrono andati
4 future indicative		11 future perfect	
andrò (anderò)	andremo	sarò andato	saremo andati
andrai	andrete	sarai andato	sarete andati
andrà	andranno	sarà andato	saranno andati
5 present conditional		12 past conditional	
andrèi (anderèi)	andremmo	sarèi andato	sarcmmo andati
andresti	andreste	saresti andato	sareste andati
andrèbbe	andrèbbero	sarèbbe andato	sarèbbero andati
6 present subjunctive		13 past subjunctive	
vada	andiamo	sia andato	siamo andati
vada	andiate	sia andato	siate andati
vada	vàdano	sia andato	síano andati
7 imperfect subjunctive		14 past perfect subjunctive	
andassi	andàssimo	fossi andato	fóssimo andati
andassi	andaste	fossi andato	foste andati
andasse	andàssero	fosse andato	fóssero andati

imperative

	—	andiamo
	va' (non andare)	andate
	vada	vàdano

Words related to this verb
Io vado a scuola ogni giorno.   I go to school every day.
andare a letto   to go to bed

17

...o go away

The Seven Simple Tenses		The Seven Compound Tenses	
Singular	Plural	Singular	Plural
1 present indicative		8 present perfect	
me ne vado (vo)	ce ne andiamo	me ne sono andato	ce ne siamo andati
te ne vai	ve ne andate	te ne sei andato	ve ne siète andati
se ne va	se ne vanno	se n'è andato	se ne sono andati
2 imperfect indicative		9 past perfect	
me ne andavo	ce ne andavamo	me n'èro andato	ce n'eravamo andati
te ne andavi	ve ne andavate	te n'èri andato	ve n'eravate andati
se ne andava	se ne andàvano	se n'èra andato	se n'erano andati
3 past absolute		10 past anterior	
me ne andai	ce ne andammo	me ne fui andato	ce ne fummo andati
te ne andasti	ve ne andaste	te ne fosti andato	ve ne foste andati
se ne andò	se ne andàrono	se ne fu andato	se ne fúrono andati
4 future indicative		11 future perfect	
me ne andrò (anderò)	ce ne andremo	me ne sarò andato	ce ne saremo andati
te ne andrai	ve ne andrete	te ne sarai andato	ve ne sarete andati
se ne andrà	se ne andranno	se ne sarà andato	e ne saranno andati
5 present conditional		12 past conditional	
me ne andrèi (anderèi)	ce ne andremmo	me ne sarèi andato	ce ne saremmo andati
te ne andresti	ve ne andreste	te ne saresti andato	ve ne sareste andati
se ne andrèbbe	se ne andrèbbero	se ne sarèbbe andato	se ne sarèbbero andati
6 present subjunctive		13 past subjunctive	
me ne vada	ce ne andiamo	me ne sia andato	ce ne siamo andati
te ne vada	ve ne andiate	te ne sia andato	ve ne siate andati
se ne vada	se ne vàdano	se ne sia andato	se ne síano andati
7 imperfect subjunctive		14 past perfect subjunctive	
me ne andassi	ce ne andàssimo	me ne fossi andato	ce ne fóssimo andati
te ne andassi	ve ne andaste	te ne fossi andato	ve ne foste andati
se ne andasse	se ne andàssero	se ne fosse andato	se ne fóssero andati

imperative	
—	andiàmocene
vàttene (non te ne andare)	andàtevene
se ne vada	se ne vàdano

Words related to this verb
Andiamocene. Let's go!
Finalmente se ne andò. Finally he went away.

to annoy, to bore

The Seven Simple Tenses		The Seven Compound Tenses	
Singular	Plural	Singular	Plural
1 present indicative		8 present perfect	
annoio	annoiamo	ho annoiata	abbiamo annoiato
annòi	annoiate	hai annoiato	avete annoiato
annoia	annòiano	ha annoiato	hanno annoiato
2 imperfect indicative		9 past perfect	
annoiavo	annoiavamo	avevo annoiato	avevamo annoiato
annoiavi	annoiavate	avevi annoiato	avevate annoiato
annoiava	annoiàvano	aveva annoiato	avévano annoiato
3 past absolute		10 past anterior	
annoiai	annoiammo	èbbi annoiato	avemmo annoiato
annoiasti	annoiaste	avesti annoiato	aveste annoiato
annoiò	annoiàrono	èbbe annoiato	èbbero annoiato
4 future indicative		11 future perfect	
annoierò	annoieremo	avrò annoiato	avremo annoiato
annoierai	annoierete	avrai annoiato	avrete annoiato
annoierà	annoieranno	avrà annoiato	avranno annoiato
5 present conditional		12 past conditional	
annoierèi	annoieremmo	avrèi annoiato	avremmo annoiato
annoieresti	annoiereste	avresti annoiato	avreste annoiato
annoierèbbe	annoierèbbero	avrèbbe annoiato	avrèbbero annoiato
6 present subjunctive		13 past subjunctive	
annòi	annoiamo	àbbia annoiato	abbiamo annoiato
annòi	annoiate	àbbia annoiato	abbiate annoiato
annòi	annòino	àbbia annoiato	àbbiano annoiato
7 imperfect subjunctive		14 past perfect subjunctive	
annoiassi	annoiàssimo	avessi annoiato	avéssimo annoiato
annoiassi	annoiaste	avessi annoiato	aveste annoiato
annoiasse	annoiàssero	avesse annoiato	avéssero annoiato

imperative

—	annoiamo
annoia (non annoiare)	annoiate
annòi	annòino

Words related to this verb
Io annoio mia sorella.   I annoy my sister.
Lui ba annoiato il maestro.   He has annoyed the teacher.

to be bored

The Seven Simple Tenses		The Seven Compound Tenses	
Singular	Plural	Singular	Plural
1 present indicative		8 present perfect	
mi annoiò	ci annoiamo	mi sono annoiato	ci siamo annoiati
ti annòi	vi annoiate	ti sèi annoiato	vi siete annoiati
si annoia	si annoiano	si è annoato	si sono annoiati
2 imperfect indicative		9 past perfect	
mi annoiavo	ci annoiavamo	mi èro annoiato	ci eravamo annoiati
ti annoiavi	vi annoiavate	ti èri annoiato	vi eravate annoiati
si annoiava	si annoiàvano	si èra annoiato	si èrano annoiati
3 past absolute		10 past anterior	
mi annoiai	ci annoiammo	mi fui annoiato	ci fummo annoiati
ti annoiasti	vi annoiaste	ti fosti annoiato	vi foste annoiati
si annoiò	si annoiàrono	si fu annoiato	si fúrono annoiati
4 future indicative		11 future perfect	
mi annoierò	ci annoieremo	mi sarò annoiato	ci saremo annoiati
ti annoierai	vi annoierete	ti sarai annoiato	vi sarete annoiati
si annoierà	si annoieranno	si sarà annoiato	si saranno annoiati
5 present conditional		12 past conditional	
mi annoierèi	ci annoieremmo	mi sarèi annoiato	ci saremmo annoiati
ti annoieresti	vi annoiereste	ti saresti annoiato	vi sareste annoiati
si annoierèbbe	si annoierèbbero	si sarèbbe annoiato	si sarèbbero annoiati
6 present subjunctive		13 past subjunctive	
mi annòi	ci annoiamo	mi sia annoiato	ci siamo annoiati
ti annòi	vi annoiate	ti sia annoiato	vi siate annoiati
si annòi	si annòino	si sia annoiato	si síano annoiati
7 imperfect subjunctive		14 past perfect subjunctive	
mi annoiassi	ci annoiassimo	mi fossi annoiato	ci fóssimo annoiati
ti annoiassi	vi annoiaste	ti fossi annoiato	vi foste annoiati
si annoiasse	si annoiàssero	si fosse annoiato	si fóssero annoiati

	imperative	
—		annoiamoci
annoiati (non ti annoiare)		annoiatevi
si annòi		si annòino

Words related to this verb
Mi annoio quando non ho niente da fare.   I get bored when I have nothing to do.
Non mi annoiare!   Don't annoy me!

to prepare, to set

The Seven Simple Tenses		The Seven Compound Tenses	
Singular	Plural	Singular	Plural
1 present indicative		8 present perfect	
apparècchio	**apparecchiamo**	ho apparecchiato	abbiamo apparecchiato
apparècchi	**apparecchiate**		
apparècchia	**apparècchiano**	hai apparecchiato	avete apparecchiato
		ha apparecchiato	hanno apparecchiato
2 imperfect indicative		9 past perfect	
apparecchiavo	**apparecchiavamo**	avevo apparecchiato	avevamo apparecchiato
apparecchiavi	**apparecchiavate**		
apparecchiava	**apparecchiàvano**	avevi apparecchiato	avevate apparecchiato
		aveva apparecchiato	avévano apparecchiato
3 past absolute		10 past anterior	
apparecchiai	**apparecchiammo**	èbbi apparecchiato	avemmo apparecchiato
apparecchiasti	**apparecchiaste**		
apparecchiò	**apparecchiàrono**	avesti apparecchiato	aveste apparecchiato
		èbbe apparecchiato	èbbero apparecchiato
4 future indicative		11 future perfect	
apparecchierò	**apparecchieremo**	avrò apparecchiato	avremo apparecchiato
apparecchierai	**apparecchierete**	avrai apparecchiato	avrete apparecchiato
apparecchierà	**apparecchie-ranno**	avrà apparecchiato	avrànno apparecchiato
5 present conditional		12 past conditional	
apparecchierèi	**apparecchie-remmo**	avrèi apparecchiato	avremmo apparecchiato
apparecchie-resti	**apparecchie-reste**	avresti apparecchiato	avreste apparecchiato
apparecchie-rèbbe	**apparecchie-rèbbero**	avrèbbe apparecchiato	avrèbbero apparecchiato
6 present subjunctive		13 past subjunctive	
apparècchi	**apparecchiamo**	àbbia apparecchiato	abbiamo apparecchiato
apparècchi	**apparecchiate**		
apparècchi	**apparècchino**	àbbia apparecchiato	abbiate apparechiatto
		àbbia apparecchiato	àbbiano apparecchiato
7 imperfect subjunctive		14 past perfect subjunctive	
apparecchiassi	**apparecchiàssimo**	avessi apparecchiato	avéssimo apparecchiato
apparecchiassi	**apparecchiaste**		
apparecchiasse	**apparecchiàssero**	avessi apparecchiato	aveste apparecchiato
		avesse apparecchiato	avéssero apparecchiato

imperative

—	**apparecchiamo**
apparècchia (non **apparecchiare**)	**apparecchiate**
apparècchi	**apparècchino**

apparire   Ger. **apparèndo**   Past Part. **appárso**

to appear, to look, to seem

The Seven Simple Tenses		The Seven Compound Tenses	
Singular	Plural	Singular	Plural
1 present indicative		8 present perfect	
appaio	**appariamo**	**sono apparso**	**siamo apparsi**
appari	**apparite**	**sèi apparso**	**siète apparsi**
appare	**appàiono**	**è apparso**	**sono apparsi**
(*Or regular:* **apparisco**, *etc.*)			
2 imperfect indicative		9 past perfect	
apparivo	**apparivamo**	**èro apparso**	**eravamo apparsi**
apparivi	**apparivate**	**èri apparso**	**eravate apparsi**
appariva	**apparívano**	**èra apparso**	**èrano apparsi**
3 past absolute		10 past anterior	
apparvi	**apparimmo**	**fui apparso**	**fummo apparsi**
apparisti	**appariste**	**fosti apparso**	**foste apparsi**
apparve	**appàrvero**	**fu apparso**	**fúrono apparsi**
(*Or regular:* **apparii**, *etc.*)			
4 future indicative		11 future perfect	
apparirò	**appariremo**	**sarò apparso**	**saremo apparsi**
apparirai	**apparirete**	**sarai apparso**	**sarete apparsi**
apparirà	**appariranno**	**sarà apparso**	**saranno apparsi**
5 present conditional		12 past conditional	
apparirèi	**appariremmo**	**sarèi apparso**	**saremmo apparsi**
appariresti	**apparireste**	**saresti apparso**	**sareste apparsi**
apparirèbbe	**apparirèbbero**	**sarèbbe apparso**	**sarèbbero apparsi**
6 present subjunctive		13 past subjunctive	
appaia	**appariamo**	**sia apparso**	**siamo apparsi**
appaia	**appariate**	**sia apparso**	**siate apparsi**
appaia	**appàiano**	**sia apparso**	**síano apparsi**
(*Or regular:* **apparisca**, *etc.*)			
7 imperfect subjunctive		14 past perfect subjunctive	
apparissi	**apparíssimo**	**fossi apparso**	**fóssimo apparsi**
apparissi	**appariste**	**fossi apparso**	**foste apparsi**
apparisse	**apparíssero**	**fosse apparso**	**fóssero apparsi**

	imperative	
		appariamo
	appari (apparisci) (non apparire)	**apparite**
	appaia (apparisca)	**appàiano (apparíscano)**

Words related to this verb

Paolo apparve al ristorante in tempo per gli spaghetti.   Paul appeared at the restaurant in time for the spaghetti.

Lui vuole apparire elegante.   He wants to look elegant.

to belong

The Seven Simple Tenses		The Seven Compound Tenses	
Singular	Plural	Singular	Plural
1 present indicative		8 present perfect	
appartèngo	apparteniamo	ho* appartenuto	abbiamo appartenuto
appartièni	appartenete	hai appartenuto	avete appartenuto
appartiène	appartèngono	ha appartenuto	hanno appartenuto
2 imperfect indicative		9 past perfect	
appartenevo	appartenevamo	avevo appartenuto	avevamo appartenuto
appartenevi	appartenevate	avevi appartenuto	avevate appartenuto
apparteneva	appartenévano	aveva appartenuto	avévano appartenuto
3 past absolute		10 past anterior	
appartenni	appartenemmo	èbbi appartenuto	avemmo appartenuto
appartenesti	apparteneste	avesti appartenuto	aveste appartenuto
appartenne	apparténnero	èbbe appartenuto	èbbero appartenuto
4 future indicative		11 future perfect	
apparterrò	apparterremo	avrò appartenuto	avremo appartenuto
apparterrai	apparterrete	avrai appartenuto	avrete appartenuto
apparterrà	apparterranno	avrà appartenuto	avranno appartenuto
5 present conditional		12 past conditional	
apparterrèi	apparterremmo	avrèi appartenuto	avremmo appartenuto
apparterresti	apparterreste	avresti appartenuto	avreste appartenuto
apparterrèbbe	apparterrèbbero		
		avrèbbe appartenuto	avrèbbero appartenuto
6 present subjunctive		13 past subjunctive	
appartènga	apparteniamo	àbbia appartenuto	abbiamo appartenuto
appartènga	apparteniate	àbbia appartenuto	abbiate appartenuto
appartènga	appartèngano	àbbia appartenuto	àbbiano appartenuto
7 imperfect subjunctive		14 past perfect subjunctive	
appartenessi	appartenéssimo	avessi appartenuto	avéssimo appartenuto
appartenessi	apparteneste	avessi appartenuto	aveste appartenuto
appartenesse	appartenéssero	avesse appartenuto	avéssero appartenuto

	imperative	
—		apparteniamo
appartièni (non appartenere)		appartenete
appartènga		appartèngano

Appartenere may have as its auxiliary *èssere*.

Words related to this verb
Questa casa mi appartiene.   This house belongs to me.
Questi vecchi dischi di jazz mi appartengono.   These old jazz records belong to me.

apprèndere   Ger. apprendèndo   Past Part. appreso

to learn

The Seven Simple Tenses		The Seven Compound Tenses	
Singular	Plural	Singular	Plural
1 present indicative		8 present perfect	
apprèndo	apprendiamo	ho appreso	abbiamo appreso
apprèndi	apprendete	hai appreso	avete appreso
apprènde	apprèndono	ha appreso	hanno appreso
2 imperfect indicative		9 past perfect	
apprendevo	apprendevamo	avevo appreso	avevamo appreso
apprendevi	apprendevate	avevi appreso	avevate appreso
apprendeva	apprendévano	aveva appreso	avévano appreso
3 past absolute		10 past anterior	
appresi	apprendemmo	èbbi appreso	avemmo appreso
apprendesti	apprendeste	avesti appreso	aveste appreso
apprese	apprésero	èbbe appreso	èbbero appreso
4 future indicative		11 future perfect	
apprenderò	apprenderemo	avrò appreso	avremo appreso
apprenderai	apprenderete	avrai appreso	avrete appreso
apprenderà	apprenderanno	avrà appreso	avranno appreso
5 present conditional		12 past conditional	
apprenderèi	apprenderemmo	avrèi appreso	avremmo appreso
apprenderesti	apprendereste	avresti appreso	avreste appreso
apprenderèbbe	apprenderèbbero	avrèbbe appreso	avrèbbero appreso
6 present subjunctive		13 past subjunctive	
apprènda	apprendiamo	àbbia appreso	abbiamo appreso
apprènda	apprendiate	àbbia appreso	abbiate appreso
apprènda	apprèndano	àbbia appreso	àbbiano appreso
7 imperfect subjunctive		14 past perfect subjunctive	
apprendessi	apprendéssimo	avessi appreso	avéssimo appreso
apprendessi	apprendeste	avessi appreso	aveste appreso
apprendesse	apprendéssero	avesse appreso	avéssero appreso

imperative		
—		apprendiamo
apprèndi (non apprèndere)		apprendete
apprènda		apprèndano

Words related to this verb
Un bambino apprende dal padre.   A child learns from his father.
L'ho appreso da fonte sicura.   I have learned it from a sure source.

to open

The Seven Simple Tenses		The Seven Compound Tenses	
Singular	Plural	Singular	Plural
1　present indicative		8　present perfect	
apro	aprimao	ho apèrto	abbiamo apèrto
apri	aprite	hai apèrto	avete apèrto
apre	àprono	ha apèrto	hanno apèrto
2　imperfect indicative		9　past perfect	
aprivo	aprivamo	avevo apèrto	avevamo apèrto
aprivi	aprivate	avevi apèrto	avevate apèrto
apriva	aprívano	aveva apèrto	avévano apèrto
3　past absolute		10　past anterior	
apèrsi	aprimmo	èbbi apèrto	avemmo apèrto
apristi	apriste	avesti apèrto	aveste apèrto
apèrse	apèrsero	èbbe apèrto	èbbero apèrto
(*Or regular:* aprii, *etc.*)			
4　future indicative		11　future perfect	
aprirò	apriremo	avrò apèrto	avremo apèrto
aprirai	aprirete	avrai apèrto	avrete apèrto
aprirà	apriranno	avrà apèrto	avranno apèrto
5　present conditional		12　past conditional	
aprirèi	apriremmo	avrèi apèrto	avremmo apèrto
apriresti	aprireste	avresti apèrto	avreste apèrto
aprirèbbe	aprirèbbero	avrèbbe apèrto	avrèbbero apèrto
6　present subjunctive		13　past subjunctive	
apra	apriamo	àbbia apèrto	abbiamo apèrto
apra	apriate	àbbia apèrto	àbbiate apèrto
apra	àprano	àbbia apèrto	àbbiano apèrto
7　imperfect subjunctive		14　past perfect subjunctive	
aprissi	apríssimo	avessi apèrto	avéssimo apèrto
aprissi	apriste	avessi apèrto	aveste apèrto
aprisse	apríssero	avesse apèrto	avéssero apèrto
		imperative	
	—		aprimao
	apri (non aprire)		aprite
	apra		àprano

Words related to this verb
Apri il regalo! Non posso più aspettare.　Open the gift! I cannot wait any longer.
Noi aprimmo il pacco.　We opened the package.

àrdere* Ger. ardèndo Past Part. arso

to burn

The Seven Simple Tenses		The Seven Compound Tenses	
Singular	Plural	Singular	Plural
1 present indicative		**8 present perfect**	
ardo	ardiamo	ho arso	abbiamo arso
ardi	ardete	hai arso	avete arso
arde	àrdono	ha arso	hanno arso
2 imperfect indicative		**9 past perfect**	
ardevo	ardevamo	avevo arso	avevamo arso
ardevi	ardevate	avevi arso	avevate arso
ardeva	ardévano	aveva arso	avévano arso
3 past absolute		**10 past anterior**	
arsi	ardemmo	èbbi arso	avemmo arso
ardesti	ardeste	avesti arso	aveste arso
arse	àrsero	èbbe arso	èbbero arso
4 future indicative		**11 future perfect**	
arderò	arderemo	avrò arso	avremo arso
arderai	arderete	avrai arso	avrete arso
arderà	arderanno	avrà arso	avranno arso
5 present conditional		**12 past conditional**	
arderèi	arderemmo	avrèi arso	avremmo arso
arderesti	ardereste	avresti arso	avreste arso
arderèbbe	arderèbbero	avrèbbe arso	avrèbbero arso
6 present subjunctive		**13 past subjunctive**	
arda	ardiamo	àbbia arso	abbiamo arso
arda	ardiate	àbbia arso	abbiate arso
arda	àrdano	àbbia arso	àbbiano arso
7 imperfect subjunctive		**14 past perfect subjunctive**	
ardessi	ardéssimo	avessi arso	avéssimo arso
ardessi	ardeste	avessi arso	aveste arso
ardesse	ardéssero	avesse arso	avéssero arso

	imperative	
—		ardiamo
ardi (non àrdere)		ardete
arda		àrdano

* When intransitive, *àrdere* is conjugated with *èssere*.

Words related to this verb
Lei arde dal desiderio di rivedere sua madre.   She burns from the desire to see her mother again.
La casa arde.   The house is burning (is on fire).

to arrest, to stop

The Seven Simple Tenses		The Seven Compound Tenses	
Singular	Plural	Singular	Plural
1 present indicative		8 present perfect	
arrèsto	arrestiamo	ho arrestato	abbiamo arrestato
arrèsti	arrestate	hai arrestato	avete arrestato
arrèsta	arrèstano	ha arrestato	hanno arrestato
2 imperfect indicative		9 past perfect	
arrestavo	arrestavamo	avevo arrestato	avevamo arrestato
arrestavi	arrestavate	avevi arrestato	avevate arrestato
arrestava	arrestàvano	aveva arrestato	avévano arrestato
3 past absolute		10 past anterior	
arrestai	arrestammo	èbbi arrestato	avemmo arrestato
arrestasti	arrestaste	avesti arrestato	aveste arrestato
arrestò	arrestàrono	èbbe arrestato	èbbero arrestato
4 future indicative		11 future perfect	
arresterò	arresteremo	avrò arrestato	avremo arrestato
arresterai	arresterete	avrai arrestato	avrete arrestato
arresterà	arresteranno	avrà arrestato	avranno arrestato
5 present conditional		12 past conditional	
arresterèi	arresteremmo	avrèi arrestato	avremmo arrestato
arresteresti	arrestereste	avresti arrestato	avreste arrestato
arresterèbbe	arresterèbbero	avrèbbe arrestato	avrèbbero arrestato
6 present subjunctive		13 past subjunctive	
arrèsti	arrestiamo	àbbia arrestato	abbiamo arrestato
arrèsti	arrestiate	àbbia arrestato	abbiate arrestato
arrèsti	arrèstino	àbbia arrestato	àbbiano arrestato
7 imperfect subjunctive		14 past perfect subjunctive	
arrestassi	arrestassimo	avessi arrestato	avéssimo arrestato
arrestassi	arrestaste	avessi arrestato	aveste arrestato
arrestasse	arrestàssero	avesse arrestato	avéssero arrestato

	imperative	
—		arrestiamo
arresta (non arrestare)		arrestate
arresti		arrèstino

Words related to this verb
Lo hanno arrestato per furto.   They arrested him for theft.
Ti faccio arrestare.   I'll have you arrested.

arrivare	Ger. **arrivando**	Past Part. **arrivato**

to arrive

The Seven Simple Tenses		The Seven Compound Tenses	
Singular	Plural	Singular	Plural
1 present indicative		8 present perfect	
arrivo	**arriviamo**	**sono arrivato**	**siamo arrivati**
arrìvi	**arrivate**	**sei arrivato**	**siete arrivati**
arriva	**arrivano**	**è arrivato**	**sono arrivati**
2 imperfect indicative		9 past perfect	
arrivavo	**arrivavamo**	**èro arrivato**	**eravamo arrivati**
arrivavi	**arrivavate**	**èri arrivato**	**eravate arrivati**
arrivava	**arrivàvano**	**èra arrivato**	**èrano arrivati**
3 past absolute		10 past anterior	
arrivai	**arrivammo**	**fui arrivato**	**fummo arrivati**
arrivasti	**arrivaste**	**fosti arrivato**	**foste arrivati**
arrivò	**arrivàrono**	**fu arrivato**	**fúrono arrivati**
4 future indicative		11 future perfect	
arriverò	**arriveremo**	**sarò arrivato**	**saremo arrivati**
arriverai	**arriverete**	**sarai arrivato**	**sarete arrivati**
arriverà	**arriveranno**	**sarà arrivato**	**saranno arrivati**
5 present conditional		12 past conditional	
arriverèi	**arriveremmo**	**sarèi arrivato**	**saremmo arrivati**
arriveresti	**arrivereste**	**saresti arrivato**	**sareste arrivati**
arriverèbbe	**arriverèbbero**	**sarèbbe arrivato**	**sarèbbero arrivati**
6 present subjunctive		13 past subjunctive	
arrìvi	**arriviamo**	**sia arrivato**	**siamo arrivati**
arrìvi	**arriviate**	**sia arrivato**	**siate arrivati**
arrìvi	**arrìvino**	**sia arrivato**	**síano arrivati**
7 imperfect subjunctive		14 past perfect subjunctive	
arrivassi	**arrivassimo**	**fossi arrivato**	**fóssimo arrivati**
arrivassi	**arrivaste**	**fossi arrivato**	**foste arrivati**
arrivasse	**arrivàssero**	**fosse arrivato**	**fóssero arrivati**

	imperative	
—		**arriviamo**
arriva (non arrivare)		**arrivate**
arrìvi		**arrìvino**

Words related to this verb
Arrivammo sani e salvi.   We arrived safe and sound.
Col coraggio si arriva ovunque.   With courage one can get anywhere.

to assail, to assault

The Seven Simple Tenses		The Seven Compound Tenses	
Singular	Plural	Singular	Plural
1 present indicative		8 present perfect	
assalgo	assaliamo	ho assalito	abbiamo assalito
assali	assalite	hai assalito	avete assalito
assale	assàlgono	ha assalito	hanno assalito
(*Or regular:* assalisco, *etc.*)			
2 imperfect indicative		9 past perfect	
assalivo	assalivamo	avevo assalito	avevamo assalito
assalivi	assalivate	avevi assalito	avevate assalito
assaliva	assalívano	aveva assalito	avévano assalito
3 past absolute		10 past anterior	
assalii	assalimmo	èbbi assalito	avemmo assalito
assalisti	assaliste	avesti assalito	aveste assalito
assalí	assalírono	èbbe assalito	èbbero assalito
4 future indicative		11 future perfect	
assalirò	assaliremo	avrò assalito	avremo assalito
assalirai	assalirete	avrai assalito	avrete assalito
assalirà	assaliranno	avrà assalito	avranno assalito
5 present conditional		12 past conditional	
assalirèi	assaliremmo	avrèi assalito	avremmo assalito
assaliresti	assalireste	avresti assalito	aveste assalito
assalirèbbe	assalirèbbero	avrèbbe assalito	avrèbbero assalito
6 present subjunctive		13 past subjunctive	
assalga	assaliamo	àbbia assalito	abbiamo assalito
assalga	assaliate	àbbia assalito	abbiate assalito
assalga	assàlgano	àbbia assalito	àbbiano assalito
(*Or regular:* assalisca, *etc.*)			
7 imperfect subjunctive		14 past perfect subjunctive	
assalissi	assalíssimo	avessi assalito	avéssimo assalito
assalissi	assaliste	avessi assalito	aveste assalito
assalisse	assalíssero	avesse assalito	avéssero assalito

imperative

—	assaliamo
assali (assalisci) (non assalire)	assalite
assalga (assalisca)	assàlgano (assalíscano)

Words related to this verb
Il nemico ci assalì. The enemy assaulted us.
Io fui assalito da molti dubbi. I was assailed by many doubts.

assístere*   Ger. **assistèndo**   Past Part. **assistito**

to assist

The Seven Simple Tenses		The Seven Compound Tenses	
Singular	Plural	Singular	Plural
1 present indicative		8 present perfect	
assisto	**assistiamo**	**ho assistito**	**abbiamo assistito**
assisti	**assistete**	**hai assistito**	**avete assistito**
assiste	**assístono**	**ha assistito**	**hanno assistito**
2 imperfect indicative		9 past perfect	
assistevo	**assistevamo**	**avevo assistito**	**avevamo assistito**
assistevi	**assistevate**	**avevi assistito**	**avevate assistito**
assisteva	**assistévano**	**aveva assistito**	**avévano assistito**
3 past absolute		10 past anterior	
assistei (assistètti)	**assistemmo**	**èbbi assistito**	**avemmo assistito**
assistesti	**assisteste**	**avesti assistito**	**aveste assistito**
assisté (assistètte)	**assistérono (assistèttero)**	**èbbe assistito**	**èbbero assistito**
4 future indicative		11 future perfect	
assisterò	**assisteremo**	**avrò assistito**	**avremo assistito**
assisterai	**assisterete**	**avrai assistito**	**avrete assistito**
assisterà	**assisteranno**	**avrà assistito**	**avranno assistito**
5 present conditional		12 past conditional	
assisterèi	**assisteremmo**	**avrèi assistito**	**avremmo assistito**
assisteresti	**assistereste**	**avresti assistito**	**avreste assistito**
assisterèbbe	**assisterèbbero**	**avrèbbe assistito**	**avrèbbero assistito**
6 present subjunctive		13 past subjunctive	
assista	**assistiamo**	**àbbia assistito**	**abbiamo assistito**
assista	**assistiate**	**àbbia assistito**	**abbiate assistito**
assista	**assístano**	**àbbia assistito**	**àbbiano assitito**
7 imperfect subjunctive		14 past perfect subjunctive	
assistessi	**assistéssimo**	**avessi assistito**	**avéssimo assistito**
assistessi	**assisteste**	**avessi assistito**	**aveste assistito**
assistesse	**assistéssero**	**avesse assistito**	**avéssero assistito**

imperative	
—	**assistiamo**
assisti (non assístere)	**assistete**
assista	**assístano**

* Like *assístere* are *consístere* (conj. with *èssere*), *esístere* (conj. with *èssere*), *insístere*, *persístere*, and *resístere*.

Words related to this verb

Io assisto mia madre ogni giorno.   I assist (help) my mother every day.
Ti assisterò il più possibile.   I will help you as much as possible.

to assume

The Seven Simple Tenses		The Seven Compound Tenses	
Singular	Plural	Singular	Plural
1 present indicative		8 present perfect	
assumo	assumiamo	ho assunto	abbiamo assunto
assumi	assumete	hai assunto	avete assunto
assume	assúmono	ha assunto	hanno assunto
2 imperfect indicative		9 past perfect	
assumevo	assumevamo	avevo assunto	avevamo assunto
assumevi	assumevate	avevi assunto	avevate assunto
assumeva	assumévano	aveva assunto	avévano assunto
3 past absolute		10 past anterior	
assunsi	assumemmo	èbbi assunto	avemmo assunto
assumesti	assumeste	avesti assunto	aveste assunto
assunse	assúnsero	èbbe assunto	èbbero assunto
4 future indicative		11 future perfect	
assumerò	assumeremo	avrò assunto	avremo assunto
assumerai	assumerete	avrai assunto	avrete assunto
assumerà	assumeranno	avrà assunto	avranno assunto
5 present conditional		12 past conditional	
assumerèi	assumeremmo	avrèi assunto	avremmo assunto
assumeresti	assumereste	avresti assunto	avreste assunto
assumerèbbe	assumerèbbero	avrèbbe assunto	avrèbbero assunto
6 present subjunctive		13 past subjunctive	
assuma	assumiamo	àbbia assunto	abbiamo assunto
assuma	assumiate	àbbia assunto	abbiate assunto
assuma	assúmano	àbbia assunto	àbbiano assunto
7 imperfect subjunctive		14 past perfect subjunctive	
assumessi	assuméssimo	avessi assunto	avéssimo assunto
assumessi	assumeste	avessi assunto	aveste assunto
assumesse	assuméssero	avesse assunto	avéssero assunto

	imperative	
—		assumiamo
assumi (non assúmere)		assumete
assuma		assúmano

Words related to this verb
Mi assumo tutta la responsabilità.   I assume all the responsibility.
Perchè non assumi un altro contabile?   Why don't you hire another accountant?

attèndere   Ger. attendèndo   Past Part. atteso

to wait for, to attend

The Seven Simple Tenses		The Seven Compound Tenses	
Singular	Plural	Singular	Plural
1　present indicative		8　present perfect	
attèndo	attendiamo	ho atteso	abbiamo atteso
attèndi	attendete	hai atteso	avete atteso
attènde	attèndono	ha atteso	hanno atteso
2　imperfect indicative		9　past perfect	
attendevo	attendevamo	avevo atteso	avevamo atteso
attendevi	attendevate	avevi atteso	avevate atteso
attendeva	attendévano	aveva atteso	avévano atteso
3　past absolute		10　past anterior	
attesi	attendemmo	èbbi atteso	avemmo atteso
attendesti	attendeste	avesti atteso	aveste atteso
attese	attésero	èbbe atteso	èbbero atteso
4　future indicative		11　future perfect	
attenderò	attenderemo	avrò atteso	avremo atteso
attenderai	attenderete	avrai atteso	avrete atteso
attenderà	attenderanno	avrà atteso	avranno atteso
5　present conditional		12　past conditional	
attenderèi	attenderemmo	avrèi atteso	avremmo atteso
attenderesti	attendereste	avresti atteso	avreste atteso
attenderèbbe	attenderèbbero	avrèbbe atteso	avrèbbero atteso
6　present subjunctive		13　past subjunctive	
attènda	attendiamo	àbbia atteso	abbiamo atteso
attènda	attendiate	àbbia atteso	abbiate atteso
attènda	attèndano	àbbia atteso	àbbiano atteso
7　imperfect subjunctive		14　past perfect subjunctive	
attendessi	attendéssimo	avessi atteso	avéssimo atteso
attendessi	attendeste	avessi atteso	aveste atteso
attendesse	attendéssero	avesse atteso	avéssero atteso

imperative	
—	attendiamo
attèndi (non attèndere)	attendete
attenda	attèndano

Words related to this verb
Non sa cosa gli attende. He does not know what's waiting for him (what to expect).
Noi attendemmo tutti con impazienza i risultati dell'esame di statistica. We all
waited impatiently for the results of the statistics exam.

Ger. **avèndo** Past Part. **avuto** **avere**

to have, to get

The Seven Simple Tenses		The Seven Compound Tenses	
Singular	Plural	Singular	Plural
1 present indicative		8 present perfect	
ho	**abbiamo**	**ho avuto**	**abbiamo avuto**
hai	**avete**	**hai avuto**	**avete avuto**
ha	**hanno**	**ha avuto**	**hanno avuto**
2 imperfect indicative		9 past perfect	
avevo	**avevamo**	**avevo avuto**	**avevamo avuto**
avevi	**avevate**	**avevi avuto**	**avevate avuto**
aveva	**avévano**	**aveva avuto**	**avévano avuto**
3 past absolute		10 past anterior	
èbbi	**avemmo**	**èbbi avuto**	**avemmo avuto**
avesti	**aveste**	**avesti avuto**	**aveste avuto**
èbbe	**èbbero**	**èbbe avuto**	**èbbero avuto**
4 future indicative		11 future perfect	
avrò	**avremo**	**avrò avuto**	**avremo avuto**
avrai	**avrete**	**avrai avuto**	**avrete avuto**
avrà	**avranno**	**avrà avuto**	**avranno avuto**
5 present conditional		12 past conditional	
avrèi	**avremmo**	**avrèi avuto**	**avremmo avuto**
avresti	**avreste**	**avresti avuto**	**avreste avuto**
avrèbbe	**avrèbbero**	**avrèbbe avuto**	**avrèbbero avuto**
6 present subjunctive		13 past subjunctive	
àbbia	**abbiamo**	**àbbia avuto**	**abbiamo avuto**
àbbia	**abbiate**	**àbbia avuto**	**abbiate avuto**
àbbia	**àbbiano**	**àbbia avuto**	**abbiano avuto**
7 imperfect subjunctive		14 past perfect subjunctive	
avessi	**avéssimo**	**avessi avuto**	**avéssimo avuto**
avessi	**aveste**	**avessi avuto**	**aveste avuto**
avesse	**avéssero**	**avesse avuto**	**avéssero avuto**

imperative	
—	**abbiamo**
abbi (non avere)	**abbiate**
àbbia	**àbbiano**

Words related to this verb
Io ho sonno. I am sleepy.
Lei ha sete. She is thirsty.

avvedersi   Ger. **avvedendosi**   Past Part. **avvedutosi**

to perceive, to notice, to become aware

The Seven Simple Tenses		The Seven Compound Tenses	
Singular	Plural	Singular	Plural
1 present indicative		8 present perfect	
mi avvedo	**ci avvediamo**	**mi sono avveduto**	**ci siamo avveduti**
ti avvedi	**vi avvedete**	**ti sèi avveduto**	**vi siète avveduti**
si avvede	**si avvédono**	**si è avveduto**	**si sono avveduti**
2 imperfect indicative		9 past perfect	
mi avvedevo	**ci avvedevamo**	**mi èro avveduto**	**ci eravamo avveduti**
ti avvedevi	**vi avvedevate**	**ti èri avveduto**	**vi eravate avveduti**
si avvedeva	**si avvedévano**	**si èra avveduto**	**si èrano avveduti**
3 past absolute		10 past anterior	
mi avvidi	**ci avvedemmo**	**mi fui avveduto**	**ci fummo avveduti**
ti avvedesti	**vi avvedeste**	**ti fosti avveduto**	**vi foste avveduti**
si avvide	**si avvidéro**	**si fu avveduto**	**si fúrono avveduti**
4 future indicative		11 future perfect	
mi avvedrò	**ci avvedremo**	**mi sarò avveduto**	**ci saremo avveduti**
ti avvedrai	**vi avvedrete**	**ti sarai avveduto**	**vi sarete avveduti**
si avvedrà	**si avvedranno**	**si sarà avveduto**	**si saranno avveduti**
5 present conditional		12 past conditional	
mi avvedrèi	**ci avvedremmo**	**mi sarèi avveduto**	**ci saremmo avveduti**
ti avvedresti	**vi avvedreste**	**ti saresti avveduto**	**vi sareste avveduti**
si avvedrèbbe	**si avvedrèbbero**	**si sarèbbe avveduto**	**si sarèbbero avveduti**
6 present subjunctive		13 past subjunctive	
mi avveda	**ci avvediamo**	**mi sia avveduto**	**ci siamo avveduti**
ti avveda	**vi avvediate**	**ti sia avveduto**	**vi siate avveduti**
si avveda	**si avvédano**	**si sia avveduto**	**si síano avveduti**
7 imperfect subjunctive		14 past perfect subjunctive	
mi avvedessi	**ci avvedéssimo**	**mi fossi avveduto**	**ci fóssimo avveduti**
ti avvedessi	**vi avvedeste**	**ti fossi avveduto**	**vi foste avveduti**
si avvedesse	**si avvedéssero**	**si fosse avveduto**	**si fóssero avveduti**

	imperative	
	—	**avvediamoci**
	avvèditi (non ti avvedere)	**avvedetevi**
	si avveda	**si avvédano**

Words related to this verb
Si avvide della verità.   He became aware of the truth.
Piansi senza avvedermene.   I cried without realizing it.

to happen, to occur

The Seven Simple Tenses		The Seven Compound Tenses	
Singular	Plural	Singular	Plural
1 present indicative		8 present perfect	
avviène	avvèngono	è avvenuto	sono avvenuti
2 imperfect indicative		9 past perfect	
avveniva	avvenívano	èra avvenuto	èrano avvenuti
3 past absolute		10 past anterior	
avvenne	avvénnero	fu avvenuto	fúrono avvenuti
4 future indicative		11 future perfect	
avverrà	avverranno	sarà avvenuto	saranno avvenuti
5 present conditional		12 past conditional	
avverrèbbe	avverrèbbero	sarèbbe avvenuto	sarèbbero avvenuti
6 present subjunctive		13 past subjunctive	
avvènga	avvèngano	sia avvenuto	síano avvenuti
7 imperfect subjunctive		14 past perfect subjunctive	
avvenisse	avveníssero	fosse avvenuto	fóssero avvenuti
		imperative	

Words related to this verb
I suoi cugini arrivano dal Canada in estate. Questo avviene una volta all'anno.
His cousins come from Canada in summer. It happens once a year.
Chi sa cosa avverrà nel futuro?   Who knows what will happen in the future?

benedire	Ger. benedicèndo	Past Part. benedetto

to bless

The Seven Simple Tenses		The Seven Compound Tenses	
Singular	Plural	Singular	Plural
1 present indicative		8 present perfect	
benedico	benediciamo	ho benedetto	abbiamo benedetto
benedici	benedite	hai benedetto	avete benedetto
benedice	benedícono	ha benedetto	hanno benedetto
2 imperfect indicative		9 past perfect	
benedicevo	benedicevamo	avevo benedetto	avevamo benedetto
benedicevi	benedicevate	avevi benedetto	avevate benedetto
benediceva	benedicévano	aveva benedetto	avévano benedetto
(Or regular: benedivo, etc.)			
3 past absolute		10 past anterior	
benedissi	benedicemmo	èbbi benedetto	avemmo benedetto
benedicesti	benediceste	avesti benedetto	aveste benedetto
benedisse	benedíssero	èbbe benedetto	èbbero benedetto
(Or regular: benedii, etc.)			
4 future indicative		11 future perfect	
benedirò	benediremo	avrò benedetto	avremo benedetto
benedirai	benedirete	avrai benedetto	avrete benedetto
benedirà	benediranno	avrà benedetto	avranno benedetto
5 present conditional		12 past conditional	
benedirèi	benediremmo	avrèi benedetto	avremmo benedetto
benediresti	benedireste	avresti benedetto	avreste benedetto
benedirèbbe	benedirèbbero	avrèbbe benedetto	avrèbbero benedetto
6 present subjunctive		13 past subjunctive	
benedica	benediciamo	àbbia benedetto	abbiamo benedetto
benedica	benediciate	àbbia benedetto	abbiate benedetto
benedica	benedícano	àbbia benedetto	àbbiano benedetto
7 imperfect subjunctive		14 past perfect subjunctive	
benedicessi	benedicéssimo	avessi benedetto	avéssimo benedetto
benedicessi	benediceste	avessi benedetto	aveste benedetto
benedicesse	benedicéssero	avesse benedetto	avéssero benedetto
(Or regular: benedissi, etc.)			

	imperative	
—		benediciamo
benedici (non benedire)		benedite
benedica		benedícano

Words related to this verb
Dio vi benedica!   God bless you!
Il sacerdote benedice i fedeli.   The priest blesses the faithful.

36

Ger. **bevèndo**   Past Part. **bevuto**   **bere (bévere)**

to drink

The Seven Simple Tenses		The Seven Compound Tenses	
Singular	Plural	Singular	Plural
1 present indicative		8 present perfect	
bevo	**beviamo**	**ho bevuto**	**abbiamo bevuto**
bevi	**bevete**	**hai bevuto**	**avete bevuto**
beve	**bévono**	**ha bevuto**	**hanno bevuto**
2 imperfect indicative		9 past perfect	
bevevo	**bevevamo**	**avevo bevuto**	**avevamo bevuto**
bevevi	**bevevate**	**avevi bevuto**	**avevate bevuto**
beveva	**bevévano**	**aveva bevuto**	**avévano bevuto**
3 past absolute		10 past anterior	
bevvi (bevètti)	**bevemmo**	**èbbi bevuto**	**avemmo bevuto**
bevesti	**beveste**	**avesti bevuto**	**aveste bevuto**
bevve (bevètte)	**bévvero (bevèttero)**	**èbbe bevuto**	**èbbero bevuto**
4 future indicative		11 future perfect	
berrò	**berremo**	**avrò bevuto**	**avremo bevuto**
berrai	**berrete**	**avrai bevuto**	**avrete bevuto**
berrà	**berranno**	**avrà bevuto**	**avranno bevuto**
5 present conditional		12 past conditional	
berrèi	**berremmo**	**avrèi bevuto**	**avremmo bevuto**
berresti	**berreste**	**avresti bevuto**	**avreste bevuto**
berrèbbe	**berrèbbero**	**avrèbbe bevuto**	**avrèbbero bevuto**
6 present subjunctive		13 past subjunctive	
beva	**beviamo**	**àbbia bevuto**	**abbiamo bevuto**
beva	**beviate**	**àbbia bevuto**	**abbiate bevuto**
beva	**bévano**	**àbbia bevuto**	**àbbiano bevuto**
7 imperfect subjunctive		14 past perfect subjunctive	
bevessi	**bevéssimo**	**avessi bevuto**	**avéssimo bevuto**
bevessi	**beveste**	**avessi bevuto**	**aveste bevuto**
bevesse	**bevéssero**	**avesse bevuto**	**avéssero bevuto**

	imperative	
—		**beviamo**
bevi (non bere)		**bevete**
beva		**bévano**

Words related to this verb

Io bevo un bicchiere di latte al giorno.   I drink a cup of milk a day.

Beviamo alla tua salute!   Let's drink to your health!

bisognare	Ger. bisognando	Past Part. bisognato

to be necessary, to have to, must

The Seven Simple Tenses	The Seven Compound Tenses

Singular	Plural	Singular	Plural
1 present indicative **bisogna**		8 present perfect **è bisognato**	
2 imperfect indicative **bisognava**		9 past perfect **èra bisognato**	
3 past absolute **bisognò**		10 past anterior **fu bisognato**	
4 future indicative **bisognerà**		11 future perfect **sarà bisognato**	
5 present conditional **bisognerèbbe**		12 past conditional **sarèbbe bisognato**	
6 present subjunctive **bisogni**		13 past subjunctive **sia bisognato**	
7 imperfect subjunctive **bisognasse**		14 past perfect subjunctive **fosse bisognato**	
		imperative	

Words related to this verb
Bisogna finire questo lavoro.   This work must be finished.
Bisogna condire l'insalata. Dov'è l'olio d'oliva?   We must season the salad. Where is the olive oil?

to boil

The Seven Simple Tenses		The Seven Compound Tenses	
Singular	Plural	Singular	Plural
1 present indicative		8 present perfect	
bòllo	bolliamo	ho bollito	abbiamo bollito
bòlli	bollite	hai bollito	avete bollito
bòlle	bòllono	ha bollito	hanno bollito
2 imperfect indicative		9 past perfect	
bollivo	bollivamo	avevo bollito	avevamo bollito
bollivi	bollivate	avevi bollito	avevate bollito
bolliva	bollívano	aveva bollito	avévano bollito
3 past absolute		10 past anterior	
bollii	bollimmo	èbbi bollito	avemmo bollito
bollisti	bolliste	avesti bollito	aveste bollito
bollí	bollírono	èbbe bollito	èbbero bollito
4 future indicative		11 future perfect	
bollirò	bolliremo	avrò bollito	avremo bollito
bollirai	bollirete	avrai bollito	avrete bollito
bollirà	bolliranno	avrà bollito	avranno bollito
5 present conditional		12 past conditional	
bollirèi	bolliremmo	avrèi bollito	avremmo bollito
bolliresti	bollireste	avresti bollito	avreste bollito
bollirèbbe	bollirèbbero	avrèbbe bollito	avrèbbero bollito
6 present subjunctive		13 past subjunctive	
bòlla	bolliamo	àbbia bollito	abbiamo bollito
bòlla	bolliate	àbbia bollito	abbiate bollito
bòlla	bòllano	àbbia bollito	àbbiano bollito
7 imperfect subjunctive		14 past perfect subjunctive	
bollissi	bollìssimo	avessi bollito	avéssimo bollito
bollissi	bolliste	avessi bollito	aveste bollito
bollisse	bollìssero	avesse bollito	avéssero bollito

imperative	
—	bolliamo
bòlli (non bollire)	bollite
bòlla	bòllano

Words related to this verb
Per quanto tempo devo bollire le patate?   How long should I boil the potatoes?
L'acqua bolle. Butta gli spaghetti!   The water boils. Throw the spaghetti in!

cadere*   Ger. **cadèndo**   Past Part. **caduto**

to fall

The Seven Simple Tenses		The Seven Compound Tenses	
Singular	Plural	Singular	Plural
1 present indicative		8 present perfect	
cado	**cadiamo**	**sono caduto**	**siamo caduti**
cadi	**cadete**	**sèi caduto**	**siète caduti**
cade	**càdono**	**è caduto**	**sono caduti**
2 imperfect indicative		9 past perfect	
cadevo	**cadevamo**	**èro caduto**	**eravamo caduti**
cadevi	**cadevate**	**èri caduto**	**eravate caduti**
cadeva	**cadévano**	**èra caduto**	**èrano caduti**
3 past absolute		10 past anterior	
caddi	**cademmo**	**fui caduto**	**fummo caduti**
cadesti	**cadeste**	**fosti caduto**	**foste caduti**
cadde	**càddero**	**fu caduto**	**fúrono caduti**
4 future indicative		11 future perfect	
cadrò	**cadremo**	**sarò caduto**	**saremo caduti**
cadrai	**cadrete**	**sarai caduto**	**sarete caduti**
cadrà	**cadranno**	**sarà caduto**	**saranno caduti**
5 present conditional		12 past conditional	
cadrèi	**cadremmo**	**sarèi caduto**	**saremmo caduti**
cadresti	**cadreste**	**saresti caduto**	**sareste caduti**
cadrèbbe	**cadrèbbero**	**sarèbbe caduto**	**sarèbbero caduti**
6 present subjunctive		13 past subjunctive	
cada	**cadiamo**	**sia caduto**	**siamo caduti**
cada	**cadiate**	**sia caduto**	**siate caduti**
cada	**càdano**	**sia caduto**	**síano caduti**
7 imperfect subjunctive		14 past perfect subjunctive	
cadessi	**cadéssimo**	**fossi caduto**	**fóssimo caduti**
cadessi	**cadeste**	**fossi caduto**	**foste caduti**
cadesse	**cadéssero**	**fosse caduto**	**fóssero caduti**

	imperative	
—		**cadiamo**
cadi (non cadere)		**cadete**
cada		**càdano**

* Like *cadere* are *accadere* (used only in the 3d person), *decadere*, *ricadere*, and *scadere*.

Words related to this verb
La pioggia cade a torrenti.   The rain falls in torrents (is falling heavily).
Io sono caduto mentre giocavo.   I fell while I was playing.

Ger. **camminando**   Past Part. **camminato**   **camminare**

to walk

The Seven Simple Tenses		The Seven compound Tenses	
Singular	Plural	Singular	Plural
1 present indicative		8 present perfect	
cammino	camminiamo	ho camminato	abbiamo camminato
cammini	camminate	hai camminato	avete camminato
cammina	camminano	ha camminato	hanno camminato
2 imperfect indicative		9 past perfect	
camminavo	camminavamo	avevo camminato	avevamo camminato
camminavi	camminavate	avevi camminato	avevate camminato
camminava	camminàvano	aveva camminato	avévano camminato
3 past absolute		10 past anterior	
camminai	camminammo	èbbi camminato	avemmo camminato
camminasti	camminaste	avesti camminato	aveste camminato
camminò	camminàrono	èbbe camminato	èbbero camminato
4 future indicative		11 future perfect	
camminerò	cammineremo	avrò camminato	avremo camminato
camminerai	camminerete	avrai camminato	avrete camminato
camminerà	cammineranno	avrà camminato	avranno camminato
5 present conditional		12 past conditional	
camminerèi	cammineremo	avrèi camminato	avremmo camminato
cammineresti	camminereste	avresti camminato	avreste camminato
camminerèbbe	camminerèbbero	avrèbbe camminato	avrèbbero camminato
6 present subjunctive		13 past subjunctive	
cammini	camminiamo	àbbia camminato	abbiamo camminato
cammini	camminiate	àbbia camminato	abbiate camminato
cammini	cammìnino	àbbia camminato	àbbiano camminato
7 imperfect subjunctive		14 past perfect subjunctive	
camminassi	camminàssimo	avessi camminato	avéssimo camminato
camminassi	camminaste	avessi camminato	aveste camminato
camminasse	camminàssero	avesse camminato	avéssero camminato

imperative	
—	camminiamo
cammina (non camminare)	camminate
cammini	cammìnino

Words related to this verb
Lei cammina ogni mattina per due ore.   She walks every morning for two hours.
Lui cammina su e giù.   He walks up and down.

cancellare   Ger. **cancellando**   Past Part. **cancellato**

to cross out, to cancel, to rub out

The Seven Simple Tenses		The Seven Compound Tenses	
Singular	Plural	Singular	Plural
1 present indicative		8 present perfect	
cancèllo	**cancelliamo**	**ho cancellato**	**abbiamo cancellato**
cancèlli	**cancellate**	**hai cancellato**	**avete cancellato**
cancèlla	**cancèllano**	**ha cancellato**	**hanno cancellato**
2 imperfect indicative		9 past perfect	
cancellavo	**cancellavamo**	**avevo cancellato**	**avevamo cancellato**
cancellavi	**cancellavate**	**avevi cancellato**	**avevate cancellato**
cancellava	**cancellàvano**	**aveva cancellato**	**avévano cancellato**
3 past absolute		10 past anterior	
cancellai	**cancellammo**	**èbbi cancellato**	**avemmo cancellato**
cancellasti	**cancellaste**	**avesti cancellato**	**aveste cancellato**
cancellò	**cancellàrono**	**èbbe cancellato**	**èbbero cancellato**
4 future indicative		11 future perfect	
cancellerò	**cancelleremo**	**avrò cancellato**	**avremo cancellato**
cancellerai	**cancellerete**	**avrai cancellato**	**avrete cancellato**
cancellerà	**cancelleranno**	**avrà cancellato**	**avranno cancellato**
5 present conditional		12 past conditional	
cancellerèi	**cancelleremmo**	**avrèi cancellato**	**avremmo cancellato**
cancelleresti	**cancellereste**	**avresti cancellato**	**avreste cancellato**
cancellerèbbe	**cancellerèbbero**	**avrèbbe cancellato**	**avrèbbero cancellato**
6 present subjunctive		13 past subjunctive	
cancèlli	**cancelliamo**	**àbbia cancellato**	**abbiamo cancellato**
cancèlli	**cancelliate**	**àbbia cancellato**	**abbiate cancellato**
cancèlli	**cancèllino**	**àbbia cancellato**	**àbbiano cancellato**
7 imperfect subjunctive		14 past perfect subjunctive	
cancellassi	**cancellàssimo**	**avessi cancellato**	**avéssimo cancellato**
cancellassi	**cancellaste**	**avessi cancellato**	**aveste cancellato**
cancellasse	**cancellàssero**	**avesse cancellato**	**avéssero cancellato**

	imperative	
—		**cancelliamo**
cancèlla (non cancellare)		**cancellate**
cancèlli		**cancèllino**

Words related to this verb

cancellare un contratto   to cancel a contract
Lo cancellai dalla mia mente perchè era un fatto troppo doloroso.   I cancelled it from my mind because it was too painful.

to understand

The Seven Simple Tenses		The Seven Compound Tenses	
Singular	Plural	Singular	Plural
1 present indicative		8 present perfect	
capisco	capiamo	ho capito	abbiamo capito
capisci	capite	hai capito	avete capito
capisce	capíscono	ha capito	hanno capito
2 imperfect indicative		9 past perfect	
capivo	capivamo	avevo capito	avevamo capito
capivi	capivate	avevi capito	avevate capito
capiva	capívano	aveva capito	avévano capito
3 past absolute		10 past anterior	
capii	capimmo	èbbi capito	avemmo capito
capisti	capiste	avesti capito	aveste capito
capí	capírono	èbbe capito	èbbero capito
4 future indicative		11 future perfect	
capirò	capiremo	avrò capito	avremo capito
capirai	capirete	avrai capito	avrete capito
capirà	capiranno	avrà capito	avranno capito
5 present conditional		12 past conditional	
capirèi	capiremmo	avrèi capito	avremmo capito
capiresti	capireste	avresti capito	avreste capito
capirèbbe	capirèbbero	avrèbbe capito	avrèbbero capito
6 present subjunctive		13 past subjunctive	
capisca	capiamo	àbbia capito	abbiamo capito
capisca	capiate	àbbia capito	abbiate capito
capisca	capíscano	àbbia capito	àbbiano capito
7 imperfect subjunctive		14 past perfect subjunctive	
capissi	capíssimo	avessi capito	avéssimo capito
capissi	capiste	avessi capito	aveste capito
capisse	capíssero	avesse capito	avéssero capito

imperative	
—	capiamo
capisci (non capire)	capite
capisca	capíscano

Words related to this verb
Loro capiscono cosa dico.   They understand what I am saying.
Capisci l'italiano?   Do you understand Italian?

cercare	Ger. **cercando**	Past Part. **cercato**

to look for, to seek

The Seven Simple Tenses		The Seven compound Tenses	
Singular	Plural	Singular	Plural
1 present indicative		8 present perfect	
cerco	cerchiamo	ho cercato	abbiamo cercato
cerchi	cercate	hai cercato	avete cercato
cerca	cércano	ha cercato	hanno cercato
2 imperfect indicative		9 past perfect	
cercavo	cercavamo	avevo cercato	avevamo cercato
cercavi	cercavate	avevi cercato	avevate cercato
cercava	cercàvano	aveva cercato	avévano cercato
3 past absolute		10 past anterior	
cercai	cercammo	èbbi cercato	avemmo cercato
cercasti	cercaste	avesti cercato	aveste cercato
cercò	cercàrono	èbbe cercato	èbbero cercato
4 future indicative		11 future perfect	
cercherò	cercheremo	avrò cercato	avremo cercato
cercherai	cercherete	avrai cercato	avrete cercato
cercherà	cercheranno	avrà cercato	avranno cercato
5 present conditional		12 past conditional	
cercherèi	cercheremmo	avrèi cercato	avremmo cercato
cercheresti	cerchereste	avresti cercato	avreste cercato
cercherèbbe	cercherèbbero	avrèbbe cercato	avrèbbero cercato
6 present subjunctive		13 past subjunctive	
cerchi	cerchiamo	àbbia cercato	abbiamo cercato
cerchi	cerchiate	àbbia cercato	abbiate cercato
cerchi	cérchino	àbbia cercato	àbbiano cercato
7 imperfect subjunctive		14 past perfect subjunctive	
cercassi	cercàssimo	avessi cercato	avéssimo cercato
cercassi	cercaste	avessi cercato	aveste cercato
cercasse	cercàssero	avesse cercato	avéssero cercato

	imperative	
—		cerchiamo
cerca (non cercare)		cercate
cerchi		cérchino

Words related to this verb
Lui cerca una soluzione.   He is looking for a solution.
Lo cercai dappertutto.   I looked everywhere for him.

to ask

The Seven Simple Tenses		The Seven Compound Tenses	
Singular	Plural	Singular	Plural
1 present indicative		8 present perfect	
chiedo (chieggo)	**chiediamo**	**ho chiesto**	**abbiamo chiesto**
chiedi	**chiedete**	**hai chiesto**	**avete chiesto**
chiede	**chiédono (chiéggono)**	**ha chiesto**	**hanno chiesto**
2 imperfect indicative		9 past perfect	
chiedevo	**chiedevamo**	**avevo chiesto**	**avevamo chiesto**
chiedevi	**chiedevate**	**avevi chiesto**	**avevate chiesto**
chiedeva	**chiedévano**	**aveva chiesto**	**avévano chiesto**
3 past absolute		10 past anterior	
chiesi	**chiedemmo**	**èbbi chiesto**	**avemmo chiesto**
chiedesti	**chiedeste**	**avesti chiesto**	**aveste chiesto**
chiese	**chiésero**	**èbbe chiesto**	**èbbero chiesto**
4 future indicative		11 future perfect	
chiederò	**chiederemo**	**avrò chiesto**	**avremo chiesto**
chiederai	**chiederete**	**avrai chiesto**	**avrete chiesto**
chiederà	**chiederanno**	**avrà chiesto**	**avranno chiesto**
5 present conditional		12 past conditional	
chiederèi	**chiederemmo**	**avrèi chiesto**	**avremmo chiesto**
chiederesti	**chiedereste**	**avresti chiesto**	**avreste chiesto**
chiederèbbe	**chiederèbbero**	**avrèbbe chiesto**	**avrèbbero chiesto**
6 present subjunctive		13 past subjunctive	
chieda (chiegga)	**chiediamo**	**àbbia chiesto**	**abbiamo chiesto**
chieda (chiegga)	**chiediate**	**àbbia chiesto**	**abbiate chiesto**
chieda (chiegga)	**chiédano (chiéggano)**	**àbbia chiesto**	**àbbiano chiesto**
7 imperfect subjunctive		14 past perfect subjunctive	
chiedessi	**chiedéssimo**	**avessi chiesto**	**avéssimo chiesto**
chiedessi	**chiedeste**	**avessi chiesto**	**aveste chiesto**
chiedesse	**chiedéssero**	**avesse chiesto**	**avéssero chiesto**

imperative

—	**chiediamo**
chiedi (non chiédere)	**chiedete**
chieda (chiegga)	**chiédano (chiéggano)**

Words related to this verb
Chiedigli che ora è.   Ask him what time it is.
Mi chiese di andare con lui.   He asked me to go with him.

chiúdere* Ger. **chiudèndo** Past Part. **chiuso**

to close, to shut

The Seven Simple Tenses		The Seven Compound Tenses	
Singular	Plural	Singular	Plural
1 present indicative		8 present perfect	
chuido	chiudiamo	ho chiuso	abbiamo chiuso
chiudi	chiudete	hai chiuso	avete chiuso
chiude	chiúdono	ha chiuso	hanno chiuso
2 imperfect indicative		9 past perfect	
chiudevo	chiudevamo	avevo chiuso	avevamo chiuso
chiudevi	chiudevate	avevi chiuso	avevate chiuso
chiudeva	chiudévano	aveva chiuso	avévano chiuso
3 past absolute		10 past anterior	
chiusi	chiudemmo	èbbi chiuso	avemmo chiuso
chiudesti	chiudeste	avesti chiuso	aveste chiuso
chiuse	chiúsero	èbbe chiuso	èbbero chiuso
4 future indicative		11 future perfect	
chiuderò	chiuderemo	avrò chiuso	avremo chiuso
chiuderai	chiuderete	avrai chiuso	avrete chiuso
chiuderà	chiuderanno	avrà chiuso	avranno chiuso
5 present conditional		12 past conditional	
chiuderèi	chiuderemmo	avrèi chiuso	avremmo chiuso
chiuderesti	chiudereste	avresti chiuso	avreste chiuso
chiuderèbbe	chiuderèbbero	avrèbbe chiuso	avrèbbero chiuso
6 present subjunctive		13 past subjunctive	
chiuda	chiudiamo	àbbia chiuso	abbiamo chiuso
chiuda	chiudiate	àbbia chiuso	abbiate chiuso
chiuda	chiúdano	àbbia chiuso	àbbiano chiuso
7 imperfect subjunctive		14 past perfect subjunctive	
chiudessi	chiudéssimo	avessi chiuso	avéssimo chiuso
chiudessi	chiudeste	avessi chiuso	aveste chiuso
chiudesse	chiudéssero	avesse chiuso	avéssero chiuso

imperative

—	chiudiamo
chiudi (non chiúdere)	chiudete
chiuda	chiúdano

* Like *chiúdere* are *conchiúdere*, *racchiúdere*, *rinchiúdere*, *schiúdere*, and *socchiúdere*.

Words related to this verb
Chiudi la porta! Ho paura dei ladri.   Close the door! I am afraid of thieves.
Lei chiude la porta quando esce.   She closes the door when she goes out.

Ger. **coglièndo**   Past Part. **còlto**   **còogliere***

to gather, to pick, to catch

The Seven Simple Tenses		The Seven Compound Tenses	
Singular	Plural	Singular	Plural
1 present indicative		8 present perfect	
còlgo	cogliamo	ho còlto	abbiamo còlto
còli	cogliete	hai còlto	avete còlto
còglie	còlgono	ha còlto	hanno còlto
2 imperfect indicative		9 past perfect	
coglievo	coglievamo	avevo còlto	avevamo còlto
coglievi	coglievate	avevi còlto	avevate còlto
coglieva	cogliévano	aveva còlto	avévano còlto
3 past absolute		10 past anterior	
còlsi	cogliemmo	èbbi còlto	avemmo còlto
cogliesti	coglieste	avesti còlto	aveste còlto
còlse	còlsero	èbbe còlto	èbbero còlto
4 future indicative		11 future perfect	
coglierò	coglieremo	avrò còlto	avremo còlto
coglierai	coglierete	avrai còlto	avrete còlto
coglierà	coglieranno	avrà còlto	avranno còlto
5 present conditional		12 past conditional	
coglierèi	coglieremmo	avrèi còlto	avremmo còlto
coglieresti	cogliereste	avresti còlto	avreste còlto
coglierèbbe	coglierèbbero	avrèbbe còlto	avrèbbero còlto
6 present subjunctive		13 past subjunctive	
còlga	cogliamo	àbbia còlto	abbiamo còlto
còlga	cogliate	àbbia còlto	abbiate còlto
còlga	còlgano	àbbia còlto	àbbiano còlto
7 imperfect subjunctive		14 past perfect subjunctive	
cogliessi	cogliéssimo	avessi còlto	avéssimo còlto
cogliessi	coglieste	avessi còlto	aveste còlto
cogliesse	cogliéssero	avesse còlto	avéssero còlto

imperative	
—	cogliamo
còli (non cògliere)	cogliete
còlga	còlgano

* Like *còogliere* are *accògliere*, *raccògliere*, and *ricògliere*.

Words related to this verb
Voi cogliete ogni opportunità per mettervi in mostra.   You pick every opportunity
to show off.
Lo colsi sul fatto.   I caught him red-handed.

cominciare	Ger. **cominciando**	Past Part. **cominciato**

to begin, to start

The Seven Simple Tenses		The Seven Compound Tenses	
Singular	Plural	Singular	Plural
1 present indicative		8 present perfect	
comìncio	cominciamo	ho cominciato	abbiamo cominciato
comìnci	cominciate	hai cominciato	avete cominciato
comìncia	comìnciano	ha cominciato	hanno cominciato
2 imperfect indicative		9 past perfect	
cominciavo	cominciavamo	avevo cominciato	avevamo cominciato
cominciavi	cominciavate	avevi cominciato	avevate cominiciato
cominciava	cominciavano	aveva cominciato	avévano cominciato
3 past absolute		10 past anterior	
cominciai	cominciammo	èbbi cominciato	avemmo cominciato
cominciasti	cominciaste	avesti cominciato	aveste cominciato
cominciò	cominciàrono	èbbe cominciato	èbbero cominciato
4 future indicative		11 future perfect	
comincerò	cominceremo	avrò cominciato	avremo cominciato
comincerai	comincerete	avrai cominciato	avrete cominciato
comincerà	cominceranno	avrà cominciato	avranno cominciato
5 present conditional		12 past conditional	
comincerèi	cominceremmo	avrèi cominciato	avremmo cominciato
cominceresti	comincereste	avresti cominciato	avreste cominciato
comincerèbbe	comincerèbbero	avrèbbe cominciato	avrèbbero cominciato
6 present subjunctive		13 past subjunctive	
comìnci	cominciamo	àbbia cominciato	abbiamo cominciato
comìnci	cominciate	àbbia cominciato	abbiate cominciato
comìnci	comìncino	àbbia cominciato	àbbiano cominciato
7 imperfect subjunctive		14 past perfect subjunctive	
cominciassi	cominciàssimo	avessi cominciato	avéssimo cominciato
cominciassi	cominciaste	avessi cominciato	aveste cominciato
cominciasse	cominciàssero	avesse cominciato	avéssero cominciato

	imperative	
	—	cominciamo
	comìncia (non cominciare)	cominciate
	comìnci	comìncino

Words related to this verb
Comincia a piovere. It's starting to rain.
Chi ben comincia, è a metà dell'opera. Well begun is half done.

The Seven Simple Tenses		The Seven Compound Tenses	
Singular	Plural	Singular	Plural
1 present indicative		8 present perfect	
commetto	commettiamo	ho commesso	abbiamo commesso
commetti	commettete	hai commesso	avete commesso
commette	comméttono	ha commesso	hanno commesso
2 imperfect indicative		9 past perfect	
commettevo	commettevamo	avevo commesso	avevamo commesso
commettevi	commettevate	avevi commesso	avevate commesso
commetteva	commettévano	aveva commesso	avévano commesso
3 past absolute		10 past anterior	
commisi	commettemmo	èbbi commesso	avemmo commesso
commettesti	commetteste	avesti commesso	aveste commesso
commise	commísero	èbbe commesso	èbbero commesso
4 future indicative		11 future perfect	
commetterò	commetteremo	avrò commesso	avremo commesso
commetterai	commetterete	avrai commesso	avrete commesso
commetterà	commetteranno	avrà commesso	avranno commesso
5 present conditional		12 past conditional	
commetterèi	commetteremmo	avrèi commesso	avremmo commesso
commetteresti	commettereste	avresti commesso	avreste commesso
commetterèbbe	commetterèbbero	avrèbbe commesso	avrèbbero commesso
6 present subjunctive		13 past subjunctive	
commetta	commettiamo	àbbia commesso	abbiamo commesso
commetta	commettiate	àbbia commesso	abbiate commesso
commetta	comméttano	àbbia commesso	àbbiano commesso
7 imperfect subjunctive		14 past perfect subjunctive	
commettessi	commettéssimo	avessi commesso	avéssimo commesso
commettessi	commetteste	avessi commesso	aveste commesso
commettesse	commettéssero	avesse commesso	avéssero commesso

imperative	
—	commettiamo
commetti (non comméttere)	commettete
commetta	comméttano

Words related to this verb
Chi non ha mai commesso un errore?   Who has never committed a mistake?
Ho commesso uno sbaglio.   I committed (made) a mistake.

commuòvere   Ger. **commovèndo**   Past Part. **commòsso**

to move, to touch, to affect

The Seven Simple Tenses		The Seven Compound Tenses	
Singular	Plural	Singular	Plural
1 present indicative		8 present perfect	
commuòvo	comm(u)oviamo	ho commòsso	abbiamo commòsso
commuòvi	comm(u)ovete	hai commòsso	avete commòsso
commuòve	commuòvono	ha commòsso	hanno commòsso
2 imperfect indicative		9 past perfect	
comm(u)ovevo	comm(u)ovevamo	avevo commòsso	avevamo commòsso
comm(u)ovevi	comm(u)ovevate	avevi commòsso	avevate commòsso
comm(u)oveva	comm(u)ovévano	aveva commòsso	avévano commòsso
3 past absolute		10 past anterior	
commòssi	comm(u)ovemmo	èbbi commòsso	avemmo commòsso
comm(u)ovesti	comm(u)oveste	avesti commòsso	aveste commòsso
commòsse	commòssero	èbbe commòsso	èbbero commòsso
4 future indicative		11 future perfect	
comm(u)overò	comm(u)overemo	avrò commòsso	avremo commòsso
comm(u)overai	comm(u)overete	avrai commòsso	avrete commòsso
comm(u)overà	comm(u)overanno	avrà commòsso	avranno commòsso
5 present conditional		12 past conditional	
comm(u)overèi	comm(u)overemmo	avrèi commòsso	avremmo commòsso
comm(u)overesti	comm(u)overeste	avresti commòsso	avreste commòsso
comm(u)overèbbe	comm(u)overèbbero	avrèbbe	avrèbbero
		commòsso	commòsso
6 present subjunctive		13 past subjunctive	
commuòva	comm(u)oviamo	àbbia commòsso	abbiamo commòsso
commuòva	comm(u)oviate	àbbia commòsso	abbiate commòsso
commuòva	commuòvano	àbbia commòsso	àbbiano commòsso
7 imperfect subjunctive		14 past perfect subjunctive	
comm(u)ovessi	comm(u)ovéssimo	avessi commòsso	avéssimo commòsso
comm(u)ovessi	comm(u)oveste	avessi commòsso	aveste commòsso
comm(u)ovesse	comm(u)ovéssero	avesse commòsso	avéssero commòsso

imperative

—	comm(u)oviamo
commuòvi (non commuòvere)	comm(u)ovete
commuòva	commuòvano

50

to appear, to cut a fine figure

The Seven Simple Tenses		The Seven Compound Tenses	
Singular	Plural	Singular	Plural
1 present indicative		8 present perfect	
compaio	compariamo	sono comparso	siamo comparsi
compari	comparite	sèi comparso	sièto comparso(i)
compare	compàiono	è comparso	sono comparsi
(*Or regular:* comparisco, *etc.*)			
2 imperfect indicative		9 past perfect	
comparivo	comparivamo	èro comparso	eravamo comparsi
comparivi	comparivate	èri comparso	eravate comparso(i)
compariva	comparívano	èra comparso	èrano comparsi
3 past absolute		10 past anterior	
comparvi	comparimmo	fui comparso	fummo comparsi
comparisti	compariste	fosti comparso	foste comparso(i)
comparve	compàrvero	fu comparso	fúrono comparsi
(*Or regular:* comparii, *etc.*			
Comparire *in the sense of* "to cut a			
fine figure" *is always regular.*)			
4 future indicative		11 future perfect	
comparirò	compariremo	saró comparso	saremo comparsi
comparirai	comparirete	sarai comparso	sarete comparso(i)
comparirà	compariranno	sará comparso	saranno comparsi
5 present conditional		12 past conditional	
comparirèi	compariremmo	sarèi comparso	saremmo comparsi
compariresti	comparireste	saresti comparso	sareste comparso(i)
comparirèbbe	comparirèbbero	sarèbbe comparso	sarèbbero comparsi
6 present subjunctive		13 past subjunctive	
compaia	compariamo	sia comparso	siamo comparsi
compaia	compariate	sia comparso	siate comparso(i)
compaia	compàiano	sia comparso	síano comparsi
(*Or regular:* comparisca, *etc.*)			
7 imperfect subjunctive		14 past perfect subjunctive	
comparissi	comparíssimo	fossi comparso	fóssimo comparsi
comparissi	compariste	fossi comparso	foste comparso(i)
comparisse	comparíssero	fosse comparso	fóssero comparsi

imperative

—	compariamo
compari (comparisci) (non comparire)	comparite
compaia (comparisca)	compàiano (comparíscano)

Words related to this verb
Lo fece per comparire gentile.   He did it to appear kind.
La nave comparve all'orizzonte.   The ship appeared on the horizon.

to please

The Seven Simple Tenses		The Seven Compound Tenses	
Singular	Plural	Singular	Plural
1 present indicative		8 present perfect	
compiàccio	compiacciamo	ho compiaciuto	abbiamo compiaciuto
	(compiaciamo)	hai compiaciuto	avete compiaciuto
compiaci	compiacete	ha compiaciuto	hanno compiaciuto
compiace	compiàcciono		
2 imperfect indicative		9 past perfect	
compiacevo	compiacevamo	avevo compiaciuto	avevamo compiaciuto
compiacevi	compiacevate	avevi compiaciuto	avevate compiaciuto
compiaceva	compiacévano	aveva compiaciuto	avévano compiaciuto
3 past absolute		10 past anterior	
compiacqui	compiacemmo	èbbi compiaciuto	avemmo compiaciuto
compiacesti	compiaceste	avesti compiaciuto	aveste compiaciuto
compiacque	compiàcquero	èbbe compiaciuto	èbbero compiaciuto
4 future indicative		11 future perfect	
compiacerò	compiaceremo	avrò compiaciuto	avremo compiaciuto
compiacerai	compiacerete	avrai compiaciuto	avrete compiaciuto
compiacerà	compiaceranno	avrà compiaciuto	avranno compiaciuto
5 present conditional		12 past conditional	
compiacerèi	compiaceremmo	avrèi compiaciuto	avremmo compiaciuto
compiaceresti	compiacereste	avresti compiaciuto	avreste compiaciuto
compiacerèbbe	compiacerèbbero	avrèbbe	avrèbbero
		compiaciuto	compiaciuto
6 present subjunctive		13 past subjunctive	
compiàccia	compiacciamo	àbbia compiaciuto	abbiamo compiaciuto
	(compiaciamo)	àbbia compiaciuto	abbiate compiaciuto
compiàccia	compiacciate	àbbia compiaciuto	àbbiano compiaciuto
	(compiaciate)		
compiàccia	compiàcciano		
7 imperfect subjunctive		14 past perfect subjunctive	
compiacessi	compiacéssimo	avessi compiaciuto	avéssimo compiaciuto
compiacessi	compiaceste	avessi compiaciuto	aveste compiaciuto
compiacesse	compiacéssero	avesse compiaciuto	avéssero compiaciuto

	imperative	
—	compiacciamo (compiaciamo)	
compiaci (non compiacere)	compiacete	
compiàccia	compiàcciano	

Words related to this verb
Lui fa di tutto per compiacere al professore.   He does everything to please his professor.

Ger. componèndo   Past Part. composto   comporre

to compose

The Seven Simple Tenses		The Seven Compound Tenses	
Singular	Plural	Singular	Plural
1 present indicative		8 present perfect	
compongo	componiamo	ho composto	abbiamo composto
componi	componete	hai composto	avete composto
compone	compóngono	ha composto	hanno composto
2 imperfect indicative		9 past perfect	
componevo	componevamo	avevo composto	avevamo composto
componevi	componevate	avevi composto	avevate composto
componeva	componévano	aveva composto	avévano composto
3 past absolute		10 past anterior	
composi	componemmo	èbbi composto	avemmo composto
componesti	componeste	avesti composto	aveste composto
compose	compósero	èbbe composto	èbbero composto
4 future indicative		11 future perfect	
comporrò	comporremo	avrò composto	avremo composto
comporrai	comporrete	avrai composto	avrete composto
comporrà	comporranno	avrà composto	avranno composto
5 present conditional		12 past conditional	
comporrèi	comporremmo	avrèi composto	avremmo composto
comporresti	comporreste	avresti composto	avreste composto
comporrèbbe	comporrèbbero	avrèbbe composto	avrèbbero composto
6 present subjunctive		13 past subjunctive	
componga	componiamo	àbbia composto	abbiamo composto
componga	componiate	àbbia composto	abbiate composto
componga	compóngano	àbbia composto	àbbiano composto
7 imperfect subjunctive		14 past perfect subjunctive	
componessi	componéssimo	avessi composto	avéssimo composto
componessi	componeste	avessi composto	aveste composto
componesse	componéssero	avesse composto	avéssero composto

	imperative	
—		componiamo
componi (non comporre)		componete
componga		compóngano

Words related to this verb

Io comporrò una sinfonia per lei.   I will compose a symphony for her.
Lui compose il numero corretto.   He dialed the right number.

53

comprare	Ger. comprando	Past Part. comprato

to buy

The Seven Simple Tenses		The Seven Compound Tenses	
Singular	Plural	Singular	Plural
1 present indicative		8 present perfect	
còmpro	compriamo	ho comprato	abbiamo comprato
còmpri	comprate	hai comprato	avete comprato
còmpra	còmprano	ha comprato	hanno comprato
2 imperfect indicative		9 past perfect	
compravo	compravamo	avevo comprato	avevamo comprato
compravi	compravate	avevi comprato	avevate comprato
comprava	compràvano	aveva comprato	avévano comprato
3 past absolute		10 past anterior	
comprai	comprammo	èbbi comprato	avemmo comprato
comprasti	compraste	avesti comprato	aveste comprato
comprò	compràrono	èbbe comprato	èbbero comprato
4 future indicative		11 future perfect	
comprerò	compreremo	avrò comprato	avremo comprato
comprerai	comprerete	avrai comprato	avrete comprato
comprerà	compreranno	avrà comprato	avranno comprato
5 present conditional		12 past conditional	
comprerei	compreremmo	avrèi comprato	avremmo comprato
compreresti	comprereste	avresti comprato	avreste comprato
comprerèbbe	comprerèbbero	avrèbbe comprato	avrèbbero comprato
6 present subjunctive		13 past subjunctive	
còmpri	compriamo	àbbia comprato	abbiamo comprato
còmpri	compriate	àbbia comprato	abbiate comprato
còmpri	còmprino	àbbia comprato	àbbiano comprato
7 imperfect subjunctive		14 past perfect subjunctive	
comprassi	compràssimo	avessi comprato	avéssimo comprato
comprassi	compraste	avessi comprato	aveste comprato
comprasse	compràssero	avesse comprato	avéssero comprato

imperative		
—		compriamo
còmpra (non comprare)		comprate
còmpri		còmprino

Words related to this verb

comprare a buon mercato   to buy cheaply
Non ho comprato niente oggi.   I did not buy anything today.

to understand

The Seven Simple Tenses		The Seven Compound Tenses	
Singular	Plural	Singular	Plural
1 present indicative		8 present perfect	
comprèndo	comprendiamo	ho compreso	abbiamo compreso
comprèndi	comprendete	hai compreso	avete compreso
comprènde	comprèndono	ha compreso	hanno compreso
2 imperfect indicative		9 past perfect	
comprendevo	comprendevamo	avevo compreso	avevamo compreso
comprendevi	comprendevate	avevi compreso	avevate compreso
comprendeva	comprendévano	aveva compreso	avévano compreso
3 past absolute		10 past anterior	
compresi	comprendemmo	èbbi compreso	avemmo compreso
comprendesti	comprendeste	avesti compreso	aveste compreso
comprese	comprésero	èbbe compreso	èbbero compreso
4 future indicative		11 future perfect	
comprenderò	comprenderemo	avrò compreso	avremo compreso
comprenderai	comprenderete	avrai compreso	avrete compreso
comprenderà	comprenderanno	avrà compreso	avranno compreso
5 present conditional		12 past conditional	
comprenderèi	comprenderemmo	avrèi compreso	avremmo compreso
comprenderesti	comprendereste	avresti compreso	avreste compreso
comprenderèbbe	comprenderèbbero	avrèbbe compreso	avrèbbero compreso
6 present subjunctive		13 past subjunctive	
comprènda	comprendiamo	àbbia compreso	abbiamo compreso
comprènda	comprendiate	àbbia compreso	abbiate compreso
comprènda	comprèndano	àbbia compreso	àbbiano compreso
7 imperfect subjunctive		14 past perfect subjunctive	
comprendessi	comprendéssimo	avessi compreso	avéssimo compreso
comprendessi	comprendeste	avessi compreso	aveste compreso
comprendesse	comprendéssero	avesse compreso	avéssero compreso

imperative

—	comprendiamo
comprèndi (non comprèndere)	comprendete
comprènda	comprèndano

Words related to this verb

Noi non comprendiamo quel che il professore dice.   We don't understand what the professor is saying.

Io comprendo il francese, non il russo.   I understand French, not Russian.

concedere   Ger. **concedendo**   Past Par. **concesso (conceduto)**

to concede, to grant, to award

The Seven Simple Tenses		The Seven Compound Tenses	
Singular	Plural	Singular	Plural
1 present indicative		8 present perfect	
concedo	**concediamo**	**ho concesso**	**abbiamo concesso**
concedi	**concedete**	**(conceduto)**	
concede	**concedono**	**hai concesso**	**avete concesso**
		ha concesso	**hanno concesso**
2 imperfect indicative		9 past perfect	
concedevo	**concedevamo**	**avevo concesso**	**avevamo concesso**
concedevi	**concedevate**	**avevi concesso**	**avevate concesso**
concedeva	**concedévano**	**aveva concesso**	**avévano concesso**
3 past absolute		10 past anterior	
concedei	**concedemmo**	**èbbi concesso**	**avemmo concesso**
(concedetti)		**avesti concesso**	**aveste concesso**
concedesti	**concedeste**	**èbbe concesso**	**èbbero concesso**
concedè	**concederono**		
(concedette)	**(concedettero)**		
4 future indicative		11 future perfect	
concederò	**concederemo**	**avrò concesso**	**avremo concesso**
concederai	**concederete**	**avrai concesso**	**avrete concesso**
concederà	**concederanno**	**avrà concesso**	**avranno concesso**
5 present conditional		12 past conditional	
concederèi	**concederemmo**	**avrèi concesso**	**avremmo concesso**
concederesti	**concedereste**	**avreste concesso**	**avreste concesso**
concederèbbe	**concederèbbero**	**avrèbbe concesso**	**avrèbbero concesso**
6 present subjunctive		13 past subjunctive	
conceda	**concediamo**	**àbbia concesso**	**abbiamo concesso**
conceda	**concediate**	**àbbia concesso**	**abbiate concesso**
conceda	**concédano**	**àbbia concesso**	**àbbiano concesso**
7 imperfect subjunctive		14 past perfect subjunctive	
concedessi	**concedéssimo**	**avessi concesso**	**avéssimo concesso**
concedessi	**concedeste**	**avessi concesso**	**aveste concesso**
concedesse	**concedéssero**	**avesse concesso**	**avéssero concesso**

imperative	
—	**concediamo**
concedi (non concedere)	**concedete**
conceda	**concédano**

Words related to this verb
La banca gli concede un prestito.   The bank awards him a loan.
Gli fu concessa una borsa di studio per andare in Italia.   He was awarded a
scholarship to go to Italy.

The Seven Simple Tenses		The Seven Compound Tenses	
Singular	Plural	Singular	Plural
1 present indicative		8 present perfect	
concludo	**concludiamo**	**ho concluso**	**abbiamo concluso**
concludi	**concludete**	**hai concluso**	**avete concluso**
conclude	**conclúdono**	**ha concluso**	**hanno concluso**
2 imperfect indicative		9 past perfect	
concludevo	**concludevamo**	**avevo concluso**	**avevamo concluso**
concludevi	**concludevate**	**avevi concluso**	**avevate concluso**
concludeva	**concludévano**	**aveva concluso**	**avévano concluso**
3 past absolute		10 past anterior	
conclusi	**concludemmo**	**èbbi concluso**	**avemmo concluso**
concludesti	**concludeste**	**avesti concluso**	**aveste concluso**
concluse	**conclúsero**	**èbbe concluso**	**èbbero concluso**
4 future indicative		11 future perfect	
concluderò	**concluderemo**	**avrò concluso**	**avremo concluso**
concluderai	**concluderete**	**avrai concluso**	**avrete concluso**
concluderà	**concluderanno**	**avrà concluso**	**avranno concluso**
5 present conditional		12 past conditional	
concluderèi	**concluderemmo**	**avrèi concluso**	**avremmo concluso**
concluderesti	**concludereste**	**avresti concluso**	**avreste concluso**
concluderèbbe	**concluderèbbero**	**avrèbbe concluso**	**avrèbbero concluso**
6 present subjunctive		13 past subjunctive	
concluda	**concludiamo**	**àbbia concluso**	**abbiamo concluso**
concluda	**concludiate**	**àbbia concluso**	**abbiate concluso**
concluda	**conclúdano**	**àbbia concluso**	**àbbiano concluso**
7 imperfect subjunctive		14 past perfect subjunctive	
concludessi	**concludéssimo**	**avessi concluso**	**avéssimo concluso**
concludessi	**concludeste**	**avessi concluso**	**aveste concluso**
concludesse	**concludéssero**	**avesse concluso**	**avéssero concluso**

	imperative	
—		**concludiamo**
concludi (non conclúdere)		**concludete**
concluda		**conclúdano**

Words related to this verb
Noi concludiamo fra cinque minuti.   We are concluding in five minutes.
Nicola ha concluso un buon affare.   Nick has concluded a good deal.

condurre*   Ger. **conducèndo**   Past Part. **condotto**

to lead, to conduct

The Seven Simple Tenses		The Seven Compound Tenses	
Singular	Plural	Singular	Plural
1 present indicative		8 present perfect	
conduco	**conduciamo**	**ho condotto**	**abbiamo condotto**
conduci	**conducete**	**hai condotto**	**avete condotto**
conduce	**condúcono**	**ha condotto**	**hanno condotto**
2 imperfect indicative		9 past perfect	
conducevo	**conducevamo**	**avevo condotto**	**avevamo condotto**
conducevi	**conducevate**	**avevi condotto**	**avevate condotto**
conduceva	**conducévano**	**aveva condotto**	**avévano condotto**
3 past absolute		10 past anterior	
condussi	**conducemmo**	**èbbi condotto**	**avemmo condotto**
conducesti	**conduceste**	**avesti condotto**	**aveste condotto**
condusse	**condússero**	**èbbe condotto**	**èbbero condotto**
4 future indicative		11 future perfect	
condurrò	**condurremo**	**avrò condotto**	**avremo condotto**
condurrai	**condurrete**	**avrai condotto**	**avrete condotto**
condurrà	**condurranno**	**avrà condotto**	**avranno condotto**
5 present conditional		12 past conditional	
condurrèi	**condurremmo**	**avrèi condotto**	**avremmo condotto**
condurresti	**condurreste**	**avresti condotto**	**avreste condotto**
condurrèbbe	**condurrèbbero**	**avrèbbe condotto**	**avrèbbero condotto**
6 present subjunctive		13 past subjunctive	
conduca	**conduciamo**	**àbbia condotto**	**abbiamo condotto**
conduca	**conduciate**	**àbbia condotto**	**abbiate condotto**
conduca	**condúcano**	**àbbia condotto**	**àbbiano condotto**
7 imperfect subjunctive		14 past perfect subjunctive	
conducessi	**conducéssimo**	**avessi condotto**	**avéssimo condotto**
conducessi	**conduceste**	**avessi condotto**	**aveste condotto**
conducesse	**conducéssero**	**avesse condotto**	**avéssero condotto**

	imperative	
—		**conduciamo**
conduci (non **condurre**)		**conducete**
conduca		**condúcano**

* Like *condurre* are *addurre, dedurre, indurre, introdurre, produrre, ridurre, sedurre, tradurre*, etc.

Words related to this verb
Lei mi conduce per la mano.   She leads me by the hand.
Li condussi a teatro perchè avevano voglia di divertirsi.   I led them to the theater because they wanted to have fun.

58

Ger. **confondèndo**   Past Part. **confuso**   **confóndere**

to confuse

The Seven Simple Tenses		The Seven Compound Tenses	
Singular	Plural	Singular	Plural
1 present indicative		8 present perfect	
confondo	confondiamo	ho confuso	abbiamo confuso
confondi	confondete	hai confuso	avete confuso
confonde	confóndono	ha confuso	hanno confuso
2 imperfect indicative		9 past perfect	
confondevo	confondevamo	avevo confuso	avevamo confuso
confondevi	confondevate	avevi confuso	avevate confuso
confondeva	confondévano	aveva confuso	avévano confuso
3 past absolute		10 past anterior	
confusi	confondemmo	èbbi confuso	avemmo confuso
confondesti	confondeste	avesti confuso	aveste confuso
confuse	confúsero	èbbe confuso	èbbero confuso
4 future indicative		11 future perfect	
confonderò	confonderemo	avrò confuso	avremo confuso
confonderai	confonderete	avrai confuso	avrete confuso
confonderà	confonderanno	avrà confuso	avranno confuso
5 present conditional		12 past conditional	
confonderèi	confonderemmo	avrèi confuso	avremmo confuso
confonderesti	confondereste	avresti confuso	avreste confuso
confonderèbbe	confonderèbbero	avrèbbe confuso	avrèbbero confuso
6 present subjunctive		13 past subjunctive	
confonda	confondiamo	àbbia confuso	abbiamo confuso
confonda	confondiate	àbbia confuso	abbiate confuso
confonda	confóndano	àbbia confuso	àbbiano confuso
7 imperfect subjunctive		14 past perfect subjunctive	
confondessi	confondéssimo	avessi confuso	avéssimo confuso
confondessi	confondeste	avessi confuso	aveste confuso
confondesse	confondéssero	avesse confuso	avéssero confuso

imperative	
—	confondiamo
confondi (non confóndere)	confondete
confonda	confóndano

Words related to this verb
Loro si confondono facilmente.   They are easily confused.
Lui confuse tutte le mie carte.   He mixed up all my papers.

59

conóscere* Ger. conoscèndo Past Part. conosciuto

to know, to meet

The Seven Simple Tenses		The Seven Compound Tenses	
Singular	Plural	Singular	Plural
1 present indicative		**8 present perfect**	
conosco	conosciamo	ho conosciuto	abbiamo conosciuto
conosci	conoscete	hai conosciuto	avete conosciuto
conosce	conóscono	ha conosciuto	hanno conosciuto
2 imperfect indicative		**9 past perfect**	
conoscevo	conoscevamo	avevo conosciuto	avevamo conosciuto
conoscevi	conoscevate	avevi conosciuto	avevate conosciuto
conosceva	conoscévano	aveva conosciuto	avévano conosciuto
3 past absolute		**10 past anterior**	
conobbi	conoscemmo	èbbi conosciuto	avemmo conosciuto
conoscesti	conosceste	avesti conosciuto	aveste conosciuto
conobbe	conóbbero	èbbe conosciuto	èbbero conosciuto
4 future indicative		**11 future perfect**	
conoscerò	conosceremo	avrò conosciuto	avremo conosciuto
conoscerai	conoscerete	avrai conosciuto	avrete conosciuto
conoscerà	conosceranno	avrà conosciuto	avranno conosciuto
5 present conditional		**12 past conditional**	
conoscerèi	conosceremmo	avrèi conosciuto	avremmo conosciuto
conosceresti	conoscereste	avresti conosciuto	avreste conosciuto
conoscerèbbe	conoscerèbbero	avrèbbe conosciuto	avrèbbero conosciuto
6 present subjunctive		**13 past subjunctive**	
conosca	conosciamo	àbbia conosciuto	abbiamo conosciuto
conosca	conosciate	àbbia conosciuto	abbiate conosciuto
conosca	conóscano	àbbia conosciuto	àbbiano conosciuto
7 imperfect subjunctive		**14 past perfect subjunctive**	
conoscessi	conoscéssimo	avessi conosciuto	avéssimo conosciuto
conoscessi	conosceste	avessi conosciuto	aveste conosciuto
conoscesse	conoscéssero	avesse conosciuto	avéssero conosciuto

imperative	
—	conosciamo
conosci (non conóscere)	conoscete
conosca	conóscano

* Like *conóscere* are *disconóscere*, *riconóscere*, and *sconóscere*.

Words related to this verb
Lui im conosce. He knows me.
Li avevo conosciuti in una discoteca di Rimini. I had met them in a disco in Rimini.

The Seven Simple Tenses		The Seven Compound Tenses	
Singular	Plural	Singular	Plural
1 present indicative		8 present perfect	
consiste	**consistono**	**è consistito**	**sono consistiti**
2 imperfect indicative		9 past perfect	
consisteva	**consistevano**	**èra consistito**	**èrano consistiti**
3 past absolute		10 past anterior	
consiste	**consisterono**	**fu consistito**	**fúrono consistiti**
4 future indicative		11 future perfect	
consisterà	**consisteranno**	**sarà consistito**	**saranno consistiti**
5 present conditional		12 past conditional	
consisterèbbe	**consisterèbbero**	**sarèbbe consistito**	**sarèbbero consistiti**
6 present subjunctive		13 past subjunctive	
consista	**consistano**	**sia consistito**	**siano consistiti**
7 imperfect subjunctive		14 past perfect subjunctive	
consistesse	**consistéssero**	**fosse consistito**	**fóssero consistiti**
		imperative	

Words related to this verb

Il libro consiste di tre storie.   The book consists of three stories.

L'appartamento consisteva in origine di due camere da letto, cucina, bagno e balcone.   The apartment originally consisted of two bedrooms, a kitchen, a bathroom, and a balcony.

contèndere   Ger. **contendèndo**   Past Part. **conteso**

to contend, to dispute

The Seven Simple Tenses		The Seven Compound Tenses	
Singular	Plural	Singular	Plural
1 present indicative		8 present perfect	
contèndo	contendiamo	ho conteso	abbiamo conteso
contèndi	contendete	hai conteso	avete conteso
contènde	contèndono	ha conteso	hanno conteso
2 imperfect indicative		9 past perfect	
contendevo	contendevamo	avevo conteso	avevamo conteso
contendevi	contendevate	avevi conteso	avevate conteso
contendeva	contendévano	aveva conteso	avévano conteso
3 past absolute		10 past anterior	
contesi	contendemmo	èbbi conteso	avemmo conteso
contendesti	contendeste	avesti conteso	aveste conteso
contese	contésero	èbbe conteso	èbbero conteso
4 future indicative		11 future perfect	
contenderò	contenderemo	avrò conteso	avremo conteso
contenderai	contenderete	avrai conteso	avrete conteso
contenderà	contenderanno	avrà conteso	avranno conteso
5 present conditional		12 past conditional	
contenderèi	contenderemmo	avrèi conteso	avremmo conteso
contenderesti	contendereste	avresti conteso	avreste conteso
contenderèbbe	contenderèbbero	avrèbbe conteso	avrèbbero conteso
6 present subjunctive		13 past subjunctive	
contènda	contendiamo	àbbia conteso	abbiamo conteso
contènda	contendiate	àbbia conteso	abbiate conteso
contènda	contendano	àbbia conteso	àbbiano conteso
7 imperfect subjunctive		14 past perfect subjunctive	
contendessi	contendéssimo	avessi conteso	avéssimo conteso
contendessi	contendeste	avessi conteso	aveste conteso
contendesse	contendéssero	avesse conteso	avéssero conteso

imperative	
—	contendiamo
contèndi (non contèndere)	contendete
contènda	contèndano

Words related to this verb
Lui contende i risultati.   He disputes the results.
Lei deve contendere con me ogni giorno.   She has to contend with me every day.

to contain

The Seven Simple Tenses		The Seven Compound Tenses	
Singular	Plural	Singular	Plural
1 present indicative		8 present perfect	
contèngo	conteniamo	ho contenuto	abbiamo contenuto
contièni	contenete	hai contenuto	avete contenuto
contiène	contèngono	ha contenuto	hanno contenuto
2 imperfect indicative		9 past perfect	
contenevo	contenevamo	avevo contenuto	avevamo contenuto
contenevi	contenevate	avevi contenuto	avevate contenuto
conteneva	contenévano	aveva contenuto	avévano contenuto
3 past absolute		10 past anterior	
contenni	contenemmo	èbbi contenuto	avemmo contenuto
contenesti	conteneste	avesti contenuto	aveste contenuto
contenne	conténnero	èbbe contenuto	èbbero contenuto
4 future indicative		11 future perfect	
conterrò	conterremo	avrò contenuto	avremo contenuto
conterrai	conterrete	avrai contenuto	avrete contenuto
conterrà	conterranno	avrà contenuto	avranno contenuto
5 present conditional		12 past conditional	
conterrèi	conterremmo	avrèi contenuto	avremmo contenuto
conterresti	conterreste	avresti contenuto	avreste contenuto
conterrèbbe	conterrèbbero	avrèbbe contenuto	avrèbbero contenuto
6 present subjunctive		13 past subjunctive	
contènga	conteniamo	àbbia contenuto	abbiamo contenuto
contènga	conteniate	àbbia contenuto	abbiate contenuto
contènga	contèngano	àbbia contenuto	àbbiano contenuto
7 imperfect subjunctive		14 past perfect subjunctive	
contenessi	contenéssimo	avessi contenuto	avéssimo contenuto
contenessi	conteneste	avressi contenuto	aveste contenuto
contenesse	contenéssero	avesse contenuto	avéssero contenuto

imperative	
—	conteniamo
contièni (non contenere)	contenete
contènga	contèngano

Words related to this verb
Il libro contiene più di trecento pagine.   The book contains more than three
hundred pages.
Che contiene quella bottiglia?   What does that bottle contain?

contraddire   Ger. **contraddicendo**   Past Part. **contraddetto**

to contradict

The Seven Simple Tenses		The Seven Compound Tenses	
Singular	Plural	Singular	Plural
1 present indicative		8 present perfect	
contraddico	**contraddiciamo**	**ho contraddetto**	**abbiamo contraddetto**
contraddici	**contraddite**	**hai contraddetto**	**avete contraddetto**
contraddice	**contraddicono**	**ha contraddetto**	**hanno contraddetto**
2 imperfect indicative		9 past perfect	
contraddicevo	**contraddicevamo**	**avevo contraddetto**	**avevamo contraddetto**
contraddicevi	**contraddicevate**	**avevi contraddetto**	**avevate contraddetto**
contraddiceva	**contraddicévano**	**aveva contraddetto**	**avévano contraddetto**
3 past absolute		10 past anterior	
contraddissi	**contraddicemmo**	**èbbi contraddetto**	**avemmo contraddetto**
contraddicesti	**contraddiceste**	**avesti contraddetto**	**aveste contraddetto**
contraddise	**contraddissero**	**èbbe contraddetto**	**èbbero contraddetto**
4 future indicative		11 future perfect	
contraddirò	**contraddiremo**	**avrò contraddetto**	**avremo contraddetto**
contraddirai	**contraddirete**	**avrai contraddetto**	**avrete contraddetto**
contraddirà	**contraddiranno**	**avrà contraddetto**	**avranno contraddetto**
5 present conditional		12 past conditional	
contraddirèi	**contraddiremmo**	**avrei contraddetto**	**avremmo**
contraddiresti	**contraddireste**		**contraddetto**
contraddirèbbe	**contraddirèbbero**	**avresti contraddetto**	**avreste contraddetto**
		avrèbbe contraddetto	**avrèbbero**
			contraddetto
6 present subjunctive		13 past subjunctive	
contraddica	**contraddiciamo**	**àbbia contraddetto**	**abbiamo contraddetto**
contraddica	**contraddiciate**	**àbbia contraddetto**	**abbiate contradetto**
contraddica	**contraddicano**	**àbbia contraddetto**	**àbbiano contraddetto**
7 imperfect subjunctive		14 past perfect subjunctive	
contraddicessi	**contraddicéssimo**	**avessi contraddetto**	**avéssimo contraddetto**
contraddicessi	**contraddiceste**	**avessi contraddetto**	**aveste contraddetto**
contraddicesse	**contraddicéssero**	**avesse contraddetto**	**avéssimo contraddetto**

imperative	
—	**contraddiciamo**
contraddici (non contraddire)	**contraddite**
contraddica	**contraddicano**

Words related to this verb
Il professore non vuole essere contraddetto.   The professor does not wish to be contradicated.

to incur, to contract, to catch

The Seven Simple Tenses		The Seven Compound Tenses	
Singular	Plural	Singular	Plural
1　present indicative		8　present perfect	
contraggo	contraiamo	ho contratto	abbiamo contratto
contrai	contraete	hai contratto	avete contratto
contrae	contràggono	ha contratto	hanno contratto
2　imperfect indicative		9　past perfect	
contraevo	contraevamo	avevo contratto	avevamo contratto
contraevi	contraevate	avevi contratto	avevano contratto
contraeva	contraévano	aveva contratto	avévano contratto
3　past absolute		10　past anterior	
contrassi	contraemmo	èbbi contratto	avemmo contratto
contraesti	contraeste	aveste contratto	aveste contratto
contrasse	contàssero	èbbe contratto	èbbero contratto
4　future indicative		11　future perfect	
contrarrò	contrarremo	avrò contratto	avremo contratto
contrarrai	contrarrete	avrai contratto	avrete contratto
contrarrà	contrarranno	avrà contratto	avranno contratto
5　present conditional		12　past conditional	
contrarrèi	contrarremmo	avrèi contratto	avremmo contratto
contrarresti	contrarreste	avresti contratto	avreste contratto
contrarrèbbe	contrarrèbbero	avrèbbe contratto	avrèbbero contratto
6　present subjunctive		13　past subjunctive	
contragga	contraiamo	àbbia contratto	abbiamo contratto
contragga	contraiate	àbbia contratto	abbiate contratto
contragga	contràggano	àbbia contratto	àbbiano contratto
7　imperfect subjunctive		14　past perfect subjunctive	
contraessi	contraéssimo	avessi contratto	avéssimo contratto
contraessi	contraeste	avessi contratto	aveste contratto
contraesse	contraéssero	avesse contratto	avéssero contratto

	imperative	
—		contraiamo
contrai (non contrarre)		contraete
contragga		contràggano

Words related to this verb
Io to contratto un raffreddore.　I contracted a cold.
Abbiamo contratto dei debiti.　We have incurred some debts.

convíncere	Ger. convincèndo	Past Part. convinto

to convince

The Seven Simple Tenses		The Seven Compound Tenses	
Singular	Plural	Singular	Plural
1 present indicative		8 present perfect	
convinco	convinciamo	ho convinto	abbiamo convinto
convinci	convincete	hai convinto	avete convinto
convince	convíncono	ha convinto	hanno convinto
2 imperfect indicative		9 past perfect	
convincevo	convincevamo	avevo convinto	avevamo convinto
convincevi	convincevate	avevi convinto	avevate convinto
convinceva	convincévano	aveva convinto	avévano convinto
3 past absolute		10 past anterior	
convinsi	convincemmo	èbbi convinto	avemmo convinto
convincesti	convinceste	avesti convinto	aveste convinto
convinse	convínsero	èbbe convinto	èbbero convinto
4 future indicative		11 future perfect	
convincerò	convinceremo	avrò convinto	avremo convinto
convincerai	convincerete	avrai convinto	avrete convinto
convincerà	convinceranno	avrà convinto	avranno convinto
5 present conditional		12 past conditional	
convincerèi	convinceremmo	avrèi convinto	avremmo convinto
convinceresti	convincereste	avresti convinto	avreste convinto
convincerèbbe	convincerèbbero	avrèbbe convinto	avrèbbero convinto
6 present subjunctive		13 past subjunctive	
convinca	convinciamo	àbbia convinto	abbiamo convinto
convinca	convinciate	àbbia convinto	abbiate convinto
convinca	convíncano	àbbia convinto	àbbiano convinto
7 imperfect subjunctive		14 past perfect subjunctive	
convincessi	convincéssimo	avessi convinto	avéssimo convinto
convincessi	convinceste	avessi convinto	aveste convinto
convincesse	convincéssero	avesse convinto	avéssero convinto

imperative	
—	convinciamo
convinci (non convíncere)	convincete
convinca	convíncano

Words related to this verb

Non mi convince affatto questo ristorante. This restaurant doesn't convince me at all.

Non lo posso convincere di venire con noi. I can't convince him to come with us.

The Seven Simple Tenses		The Seven Compound Tenses	
Singular	Plural	Singular	Plural
1 present indicative		8 present perfect	
còpro	copriamo	ho copèrto	abbiamo copèrto
còpri	coprite	hai copèrto	avete copèrto
còpre	còprono	ha copèrto	hanno copèrto
2 imperfect indicative		9 past perfect	
coprivo	coprivamo	avevo copèrto	avevamo copèrto
coprivi	coprivate	avevi copèrto	avevate copèrto
copriva	coprívano	aveva copèrto	avévano copèrto
3 past absolute		10 past anterior	
copèrsi	coprimmo	èbbi copèrto	avemmo copèrto
copristi	copriste	avesti copèrto	aveste copèrto
copèrse	copèrsero	èbbe copèrto	èbbero copèrto
(*Or regular:* coprii, *etc.*)			
4 future indicative		11 future perfect	
coprirò	copriremo	avrò copèrto	avremo copèrto
coprirai	coprirete	avrai copèrto	avrete copèrto
coprirà	copriranno	avrà copèrto	avranno copèrto
5 present conditional		12 past conditional	
coprirèi	copriremmo	avrèi copèrto	avremmo copèrto
copriresti	coprireste	avresti copèrto	avreste copèrto
coprirèbbe	coprirèbbero	avrèbbe copèrto	avrèbbero copèrto
6 present subjunctive		13 past subjunctive	
còpra	copriamo	àbbia copèrto	abbiamo copèrto
còpra	copriate	àbbia copèrto	abbiate copèrto
còpra	còprano	àbbia copèrto	àbbiano copèrto
7 imperfect subjunctive		14 past perfect subjunctive	
coprissi	copríssimo	avessi copèrto	avéssimo copèrto
coprissi	copriste	avessi copèrto	aveste copèrto
coprisse	copríssero	avesse copèrto	avéssero copèrto

	imperative	
—		copriamo
còpri (non coprire)		coprite
còpra		còprano

Words related to this verb
Lui copre la seatola. He covers the box.
I mobili sono coperti. The furniture is covered.

corrèggere	Ger. correggèndo	Past Part. corrètto

to correct

The Seven Simple Tenses		The Seven Compound Tenses	
Singular	Plural	Singular	Plural
1 present indicative		8 present perfect	
corrèggo	correggiamo	ho corrètto	abbiamo corrètto
corrèggi	correggete	hai corrètto	avete corrètto
corrègge	corrèggono	ha corrètto	hanno corrètto
2 imperfect indicative		9 past perfect	
correggevo	correggevamo	avevo corrètto	avevamo corrètto
correggevi	correggevate	avevi corrètto	avevate corrètto
correggeva	correggévano	aveva corrètto	avévano corrètto
3 past absolute		10 past anterior	
corrèssi	correggemmo	èbbi corrètto	avemmo corrètto
correggesti	correggeste	avesti corrètto	aveste corrètto
corrèsse	corrèssero	èbbe corrètto	èbbero corrètto
4 future indicative		11 future perfect	
correggerò	correggeremo	avrò corrètto	avremo corrètto
correggerai	correggerete	avrai corrètto	avrete corrètto
correggerà	correggeranno	avrà corrètto	avranno corrètto
5 present conditional		12 past conditional	
correggerèi	correggeremmo	avrèi corrètto	avremmo corrètto
correggeresti	correggereste	avresti corrètto	aveste corrètto
correggerèbbe	correggerèbbero	avrèbbe corrètto	avrèbbero corrètto
6 present subjunctive		13 past subjunctive	
corrègga	correggiamo	àbbia corrètto	abbiamo corrètto
corrègga	correggiate	àbbia corrètto	abbiate corrètto
corrègga	corrèggano	àbbia corrètto	àbbiano corrètto
7 imperfect subjunctive		14 past perfect subjunctive	
correggessi	correggéssimo	avessi corrètto	avéssimo corrètto
correggessi	correggeste	avessi corrètto	aveste corrètto
correggesse	correggéssero	avesse corrètto	avéssero corrètto

	imperative	
		correggiamo
	corrèggi (non corrèggere)	correggete
	corrègga	corrèggano

Words related to this verb
La maestra corregge gli esami.   The teacher corrects the exams.
Ho coretto la sua pronunzia.   I corrected his pronunciation.

to run

The Seven Simple Tenses		The Seven Compound Tenses	
Singular	Plural	Singular	Plural
1 present indicative		8 present perfect	
corro	corriamo	ho corso	abbiamo corso
corri	correte	hai corso	avete corso
corre	córrono	ha corso	hanno corso
2 imperfect indicative		9 past perfect	
correvo	correvamo	avevo corso	avevamo corso
correvi	correvate	avevi corso	avevate corso
correva	corrévano	aveva corso	avévano corso
3 past absolute		10 past anterior	
corsi	corremmo	èbbi corso	avemmo corso
corresti	correste	avesti corso	aveste corso
corse	córsero	èbbe corso	èbbero corso
4 future indicative		11 future perfect	
correrò	correremo	avrò corso	avremo corso
correrai	correrete	avrai corso	avrete corso
correrà	correranno	avrà corso	avranno corso
5 present conditional		12 past conditional	
correrèi	correremmo	avrèi corso	avremmo corso
correresti	correreste	avresti corso	avreste corso
correrèbbe	correrèbbero	avrèbbe corso	avrèbbero corso
6 present subjunctive		13 past subjunctive	
corra	corriamo	àbbia corso	abbiamo corso
corra	corriate	àbbia corso	abbiate corso
corra	córrano	àbbia corso	àbbiano corso
7 imperfect subjunctive		14 past perfect subjunctive	
corressi	corréssimo	avessi corso	avéssimo corso
corressi	correste	avessi corso	aveste corso
corresse	corréssero	avesse corso	avéssero corso

imperative

—	corriamo
corri (non córrere)	correte
corra	córrano

---

* Sometimes conjugated with *èssere*. See introduction. Like *córrere* are *accórrere* (conj. with *èssere*), *concórrere*, *discórrere*, *occórrere* (conj. with *èssere*), *soccórrere*, etc.

Words related to this verb

Il ragazzo corre felice.   The boy runs happily.

Pamela corre tutte le mattine per prendere la metropolitana.   Pamela runs every morning to catch the subway.

corrispondere   Ger. **corrispondèndo**   Past Part. **corrispòsto**

to correspond; to agree

The Seven Simple Tenses		The Seven Compound Tenses	
Singular	Plural	Singular	Plural
1 present indicative		8 present perfect	
corrispondo	corrispondiamo	ho corrispòsto	abbiamo corrispòsto
corrispondi	corrispondete	hai corrispòsto	avete corrispòsto
corrisponde	corrispóndono	ha corrispòsto	hanno corrispòsto
2 imperfect indicative		9 past perfect	
corrispondevo	corrispondevamo	avevo corrispòsto	avevamo corrispòsto
corrispondevi	corrispondevate	avevi corrispòsto	avevate corrispòsto
corrispondeva	corrispondévano	aveva corrispòsto	avévano corrispòsto
3 past absolute		10 past anterior	
corrisposi	corrispondemmo	èbbi corrispòsto	avemmo corrispòsto
corrispondesti	corrispondeste	avesti corrispòsto	aveste corrispòsto
corrispose	corrispósero	èbbe corrispòsto	èbbero corrispòsto
4 future indicative		11 future perfect	
corrisponderò	corrisponderemo	avrò corrispòsto	avremo corrispòsto
corrisponderai	corrisponderete	avrai corrispòsto	avrete corrispòsto
corrisponderà	corrisponderanno	avrà corrispòsto	avranno corrispòsto
5 present conditional		12 past conditional	
corrisponderèi	corrisponderemmo	avrèi corrispòsto	avremmo corrispòsto
corrisponderesti	corrispondereste	avresti corrispòsto	avreste corrispòsto
corrisponderèbbe	corrisponderèbbero	avrèbbe corrispòsto	avrèbbero corrispòsto
6 present subjunctive		13 past subjunctive	
corrisponda	corrispondiamo	àbbia corrispòsto	abbiamo corrispòsto
corrisponda	corrispondiate	àbbia corrispòsto	avete corrispòsto
corrisponda	corrispóndano	àbbia corrispòsto	àbbia corrispòsto
7 imperfect subjunctive		14 past perfect subjunctive	
corrispondessi	corrispondéssimo	avessi corrispòsto	avéssimo corrispòsto
corrispondessi	corrispondeste	avessi corrispòsto	aveste corrispòsto
corrispondesse	corrispondéssero	avesse corrispòsto	avéssero corrispòsto

	imperative	
—		corrispondiamo
corrispondi (non corrispondere)		corrispondete
corrisponda		corrispóndano

Words related to this verb
Io corrispondo con Il mio zio.   I correspond with my uncle.
Queste cifre corrispondono.   These figures agree (tally).

70

to corrupt

The Seven Simple Tenses		The Seven Compound Tenses	
Singular	Plural	Singular	Plural
1 present indicative		8 present perfect	
corrompo	**corrompiamo**	**ho corrotto**	**abbiamo corrotto**
corrompi	**corrompete**	**hai corrotto**	**avete corrotto**
corrompe	**corrómpono**	**ha corrotto**	**hanno corrotto**
2 imperfect indicative		9 past perfect	
corrompevo	**corrompevamo**	**avevo corrotto**	**avevamo corrotto**
corrompevi	**corrompevate**	**avevi corrotto**	**avevate corrotto**
corrompeva	**corrompévano**	**aveva corrotto**	**avévano corrotto**
3 past absolute		10 past anterior	
corruppi	**corrompemmo**	**èbbi corrotto**	**avemmo corrotto**
corrompesti	**corrompeste**	**avesti corrotto**	**aveste corrotto**
corruppe	**corrúppero**	**èbbe corrotto**	**èbbero corrotto**
4 future indicative		11 future perfect	
corromperò	**corromperemo**	**avrò corrotto**	**avremo corrotto**
corromperai	**corromperete**	**avrai corrotto**	**avrete corrotto**
corromperà	**corromperanno**	**avrà corrotto**	**avranno corrotto**
5 present conditional		12 past conditional	
corromperèi	**corromperemmo**	**avrèi corrotto**	**avrennno corrotto**
corromperesti	**corrompereste**	**avresti corrotto**	**avreste corrotto**
corromperèbbe	**corromperèbbero**	**avrèbbe corrotto**	**avrèbbero corrotto**
6 present subjunctive		13 past subjunctive	
corrompa	**corrompiamo**	**àbbia corrotto**	**abbiamo corrotto**
corrompa	**corrompiate**	**àbbia corrotto**	**abbiate corrotto**
corrompa	**corrómpano**	**àbbia corrotto**	**àbbiano corrotto**
7 imperfect subjunctive		14 past perfect subjunctive	
corrompessi	**corrompéssimo**	**avessi corrotto**	**avéssimo corrotto**
corrompessi	**corrompeste**	**avessi corrotto**	**aveste corrotto**
corrompesse	**corrompéssero**	**avesse corrotto**	**avéssero corrotto**

imperative

—	**corrompiamo**
corrompi (non **corrómpere**)	**corrompete**
corrompa	**corrómpano**

Words related to this verb
L uomo è corrotto.   The man is corrupt.
Si fa corrompere dal denaro.   He allows himself to be corrupted by money.

to force, to compel

The Seven Simple Tenses		The Seven Compound Tenses	
Singular	Plural	Singular	Plural
1　present indicative		8　present perfect	
costringo	costringiamo	ho costretto	abbiamo costretto
costringi	costringete	hai costretto	avete costretto
costringe	costríngono	ha costretto	hanno costretto
2　imperfect indicative		9　past perfect	
costringevo	costringevamo	avevo costretto	avevamo costretto
costringevi	costringevate	avevi costretto	avevate costretto
costringeva	costringévano	aveva costretto	avévano costretto
3　past absolute		10　past anterior	
costrinsi	costringemmo	èbbi costretto	avemmo costretto
costringesti	costringeste	avesti costretto	aveste costretto
costrinse	costrínsero	èbbe costretto	èbbero costretto
4　future indicative		11　future perfect	
costringerò	costringeremo	avrò costretto	avremo costretto
costringerai	costringerete	avrai costretto	avrete costretto
costringerà	costringeranno	avrà costretto	avranno costretto
5　present conditional		12　past conditional	
costringerèi	costringeremmo	avrèi costretto	avremmo costretto
costringeresti	costringereste	avresti costretto	avreste costretto
costringerèbbe	costringerèbbero	avrèbbe costretto	avrèbbero costretto
6　present subjunctive		13　past subjunctive	
costringa	costringiamo	àbbia costretto	abbiamo costretto
costringa	costringiate	àbbia costretto	abbiate costretto
costringa	costríngano	àbbia costretto	àbbiano costretto
7　imperfect subjunctive		14　past perfect subjunctive	
costringessi	costringéssimo	avessi costretto	avéssimo costretto
costringessi	costringeste	avessi costretto	aveste costretto
costringesse	costringéssero	avesse costretto	avéssero costretto

imperative	
—	costringiamo
costringi (non costríngere)	costringete
costringa	costríngano

Words related to this verb

La necessità lo costringe a lavorare.　Necessity forces him to work.
Io sono costretta a vivere in una città industriale.　I am forced to live in an industrial town.

Ger. costruèndo Past Part. costruito costruire

to build, to construct

The Seven Simple Tenses		The Seven Compound Tenses	
Singular	Plural	Singular	Plural
1 present indicative		8 present perfect	
costruisco	costruiamo	ho costruito	abbiamo costruito
costruisci	costruite	hai costruito	avete costruito
costruisce	costruíscono	ha costruito	hanno costruito
2 imperfect indicative		9 past perfect	
costruivo	costruivamo	avevo costruito	avevamo costruito
costruivi	costruivate	avevi costruito	avevate costruito
costruiva	costruívano	aveva costruito	avévano costruito
3 past absolute		10 past anterior	
costruii	costruimmo	èbbi costruito	avemmo costruito
costruisti	costruiste	avesti costruito	aveste costruito
costruí	costruírono	èbbe costruito	èbbero costruito
(*Also* costrussi, costrusse,			
costrússero)			
4 future indicative		11 future perfect	
costruirò	costruiremo	avrò costruito	avremo costruito
costruirai	costruirete	avrai costruito	avrete costruito
costruirà	costruiranno	avrà costruito	avranno costruito
5 present conditional		12 past conditional	
costruirèi	costruiremmo	avrèi costruito	avremmo costruito
costruiresti	costruireste	avresti costruito	avreste costruito
costruirèbbe	costruirèbbero	avrèbbe costruito	avrèbbero costruito
6 present subjunctive		13 past subjunctive	
costruisca	costruiamo	àbbia costruito	abbiamo costruito
costruisca	costruiate	àbbia costruito	abbiate costruito
costruisca	costruíscano	àbbia costruito	àbbiano costruito
7 imperfect subjunctive		14 past perfect subjunctive	
costruissi	costruíssimo	avessi costruito	avéssimo costruito
costruissi	costruiste	avessi costruito	aveste costruito
costruisse	costruíssero	avesse costruito	avéssero costruito

imperative		
—		costruiamo
costruisci (non costruire)		costruite
costruisca		costruíscano

Words related to this verb
Ha costruito una bella casa.   He built a beautiful house.
È il suo lavoro costruire case.   His work is to build houses.

credere   Ger. **credendo**   Past Part. **creduto**

to believe

The Seven Simple Tenses		The Seven Compound Tenses	
Singular	Plural	Singular	Plural
1 present indicative		8 present perfect	
crèdo	**crediamo**	**ho creduto**	**abbiamo creduto**
crèdi	**credete**	**hai creduto**	**avete creduto**
crède	**credono**	**ha creduto**	**hanno creduto**
2 imperfect indicative		9 past perfect	
credevo	**credevamo**	**avevo creduto**	**avevamo creduto**
credevi	**credevate**	**avevi creduto**	**avevate creduto**
credeva	**credevano**	**aveva creduto**	**avévano creduto**
3 past absolute		10 past anterior	
credèi (credetti)	**credemmo**	**èbbi creduto**	**avemmo creduto**
credesti	**credeste**	**avesti creduto**	**aveste creduto**
credè (credette)	**credèrono (credèttero)**	**èbbe creduto**	**èbbero creduto**
4 future indicative		11 future perfect	
crederò	**crederemo**	**avrò creduto**	**avremo creduto**
crederai	**crederete**	**avrai creduto**	**avrete creduto**
crederà	**crederanno**	**avrà creduto**	**avranno creduto**
5 present conditional		12 past conditional	
crederèi	**crederemmo**	**avrèi creduto**	**avremmo creduto**
crederesti	**credereste**	**avresti creduto**	**avreste creduto**
crederèbbe	**crederèbbero**	**avrèbbe creduto**	**avrèbbero creduto**
6 present subjunctive		13 past subjunctive	
creda	**crediamo**	**àbbia creduto**	**abbiamo creduto**
creda	**crediate**	**àbbia creduto**	**abbiate creduto**
creda	**credano**	**àbbia creduto**	**àbbiano creduto**
7 imperfect subjunctive		14 past perfect subjunctive	
credessi	**credèssimo**	**avessi creduto**	**avéssimo creduto**
credessi	**credeste**	**avessi creduto**	**aveste creduto**
credesse	**credèssero**	**avesse creduto**	**avéssero creduto**

imperative

—	**crediamo**
crèdi (non credere)	**credete**
crèda	**credano**

Words related to this verb
Non credo nella fortuna.   I don't believe in luck.
credere in Dio   to believe in God
credere ai fantasmi   to believe in ghosts

Ger. crescèndo	Past Part. cresciuto	créscere*

to grow, to increase

The Seven Simple Tenses		The Seven Compound Tenses	
Singular	Plural	Singular	Plural
1 present indicative		8 present perfect	
cresco	cresciamo	sono cresciuto	siamo cresciuti
cresci	crescete	sèi cresciuto	sièti cresciuti
cresce	créscono	è cresciuto	sono cresciuti
2 imperfect indicative		9 past perfect	
crescevo	crescevamo	èro cresciuto	eravamo cresciuti
crescevi	crescevate	èri cresciuto	eravate cresciuti
cresceva	crescévano	èra cresciuto	èrano crsciuti
3 past absolute		10 past anterior	
crebbi	crescemmo	fui cresciuto	fummo cresciuti
crescesti	cresceste	fosti cresciuto	foste cresciuti
crebbe	crébbero	fu cresciuto	fúrono cresciuti
4 future indicative		11 future perfect	
crescerò	cresceremo	sarò cresciuto	saremo cresciuti
crescerai	crescerete	sarai cresciuto	sarete cresciuti
crescerà	cresceranno	sarà cresciuto	saranno cresciuti
5 present conditional		12 past conditional	
crescerèi	cresceremmo	sarèi cresciuto	saremmo cresciuti
cresceresti	crescereste	saresti cresciuto	sareste cresciuti
crescerèbbe	crescerèbbero	sarèbbe cresciuto	sarèbbero cresciuti
6 present subjunctive		13 past subjunctive	
cresca	cresciamo	sia cresciuto	siamo cresciuti
cresca	cresciate	sia cresciuto	siate cresciuti
cresca	créscano	sia cresciuto	síano cresciuti
7 imperfect subjunctive		14 past perfect subjunctive	
crescessi	cresséssimo	fossi cresciuto	fóssimo cresciuti
crescessi	cresceste	fossi cresciuto	foste cresciuti
crescesse	crescéssero	fosse cresciuto	fóssero cresciuti

imperative

—	cresciamo
cresci (non créscere)	crescete
cresca	créscano

* Like *créscere* are *accréscere* (with *avere*), *decréscere*, and *rincréscere*.

Words related to this verb
Il bambino è cresciuto molto.   The child has grown a lot.
Il fiume cresceva.   The river was rising.

75

cucire	Ger. cucèndo	Past Part. cucito

to sew

The Seven Simple Tenses		The Seven Compound Tenses	
Singular	Plural	Singular	Plural
1 present indicative		8 present perfect	
cucio	cuciamo	ho cucito	abbiamo cucito
cuci	cucite	hai cucito	avete cucito
cuce	cúciono	ha cucito	hanno cucito
2 imperfect indicative		9 past perfect	
cucivo	cucivamo	avevo cucito	avevamo cucito
cucivi	cucivate	avevi cucito	avevate cucito
cuciva	cucívano	aveva cucito	avévano cucito
3 past absolute		10 past anterior	
cucii	cucimmo	èbbi cucito	avemmo cucito
cucisti	cuciste	avesti cucito	aveste cucito
cucí	cucírono	èbbe cucito	èbbero cucito
4 future indicative		11 future perfect	
cucirò	cuciremo	avrò cucito	avremo cucito
cucirai	cucirete	avrai cucito	avrete cucito
cucirà	cuciranno	avrà cucito	avranno cucito
5 present conditional		12 past conditional	
cucirèi	cuciremmo	avrèi cucito	avremmo cucito
cuciresti	cucireste	avresti cucito	avreste cucito
cucirèbbe	cucirèbbero	avrèbbe cucito	avrèbbero cucito
6 present subjunctive		13 past subjunctive	
cucia	cuciamo	àbbia cucito	abbiamo cucito
cucia	cuciate	àbbia cucito	abbiate cucito
cucia	cúciano	àbbia cucito	àbbiano cucito
7 imperfect subjunctive		14 past perfect subjunctive	
cucissi	cucíssimo	avessi cucito	avéssimo cucito
cucissi	cuciste	avessi cucito	aveste cucito
cucisse	cucíssero	avesse cucito	avéssero cucito

imperative	
—	cuciamo
cuci (non cucire)	cucite
cucia	cúciano

Words related to this verb
Io cucio i miei vestiti.   I sew my own dresses.
Lono non sanno cucire.   They don't know how to sew.

The Seven Simple Tenses		The Seven Compound Tenses	
Singular	Plural	Singular	Plural
1 present indicative		8 present perfect	
cuòcio (cuòco)	cociamo (cuociamo)	ho còtto	abbiamo còtto
cuòci	cocete (cuocete)	hai còtto	avete còtto
cuòce	cuòciono (cuòcono)	ha còtto	hanno còtto
2 imperfect indicative		9 past perfect	
cocevo (cuocevo)	cocevamo (cuocevamo)	avevo còtto	avevamo còtto
cocevi (cuocevi)	cocevate (cuocevate)	avevi còtto	avevate còtto
coceva (cuoceva)	cocévano (cuocévano)	aveva còtto	avévano còtto
3 past absolute		10 past anterior	
còssi	cocemmo (cuocemmo)	èbbi còtto	avemmo còtto
cocesti (cuocesti)	coceste (cuoceste)	avesti còtto	aveste còtto
còsse	còssero	èbbe còtto	èbbero còtto
4 future indicative		11 future perfect	
cocerò (cuocerò)	coceremo (cuoceremo)	avrò còtto	avremo còtto
cocerai (cuocerai)	cocerete (cuocerete)	avrai còtto	avrete còtto
cocerà (cuocerà)	coceranno (cuoceranno)	avrà còtto	avranno còtto
5 present conditional		12 past conditional	
cocerèi (cuocerèi)	(cuoceremmo)	avrèi còtto	avremmo còtto
coceresti (cuoceresti)	cocereste (cuocereste)	avresti còtto	avreste còtto
cocerèbbe	cocerèbbero'	avrèbbe còtto	avrèbbero
cocerèmmo (cuocerèbbe)	(cuocerèbbero)		còtto
6 present subjunctive		13 past subjunctive	
cuòcia (cuòca)	cociamo (cuociamo)	àbbia còtto	abbiamo còtto
cuòcia (cuòca)	cociate (cuociate)	àbbia còtto	abbiate còtto
cuòcia (cuòca)	cuòciano (cuòcano)	àbbia còtto	àbbiano còtto
7 imperfect subjunctive		14 past perfect subjunctive	
cocessi (cuocessi)	cocéssimo (cuocéssimo)	avessi còtto	avéssimo còtto
cocessi (cuocessi)	coceste (cuoceste)	avessi còtto	aveste còtto
cocesse (cuocesse)	cocéssero (cuocéssero)	avesse còtto	avéssero còtto

	imperative	
—	cociamo (cuociamo)	
cuòci (non cuòcere)	cocete (cuocete)	
cuòcia (cuòca)	cuòciano (cuòcano)	

Words related to this verb
Io cuocio le uova ogni giorno.   I cook eggs every day.
Lui cucina bene.   He cooks well.

dare   Ger. **dando**   Past Part. **dato**

to give

The Seven Simple Tenses		The Seven Compound Tenses	
Singular	Plural	Singular	Plural
1 present indicative		8 present perfect	
do	**diamo**	**ho dato**	**abbiamo dato**
dai	**date**	**hai dato**	**avete dato**
dà	**danno**	**ha dato**	**hanno dato**
2 imperfect indicative		9 past perfect	
davo	**davamo**	**avevo dato**	**avevamo dato**
davi	**davate**	**avevi dato**	**avevate dato**
dava	**dàvano**	**aveva dato**	**avévano dato**
3 past absolute		10 past anterior	
dièdi (dètti)	**demmo**	**èbbi dato**	**avemmo dato**
desti	**deste**	**avesti dato**	**aveste dato**
diède (dètte)	**dièdero (dèttero)**	**èbbe dato**	**èbbero dato**
4 future indicative		11 future perfect	
darò	**daremo**	**avrò dato**	**avremo dato**
darai	**darete**	**avrai dato**	**avrete dato**
darà	**daranno**	**avrà dato**	**avranno dato**
5 present conditional		12 past conditional	
darèi	**daremmo**	**avrèi dato**	**avremmo dato**
daresti	**dareste**	**avresti dato**	**avreste dato**
darèbbe	**darèbbero**	**avrèbbe dato**	**avrèbbero dato**
6 present subjunctive		13 past subjunctive	
dia	**diamo**	**àbbia dato**	**abbiamo dato**
dia	**diate**	**àbbia dato**	**abbiate dato**
dia	**díano**	**àbbia dato**	**àbbiano dato**
7 imperfect subjunctive		14 past perfect subjunctive	
dessi	**déssimo**	**avessi dato**	**avéssimo dato**
dessi	**deste**	**avessi dato**	**aveste dato**
desse	**déssero**	**avesse dato**	**avéssero dato**

	imperative
—	**diamo**
da' (non dare)	**date**
dia	**díano**

Words related to this verb
Paolo dà i soldi a Pietro.   Paul gives the money to Peter.
Mi ha dato da mangiare.   He gave me food to eat.

to decide

The Seven Simple Tenses		The Seven Compound Tenses	
Singular	Plural	Singular	Plural
1 present indicative		8 present perfect	
decido	decidiamo	ho deciso	abbiamo deciso
decidi	decidete	hai deciso	avete deciso
decide	decídono	ha deciso	hanno deciso
2 imperfect indicative		9 past perfect	
decidevo	decidevamo	avevo deciso	avevamo deciso
decidevi	decidevate	avevi deciso	avevate deciso
decideva	decidévano	aveva deciso	avévano deciso
3 past absolute		10 past anterior	
decisi	decidemmo	èbbi deciso	avemmo deciso
decidesti	decideste	avesti deciso	aveste deciso
decise	decísero	èbbe deciso	èbbero deciso
4 future indicative		11 future perfect	
deciderò	decideremo	avrò deciso	avremo deciso
deciderai	deciderete	avrai deciso	avrete deciso
deciderà	decideranno	avrà deciso	avranno deciso
5 present conditional		12 past conditional	
deciderèi	decideremmo	avrèi deciso	avremmo deciso
decideresti	decidereste	avresti deciso	avreste deciso
deciderèbbe	deciderèbbero	avrèbbe deciso	avrèbbero deciso
6 present subjunctive		13 past subjunctive	
decida	decidiamo	àbbia deciso	abbiamo deciso
decida	decidiate	àbbia deciso	abbiate deciso
decida	decídano	àbbia deciso	àbbiano deciso
7 imperfect subjunctive		14 past perfect subjunctive	
decidessi	decidéssimo	avessi deciso	avéssimo deciso
decidessi	decideste	avessi deciso	aveste deciso
decidesse	decidéssero	avesse deciso	avéssero deciso

	imperative
—	decidiamo
decidi (non decídere)	decidete
decida	decídano

Words related to this verb
Lui deve decidere cosa vuole fare.   He has to decide what he wants to do.
Lei decise di fare un viaggio.   She decided to take a trip.

descrívere   Ger. **descrivèndo**   Past Part. **descritto**

to describe

The Seven Simple Tenses		The Seven Compound Tenses	
Singular	Plural	Singular	Plural
1 present indicative		8 present perfect	
descrivo	descriviamo	ho descritto	abbiamo descritto
descrivi	descrivete	hai descritto	avete descritto
descrive	descrívono	ha descritto	hanno descritto
2 imperfect indicative		9 past perfect	
descrivevo	descrivevamo	avevo descritto	avevamo descritto
descrivevi	descrivevate	avevi descritto	avevate descritto
descriveva	descrivévano	aveva descritto	avévano descritto
3 past absolute		10 past anterior	
descrissi	descrivemmo	èbbi descritto	avemmo descritto
descrivesti	descriveste	avesti descritto	aveste descritto
descrisse	descríssero	èbbe descritto	èbbero descritto
4 future indicative		11 future perfect	
descriverò	descriveremo	avrò descritto	avremo descritto
descriverai	descriverete	avrai descritto	avrete descritto
descriverà	descriveranno	avrà descritto	avranno descritto
5 present conditional		12 past conditional	
descriverèi	descriveremmo	avrèi descritto	avremmo descritto
descriveresti	descrivereste	avresti descritto	avreste descritto
descriverèbbe	descriverèbbero	avrèbbe descritto	avrèbbero descritto
6 present subjunctive		13 past subjunctive	
descriva	descriviamo	àbbia descritto	abbiamo descritto
descriva	descriviate	àbbia descritto	abbiate descritto
descriva	descrívano	àbbia descritto	àbbiano descritto
7 imperfect subjunctive		14 past perfect subjunctive	
descrivessi	descrivéssimo	avessi descritto	avéssimo descritto
descrivessi	descriveste	avessi descritto	aveste descritto
descrivesse	descrivéssero	avesse descritto	avéssero descritto

imperative	
—	descriviamo
descrivi (non descrívere)	descrivete
descriva	descrívano

Words related to this verb
Lui ha descritto bene la situazione.   He described the situation well.
Lo scrittore descrive il palazzo.   The writer describes the building.

to wish, to want, to desire

The Seven Simple Tenses		The Seven Compound Tenses	
Singular	Plural	Singular	Plural
1 present indicative		8 present perfect	
desìdero	desideriamo	ho desiderato	abbiamo desiderato
desìderi	desiderate	hai desiderato	avete desiderato
desìdera	desìderano	ha desiderato	hanno desiderato
2 imperfect indicative		9 past perfect	
desideravo	desideravamo	avevo desiderato	avevamo desiderato
desideravi	desideravate	avevi desiderato	avevate desiderato
desiderava	desideràvano	aveva desiderato	avévano desiderato
3 past absolute		10 past anterior	
desiderai	desiderammo	èbbi desiderato	avemmo desiderato
desiderasti	desideraste	avesti desiderato	aveste desiderato
desiderò	desiderarono	èbbe desiderato	èbbero desiderato
4 future indicative		11 future perfect	
desidererò	desidereremo	avrò desiderato	avremo desiderato
desidererai	desidererete	avrai desiderato	avrete desiderato
desidererà	desidereranno	avrà desiderato	avranno desiderato
5 present conditional		12 past conditional	
desidererèi	desidereremmo	avrèi desiderato	avremmo desiderato
desidereresti	desiderereste	avresti desiderato	avreste desiderato
desidererèbbe	desidererèbbero	avrèbbe desiderato	avrèbbero desiderato
6 present subjunctive		13 past subjunctive	
desìderi	desideriamo	àbbia desiderato	abbiamo desiderato
desìderi	desideriate	àbbia desiderato	abbiate desiderato
desìderi	desìderino	àbbia desiderato	àbbiano desiderato
7 imperfect subjunctive		14 past perfect subjunctive	
desiderassi	desideràssimo	avessi desiderato	avéssimo desiderato
desiderassi	desideraste	avessi desiderato	aveste desiderato
desiderasse	desideràssero	avesse desiderato	avéssero desiderato

	imperative	
—		desideriamo
desìdera (non desiderare)		desiderate
desìderi		desìderino

Words related to this verb
Desidero un bicchiere d'acqua.   I want a glass of water.
Desidera aspettare?   Do you wish to wait?

difèndere	Ger. difendèndo		Past Part. difeso

to defend, to guard against

The Seven Simple Tenses		The Seven Compound Tenses	
Singular	Plural	Singular	Plural
1 present indicative		8 present perfect	
difèndo	difendiamo	ho difeso	abbiamo difeso
difèndi	difendete	hai difeso	avete difeso
difènde	difèndono	ha difeso	hanno difeso
2 imperfect indicative		9 past perfect	
difendevo	difendevamo	avevo difeso	avevamo difeso
difendevi	difendevate	avevi difeso	avevate difeso
difendeva	difendévano	aveva difeso	avévano difeso
3 past absolute		10 past anterior	
difesi	difendemmo	èbbi difeso	avemmo difeso
difendesti	difendeste	avesti difeso	aveste difeso
difese	difèsero	èbbe difeso	èbbero difeso
4 future indicative		11 future perfect	
difenderò	difenderemo	avrò difeso	avremo difeso
difenderai	difenderete	avrai difeso	avrete difeso
difenderà	difenderanno	avrà difeso	avranno difeso
5 present conditional		12 past conditional	
difenderèi	difenderemmo	avrèi difeso	avremmo difeso
difenderesti	difendereste	avresti difeso	avreste difeso
difenderèbbe	difenderèbbero	avrèbbe difeso	avrèbbero difeso
6 present subjunctive		13 past subjunctive	
difènda	difendiamo	àbbia difeso	abbiamo difeso
difènda	difendiate	àbbia difeso	abbiate difeso
difènda	difèndano	àbbia difeso	àbbiano difeso
7 imperfect subjunctive		14 past perfect subjunctive	
difendessi	difendéssimo	avessi difeso	avéssimo difeso
difendessi	difendeste	avessi difeso	aveste difeso
difendesse	difendéssero	avesse difeso	avéssero difeso

imperative	
—	difendiamo
difèndi (non difèndere)	difendete
difènda	difèndano

Words related to this verb
Si difende dalla censura. He guards against censure.
La ragazza difende le sue amiche. The girl defends her friends.

to diffuse, to spread

The Seven Simple Tenses		The Seven Compound Tenses	
Singular	Plural	Singular	Plural
1 present indicative		8 present perfect	
diffondo	diffondiamo	ho diffuso	abbiamo diffuso
diffondi	diffondete	hai diffuso	avete diffuso
diffonde	diffóndono	ha diffuso	hanno diffuso
2 imperfect indicative		9 past perfect	
diffondevo	diffondevamo	avevo diffuso	avevamo diffuso
diffondevi	diffondevate	avevi diffuso	avevate diffuso
diffondeva	diffondévano	aveva diffuso	avévano diffuso
3 past absolute		10 past anterior	
diffusi	diffondemmo	èbbi diffuso	avemmo diffuso
diffondesti	diffondeste	avesti diffuso	aveste diffuso
diffuse	diffúsero	èbbe diffuso	èbbero diffuso
4 future indicative		11 future perfect	
diffonderò	diffonderemo	avrò diffuso	avremo diffuso
diffonderai	diffonderete	avrai diffuso	avrete diffuso
diffonderà	diffonderanno	avrà diffuso	avranno diffuso
5 present conditional		12 past conditional	
diffondrèi	diffonderemmo	avrèi diffuso	avremmo diffuso
diffonderesti	diffondereste	avresti diffuso	avreste diffuso
diffonderèbbe	diffonderèbbero	avrèbbe diffuso	avrèbbero diffuso
6 present subjunctive		13 past subjunctive	
diffonda	diffondiamo	àbbia diffuso	abbiamo diffuso
diffonda	diffondiate	àbbia diffuso	abbiate diffuso
diffonda	diffóndano	àbbia diffuso	àbbiano diffuso
7 imperfect subjunctive		14 past perfect subjunctive	
diffondessi	diffondéssimo	avessi diffuso	avéssimo diffuso
diffondessi	diffondeste	avessi diffuso	aveste diffuso
diffondesse	diffondéssero	avesse diffuso	avéssero diffuso

imperative

—	diffondiamo
diffondi (non diffóndere)	diffondete
diffonda	diffóndano

Words related to this verb
Lei diffonde bugie.   She spreads lies.
Le notizie sono diffuse dal giornale.   The news is spread by the newspapers.

83

dimenticare   Ger. **dimenticando**   Past Part. **dimenticato**

to forget

The Seven Simple Tenses		The Seven Compound Tenses	
Singular	Plurall	Singular	Plural
1 present indicative		8 present perfect	
dimèntico	**dimentichiamo**	**ho dimenticato**	**abbiamo dimenticato**
dimèntichi	**dimenticate**	**hai dimenticato**	**avete dimenticato**
dimèntica	**dimenticano**	**ha dimenticato**	**hanno dimenticato**
2 imperfect indicative		9 past perfect	
dimenticavo	**dimenticavamo**	**avevo diemnticato**	**avevamo dimenticato**
dimenticavi	**dimenticavate**	**avevi dimenticato**	**avevate dimenticato**
dimenticava	**dimenticavano**	**aveva dimenticato**	**avévano dimenticato**
3 past absolute		10 past anterior	
dimenticai	**dimenticammo**	**èbbi dimenticato**	**avemmo dimenticato**
dimenticasti	**dimenticaste**	**avesti dimenticato**	**aveste dimenticato**
dimenticò	**dimenticarono**	**èbbe dimenticato**	**èbbero dimenticato**
4 future indicative		11 future perfect	
dimenticherò	**dimenticheremo**	**avrò dimenticato**	**avremo dimenticato**
dimenticherai	**dimenticherete**	**avrai dimenticato**	**avrete dimenticato**
dimenticherà	**dimenticheranno**	**avrà dimenticato**	**avranno dimenticato**
5 present conditional		12 past conditional	
dimenticherèi	**dimentiche-**	**avrèi dimenticato**	**avremmo dimenticato**
	remmo	**avresti dimenticato**	**avreste dimenticato**
dimenti-	**diemntichereste**	**avrèbbe**	**avrèbbero**
cheresti		**dimenticato**	**dimenticato**
dimenti-	**dimentiche-**		
cherèbbe	**rèbbero**		
6 present subjunctive		13 past subjunctive	
dimèntichi	**dimentichiamo**	**àbbia dimenticato**	**abbiamo dimenticato**
dimèntichi	**dimentichiate**	**àbbia dimenticato**	**abbiate dimenticato**
dimèntichi	**dimèntichino**	**àbbia dimenticato**	**àbbiano dimenticato**
7 imperfect subjunctive		14 past perfect subjunctive	
dimenticassi	**dimenticàssimo**	**avessi dimenticato**	**avéssimo dimenticato**
dimenticassi	**dimenticaste**	**avessi dimenticato**	**aveste dimenticato**
dimenticasse	**dimenticàssero**	**avesse dimenticato**	**avéssero dimenticato**

imperative

—	**dimentichiamo**
dimènta (non dimenticare)	**dimenticate**
dimèntichi	**dimèntichino**

to depend

The Seven Simple Tenses		The Seven Compound Tenses	
Singular	Plural	Singular	Plural
1 present indicative		8 present perfect	
dipèndo	dipendiamo	sono dipeso	siamo dipesi
dipèndi	dipendete	sèi dipeso	siète dipesi
dipènde	dipèndono	è dipeso	sono dipesi
2 imperfect indicative		9 past perfect	
dipendevo	dipednvamo	èro dipeso	eravamo dipesi
dipendevi	dipendevate	èri dipeso	eravate dipesi
dipendeva	dipendévano	èri dipeso	èrano dipesi
3 past absolute		10 past anterior	
dipesi	dipendemmo	fui dipeso	fummo dipesi
dipendesti	dipendeste	fosti dipeso	foste dipesi
dipese	dipésero	fu dipeso	fùrono dipesi
4 future indicative		11 future perfect	
dipenderò	dipenderemo	sarò dipeso	saremo dipesi
dipenderai	dipenderete	sarai dipeso	sarete dipesi
dipenderà	dipenderanno	sarà dipeso	saranno dipesi
5 present conditional		12 past conditional	
dipenderèi	dipenderemmo	sarèi dipeso	saremmo dipesi
dipenderesti	dipendereste	saresti dipeso	sareste dipesi
dipenderèbbe	dipenderèbbero	sarèbbe dipeso	sarèbbero dipesi
6 present subjunctive		13 past subjunctive	
dipènda	dipendiamo	sia dipeso	siamo dipesi
dipènda	dipendiate	sia dipeso	siate dipesi
dipènda	dipèndano	sia dipeso	siano dipesi
7 imperfect subjunctive		14 past perfect subjunctive	
dipendessi	dipendéssimo	fossi dipeso	fóssimo dipesi
dipendessi	dipendeste	fossi dipeso	foste dipesi
dipendesse	dipendéssero	fosse dipeso	fóssero dipesi

	imperative	
—	dipendiamo	
dipèndi (non dipèndere)	dipendete	
dipènda	dipèndano	

Words related to this verb
Dipende dalle circostanze.   It depends on the circumstances.
Il ragazzo dipende dalla madre.   The child depends on his mother.

dipíngere   Ger. dipingèndo   Past Part. **dipinto**

to paint, to depict

The Seven Simple Tenses		The Seven Compound Tenses	
Singular	Plural	Singular	Plural
1 present indicative		**8 present perfect**	
dipingo	dipingiamo	ho dipinto	abbiamo dipinto
dipingi	dipingete	hai dipinto	avete dipinto
dipinge	dipíngono	ha dipinto	hanno dipinto
2 imperfect indicative		**9 past perfect**	
dipingevo	dipingevamo	avevo dipinto	avevamo dipinto
dipingevi	dipingevate	avevi dipinto	avevate dipinto
dipingeva	dipingévano	aveva dipinto	avévano dipinto
3 past absolute		**10 past anterior**	
dipinsi	dipingemmo	èbbi dipinto	avemmo dipinto
dipingesti	dipingeste	avesti dipinto	aveste dipinto
dipinse	dipínsero	èbbe dipinto	èbbero dipinto
4 future indicative		**11 future perfect**	
dipingerò	dipingeremo	avrò dipinto	avremo dipinto
dipingerai	dipingerete	avrai dipinto	avrete dipinto
dipingerà	dipingeranno	avrà dipinto	avranno dipinto
5 present conditional		**12 past conditional**	
dipingerèi	dipingeremmo	avrèi dipinto	avremmo dipinto
dipingeresti	dipingereste	avresti dipinto	avreste dipinto
dipingerèbbe	dipingerèbbero	avrèbbe dipinto	avrèbbero dipinto
6 present subjunctive		**13 past subjunctive**	
dipinga	dipingiamo	àbbia dipinto	abbiamo dipinto
dipinga	dipingiate	àbbia dipinto	abbiate dipinto
dipinga	dipígano	àbbia dipinto	àbbiano dipinto
7 imperfect subjunctive		**14 past perfect subjunctive**	
dipingessi	dipingéssimo	avessi dipinto	avéssimo dipinto
dipingessi	dipingeste	avessi dipinto	aveste dipinto
dipingesse	dipingéssero	avesse dipinto	avéssero dipinto

imperative

—	dipingiamo
dipingi (non dipíngere)	dipingete
dipinga	dipíngano

Words related to this verb
Michelangelo ha dipinto *Il Giudisio Universale.*   Michelangelo painted *The Last Judgment.*
Il ragazzo dipinge bene.   The boy paints well.

Ger. dicèndo   Past Part. detto   dire*

to say, to tell

The Seven Simple Tenses		The Seven Compound Tenses	
Singular	Plural	Singular	Plural
1 present indicative		8 present perfect	
dico	diciamo	ho detto	abbiamo detto
dici	dite	hai detto	avete detto
dice	dícono	ha detto	hanno detto
2 imperfect indicative		9 past perfect	
dicevo	dicevamo	avevo detto	avevamo detto
dicevi	dicevate	avevi detto	avevate detto
diceva	dicévano	aveva detto	avévano detto
3 past absolute		10 past anterior	
dissi	dicemmo	èbbi detto	avemmo detto
dicesti	diceste	avesti detto	aveste detto
disse	díssero	èbbe detto	èbbero detto
4 future indicative		11 future perfect	
dirò	diremo	avrò detto	avremo detto
dirai	direte	avrai detto	avrete detto
dirà	diranno	avrà detto	avranno detto
5 present conditional		12 past conditional	
dirèi	diremmo	avrèi detto	avremmo detto
diresti	direste	avresti detto	avreste detto
dirèbbe	dirèbbero	avrèbbe detto	avrèbbero detto
6 present subjunctive		13 past subjunctive	
dica	diciamo	àbbia detto	abbiamo detto
dica	diciate	àbbia detto	abbiate detto
dica	dícano	àbbia detto	àbbiano detto
7 imperfect subjunctive		14 past perfect subjunctive	
dicessi	dicéssimo	avessi detto	avéssimo detto
dicessi	diceste	avessi detto	aveste detto
dicesse	dicéssero	avesse detto	avéssero detto

imperative	
—	diciamo
di' (non dire)	dite
dica	dícano

* Like *dire* are *disdire*, *interdire*, *predire*, and *ridire*, except for *disdici*, etc. in the Imperative.

Words related to this verb
Che dice il maestro?   What is the teacher saying?
Che ti ho detto?   What did I tell you?

87

dirígere   Ger. **dirigèndo**   Past Part. **dirètto**

to direct

The Seven Simple Tenses		The Seven Compound Tenses	
Singular	Plural	Singular	Plural
1 present indicative		8 present perfect	
dirigo	dirigiamo	ho dirètto	abbiamo dirètto
dirigi	dirigete	hai dirètto	avete dirètto
dirige	dirígono	ha dirètto	hanno dirètto
2 imperfect indicative		9 past perfect	
dirigevo	dirigevamo	avevo dirètto	avevamo dirètto
dirigevi	dirigevate	avevi dirètto	avevate dirètto
dirigeva	dirigévano	aveva dirètto	avévano dirètto
3 past absolute		10 past anterior	
dirèssi	dirigemmo	èbbi dirètto	avemmo dirètto
dirigesti	dirigeste	avesti dirètto	aveste dirètto
dirèsse	dirèssero	èbbe dirètto	èbbero dirètto
4 future indicative		11 future perfect	
dirigerò	dirigeremo	avrò dirètto	avremo dirètto
dirigerai	dirigerete	avrai dirètto	avrete dirètto
dirigerà	dirigeranno	avrà diretto	avranno dirètto
5 present conditional		12 past conditional	
dirigerèi	dirigeremmo	avrèi dirètto	avremmo dirètto
dirigeresti	dirigereste	avresti dirètto	avreste dirètto
dirigerèbbe	dirigerèbbero	avrèbbe dirètto	avrèbbero dirètto
6 present subjunctive		13 past subjunctive	
diriga	dirigiamo	àbbia dirètto	abbiamo dirètto
diriga	dirigiate	àbbia dirètto	abbiate dirètto
diriga	dirígano	àbbia dirètto	àbbiano dirètto
7 imperfect subjunctive		14 past perfect subjunctive	
dirigessi	dirigéssimo	avessi dirètto	avéssimo dirètto
dirigessi	dirigeste	avessi dirètto	aveste dirètto
dirigesse	dirigéssero	avesse dirètto	avéssero dirètto

imperative	
—	dirigiamo
dirigi (non dirígere)	dirigete
diriga	dirígano

Words related to this verb
Il poliziotto dirige il traffico. The policeman directs the traffic.
Lui mi diresse verso casa. He directed me home.

to go down, to descend, to come down

The Seven Simple Tenses		The Seven Compound Tenses	
Singular	Plural	Singular	Plural
1 present indicative		8 present perfect	
discendo	discendiamo	sono disceso	siamo discesi
discendi	discendete	sèi disceso	siète discesi
discende	discéndono	è disceso	sono discesi
2 imperfect indicative		9 past perfect	
discendevo	discendevamo	èro disceso	eravamo discesi
discendevi	discendevate	èri disceso	eravate discesi
discendeva	discendévano	èra disceso	èrano discesi
3 past absolute		10 past anterior	
discesi	discendemmo	fui disceso	fummo discesi
discendesti	discendeste	fosti disceso	foste discesi
discese	discésero	fu disceso	fúrono discesi
4 future indicative		11 future perfect	
discenderò	discenderemo	sarò disceso	saremo discesi
discenderai	discenderete	sarai disceso	sarete discesi
discenderà	discenderanno	sarà disceso	saranno discesi
5 present conditional		12 past conditional	
discenderèi	discenderemmo	sarèi disceso	sarèmmo discesi
discenderesti	discendereste	saresti disceso	sareste discesi
discenderèbbe	discenderèbbero	sarèbbe disceso	sarèbbero discesi
6 present subjunctive		13 past subjunctive	
discenda	discendiamo	sia disceso	siamo discesi
discenda	discendiate	sia disceso	siate discesi
discenda	discéndano	sia disceso	síano discesi
7 imperfect subjunctive		14 past perfect subjunctive	
discendessi	discendéssimo	fossi disceso	fòssimo discesi
discendessi	discendeste	fossi disceso	foste discesi
discendesse	discendéssero	fosse disceso	fóssero discesi

imperative

—	discendiamo
discendi (non discéndere)	discendete
discenda	discéndano

Words related to this verb
Marco discese in fretta dal terzo piano.   Mark descended hurriedly from the third floor.
Lui è disceso presto.   He came down early.

discórrere Ger. discorrèndo Past Part. discorso

to talk, to chat

The Seven Simple Tenses		The Seven Compound Tenses	
Singular	Plural	Singular	Plural
1 present indicative		8 present perfect	
discorro	discorriamo	ho discorso	abbiamo discorso
discorri	discorrete	hai discorso	avete discorso
discorre	discórrono	ha discorso	hanno discorso
2 imperfect indicative		9 past perfect	
discorrevo	discorrevamo	avevo discorso	avevamo discorso
discorrevi	discorrevate	avevi discorso	avevate discorso
discorreva	discorrévano	aveva discorso	avévano discorso
3 past absolute		10 past anterior	
discorsi	discorremmo	èbbi discorso	avemmo discorso
discorresti	discorreste	avesti discorso	aveste discorso
discorse	discórsero	èbbe discorso	èbbero discorso
4 future indicative		11 future perfect	
discorrerò	discorreremo	avrò discorso	avremo discorso
discorrerai	discorrerete	avrai discorso	avrete discorso
discorrerà	discorreranno	avrà discorso	avranno discorso
5 present conditional		12 past conditional	
discorrerèi	discorreremmo	avrèi discorso	avremmo discorso
discorreresti	discorrereste	avresti discorso	avreste discorso
discorrerèbbe	discorrerèbbero	avrèbbe discorso	avrèbbero discorso
6 present subjunctive		13 past subjunctive	
discorra	discorriamo	àbbia discorso	abbiamo discorso
discorra	discorriate	àbbia discorso	abbiate discorso
discorra	discórrano	àbbia discorso	àbbiano discorso
7 imperfect subjunctive		14 past perfect subjunctive	
discorressi	discorréssimo	avessi discorso	avéssimo discorso
discorressi	discorreste	avessi discorso	aveste discorso
discorresse	discorréssero	avesse discorso	avéssero discorso

imperative	
—	discorriamo
discorri (non discórrere)	discorrete
discorra	discórrano

Words related to this verb

Discorre al telefono con l'amica.   She chats with her friend on the phone.
Che discorri a fare delle notizie di attualità se non leggi il giornale e non guardi la televisione?   Why do you talk about the news if you neither read the newspaper nor watch the TV?

to dissolve, to separate

The Seven Simple Tenses		The Seven Compound Tenses	
Singular	Plural	Singular	Plural
1 present indicative		8 present perfect	
dissòlvo	**dissolviamo**	**ho dissolto (dissoluto)**	**abbiamo dissolto**
dissòlvi	**dissolvete**	**hai dissolto (dissoluto)**	**avete dissolto**
dissòlve	**dissòlvono**	**ha dissolto (dissoluto)**	**hanno dissolto**
2 imperfect indicative		9 past perfect	
dissolvevo	**dissolvevamo**	**avevo dissolto (dissoluto)**	**avevamo dissolto**
dissolvevi	**dissolvevate**	**avevi dissolto (dissoluto)**	**avevate dissolto**
dissolveva	**dissolvévano**	**aveva dissolto (dissoluto)**	**avévano dissolto**
3 past absolute		10 past anterior	
dissolsi	**dissolvemmo**	**èbbi dissolto (dissoluto)**	**avemmo dissolto**
dissolvesti	**dissolveste**	**avesti dissolto (dissoluto)**	**aveste dissolto**
dissolse	**dissólsero**	**èbbe dissolto (dissoluto)**	**èbbero dissolto**
4 future indicative		11 future perfect	
dissolverò	**dissolveremo**	**avrò dissolto (dissoluto)**	**avremo dissolto**
dissolverai	**dissolverete**	**avrai dissolto (dissoluto)**	**avrete dissolto**
dissolverà	**dissolveranno**	**avrà dissolto (dissoluto)**	**avranno dissolto**
5 present conditional		12 past conditional	
dissolverèi	**dissolveremmo**	**avrèi dissolto (dissoluto)**	**avremmo dissolto**
dissolveresti	**dissolvereste**	**avresti dissolto (dissoluto)**	**avreste dissolto**
dissolverèbbe	**dissolverèbbero**	**avrèbbe dissolto (dissoluto)**	**avrèbbero dissolto**
6 present subjunctive		13 past subjunctive	
dissòlva	**dissolviamo**	**àbbia dissolto (dissoluto)**	**abbiamo dissolto**
dissòlva	**dissolviate**	**àbbia dissolto (dissoluto)**	**abbiate dissolto**
dissòlva	**dissòlvano**	**àbbia dissolto (dissoluto)**	**àbbiano dissolto**
7 imperfect subjunctive		14 past perfect subjunctive	
dissolvessi	**dissolvéssimo**	**avessi dissolto (dissoluto)**	**avéssimo dissolto**
dissolvessi	**dissolveste**	**avessi dissolto (dissoluto)**	**aveste dissolto**
dissolvesse	**dissolvéssero**	**avesse dissolto (dissoluto)**	**avéssero dissolto**

	imperative	
—		**dissolviamo**
dissòlvi (non dissolvere)		**dissolvete**
dissòlva		**dissòlvano**

Words related to this verb
dissolvere un matrimonio   to dissolve a marriage
dissolvere un dubbio   to dispel a doubt

discútere   Ger. **discutèndo**   Past Part. **discusso**

to discuss

The Seven Simple Tenses		The Seven Compound Tenses	
Singular	Plural	Singular	Plural
1 present indicative		8 present perfect	
discuto	**discutiamo**	**ho discusso**	**abbiamo discusso**
discuti	**discutete**	**hai discusso**	**avete discusso**
discute	**discútono**	**ha discusso**	**hanno discusso**
2 imperfect indicative		9 past perfect	
discutevo	**discutevamo**	**avevo discusso**	**avevamo discusso**
discutevi	**discutevate**	**avevi discusso**	**avevate discusso**
discuteva	**discutévano**	**aveva discusso**	**avévano discusso**
3 past absolute		10 past anterior	
discussi	**discutemmo**	**èbbi discusso**	**avemmo discusso**
discutesti	**discuteste**	**avesti discusso**	**aveste discusso**
discusse	**discússero**	**èbbe discusso**	**èbbero discusso**
4 future indicative		11 future perfect	
discuterò	**discuteremo**	**avrò discusso**	**avremo discusso**
discuterai	**discuterete**	**avrai discusso**	**avrete discusso**
discuterà	**discuteranno**	**avrà discusso**	**avranno discusso**
5 present conditional		12 past conditional	
discuterèi	**discuteremmo**	**avrèi discusso**	**avremmo discusso**
discuteresti	**discutereste**	**avresti discusso**	**avreste discusso**
discuterèbbe	**discuterèbbero**	**avrèbbe discusso**	**avrèbbero discusso**
6 present subjunctive		13 past subjunctive	
discuta	**discutiamo**	**àbbia discusso**	**abbiamo discusso**
discuta	**discutiate**	**àbbia discusso**	**abbiate discusso**
discuta	**discútano**	**àbbia discusso**	**àbbiano discusso**
7 imperfect subjunctive		14 past perfect subjunctive	
discutessi	**discutéssimo**	**avessi discusso**	**avéssimo discusso**
discutessi	**discuteste**	**avessi discusso**	**aveste discusso**
discutesse	**discutéssero**	**avesse discusso**	**avéssero discusso**

	imperative	
	—	**discutiamo**
	discuti (non discútere)	**discutete**
	discuta	**discútano**

Words related to this verb
Il ragazzo discute di tutto con suo padre.   The boy discusses everything with his father.
Lui non vuole discutere niente con me.   He doesn't want to discuss anything with me.

to undo

The Seven Simple Tenses		The Seven Compound Tenses	
Singular	Plural	Singular	Plural
1 present indicative		8 present perfect	
disfaccio (disfò)	**disfacciamo**	**ho disfatto**	**abbiamo disfatto**
disfai	**disfate**	**hai disfatto**	**avete disfatto**
disfà	**disfanno**	**ha disfatto**	**hanno disfatto**
(*Or regular:* disfo, *etc.*)			
2 imperfect indicative		9 past perfect	
disfacevo	**disfacevamo**	**avevo disfatto**	**avevamo disfatto**
disfacevi	**disfacevate**	**avevi disfatto**	**avevate disfatto**
disfaceva	**disfacévano**	**aveva disfatto**	**avévano disfatto**
3 past absolute		10 past anterior	
disfeci	**disfacemmo**	**èbbi disfatto**	**avemmo disfatto**
disfacesti	**disfaceste**	**avesti disfatto**	**aveste disfatto**
disfece	**disfécero**	**èbbe disfatto**	**èbbero disfatto**
4 future indicative		11 future perfect	
disfarò	**disfaremo**	**avrò disfatto**	**avremo disfatto**
disfarai	**disfarete**	**avrai disfatto**	**avrete disfatto**
disfarà	**disfaranno**	**avrà disfatto**	**avranno disfatto**
(*Or regular:* disferò, *etc.*)			
5 present conditional		12 past conditional	
disfarèi	**disfaremmo**	**avrèi disfatto**	**avremmo disfatto**
disfaresti	**disfareste**	**avresti disfatto**	**avreste disfatto**
disfarèbbe	**disfarèbbero**	**avrèbbe disfatto**	**avrèbbero disfatto**
(*Or regular:* disferèi, *etc.*)			
6 present subjunctive		13 past subjunctive	
disfaccia	**disfacciamo**	**àbbia disfatto**	**abbiamo disfatto**
disfaccia	**disfacciate**	**àbbia disfatto**	**abbiate disfatto**
disfaccia	**disfàcciano**	**àbbia disfatto**	**àbbiano disfatto**
(*Or regular:* disfi, *etc.*)			
7 imperfect subjunctive		14 past perfect subjunctive	
disfacessi	**disfacéssimo**	**avessi disfatto**	**avéssimo disfatto**
disfacessi	**disfaceste**	**avessi disfatto**	**aveste disfatto**
disfacesse	**disfacéssero**	**avesse disfatto**	**avéssero disfatto**

	imperative	
—	**disfacciamo (disfiamo)**	
disfa' (non disfare)	**disfate**	
disfaccia (disfi)	**disfàcciano (dísfino)**	

Words related to this verb
In cinque minuti lui ha disfatto tutto il nostro lavoro.   In five minutes he undid all our work.
Lui disfa il nodo.   He undoes the knot.

dispiacere   Ger. **dispiacèndo**   Past Part. **dispiaciuto**

to displease, to be sorry

The Seven Simple Tenses		The Seven Compound Tenses	
Singular	Plural	Singular	Plural
1 present indicative		8 present perfect	
dispiaccio	**dispiacciamo**	**sono dispiaciuto**	**siamo dispiaciuti**
	(**dispiaciamo**)	**sèi dispiaciuto**	**siète dispiaciuti**
dispiaci	**dispiacete**	**è dispiaciuto**	**sono dispiaciuti**
dispiace	**dispiàcciono**		
2 imperfect indicative		9 past perfect	
dispiacevo	**dispiacevamo**	**èro dispiaciuto**	**eravamo dispiaciuti**
dispiacevi	**dispiacevate**	**èri dispiaciuto**	**eravate dispiaciuti**
dispiaceva	**dispiacévano**	**èra dispiaciuto**	**èrano dispiaciuti**
3 past absolute		10 past anterior	
dispiacqui	**dispiacemmo**	**fui dispiaciuto**	**fummo dispiaciuti**
dispiacesti	**dispiaceste**	**fosti dispiaciuto**	**foste dispiaciuti**
dispiacque	**dispiàcquero**	**fu dispiaciuto**	**fúrono dispiaciuti**
4 future indicative		11 future perfect	
dispiacerò	**dispiaceremo**	**sarò dispiaciuto**	**saremo dispiaciuti**
dispiacerai	**dispiacerete**	**sarai dispiaciuto**	**sarete dispiaciuti**
dispiacerà	**dispiaceranno**	**sarà dispiaciuto**	**saranno dispiaciuti**
5 present conditional		12 past conditional	
dispiacerèi	**dispiaceremmo**	**sarèi dispiaciuto**	**saremmo dispiaciuti**
dispiaceresti	**dispiacereste**	**saresti dispiaciuto**	**sareste dispiaciuti**
dispiacerèbbe	**dispiacerèbbero**	**sarèbbe dispiaciuto**	**sarèbbero dispiaciuti**
6 present subjunctive		13 past subjunctive	
dispiaccia	**dispiacciamo**	**sia dispiaciuto**	**siamo dispiaciuti**
	(**dispiaciamo**)	**sia dispiaciuto**	**siate dispiaciuti**
dispiaccia	**dispiacciate**	**sia dispiaciuto**	**síano dispiaciuti**
	(**dispiaciate**)		
dispiaccia	**dispiàcciano**		
7 imperfect subjunctive		14 past perfect subjunctive	
dispiacessi	**dispiacéssimo**	**fossi dispiaciuto**	**fóssimo dispiaciuti**
dispiacessi	**dispiaceste**	**fossi dispiaciuto**	**foste dispiaciuti**
dispiacesse	**dispiacéssero**	**fosse dispiaciuto**	**fóssero dispiaciuti**

imperative	
—	**dispiacciamo** (**dispiaciamo**)
dispiaci (non **dispiacere**)	**dispiacete**
dispiaccia	**dispiàcciano**

Words related to this verb

Mi dispiace, ma non posso venire alla festa.   I'm sorry, but I can't come to the party.

Gli dispiacquero le tue accuse.   He was displeased by your accusations.

to arrange, to dispose

The Seven Simple Tenses		The Seven Compound Tenses	
Singular	Plural	Singular	Plural
1 present indicative		8 present perfect	
dispongo	**disponiamo**	**ho disposto**	**abbiamo disposto**
disponi	**disponete**	**hai disposto**	**avete disposto**
dispone	**dispóngono**	**ha disposto**	**hanno disposto**
2 imperfect indicative		9 past perfect	
disponevo	**disponevamo**	**avevo disposto**	**avevamo disposto**
disponevi	**disponevate**	**avevi disposto**	**avevate disposto**
disponeva	**disponévano**	**aveva disposto**	**avévano disposto**
3 past absolute		10 past anterior	
disposi	**disponemmo**	**èbbi disposto**	**avemmo disposto**
disponesti	**disponeste**	**avesti disposto**	**aveste disposto**
dispose	**dispósero**	**èbbe disposto**	**èbbero disposto**
4 future indicative		11 future perfect	
disporrò	**disporremo**	**avrò disposto**	**avremo disposto**
disporrai	**disporrete**	**avrai disposto**	**avrete disposto**
disporrà	**disporranno**	**avrà disposto**	**avranno disposto**
5 present conditional		12 past conditional	
disporrèi	**disporremmo**	**avrèi disposto**	**avremmo disposto**
disporresti	**disporreste**	**avresti disposto**	**avreste disposto**
disporrèbbe	**disporrèbbero**	**avrèbbe disposto**	**avrèbbero disposto**
6 present subjunctive		13 past subjunctive	
disponga	**disponiamo**	**àbbia disposto**	**abbiamo disposto**
disponga	**disponiate**	**àbbia disposto**	**abbiate disposto**
disponga	**dispóngano**	**àbbia disposto**	**àbbiano disposto**
7 imperfect subjunctive		14 past perfect subjunctive	
disponessi	**disponéssimo**	**avessi disposto**	**avéssimo disposto**
disponessi	**disponeste**	**avessi disposto**	**aveste disposto**
disponesse	**disponéssero**	**avesse disposto**	**avéssero disposto**

imperative

—	**disponiamo**
disponi (non **disporre**)	**disponete**
disponga	**dispóngano**

Words related to this verb

La ragazza dispone i fiori nel vaso.   The girl arranges the flowers in the vase.
Lui dispose tutto per la partenza.   He arranged everything for the departure.
Lei dispone di molto denaro ogni giorno.   She disposes of a lot of money every day.

95

distínguere	Ger. distinguèndo	Past Part. distinto

to distinguish

The Seven Simple Tenses		The Seven Compound Tenses	
Singular	Plural	Singular	Plural
1 present indicative		8 present perfect	
distinguo	distinguiamo	ho distinto	abbiamo distinto
distingui	distinguete	hai distinto	avete distinto
distingue	distínguono	ha distinto	hanno distinto
2 imperfect indicative		9 past perfect	
distinguevo	distinguevamo	avevo distinto	avevamo distinto
distinguevi	distinguevate	avevi distinto	avevate distinto
distingueva	distinguévano	aveva distinto	avévano distinto
3 past absolute		10 past anterior	
distinsi	distinguemmo	èbbi distinto	avemmo distinto
distinguesti	distingueste	avesti distinto	aveste distinto
distinse	distínsero	èbbe distinto	èbbero distinto
4 future indicative		11 future perfect	
distinguerò	distingueremo	avrò distinto	avremo distinto
distinguerai	distinguerete	avrai distinto	avrete distinto
distinguerà	distingueranno	avrà distinto	avranno distinto
5 present conditional		12 past conditional	
distinguerèi	distingueremmo	avrèi distinto	avremmo distinto
distingueresti	distinguereste	avresti distinto	avreste distinto
distinguerèbbe	distinguerèbbero	avrèbbe distinto	avrèbbero distinto
6 present subjunctive		13 past subjunctive	
distingua	distinguiamo	àbbia distinto	abbiamo distinto
distingua	distinguiate	àbbia distinto	abbiate distinto
distingua	distínguano	àbbia distinto	àbbiano distinto
7 imperfect subjunctive		14 past perfect subjunctive	
distinguessi	distinguéssimo	avessi distinto	avéssimo distinto
distinguessi	distingueste	avessi distinto	aveste distinto
distinguesse	distinguéssero	avesse distinto	avéssero distinto

imperative

—	distinguiamo
distingui (non distínguere)	distinguete
distingua	distínguano

Words related to this verb
Lui non può distinguere i colori. He cannot distinguish colors.
Io distinguo la tua voce facilmente. I distinguish your voice easily.

The Seven Simple Tenses		The Seven Compound Tenses	
Singular	Plural	Singular	Plural
1 present indicative		8 present perfect	
distraggo	**distraiamo**	**ho distratto**	**abbiamo distratto**
	(distragghiamo)	**hai distratto**	**avete distratto**
distrai	**distraete**	**ha distratto**	**hanno distratto**
distrae	**distràggono**		
2 imperfect indicative		9 past perfect	
distraevo	**distraevamo**	**avevo distratto**	**avevamo distratto**
distraevi	**distraevate**	**avevi distratto**	**avevate distratto**
distraeva	**distraévano**	**aveva distratto**	**avévano distratto**
3 past absolute		10 past anterior	
distrassi	**distraemmo**	**èbbi distratto**	**avemmo distratto**
distraesti	**distraeste**	**avesti distratto**	**aveste distratto**
distrasse	**distràssero**	**èbbe distratto**	**èbbero distratto**
4 future indicative		11 future perfect	
distrarrò	**distrarremo**	**avrò distratto**	**avremo distratto**
distrarrai	**distrarrete**	**avrai distratto**	**avrete distratto**
distrarrà	**distrarranno**	**avrà distratto**	**avranno distratto**
5 present conditional		12 past conditional	
distrarrèi	**distrarremmo**	**avrèi distratto**	**avremmo distratto**
distrarresti	**distrarreste**	**avresti distratto**	**avreste distratto**
distrarrèbbe	**distrarrèbbero**	**avrèbbe distratto**	**avrèbbero distratto**
6 present subjunctive		13 past subjunctive	
distragga	**distraiamo**	**àbbia distratto**	**abbiamo distratto**
	(distragghiamo)	**àbbia distratto**	**abbiate distratto**
distragga	**distraiate (distragghiate)**	**àbbia distratto**	**àbbiano distratto**
distragga	**distràggano**		
7 imperfect subjunctive		14 past perfect subjunctive	
distraessi	**distraéssimo**	**avessi distratto**	**avéssimo distratto**
distraessi	**distraeste**	**avessi distratto**	**aveste distratto**
distraesse	**distraéssero**	**avesse distratto**	**avéssero distratto**

	imperative	
	—	**distraiamo (distragghiamo)**
	distrai (non distrarre)	**distraete**
	distragga	**distràggano**

Words related to this verb

La mamma distrae il bambino.   The mother distracts the child.
Il ragazzo mi distrasse con delle storie.   The boy distracted me with some stories.

97

distrúggere Ger. **distruggèndo** Past Part. **distrutto**

to destroy

The Seven Simple Tenses		The Seven Compound Tenses	
Singular	Plural	Singular	Plural
1 present indicative		8 present perfect	
distruggo	distruggiamo	ho distrutto	abbiamo distrutto
distruggi	distruggete	hai distrutto	avete distrutto
distrugge	distrúggono	ha distrutto	hanno distrutto
2 imperfect indicative		9 past perfect	
distruggevo	distruggevamo	avevo distrutto	avevamo distrutto
distruggevi	distruggevate	avevi distrutto	avevate distrutto
distruggeva	distruggévano	aveva distrutto	avévano distrutto
3 past absolute		10 past anterior	
distrussi	distruggemmo	èbbi distrutto	avemmo distrutto
distruggesti	distruggeste	avesti distrutto	aveste distrutto
distrusse	distrússero	èbbe distrutto	èbbero distrutto
4 future indicative		11 future perfect	
distruggerò	distruggeremo	avrò distrutto	avremo distrutto
distruggerai	distruggerete	avrai distrutto	avrete distrutto
distruggerà	distruggeranno	avrà distrutto	avranno distrutto
5 present conditional		12 past conditional	
distruggerèi	distruggeremmo	avrèi distrutto	avremmo distrutto
distruggeresti	distruggereste	avresti distrutto	avreste distrutto
distruggerèbbe	distruggerèbbero	avrèbbe distrutto	avrèbbero distrutto
6 present subjunctive		13 past subjunctive	
distrugga	distruggiamo	àbbia distrutto	abbiamo distrutto
distrugga	distruggiate	àbbia distrutto	abbiate distrutto
distrugga	distrúggano	àbbia distrutto	àbbiano distrutto
7 imperfect subjunctive		14 past perfect subjunctive	
distruggessi	distruggéssimo	avessi distrutto	avéssimo distrutto
distruggessi	distruggeste	avessi distrutto	aveste distrutto
distruggesse	distruggéssero	avesse distrutto	avéssero distrutto

	imperative	
—		distruggiamo
distruggi (non distrúggere)		distruggete
distrugga		distrúggano

Words related to this verb
Il ragazzo distrugge il giocattolo.   The child is destroying the toy.
L'esercito del nemico fu distrutto.   The enemy's army was destroyed.

to become

The Seven Simple Tenses		The Seven Compound Tenses	
Singular	Plural	Singular	Plural
1 present indicative		8 present perfect	
divèngo	diveniamo	sono divenuto	siamo divenuti
divièni	divenite	sèi divenuto	siète divenuti
divière	divèngono	è divenuto	sono divenuti
2 imperfect indicative		9 past perfect	
divenivo	divenivamo	èro divenuto	eravamo divenuti
divenivi	divenivate	èri divenuto	eravate divenuti
diveniva	divenívano	èra divenuto	èrano divenuti
3 past absolute		10 past anterior	
divenni	divenimmo	fui divenuto	fummo divenuti
divenisti	diveniste	fosti divenuto	foste divenuti
divenne	divénnero	fu divenuto	fúrono divenuti
4 future indicative		11 future perfect	
diverrò	diverremo	sarò divenuto	saremo divenuti
diverrai	diverrete	sarai divenuto	sarete divenuti
diverrà	diverranno	sarà divenuto	saranno divenuti
5 present conditional		12 past conditional	
dIverrèi	diverremmo	sarèi divenuto	saremmo divenuti
diverresti	diverreste	saresti divenuto	sareste divenuti
diverrèbbe	diverrèbbero	sarèbbe divenuto	sarèbbero divenuti
6 present subjunctive		13 past subjunctive	
divènga	diveniamo	sia divenuto	siamo divenuti
divènga	diveniate	sia divenuto	siate divenuti
divènga	divèngano	sia divenuto	síano divenuti
7 imperfect subjunctive		14 past perfect subjunctive	
divenissi	diveníssimo	fossi divenuto	fóssimo divenuti
divenissi	diveniste	fossi divenuto	foste divenuti
divenisse	diveníssero	fosse divenuto	fóssero divenuti

imperative	
—	diveniamo
divièni (non divenire)	divenite
divènga	divèngano

Words related to this verb
Lui divenne il rettore dell'università.   He became president of the university.
Mi fai divenire matto!   You drive me mad!

diventare   Ger. **diventando**   Past Part. **diventato**

to become

The Seven Simple Tenses		The Seven Compound Tenses	
Singular	Plural	Singular	Plural
1 present indicative		8 present perfect	
divènto	**diventiamo**	**sono diventato**	**siamo diventati**
divènti	**diventate**	**sèi diventato**	**siete diventati**
divènta	**divèntano**	**è diventato**	**sono diventati**
2 imperfect indicative		9 past perfect	
diventavo	**diventavamo**	**èro diventato**	**eravamo diventati**
diventavi	**diventavate**	**èri diventato**	**eravate diventati**
diventava	**diventàvano**	**èra diventato**	**èrano diventati**
3 past absolute		10 past anterior	
diventai	**diventammo**	**fui diventato**	**fummo diventati**
diventasti	**diventaste**	**fosti diventato**	**foste diventati**
diventò	**diventárono**	**fu diventato**	**fúrono diventati**
4 future indicative		11 future perfect	
diventerò	**diventeremo**	**sarò diventato**	**saremo diventati**
diventerai	**diventerete**	**sarai diventato**	**sarete diventati**
diventerà	**diventeranno**	**sarà diventato**	**saranno diventati**
5 present conditional		12 past conditional	
diventerèi	**diventeremmo**	**sarèi diventato**	**saremmo diventati**
diventeresti	**diventereste**	**saresti diventato**	**sareste diventati**
diventerèbbe	**diventerèbbero**	**sarèbbe diventato**	**sarèbbero diventati**
6 present subjunctive		13 past subjunctive	
divènti	**diventiamo**	**sia diventato**	**siamo diventati**
divènti	**diventiate**	**sia diventato**	**siate diventati**
divènti	**divèntino**	**sia diventato**	**síano diventati**
7 imperfect subjunctive		14 past perfect subjunctive	
diventassi	**diventassimo**	**fossi diventato**	**fóssimo diventati**
diventassi	**diventaste**	**fossi diventato**	**foste diventati**
diventasse	**diventàssero**	**fosse diventato**	**fóssero diventati**

	imperative	
—	**diventiamo**
divènta (non **diventare**)	**diventate**
divènti	**divèntino**

Words related to this verb
È diventato famoso. He become famous.
Diventiamo vecchi. We are becoming old.

to have a good time, to amuse onself, to enjoy onself

The Seven Simple Tenses		The Seven Compound Tenses	
Singular	Plural	Singular	Plural
1 present indicative		8 present perfect	
mi divèrto	**ci divertiamo**	**mi sono divertito**	**ci siamo divertiti**
ti divèrti	**vi divertite**	**ti sèi divertito**	**vi siète divertiti**
si divèrte	**si divèrtono**	**si è divertito**	**si sono divertiti**
2 imperfect indicative		9 past perfect	
mi divertivo	**ci divertivamo**	**mi èro divertito**	**ci eravamo divertiti**
ti divertivi	**vi divertivate**	**ti èri divertito**	**vi eravate divertiti**
si divertiva	**si divertívano**	**si èra divertito**	**si èrano divertiti**
3 past absolute		10 past anterior	
mi divertii	**ci divertimmo**	**mi fui divertito**	**ci fummo divertiti**
ti divertisti	**vi divertiste**	**ti fosti divertito**	**vi foste divertiti**
si divertí	**si divertírono**	**si fu divertito**	**si fúrono divertiti**
4 future indicative		11 future perfect	
mi divertirò	**ci divertiremo**	**mi sarò divertito**	**ci saremo divertiti**
ti divertirai	**vi divertirete**	**ti sarai divertito**	**vi sarete divertiti**
si divertirà	**si divertiranno**	**si sarà divertito**	**si saranno divertiti**
5 present conditional		12 past conditional	
mi divertirèi	**ci divertiremmo**	**mi sarèi divertito**	**ci saremmo divertiti**
ti divertiresti	**vi divertireste**	**ti saresti divertito**	**vi sareste divertiti**
si divertirèbbe	**si divertirèbbero**	**si sarèbbe divertito**	**si sarèbbero divertiti**
6 present subjunctive		13 past subjunctive	
mi divèrta	**ci divertiamo**	**mi sia divertito**	**ci siamo divertiti**
ti divèrta	**vi divertiate**	**ti sia divertito**	**vi siate divertiti**
si divèrta	**si divèrtano**	**si sia divertito**	**si síano divertiti**
7 imperfect subjunctive		14 past perfect subjunctive	
mi divertissi	**ci divertíssimo**	**mi fossi divertito**	**ci fóssimo divertiti**
ti divertissi	**vi divertiste**	**ti fossi divertito**	**vi foste divertiti**
si divertisse	**si divertíssero**	**si fosse divertito**	**si fóssero divertiti**

	imperative	
—		**divertiàmoci**
divèrtiti (non ti divertire)		**divertítevi**
si divèrta		**si divèrtano**

Words related to this verb
Il ragazzo si diverte da solo.   The child amuses himself.
Noi non ci divertiamo a scuola.   We don't enjoy ourselves at school.

to divide

The Seven Simple Tenses		The Seven Compound Tenses	
Singular	Plural	Singular	Plural
1 present indicative		8 present perfect	
divido	dividiamo	ho diviso	abbiamo diviso
dividi	dividete	hai diviso	avete diviso
divide	divídono	ha diviso	hanno diviso
2 imperfect indicative		9 past perfect	
dividevo	dividevamo	avevo diviso	avevamo diviso
dividevi	dividevate	avevi diviso	avevate diviso
divideva	dividévano	aveva diviso	avévano diviso
3 past absolute		10 past anterior	
divisi	dividemmo	èbbi diviso	avemmo diviso
dividesti	divideste	avesti diviso	aveste diviso
divise	divísero	èbbe diviso	èbbero diviso
4 future indicative		11 future perfect	
dividerò	divideremo	avrò diviso	avremo diviso
dividerai	dividerete	avrai diviso	avrete diviso
dividerà	divideranno	avrà diviso	avranno diviso
5 present conditional		12 past conditional	
dividerèi	divideremmo	avrèi diviso	avremmo diviso
divideresti	dividereste	avresti diviso	avreste diviso
dividerèbbe	dividerèbbero	avrèbbe diviso	avrèbbero diviso
6 present subjunctive		13 past subjunctive	
divida	dividiamo	àbbia diviso	abbiamo diviso
divida	dividiate	àbbia diviso	abbiate diviso
divida	divídano	àbbia diviso	àbbiano diviso
7 imperfect subjunctive		14 past perfect subjunctive	
dividessi	dividéssimo	avessi diviso	avéssimo diviso
dividessi	divideste	avessi diviso	aveste diviso
dividesse	dividéssero	avesse diviso	avéssero diviso

imperative	
—	dividiamo
dividi (non divídere)	dividete
divida	divídano

Words related to this verb
Quattro diviso due fa due.   Four divided by two is two.
Loro dividono il panino.   They divide the sandwich.

to suffer pain, to ache

The Seven Simple Tenses		The Seven Compound Tenses	
Singular	Plural	Singular	Plural
1 present indicative		8 present perfect	
dòlgo	doliamo (dogliamo)	ho* doluto	abbiamo doluto
duòli	dolete	hai doluto	avete doluto
duòle	dòlgono	ha doluto	hanno doluto
2 imperfect indicative		9 past perfect	
dolevo	dolevamo	avevo doluto	avevamo doluto
dolevi	dolevate	avevi doluto	avevate doluto
doleva	dolévane	aveva doluto	avévano doluto
3 past absolute		10 past anterior	
dòlsi	dolemmo	èbbi doluto	avemmo doluto
dolesti	doleste	avesti doluto	aveste doluto
dòlse	dòlsero	èbbe doluto	èbbero doluto
4 future indicative		11 future perfect	
dorrò	dorremo	avrò doluto	avremo doluto
dorrai	dorrete	avrai doluto	avrete doluto
dorrà	dorranno	avrà doluto	avranno doluto
5 present conditional		12 past conditional	
dorrèi	dorremmo	avrèi doluto	avremmo doluto
dorresti	dorreste	avresti doluto	avreste doluto
dorrèbbe	dorrèbbero	avrèbbe doluto	avrèbbero doluto
6 present subjunctive		13 past subjunctive	
dòlga	doliamo (dogliamo)	àbbia doluto	abbiamo doluto
dòlga	doliate (dogliate)	àbbia doluto	abbiate doluto
dòlga	dòlgano	àbbia doluto	àbbiano doluto
7 imperfect subjunctive		14 past perfect subjunctive	
dolessi	doléssimo	avessi doluto	avéssimo doluto
dolessi	doleste	avessi doluto	aveste doluto
dolesse	doléssero	avesse doluto	avéssero doluto

	imperative	
		doliamo (dogliamo)
	duòli (non dolere)	dolete
	dòlga	dòlgano

* *Dolere* is also conjugated with *èssere*.

Words related to this verb
Mi duole la testa.   I have a headache.
Se ti dolesse il braccio come a me, non rideresti.   If your arm hurt like mine does,
you would not laugh.

domandare   Ger. **domandando**   Past Part. **domandato**

to ask (for), to demand, to beg

The Seven Simple Tenses		The Seven Compound Tenses	
Singular	Plural	Singular	Plural
1　present indicative		8　present perfect	
domàndo	domandiamo	ho domandato	abbiamo domandato
domàndi	domandate	hai domandato	avete domandato
domànda	domàndano	ha domandato	hanno domandato
2　imperfect indicative		9　past perfect	
domandavo	domandavamo	avevo domandato	avevamo domandato
domandavi	domandavate	avevi domandato	avevate domandato
domandava	domandàvano	aveva domandato	avévano domandato
3　past absolute		10　past anterior	
domandai	domandammo	èbbi domandato	avemmo domandato
domandasti	domandaste	avesti domandato	aveste domandato
domandò	domandàrono	èbbe domandato	èbbero domandato
4　future indicative		11　future perfect	
domanderò	domanderemo	avrò domandato	avremo domandato
domanderai	domanderete	avrai domandato	avrete domandato
domanderà	domanderanno	avrà domandato	avranno domandato
5　present conditional		12　past conditional	
domanderèi	domanderemmo	avrèi domandato	avremmo domandato
domanderesti	domandereste	avresti domandato	avreste domandato
domanderèbbe	domanderèbbero	avrèbbe domandato	avrèbbero domandato
6　present subjunctive		13　past subjunctive	
domàndi	domandiamo	àbbia domandato	abbiamo domandato
domàndi	domandiate	àbbia domandato	abbiate domandato
domàndi	domàndino	àbbia domandato	àbbiano domandato
7　imperfect subjunctive		14　past perfect subjunctive	
domandassi	domandàssimo	avessi domandato	avéssimo domandato
domandassi	domandaste	avessi domandato	aveste domandato
domandasse	domandàssero	avesse domandato	avéssero domandato

	imperative	
—		domandiamo
domànda (non domandare)		domandate
domàndi		domàndino

Words related to this verb
fare una domanda　to ask a question
domande e risposte　questions and answers

The Seven Simple Tenses		The Seven Compound Tenses	
Singular	Plural	Singular	Plural
1 present indicative		8 present perfect	
dòrmo	**dormiamo**	**ho dormito**	**abbiamo dormito**
dòrmi	**dormite**	**hai dormito**	**avete dormito**
dòrme	**dormono**	**ha dormito**	**hanno dormito**
2 imperfect indicative		9 past perfect	
dormivo	**dormivamo**	**avevo dormito**	**avevamo dormito**
dormivi	**dormivate**	**avevi dormito**	**avevate dormito**
dormiva	**dormivano**	**aveva dormito**	**avévano dormito**
3 past absolute		10 past anterior	
dormii	**dormimmo**	**èbbi dormito**	**avemmo dormito**
dormisti	**dormiste**	**avesti dormito**	**aveste dormito**
dormì	**dormírono**	**èbbe dormito**	**èbbero dormito**
4 future indicative		11 future perfect	
dormirò	**dormiremo**	**avrò dormito**	**avremo dormito**
dormirai	**dormirete**	**avrai dormito**	**avrete dormito**
dormirà	**dormiranno**	**avrà dormito**	**avranno dormito**
5 present conditional		12 past conditional	
dormirèi	**dormiremmo**	**avrèi dormito**	**avremmo dormito**
dormiresti	**dormireste**	**avresti dormito**	**avreste dormito**
dormirèbbe	**dormirèbbero**	**avrèbbe dormito**	**avrèbbero dormito**
6 present subjunctive		13 past subjunctive	
dòrma	**dormiamo**	**àbbia dormito**	**abbiamo dormito**
dòrma	**dormiate**	**àbbia dormito**	**abbiate dormito**
dòrma	**dòrmano**	**àbbia dormito**	**àbbiano dormito**
7 imperfect subjunctive		14 past perfect subjunctive	
dormissi	**dormìssimo**	**avessi dormito**	**avessimo dormito**
dormissi	**dormiste**	**avessi dormito**	**aveste dormito**
dormisse	**dormìssero**	**avesse dormito**	**avessero dormito**

imperative

—	**dormiamo**
dòrmi (non dormire)	**dormite**
dòrma	**dòrmano**

Words related to this verb
Io dormo bene ogni notte.   I sleep well every night.
dormire come un ghiro   to sleep like a log

105

| dovere | Ger. **dovèndo** | Past Part. **dovuto** |

to have to, must, ought, should; owe

The Seven Simple Tenses		The Seven Compound Tenses	
Singular	Plural	Singular	Plural
1 present indicative		8 present perfect	
devo (debbo)	**dobbiamo**	**ho* dovuto**	**abbiamo dovuto**
devi	**dovete**	**hai dovuto**	**avete dovuto**
deve	**dévono (débbono)**	**ha dovuto**	**hanno dovuto**
2 imperfect indicative		9 past perfect	
dovevo	**dovevamo**	**avevo dovuto**	**avevamo dovuto**
dovevi	**dovevate**	**avevi dovuto**	**avevate dovuto**
doveva	**dovévano**	**aveva dovuto**	**avévano dovuto**
3 past absolute		10 past anterior	
dovei (dovètti)	**dovemmo**	**èbbi dovuto**	**avemmo dovuto**
dovesti	**doveste**	**avesti dovuto**	**aveste dovuto**
dové (dovètte)	**dovérono (dovèttero)**	**èbbe dovuto**	**èbbero dovuto**
4 future indicative		11 future perfect	
dovrò	**dovremo**	**avrò dovuto**	**avremo dovuto**
dovrai	**dovrete**	**avrai dovuto**	**avrete dovuto**
dovrà	**dovranno**	**avrà dovuto**	**avranno dovuto**
5 present conditional		12 past conditional	
dovrèi	**dovremmo**	**avrèi dovuto**	**avremmo dovuto**
dovresti	**dovreste**	**avresti dovuto**	**avreste dovuto**
dovrèbbe	**dovrèbbero**	**avrèbbe dovuto**	**avrèbbero dovuto**
6 present subjunctive		13 past subjunctive	
deva (debba)	**dobbiamo**	**àbbia dovuto**	**abbiamo dovuto**
deva (debba)	**dobbiate**	**àbbia dovuto**	**abbiate dovuto**
deva (debba)	**dévano (débbano)**	**àbbia dovuto**	**àbbiano dovuto**
7 imperfect subjunctive		14 past perfect subjunctive	
dovessi	**dovéssimo**	**avessi dovuto**	**avéssimo dovuto**
dovessi	**doveste**	**avessi dovuto**	**aveste dovuto**
dovesse	**dovéssero**	**avesse dovuto**	**avéssero dovuto**

imperative

* *Dovere* takes *èssere* when the following infinitive requires it.

Words related to this verb
Io devo andare a scuola.   I must go to school.
Maria deve andare a dormire presto.   Mary must go to sleep early.

to elect, to choose

The Seven Simple Tenses		The Seven Compound Tenses	
Singular	Plural	Singular	Plural
1 present indicative		8 present perfect	
elèggo	eleggiamo	ho elètto	abbiamo elètto
elèggi	eleggete	hai elètto	avete elètto
elègge	elèggono	ha elètto	hanno elètto
2 imperfect indicative		9 past perfect	
eleggevo	eleggevamo	avevo elètto	avevamo elètto
eleggevi	eleggevate	avevi elètto	avevate elètto
eleggeva	eleggévano	aveva elètto	avévano elètto
3 past absolute		10 past anterior	
clèssi	eleggemmo	èbbi elètto	avemmo elètto
eleggesti	eleggeste	avesti clètto	aveste elètto
elèsse	elèssero	èbbe elètto	èbbero elètto
4 future indicative		11 future perfect	
eleggerò	eleggeremo	avrò elètto	avremo elètto
eleggerai	eleggerete	avrai elètto	avrete elètto
eleggerà	eleggeranno	avrà elètto	avranno elètto
5 present conditional		12 past conditional	
eleggerèi	eleggercmmo	avrèi elètto	avremmo elètto
eleggeresti	eleggereste	avresti elètto	avreste clètto
eleggerèbbe	eleggerèbbero	avrèbbe elètto	avrèbbero elètto
6 present subjunctive		13 past subjunctive	
clègga	eleggiamo	àbbia elètto	abbiamo elètto
elègga	eleggiate	àbbia clètto	abbiate elètto
elègga	elèggano	àbbia elètto	àbbiano elètto
7 imperfect subjunctive		14 past perfect subjunctive	
eleggessi	eleggéssimo	avessi elètto	avéssimo elètto
eleggessi	eleggeste	avessi elètto	aveste elètto
eleggesse	eleggéssero	avesse elètto	avéssero elètto

	imperative	
—		eleggiamo
elèggi (non elèggere)		eleggete
elègga		elèggano

Words related to this verb
Noi eleggiamo un presidente ogni quattro anni.   We elect a president every four years.
Io eleggo di stare a casa oggi.   I choose to stay home today.

to emerge

The Seven Simple Tenses		The Seven Compound Tenses	
Singular	Plural	Singular	Plural
1 present indicative		8 present perfect	
emèrgo	emergiamo	sono emèrso	siamo emèrsi
emèrgi	emergete	sèi emèrso	sièto emèrsi
emèrge	emèrgono	è emèrso	sono emèrsi
2 imperfect indicative		9 past perfect	
emergevo	emergevamo	èro emèrso	eravamo emèrsi
emergevi	emergevate	èri emèrso	eravate emèrsi
emergeva	emergévano	èra emèrso	ièrano emèrsi
3 past absolute		10 past anterior	
emèrsi	emergemmo	fui emèrso	fummo emèrsi
emergesti	emergeste	fosti emèrso	foste emèrsi
emèrse	emèrsero	fui emèrso	fúrono emèrsi
4 future indicative		11 future perfect	
emergerò	emergeremo	sarò emèrso	saremo emèrsi
emergerai	emergerete	sarai emèrso	sarete emèrsi
emergerà	emergeranno	sarà emèrso	saranno emèrsi
5 present conditional		12 past conditional	
emergerèi	emergeremmo	sarèi emèrso	saremmo emèrsi
emergeresti	emergereste	saresti emèrso	sareste emèrsi
emergerèbbe	emergerèbbero	sarèbbe emèrso	sarèbbero emèrsi
6 present subjunctive		13 past subjunctive	
emèrga	emergiamo	sia emèrso	siamo emèrsi
emèrga	emergiate	sia emèrso	siate emèrsi
emèrga	emèrgano	sia emèrso	síano emèrsi
7 imperfect subjunctive		14 past perfect subjunctive	
emergessi	emergéssimo	fossi emèrso	fóssimo emèrsi
emergessi	emergeste	fossi emèrso	foste emèrsi
emergesse	emergéssero	fosse emèrso	fóssero emèrsi

imperative	
—	emergiamo
emèrgi (non emèrgere)	emergete
emèrga	emèrgano

Words related to this verb
Lui emerse vittorioso.   He emerged victorious.
Il topo emerge di notte.   The mouse comes out at night.

to exist, to be

The Seven Simple Tenses		The Seven Compound Tenses	
Singular	Plural	Singular	Plural
1　present indicative		8　present perfect	
esisto	esistiamo	sono esistito	siamo esistiti
esisti	esistere	sei esistito	siete esistiti
esiste	esístono	è esistito	sono esistiti
2　imperfect indicative		9　past perfect	
esistevo	esistevamo	èro esistito	eravamo esistiti
esistevi	esistevate	èri esistito	eravate esistiti
esisteva	esistévano	èra esistito	érano esistiti
3　past absolute		10　past anterior	
esistei (esistètti)	esistemmo	fui esistito	fummo esistiti
esistesti	esisteste	fosti esistito	foste esistiti
esistè (esistètte)	esistérono (esistèttero)	fu esistito	fúrono esistiti
4　future indicative		11　future perfect	
esisterò	esisteremo	sarò esistito	saremo esistiti
esisterai	esisterete	sarai esistito	sarete esistiti
esisterà	esisteranno	sarà esistito	saranno esistiti
5　present conditional		12　past conditional	
esisterèi	esistcrcmmo	sarèi esistito	saremmo esistiti
esisteresti	esistereste	saresti esistito	sareste esistiti
esisterèbbe	esisterèbbero	sarèbbe esistito	sarèbbero esistiti
6　present subjunctive		13　past subjunctive	
esista	esistiamo	sia esistito	saimo esistiti
esista	esistiate	sia esistito	siate esistiti
esista	esístano	sia esistito	siano esistiti
7　imperfect subjunctive		14　past perfect subjunctive	
esistessi	esistéssimo	fossi esistito	fóssimo esistiti
esistessi	esisteste	fossi esistito	foste esistiti
esistesse	esistéssero	fosse esistito	fóssero esistiti

imperative	
—	esistiamo
esisti (non esistere)	esistete
esista	esístano

Words related to this verb
Credo che la bontà esista.　I believe that goodness exists.
Queste cose non esistono piú.　These things no longer exist.

esprímere   Ger. **esprimèndo**   Past Part. **esprèsso**

to express

The Seven Simple Tenses		The Seven Compound Tenses	
Singular	Plural	Singular	Plural
1 present indicative		8 present perfect	
esprimo	**esprimiamo**	**ho esprèsso**	**abbiamo esprèsso**
esprimi	**esprimete**	**hai esprèsso**	**avete esprèsso**
esprime	**esprímono**	**ha esprèsso**	**hanno esprèsso**
2 imperfect indicative		9 past perfect	
esprimevo	**esprimevamo**	**avevo esprèsso**	**avevamo esprèsso**
esprimevi	**esprimevate**	**avevi esprèsso**	**avevate esprèsso**
esprimeva	**esprimévano**	**aveva esprèsso**	**avévano esprèsso**
3 past absolute		10 past anterior	
esprèssi	**esprimemmo**	**èbbi esprèsso**	**avemmo esprèsso**
esprimesti	**esprimeste**	**avesti esprèsso**	**aveste esprèsso**
esprèsse	**esprèssero**	**èbbe esprèsso**	**èbbero esprèsso**
4 future indicative		11 future perfect	
esprimerò	**esprimeremo**	**avrò esprèsso**	**avremo esprèsso**
esprimerai	**esprimerete**	**avrai esprèsso**	**avrete esprèsso**
esprimerà	**esprimeranno**	**avrà esprèsso**	**avranno esprèsso**
5 present conditional		12 past conditional	
esprimerèi	**esprimeremmo**	**avrèi esprèsso**	**avremmo esprèsso**
esprimeresti	**esprimereste**	**avesti esprèsso**	**avreste esprèsso**
esprimerèbbe	**esprimerèbbero**	**avrèbbe esprèsso**	**avrèbbero esprèsso**
6 present subjunctive		13 past subjunctive	
esprima	**esprimiamo**	**àbbia esprèsso**	**abbiamo esprèsso**
esprima	**esprimiate**	**àbbia esprèsso**	**abbiate esprèsso**
esprima	**esprímano**	**àbbia esprèsso**	**àbbiano esprèsso**
7 imperfect subjunctive		14 past perfect subjunctive	
esprimessi	**espriméssimo**	**avessi esprèsso**	**avéssimo esprèsso**
esprimessi	**esprimeste**	**avessi esprèsso**	**aveste esprèsso**
esprimesse	**espriméssero**	**avesse esprèsso**	**avéssero esprèsso**

	imperative	
—		**esprimiamo**
esprimi (non esprímere)		**esprimete**
esprima		**esprímano**

Words related to this verb
esprimere i propri sentimenti   to express one's feelings
Non posso esprimermi bene in italiano.   I cannot express myself well in Italian.

The Seven Simple Tenses		The Seven Compound Tenses	
Singular	Plural	Singular	Plural
1 present indicative		8 present perfect	
sono	siamo	sono stato	siamo stati
sèi	sième	sèi stato	sième stato (i)
è	sono	è stato	sono stati
2 imperfect indicative		9 past anterior	
èro	eravamo	èro stato	eravamo stati
èri	eravate	èri stato	eravate stati
èra	èrano	èra stato	èrano stati
3 past absolute		10 future perfect	
fui	fummo	fui stato	fummo stati
fosti	foste	fosti stato	foste stati
fu	fúrono	fu stato	fúrono stati
4 future indicative		11 past conditional	
sarò	saremo	sarò stato	saremo stati
sarai	sarete	sarai stato	sarete stati
sarà	saranno	sarà stato	saranno stati
5 present conditional		12 past subjunctive	
sarèi	saremmo	sarèi stato	saremmo stati
saresti	sareste	saresti stato	sareste stati
sarèbbe	sarèbbero	sarèbbe stato	sarèbbero stati
6 present subjunctive		13 past subjunctive	
sia	siamo	sia stato	siamo stati
sia	siate	sia stato	siate stati
sia	síano	sia stato	síano stati
7 imperfect subjunctive		14 past perfect subjunctive	
fossi	fóssimo	fossi stato	fóssimo stati
fossi	foste	fossi stato	foste stati
fosse	fóssero	fosse stato	fóssero stati

	imperative	
—		siamo
sii (non èssere)		siate
sia		síano

Words related to this verb
Io sono qui.   I am here.
essere stanco(a)   to be tired

estèndere   Ger. estendèndo   Past Part. esteso

to extend

The Seven Simple Tenses		The Seven Compound Tenses	
Singular	Plural	Singular	Plural
1 present indicative		8 present perfect	
estèndo	estendiamo	ho esteso	abbiamo esteso
estèndi	estendete	hai esteso	avete esteso
estènde	estèndono	ha esteso	hanno esteso
2 imperfect indicative		9 past perfect	
estendevo	estendevamo	avevo esteso	avevamo esteso
estendevi	estendevate	avevi esteso	avevate esteso
estèndeva	estendévano	aveva esteso	avévano esteso
3 past absolute		10 past anterior	
estesi	estendemmo	èbbi esteso	avemmo esteso
estendesti	estendeste	avesti esteso	aveste esteso
estese	estésero	èbbe esteso	èbbero esteso
4 future indicative		11 future perfect	
estenderò	estenderemo	avrò esteso	avremo esteso
estenderai	estenderete	avrai esteso	avrete esteso
estenderà	estenderanno	avrà esteso	avranno esteso
5 present conditional		12 past conditional	
estenderèi	estenderemmo	avrèi esteso	avremmo esteso
estenderesti	estendereste	avresti esteso	avreste esteso
estenderèbbe	estenderèbbero	avrèbbe esteso	avrèbbero esteso
6 present subjunctive		13 past subjunctive	
estènda	estendiamo	àbbia esteso	abbiamo esteso
estènda	estendiate	àbbia esteso	abbiate esteso
estènda	estèndano	àbbia esteso	àbbiano esteso
7 imperfect subjunctive		14 past perfect subjunctive	
estendessi	estendéssimo	avessi esteso	avéssimo esteso
estendessi	estendeste	avessi esteso	aveste esteso
estendesse	estendéssero	avesse esteso	avéssero esteso

	imperative	
—		estendiamo
estèndi (non estèdere)		estendete
estènda		estèndano

Words related to this verb
estendere il proprio potere   to extend (increase) one's power
Lui vuole estendere la casa.   He wants to expand (enlarge) the house.

to do, to make

The Seven Simple Tenses		The Seven Compound Tenses	
Singular	Plural	Singular	Plural
1 present indicative		8 present perfect	
faccio (fo)	**facciamo**	**ho fatto**	**abbiamo fatto**
fai	**fate**	**hai fatto**	**avete fatto**
fa	**fanno**	**ha fatto**	**hanno fatto**
2 imperfect indicative		9 past perfect	
facevo	**facevamo**	**avevo fatto**	**avevamo fatto**
facevi	**facevate**	**avevi fatto**	**avevate fatto**
faceva	**facévano**	**aveva fatto**	**avévano fatto**
3 past absolute		10 past anterior	
feci	**facemmo**	**èbbi fatto**	**avemmo fatto**
facesti	**faceste**	**avesti fatto**	**aveste fatto**
fece	**fécero**	**èbbe fatto**	**èbbero fatto**
4 future indicative		11 future perfect	
farò	**faremo**	**avrò fatto**	**avremo fatto**
farai	**farete**	**avrai fatto**	**avrete fatto**
farà	**faranno**	**avrà fatto**	**avranno fatto**
5 present conditional		12 past conditional	
farèi	**faremmo**	**avrèi fatto**	**avremmo fatto**
faresti	**fareste**	**avresti fatto**	**avreste fatto**
farèbbe	**farèbbero**	**avrèbbe fatto**	**avrèbbero fatto**
6 present subjunctive		13 past subjunctive	
faccia	**facciamo**	**àbbia fatto**	**abbiamo fatto**
faccia	**facciate**	**àbbia fatto**	**abbiate fatto**
faccia	**fàcciano**	**àbbia fatto**	**àbbiano fatto**
7 imperfect subjunctive		14 past perfect subjunctive	
facessi	**facéssimo**	**avessi fatto**	**avéssimo fatto**
facessi	**faceste**	**avessi fatto**	**aveste fatto**
facesse	**facéssero**	**avesse fatto**	**avéssero fatto**

	imperative	
—	**facciamo**
fa' (non fare)	**fate**
faccia	**fàcciano**

* Like *fare* are *contraffare*, *rifare*, *sfare*, *sopraffare*, and *stupefare*; but all these compounds (except *sfare*) require an accent on the forms in *-fo* and *-fa*.

Words related to this verb
Cosa fai?   What are you doing?
Lui non fa altro che sognare.   He does nothing but dream.

fermarsi   Ger. **fermandosi**   Past Part. **fermatosi**

to stop

The Seven Simple Tenses		The Seven Compound Tenses	
Singular	Plural	Singular	Plural
1 present indicative		8 present perfect	
mi fèrmo	ci fermiamo	mi sono fermato	ci siamo fermati
ti fèrmi	vi fermate	ti sei fermato	vi siete fermati
si fèrma	si fermano	si è fermato	si sono fermati
2 imperfect indicative		9 past perfect	
mi fermavo	ci fermavamo	mi èro fermato	ci eravamo fermati
ti fermavi	vi fermavate	ti èri fermato	vi eravate fermati
si fermava	si fermàvano	si èra fermato	si èrano fermati
3 past absolute		10 past anterior	
mi fermai	ci fermammo	mi fui fermato	ci fummo fermati
ti fermasti	vi fermaste	ti fosti fermato	vi foste fermati
si fermò	si fermarono	si fu fermato	si fúrono fermati
4 future indicative		11 future perfect	
mi fermerò	ci fermeremo	mi sarò fermato	cl saremo fermati
ti fermerai	vi fermerete	ti sarai fermato	vi sarete fermati
si fermerà	si fermeranno	si sarà fermato	si saranno fermati
5 present conditional		12 past conditional	
mi fermerèi	ci fermeremmo	mi sarèi fermato	ci saremmo fermati
ti fermeresti	vi fermereste	ti saresti fermato	vi sareste fermati
si fermerèbbe	si fermerèbbero	si sarèbbe fermato	si sarèbbero fermati
6 present subjunctive		13 past subjunctive	
mi fèrmi	ci fermiamo	mi sia fermato	ci siamo fermati
ti fèrmi	vi fermiate	ti sia fermato	vi siate fermati
si fèrmi	si fèrmino	si sia fermato	si síano fermati
7 imperfect subjunctive		14 past perfect subjunctive	
mi fermassi	ci fermàssimo	mi fossi fermato	ci fóssimo fermati
ti fermassi	vi fermaste	ti fossi fermato	vi foste fermati
si fermasse	si fermàssero	si fosse fermato	si fóssero fermati

imperative	
—	fermiamoci
fèrmati (non ti fermare)	fermatevi
si fermi	si fèrmino

Words related to this verb
Ci fermiamo alle nove. We stop at nine.
Fermati, ladro! Stop, thief!

114

to fix, to fasten

The Seven Simple Tenses		The Seven Compound Tenses	
Singular	Plural	Singular	Plural
1 present indicative		8 present perfect	
figgo	**figgiamo**	**ho fitto**	**abbiamo fitto**
figgi	**figgete**	**hai fitto**	**avete fitto**
figge	**figgono**	**ha fitto**	**hanno fitto**
2 imperfect indicative		9 past perfect	
figgevo	**figgevamo**	**avevo fitto**	**avevamo fitto**
figgevi	**figgevate**	**avevi fitto**	**avevate fitto**
figgeva	**figgévano**	**aveva fitto**	**avévano fitto**
3 past absolute	**fissi** **figgemmo**	10 past anterior	
fissi	**figgemmo**	**èbbi fitto**	**avemmo fitto**
figgesti	**figgeste**	**avesti fitto**	**aveste fitto**
fisse	**físsero**	**èbbe fitto**	**èbbero fitto**
4 future indicative		11 future perfect	
figgerò	**figgeremo**	**avrò fitto**	**avremo fitto**
figgerai	**figgerete**	**avrai fitto**	**avrete fitto**
figgerà	**figgeranno**	**avrà fitto**	**avranno fitto**
5 present conditional		12 past conditional	
figgerèi	**figgeremmo**	**avrèi fitto**	**avremmo fitto**
figgeresti	**figgereste**	**avresti fitto**	**avreste fitto**
figgerèbbe	**figgerèbbero**	**avrèbbe fitto**	**avrèbbero fitto**
6 present subjunctive		13 past subjunctive	
figga	**figgiamo**	**àbbia fitto**	**abbiamo fitto**
figga	**figgiate**	**àbbia fitto**	**abbiate fitto**
figga	**fíggano**	**àbbia fitto**	**àbbiano fitto**
7 imperfect subjunctive		14 past perfect subjunctive	
figgessi	**figgéssimo**	**avessi fitto**	**avéssimo fitto**
figgessi	**figgeste**	**avessi fitto**	**aveste fitto**
figgesse	**figgéssero**	**avesse fitto**	**avéssero fitto**

imperative

—	**figgiamo**
figgi (non fíggere)	**fíggete**
figga	**fíggano**

* The compounds of *figgere* are the same except for some past participles. The past participles of the compounds are as follows: *affisso, confitto, crocefisso, prefisso, sconfitto, trafitto*.

Words related to this verb
Io figgo il quadro al muro.   I fix the picture to the wall.
Lui figge gli occhi su me.   He fixes his eyes on (stares at) me.

to feign, to pretend

The Seven Simple Tenses		The Seven Compound Tenses	
Singular	Plural	Singular	Plural
1 present indicative		8 present perfect	
fingo	fingiamo	ho finto	abbiamo finto
fingi	fingete	hai finto	avete finto
finge	fíngono	ha finto	hanno finto
2 imperfect indicative		9 past perfect	
fingevo	fingevamo	avevo finto	avevamo finto
fingevi	fingevate	avevi finto	avevate finto
fingeva	fingévano	aveva finto	avévano finto
3 past absolute		10 past anterior	
finsi	fingemmo	èbbi finto	avemmo finto
fingesti	fingeste	avesti finto	aveste finto
finse	fínsero	èbbe finto	èbbero finto
4 future indicative		11 future perfect	
fingerò	fingeremo	avrò finto	avremo finto
fingerai	fingerete	avrai finto	avrete finto
fingerà	fingeranno	avrà finto	avranno finto
5 present conditional		12 past conditional	
fingerèi	fingeremmo	avrèi finto	avremmo finto
fingeresti	fingereste	avresti finto	avreste finto
fingerèbbe	fingerèbbero	avrèbbe finto	avrèbbero finto
6 present subjunctive		13 past subjunctive	
finga	fingiamo	àbbia finto	abbiamo finto
finga	fingiate	àbbia finto	abbiate finto
finga	fíngano	àbbia finto	àbbiano finto
7 imperfect subjunctive		14 past perfect subjunctive	
fingessi	fingéssimo	avessi finto	avéssimo finto
fingessi	fingeste	avessi finto	aveste finto
fingesse	fingéssero	avesse finto	avéssero finto

	imperative	
—		fingiamo
fingi (non fíngere)		fingete
finga		fíngano

Words related to this verb
Lei finge di dormire.   She is pretending to sleep.
fingere indifferenza   to feign indifference

The Seven Simple Tenses		The Seven Compound Tenses	
Singular	Plural	Singular	Plural
1 present indicative		**8 present perfect**	
finìsco	**finiamo**	**ho finito**	**abbiamo finito**
finìsci	**finite**	**hai finito**	**avete finito**
finìsce	**finìscono**	**ha finito**	**hanno finito**
2 imperfect indicative		**9 past perfect**	
finivo	**finivamo**	**avevo finito**	**avevamo finito**
finivi	**finivate**	**avevi finito**	**avevate finito**
finiva	**finìvano**	**aveva finito**	**avévano finito**
3 past absolute		**10 past anterior**	
finìi	**finimmo**	**èbbi finito**	**avemmo finito**
finisti	**finiste**	**avesti finito**	**aveste finito**
finì	**finìrono**	**èbbe finito**	**èbbero finito**
4 future indicative		**11 future perfect**	
finirò	**finiremo**	**avrò finito**	**avremo finito**
finirai	**finirete**	**avrai finito**	**avrete finito**
finirà	**finiranno**	**avrà finito**	**avranno finito**
5 present conditional		**12 past conditional**	
finirèi	**finiremmo**	**avrèi finito**	**avremmo finito**
finiresti	**finireste**	**avresti finito**	**avreste finito**
finirèbbe	**finirèbbero**	**avrèbbe finito**	**avrèbbero finito**
6 present subjunctive		**13 past subjunctive**	
finisca	**finiamo**	**àbbia finito**	**abbiamo finito**
finisca	**finiàte**	**àbbia finito**	**abbiate finito**
finisca	**finìscano**	**àbbia finito**	**àbbiano finito**
7 imperfect subjunctive		**14 past perfect subjunctive**	
finissi	**finìssimo**	**avessi finito**	**avéssimo finito**
finissi	**finiste**	**avessi finito**	**aveste finito**
finisse	**finìssero**	**avesse finito**	**avéssero finito**

imperative

—	**finiamo**
finìsci (non finire)	**finite**
finìsca	**finìscano**

Words related to this verb
Tutto è bene ciò che finisce bene.   All's well that ends well.
Come finisce il libro?   How does the book end?

fóndere* Ger. **fondèndo** Past Part. **fuso**

to fuse, to melt

The Seven Simple Tenses		The Seven Compound Tenses	
Singular	Plural	Singular	Plural
1 present indicative		8 present perfect	
fondo	fondiamo	ho fuso	abbiamo fuso
fondi	fondete	hai fuso	avete fuso
fonde	fóndono	ha fuso	hanno fuso
2 imperfect indicative		9 past perfect	
fondevo	fondevamo	avevo fuso	avevamo fuso
fondevi	fondevate	avevi fuso	avevate fuso
fondeva	fondévano	aveva fuso	avévano fuso
3 past absolute		10 past anterior	
fusi	fondemmo	èbbi fuso	avemmo fuso
fondesti	fondeste	avesti fuso	aveste fuso
fuse	fúsero	èbbe fuso	èbbero fuso
4 future indicative		11 future perfect	
fonderò	fonderemo	avrò fuso	avremo fuso
fonderai	fonderete	avrai fuso	avrete fuso
fonderà	fonderanno	avrà fuso	avranno fuso
5 present conditional		12 past conditional	
fonderèi	fonderemmo	avrèi fuso	avremmo fuso
fonderesti	fondereste	avresti fuso	avreste fuso
fonderèbbe	fonderèbbero	avrèbbe fuso	avrèbbero fuso
6 present subjunctive		13 past subjunctive	
fonda	fondiamo	àbbia fuso	abbiamo fuso
fonda	fondiate	àbbia fuso	abbiate fuso
fonda	fóndano	àbbia fuso	àbbiano fuso
7 imperfect subjunctive		14 past perfect subjunctive	
fondessi	fondéssimo	avessi fuso	avéssimo fuso
fondessi	fondeste	avessi fuso	aveste fuso
fondesse	fondéssero	avesse fuso	avéssero fuso

imperative	
—	fondiamo
fondi (non fóndere)	fondete
fonda	fóndano

* Like *fóndere* are *confóndere*, *diffóndere*, *infóndere*, *rifóndere*, *trasfóndere*, etc.

Words related to this verb
Il sole fonde la neve. The sun melts the snow.
Lui fonderà i pezzi di metallo. He will fuse the pieces of metal.

to fry

The Seven Simple Tenses		The Seven Compound Tenses	
Singular	Plural	Singular	Plural
1 present indicative		8 present perfect	
friggo	**friggiamo**	**ho fritto**	**abbiamo fritto**
friggi	**friggete**	**hai fritto**	**avete fritto**
frigge	**fríggono**	**ha fritto**	**hanno fritto**
2 imperfect indicative		9 past perfect	
friggevo	**friggevamo**	**avevo fritto**	**avevamo fritto**
friggevi	**friggevate**	**avevi fritto**	**avevate fritto**
friggeva	**friggévano**	**aveva fritto**	**avévano fritto**
3 past absolute		10 past anterior	
frissi	**friggemmo**	**èbbi fritto**	**avemmo fritto**
friggesti	**friggeste**	**avesti fritto**	**aveste fritto**
frisse	**fríssero**	**èbbe fritto**	**èbbero fritto**
4 future indicative		11 future perfect	
friggerò	**friggeremo**	**avrò fritto**	**avremo fritto**
friggerai	**friggerete**	**ávral fritto**	**avrete fritto**
friggerà	**friggeranno**	**avrà fritto**	**avranno fritto**
5 present conditional		12 past conditional	
friggerèi	**friggeremmo**	**avrèi fritto**	**avremmo fritto**
friggeresti	**friggereste**	**avresti fritto**	**avreste frItto**
friggerèbbe	**friggerèbbero**	**avrèbbe fritto**	**avrèbbero fritto**
6 present subjunctive		13 past subjunctive	
frigga	**friggiamo**	**àbbia fritto**	**abbiamo fritto**
frigga	**friggiate**	**àbbia fritto**	**abbiate fritto**
frigga	**fríggano**	**àbbia fritto**	**àbbiano fritto**
7 imperfect subjunctive		14 past perfect subjunctive	
friggessi	**friggéssimo**	**avessi fritto**	**avéssimo fritto**
friggessi	**friggeste**	**avessi fritto**	**aveste fritto**
friggesse	**friggéssero**	**avesse fritto**	**avéssero fritto**

	imperative	
—		**friggiamo**
friggi (non fríggere)		**friggete**
frigga		**fríggano**

Words related to this verb
Lui non sa friggere le uova.   He does not know how to fry eggs.
Questa carne frigge bene.   This meat fries well.
padella per friggere   frying pan

giacere   Ger. **giacèndo**   Past Part. **giaciuto**

to lie

The Seven Simple Tenses		The Seven Compound Tenses	
Singular	Plural	Singular	Plural
1 present indicative		8 present perfect	
giaccio	giacciamo (giaciamo)	sono giaciuto	siamo giaciuti
giaci	giacete	sèi giaciuto	siète giaciuti
giace	giàcciono	è giaciuto	sono giaciuti
2 imperfect indicative		9 past perfect	
giacevo	giacevamo	èro giaciuto	eravamo giaciuti
giacevi	giacevate	èri giaciuto	eravate giaciuti
giaceva	giacévano	èra giaciuto	èrano giaciuti
3 past absolute		10 past anterior	
giacqui	giacemmo	fui giaciuto	fummo giaciuti
giacesti	giaceste	fosti giaciuto	foste giaciuti
giacque	giàcquero	fu giaciuto	fúrono giaciuti
4 future indicative		11 future perfect	
giacerò	giaceremo	sarò giaciuto	saremo giaciuti
giacerai	giacerete	sarai giaciuto	sarete giaciuti
giacerà	giaceranno	sarà giaciuto	saranno giaciuti
5 present conditional		12 past conditional	
giacerèi	giaceremmo	sarèi giaciuto	saremmo giaciuti
giaceresti	giacereste	saresti giaciuto	sareste giaciuti
giacerèbbe	giacerèbbero	sarèbbe giaciuto	sarèbbero giaciuti
6 present subjunctive		13 past subjunctive	
giaccia	giacciamo (giaciamo)	sia giaciuto	siamo giaciuti
giaccia	giacciate (giaciate)	sia giaciuto	siate giacitui
giaccia	giàcciano	sia giacituo	síano giaciuti
7 imperfect subjunctive		14 past perfect subjunctive	
giacessi	giacéssimo	fossi giaciuto	fóssimo giaciuti
giacessi	giaceste	fossi giaciuto	foste giaciuti
giacesse	giacéssero	fosse giaciuto	fóssero giaciuti

	imperative	
—		giacciamo (giaciamo)
giaci (non giacere)		giacete
giaccia		giàcciano

* Also conjugated with *avere*.

Words related to this verb
Lui giace a letto.   He is lying in bed.
Lei giaceva a terra quando la vidi.   She was lying on the ground when I saw her.

to play (a game)

The Seven Simple Tenses		The Seven Compound Tenses	
Singular	Plural	Singular	Plural
1 present indicative		8 present perfect	
giòco	**giochiamo**	**ho giocato**	**abbiamo giocato**
giòchi	**giocate**	**hai giocato**	**avete giocato**
giòca	**giocano**	**ha giocato**	**hanno giocato**
2 imperfect indicative		9 past perfect	
giocavo	**giocavamo**	**avevo giocato**	**avevamo giocato**
giocavi	**giocavate**	**avevi giocato**	**avevate giocato**
giocava	**giocavano**	**aveva giocato**	**avévano giocato**
3 past absolute		10 past anterior	
giocai	**giocammo**	**èbbi giocato**	**avemmo giocato**
giocasti	**giocaste**	**avesti giocato**	**aveste giocato**
giocò	**giocarono**	**èbbe giocato**	**èbbero giocato**
4 future indicative		11 future perfect	
giocherò	**giocheremo**	**avrò giocato**	**avremo giocato**
giocherai	**giocherete**	**avrai giocato**	**avrete giocato**
giocherà	**giocheranno**	**avrà giocato**	**avranno giocato**
5 present conditional		12 past conditional	
giocherèi	**giocheremmo**	**avrèi giocato**	**avremmo giocato**
giocheresti	**giochereste**	**avresti giocato**	**avreste giocato**
giocherèbbe	**giocherèbbero**	**avrèbbe giocato**	**avrèbbero giocato**
6 present subjunctive		13 past subjunctive	
giòchi	**giochiamo**	**àbbia giocato**	**abbiamo giocato**
giòchi	**giochiate**	**àbbia giocato**	**abbiate giocato**
giòchi	**giòchino**	**àbbia giocato**	**àbbiano giocato**
7 imperfect subjunctive		14 past perfect subjunctive	
giocassi	**giocàssimo**	**avessi giocato**	**avéssimo giocato**
giocassi	**giocaste**	**avessi giocato**	**aveste giocato**
giocasse	**giocàssero**	**avesse giocato**	**avéssero giocato**

imperative

—	**giochiamo**
giòca (non giocare)	**giocate**
giòchi	**giòchino**

Words related to this verb
giocare a carte   to play cards
giocare sulle parole   to play on words

girare	Ger. girando	Past Part. girato

to turn

The Seven Simple Tenses		The Seven Compound Tenses	
Singular	Plural	Singular	Plural
1 present indicative		**8 present perfect**	
gìro	giriamo	ho girato	abbiamo girato
giri	girate	hai girato	avete girato
gìra	girano	ha girato	hanno girato
2 imperfect indicative		**9 past perfect**	
giravo	giravamo	avevo girato	avevamo girato
giravi	giravate	avevi girato	avevate girato
girava	giravano	aveva girato	avévano girato
3 past absolute		**10 past anterior**	
girai	girammo	èbbi girato	avemmo girato
girasti	giraste	avesti girato	aveste girato
girò	girarono	èbbe girato	èbbero girato
4 future indicative		**11 future perfect**	
girerò	gireremo	avrò girato	avremo girato
girerai	girerete	avrai girato	avrete girato
girerà	gireranno	avrà girato	avranno girato
5 present conditional		**12 past conditional**	
girerèi	gireremmo	avrèi girato	avremmo girato
gireresti	girereste	avresti girato	avreste girato
girerèbbe	girerèbbero	avrèbbe girato	avrèbbero girato
6 present subjunctive		**13 past subjunctive**	
gìri	giriamo	àbbia girato	abbiamo girato
gìri	giriate	àbbia girato	abbiate girato
gìri	gìrino	àbbia girato	àbbiano girato
7 imperfect subjunctive		**14 past perfect subjunctive**	
girassi	giràssimo	avessi girato	avéssimo girato
girassi	giraste	avessi girato	aveste girato
girasse	giràssero	avesse girato	avèssero girato

	imperative	
—	giriamo
gìra (non girare)	girate
gìri	gìrino

Words related to this verb
girare la chiave nella serratura   to turn the key in the lock
girare lo sguardo per la stanza   to cast one's eye around the room
girare la pagina   to turn the page

to arrive

The Seven Simple Tenses		The Seven Compound Tenses	
Singular	Plural	Singular	Plural
1 present indicative		8 present perfect	
giungo	giungiamo	sono giunto	siamo giunti
giungi	giungete	sèi giunto	siète giunto(i)
giunge	giúngono	è giunto	sono giunti
2 imperfect indicative		9 past perfect	
giungevo	giungevamo	èro giunto	eravamo giunti
giungevi	giungevate	èri giunto	eravate giunto(i)
giungeva	giungévano	èra giunto	èrano giunti
3 past absolute		10 past anterior	
giunsi	giungemmo	fui giunto	fummo giunti
giungesti	giungeste	fosti giunto	foste giunto(i)
giunse	giúnsero	fu giunto	fúrono giunti
4 future indicative		11 future perfect	
giungerò	giungeremo	sarò giunto	saremo giunti
giungerai	giungerete	sarai giunto	sarete giunto(i)
giungerà	giungeranno	sarà giunto	saranno giunti
5 present conditional		12 past conditional	
giungerèi	giungeremmo	sarèi giunto	saremmo giunti
giungeresti	giungereste	saresti giunto	sareste giunto(i)
giungerèbbe	giungerèbbero	sarèbbe giunto	sarèbbero giunti
6 present subjunctive		13 past subjunctive	
giunga	giungiamo	sia giunto	siamo giunti
giunga	giungiate	sia giunto	siate giunto(i)
giunga	giúngano	sia giunto	siano giunti
7 imperfect subjunctive		14 past perfect subjunctive	
giungessi	giungéssimo	fossi giunto	fóssimo giunti
giungessi	giungeste	fossi giunto	foste giunto(i)
giungesse	giungéssero	fosse giunto	fóssero giunti

imperative

	giungiamo
giungi (non giúngere)	giungete
giunga	giúngano

* Like *giúngere*, are *aggiúngere*, *congiúngere*, *disgiúngere*, *raggiúngere*, *soggiúngere*, and *sopraggiúngere*, all of which (except the last) require *avere*.

Words related to this verb
Io sono giunto(a) tardi alla festa.   I arrived late at the party.
Giunsi in Italia il primo agosto.   I arrived in Italy on August first.

godere	Ger. godèndo	Past Part. goduto

to enjoy

The Seven Simple Tenses		The Seven Compound Tenses	
Singular	Plural	Singular	Plural
1 present indicative		8 present perfect	
gòdo	godiamo	ho goduto	abbiamo goduto
gòdi	godete	hai goduto	avete goduto
gòde	gòdono	ha goduto	hanno goduto
2 imperfect indicative		9 past perfect	
godevo	godevamo	avevo goduto	avevamo goduto
godevi	godevate	avevi goduto	avevate goduto
godeva	godévano	aveva goduto	avévano goduto
3 past absolute		10 past anterior	
godei (godètti)	godemmo	èbbi goduto	avemmo goduto
godesti	godeste	avesti goduto	aveste goduto
godé (godètte)	godérono (godèttero)	èbbe goduto	èbbero goduto
4 future indicative		11 future perfect	
godrò	godremo	avrò goduto	avremo goduto
godrai	godrete	avrai goduto	avrete goduto
godrà	godranno	avrà goduto	avranno goduto
5 present conditional		12 past conditional	
godrèi	godremmo	avrèi goduto	avremmo goduto
godresti	godreste	avresti goduto	avreste goduto
godrèbbe	godrèbbero	avrèbbe goduto	avrèbbero goduto
6 present subjunctive		13 past subjunctive	
gòda	godiamo	àbbia goduto	abbiamo goduto
gòda	godiate	àbbia goduto	abbiate goduto
gòda	gòdano	àbbia goduto	àbbiano goduto
7 imperfect subjunctive		14 past perfect subjunctive	
godessi	godéssimo	avessi goduto	avéssimo goduto
godessi	godeste	avessi goduto	aveste goduto
godesse	godéssero	avesse goduto	avéssero goduto

imperative		
—	godiamo	
gòdi (non godere)	godete	
gòda	gòdano	

Words related to this verb
Lui gode la vita.   He enjoys life.
Ho goduto ogni momento del viaggio.   I enjoyed every minute of the trip.

to look at

The Seven Simple Tenses		The Seven Compound Tenses	
Singular	Plural	Singular	Plural
1 present indicative		8 present perfect	
guàrdo	guardiamo	ho guardato	abbiamo guardato
guàrdi	guardate	hai guardato	avete guardato
guàrda	guàrdano	ha guardato	hanno guardato
2 imperfect indicative		9 past perfect	
guardavo	guardavamo	avevo guardato	avevamo guardato
guardavi	guardavate	avevi guardato	avevate guardato
guardava	guardàvano	aveva guardato	avévano guardato
3 past absolute		10 past anterior	
guardai	guardammo	èbbi guardato	avemmo guardato
guardasti	guardaste	avesti guardato	aveste guardato
guardò	guardarono	èbbe guardato	èbbero guardato
4 future indicative		11 future perfect	
guarderò	guarderemo	avrò guardato	avremo guardato
guarderai	guarderete	avrai guardato	avrete guardato
guarderà	guarderanno	avrà guardato	avranno guardato
5 present conditional		12 past conditional	
guarderei	guarderemmo	avrèi guardato	avremmo guardato
guarderesti	guardereste	avresti guardato	avreste guardato
guarderèbbe	guarderèbbero	avrèbbe guardato	avrèbbero guardato
6 present subjunctive		13 past subjunctive	
guàrdi	guardiamo	àbbia guardato	abbiamo guardato
guàrdi	guardiate	àbbia guardato	abbiate guardato
guàrdi	guàrdino	àbbia guardato	àbbiano guardato
7 imperfect subjunctive		14 past perfect subjunctive	
guardassi	guardàssimo	avessi guardato	avéssimo guardato
guardassi	guardaste	avessi guardato	aveste guardato
guardasse	guardàssero	avesse guardato	avéssero guardato

	imperative	
—		guardiamo
	guàrda (non guardare)	guardate
	guàrdi	guàrdino

Words related to this verb
Guardate quella casa!   Look at that house!
Lui guarda il paesaggio.   He is looking at the view.

illúdere Ger. illudèndo Past Part. illuso

to deceive, to delude

The Seven Simple Tenses		The Seven Compound Tenses	
Singular	Plural	Singular	Plural
1 present indicative		8 present perfect	
illudo	**illudiamo**	**ho illuso**	**abbiamo illuso**
illudi	**illudete**	**hai illuso**	**avete illuso**
illude	**illúdono**	**ha illuso**	**hanno illuso**
2 imperfect indicative		9 past perfect	
illudevo	**illudevamo**	**avevo illuso**	**avevamo illuso**
illudevi	**illudevate**	**avevi illuso**	**avevate illuso**
illudeva	**illudévano**	**aveva illuso**	**avévano illuso**
3 past absolute		10 past anterior	
illusi	**illudemmo**	**èbbi illuso**	**avemmo illuso**
illudesti	**illudeste**	**avesti illuso**	**aveste illuso**
illuse	**illúsero**	**èbbe illuso**	**èbbero illuso**
4 future indicative		11 future perfect	
illuderò	**illuderemo**	**avrò illuso**	**avremo illuso**
illuderai	**illuderete**	**avrai illuso**	**avrete illuso**
illuderà	**illuderanno**	**avrà illuso**	**avranno illuso**
5 present conditional		12 past conditional	
illuderèi	**illuderemmo**	**avrèi illuso**	**avremmo illuso**
illuderesti	**illudereste**	**avresti illuso**	**avreste illuso**
illuderèbbe	**illuderèbbero**	**avrèbbe illuso**	**avrèbbero illuso**
6 present subjunctive		13 past subjunctive	
illuda	**illudiamo**	**àbbia illuso**	**abbiamo illuso**
illuda	**illudiate**	**àbbia illuso**	**abbiate illuso**
illuda	**illúdano**	**àbbia illuso**	**àbbiano illuso**
7 imperfect subjunctive		14 past perfect subjunctive	
illudessi	**illudéssimo**	**avessi illuso**	**avéssimo illuso**
illudessi	**illudeste**	**avessi illuso**	**aveste illuso**
illudesse	**illudéssero**	**avesse illuso**	**avéssero illuso**

	imperative	
	—	**illudiamo**
	illudi (non illúdere)	**illudete**
	illuda	**illúdano**

Words related to this verb
Lui si illude se crede questo.   He is deceiving himself if he believes this.
Lui vuole illudere la fidanzata.   He wants to deceive his fiancée.

126

to plunge, to immerse

The Seven Simple Tenses		The Seven Compound Tenses	
Singular	Plural	Singular	Plural
1 present indicative		8 present perfect	
immèrgo	immergiamo	ho immèrso	abbiamo immèrso
immèrgi	immergete	hai immèrso	avete immèrso
immèrge	immèrgono	ha immèrso	hanno immèrso
2 imperfect indicative		9 past perfect	
immergevo	immergevamo	avevo immèrso	avevamo immèrso
immergevi	immergevate	avevi immèrso	avevate immèrso
immergeva	immergévano	aveva immèrso	avévano immèrso
3 past absolute		10 past anterior	
immèrsi	immergemmo	èbbi immèrso	avemmo immèrso
immergesti	immergeste	avesti immèrso	aveste immèrso
immèrse	immèrsero	èbbe immèrso	èbbero immèrso
4 future indicative		11 future perfect	
immergerò	immergeremo	avrò immèrso	avremo immèrso
immergerai	immergerete	avrai immèrso	avrete immèrso
immergerà	immergeranno	avrà immèrso	avranno immèrso
5 present conditional		12 past conditional	
immergerèi	immergeremmo	avrèi immèrso	avremmo immèrso
immergeresti	immergereste	avresti immèrso	avreste immèrso
immergerèbbe	immergerèbbero	avrèbbe immèrso	avrèbbero immèrso
6 present subjunctive		13 past subjunctive	
immèrga	immergiamo	àbbia immèrso	abbiamo immèrso
immèrga	immergiate	àbbia immèrso	abbiate immèrso
immèrga	immèrgano	àbbia immèrso	àbbiano immèrso
7 imperfect subjunctive		14 past perfect subjunctive	
immergessi	immergéssimo	avessi immèrso	avéssimo immèrso
immergessi	immergeste	avessi immèrso	aveste immèrso
immergesse	immergéssero	avesse immèrso	avéssero immèrso

imperative	
—	immergiamo
immèrgi (non immèrgere)	immergete
immèrga	immèrgano

Words related to this verb
Lui si è immerso nell'acqua.   He immersed himself in the water.
Io immersi la stanza nell'oscurità.   I plunged the room into darkness.

imparare	Ger. imparando	Past Part. imparato

to learn

The Seven Simple Tenses		The Seven Compound Tenses	
Singular	Plural	Singular	Plural
1 present indicative		8 present perfect	
impàro	impariamo	ho imparato	abbiamo imparato
impàri	imparate	hai imparato	avete imparato
impàra	impàrano	ha imparato	hanno imparato
2 imperfect indicative		9 past perfect	
imparavo	imparavamo	avevo imparato	avevamo imparato
imparavi	imparavate	avevi imparato	avevate imparato
imparava	imparàvano	aveva imparato	avévano imparato
3 past absolute		10 past anterior	
imparai	imparammo	èbbi imparato	avemmo imparato
imparasti	imparaste	avesti imparato	aveste imparato
imparò	imparàrono	èbbe imparato	èbbero imparato
4 future indicative		11 future perfect	
imparerò	impareremo	avrò imparato	avremo imparato
imparerai	imparerete	avrai imparato	avrete imparato
imparerà	impareranno	avrà imparato	avranno imparato
5 present conditional		12 past conditional	
imparerèi	impareremmo	avrèi imparato	avremmo imparato
impareresti	imparereste	avresti imparato	avreste imparato
imparerèbbe	imparerèbbero	avrèbbe imparato	avrèbbero imparato
6 present subjunctive		13 past subjunctive	
impàri	impariamo	àbbia imparato	abbiamo imparato
impàri	impariate	àbbia imparato	abbiate imparato
impàri	impàrino	àbbia imparato	àbbiano imparato
7 imperfect subjunctive		14 past perfect subjunctive	
imparassi	imparàssimo	avessi imparato	avéssimo imparato
imparassi	imparaste	avessi imparato	aveste imparato
imparasse	imparàssero	avesse imparato	avéssero imparato

	imperative	
—		impariamo
impàra (non imparare)		imparate
impàri		impàrino

Words related to this verb
Ho imparato la storia.   I learned the story.
imparare a memoria   to learn by heart
imparare a vivere   to learn manners

to impose

The Seven Simple Tenses		The Seven Compound Tenses	
Singular	Plural	Singular	Plural
1 present indicative		8 present perfect	
impongo	imponiamo	ho imposto	abbiamo imposto
imponi	imponete	hai imposto	avete imposto
impone	impóngono	ha imposto	hanno imposto
2 imperfect indicative		9 past perfect	
imponevo	imponevamo	avevo imposto	avevamo imposto
imponevi	imponevate	avevi imposto	avevate imposto
imponeva	imponévano	aveva imposto	avévano imposto
3 past absolute		10 past anterior	
imposi	imponemmo	èbbi imposto	avemmo imposto
imponesti	imponeste	avesti imposto	aveste imposto
impose	impósero	èbbe imposto	èbbero imposto
4 future indicative		11 future perfect	
imporrò	imporremo	avrò imposto	avremo imposto
imporrai	imporrete	avrai imposto	avrete imposto
imporrà	imporranno	avrà imposto	avranno imposto
5 present conditional		12 past conditional	
imporrèi	imporremmo	avrèi imposto	avremmo imposto
imporresti	imporreste	avresti imposto	avreste imposto
imporrèbbe	imporrèbbero	avrèbbe imposto	avrèbbero imposto
6 present subjunctive		13 past subjunctive	
imponga	imponiamo	àbbia imposto	abbiamo imposto
imponga	imponiate	àbbia imposto	abbiate imposto
imponga	impóngano	àbbia imposto	àbbiano imposto
7 imperfect subjunctive		14 past perfect subjunctive	
imponessi	imponéssimo	avessi imposto	avéssimo imposto
imponessi	imponeste	avessi imposto	aveste imposto
imponesse	imponéssero	avesse imposto	avéssero imposto

imperative	
—	imponiamo
imponi (non imporre)	imponete
imponga	impóngano

Words related to this verb
Lui impone la sua volontà su di tutti.   He imposes his will on everyone.
Lei ci impose un obbligo.   She imposed an obligation on us.

imprímere	Ger. imprimèndo		Past Part. imprèsso

to impress; to print, to stamp

The Seven Simple Tenses		The Seven Compound Tenses	
Singular	Plural	Singular	Plural
1 present indicative		8 present perfect	
imprimo	imprimiamo	ho imprèsso	abbiamo imprèsso
imprimi	imprimete	hai imprèsso	avete imprèsso
imprime	imprímono	ha imprèsso	hanno imprèsso
2 imperfect indicative		9 past perfect	
imprimevo	imprimevamo	avevo imprèsso	avevamo imprèsso
imprimevi	imprimevate	avevi imprèsso	avevate imprèsso
imprimeva	imprimévano	aveva imprèsso	avévano imprèsso
3 past absolute		10 past anterior	
imprèssi	imprimemmo	èbbi imprèsso	avemmo imprèsso
imprimesti	imprimeste	avesti imprèsso	aveste imprèsso
imprèsse	imprèssero	èbbe imprèsso	èbbero imprèsso
4 future indicative		11 future perfect	
imprimerò	imprimeremo	avrò imprèsso	avremo imprèsso
imprimerai	imprimerete	avrai imprèsso	avrete imprèsso
imprimerà	imprimeranno	avrà imprèsso	avranno imprèsso
5 present conditional		12 past conditional	
imprimerèi	imprimeremmo	avrèi imprèsso	avremmo imprèsso
imprimeresti	imprimereste	avresti imprèsso	avreste imprèsso
imprimerèbbe	imprimerèbbero	avrèbbe imprèsso	avrèbbero imprèsso
6 present subjunctive		13 past subjunctive	
imprima	imprimiamo	àbbia imprèsso	abbiamo imprèsso
imprima	imprimiate	àbbia imprèsso	abbiate imprèsso
imprima	imprímano	àbbia imprèsso	àbbiano imprèsso
7 imperfect subjunctive		14 past perfect subjunctive	
imprimessi	impriméssimo	avessi imprèsso	avéssimo imprèsso
imprimessi	imprimeste	avessi imprèsso	aveste imprèsso
imprimesse	impriméssero	avesse imprèsso	avéssero imprèsso

imperative	
—	imprimiamo
imprimi (non imprímere)	imprimete
imprima	imprímano

Words related to this verb
Con i piedi bagnati, i bambini imprimono le orme sul tappeto. With wet feet, the children leave footprints on the carpet.
Voglio imprimere questo fatto su di te. I want to impress this fact on you.

The Seven Simple Tenses		The Seven Compound Tenses	
Singular	Plural	Singular	Plural
1 present indicative		8 present perfect	
includo	includiamo	ho incluso	abbiamo incluso
includi	includete	hai incluso	avete incluso
include	inclúdono	ha incluso	hanno incluso
2 imperfect indicative		9 past perfect	
includevo	includevamo	avevo incluso	avevamo incluso
includevi	includevate	avevi incluso	avevate incluso
includeva	includévano	aveva incluso	avévano incluso
3 past absolute		10 past anterior	
inclusi	includemmo	èbbi incluso	avemmo incluso
includesti	includeste	avesti incluso	aveste incluso
incluse	inclúsero	èbbe incluso	èbbero incluso
4 future indicative		11 future perfect	
includerò	includeremo	avrò incluso	avremo incluso
includerai	includerete	avrai incluso	avrete incluso
includerà	includeranno	avrà incluso	avranno incluso
5 present conditional		12 past conditional	
includerèi	includeremmo	avrèi incluso	avremmo incluso
includeresti	includereste	avresti incluso	avreste incluso
includerèbbe	includerèbbero	avrèbbe incluso	avrèbbero incluso
6 present subjunctive		13 past subjunctive	
includa	includiamo	àbbia incluso	abbiamo incluso
includa	includiate	àbbia incluso	abbiate incluso
includa	inclúdano	àbbia incluso	àbbiano incluso
7 imperfect subjunctive		14 past perfect subjunctive	
includessi	includéssimo	avessi incluso	avéssimo incluso
includessi	includeste	avessi incluso	aveste incluso
includesse	includéssero	avesse incluso	avéssero incluso

	imperative	
—		includiamo
includi (non inclúdere)		includete
includa		inclúdano

Words related to this verb
Io includerò il libro nel pacco.   I will include the book in the package.
Io sono incluso(a) fra gli invitati.   I am included among the guests.

incontrare   Ger. **incontrando**   Past Part. **incontrato**

to meet

The Seven Simple Tenses		The Seven Compound Tenses	
Singular	Plural	Singular	Plural
1 present indicative		8 present perfect	
incontro	incontriamo	ho incontrato	abbiamo incontrato
incontri	incontrate	hai incontrato	avete incontrato
incontra	incontrano	ha incontrato	hanno incontrato
2 imperfect indicative		9 past perfect	
incontravo	incontravamo	avevo incontrato	avevamo incontrato
incontravi	incontravate	avevi incontrato	avevate incontrato
incontrava	incontràvano	aveva incontrato	avévano incontrato
3 past absolute		10 past anterior	
incontrai	incontrammo	èbbi incontrato	avemmo incontrato
incontrasti	incontraste	avesti incontrato	aveste incontrato
incontrò	incontràrono	èbbe incontrato	èbbero incontrato
4 future indicative		11 future perfect	
incontrerò	incontreremo	avrò incontrato	avremo incontrato
incontrerai	incontrerete	avrai incontrato	avrete incontrato
incontrerà	incontreranno	avrà incontrato	avranno incontrato
5 present conditional		12 past conditional	
incontrerèi	incontreremmo	avrèi incontrato	avremmo incontrato
incontreresti	incontrereste	avresti incontrato	avreste incontrato
incontrerèbbe	incontrerèbbero	avrèbbe incontrato	avrèbbero incontrato
6 present subjunctive		13 past subjunctive	
incontri	incontriamo	àbbia incontrato	abbiamo incontrato
incontri	incontriate	àbbia incontrato	abbiate incontrato
incontri	incontrino	àbbia incontrato	àbbiano incontrato
7 imperfect subjunctive		14 past perfect subjunctive	
incontrassi	incontràssimo	avessi incontrato	avéssimo incontrato
incontrassi	incontraste	avessi incontrato	aveste incontrato
incontrasse	incontràssero	avesse incontrato	avéssero incontrato

	imperative	
—		incontriamo
incontra (non incontrate)		incontrate
incontri		incontrino

Words related to this verb
L'ho incontrata in discoteca.   I met her in the disco.
Ci incontriamo ogni giorno.   We meet every day.

to indicate, to point at, to show

The Seven Simple Tenses		The Seven Compound Tenses	
Singular	Plural	Singular	Plural
1 present indicative		8 present perfect	
ìndico	**indichiamo**	**ho indicato**	**abbiamo indicato**
ìndichi	**indicate**	**hai indicato**	**avete indicato**
ìndica	**ìndicano**	**ha indicato**	**hanno indicato**
2 imperfect indicative		9 past perfect	
indicavo	**indicavamo**	**avevo indicato**	**avevamo indicato**
indicavi	**indicavate**	**avevi indicato**	**avevate indicato**
indicava	**indicàvano**	**aveva indicato**	**avévano indicato**
3 past absolute		10 past anterior	
indicai	**indicammo**	**èbbi indicato**	**avemmo indicato**
indicasti	**indicaste**	**avesti indicato**	**aveste indicato**
indicò	**indicàrono**	**èbbe indicato**	**èbbero indicato**
4 future indicative		11 future perfect	
indicherò	**Indicheremo**	**avrò indicato**	**avremo indicato**
indicherai	**indicherete**	**avrai indicato**	**avrete indicato**
indicherà	**indicheranno**	**avrà indicato**	**avranno indicato**
5 present conditional		12 past conditional	
indicherèi	**indicheremmo**	**avrèi indicato**	**avremmo indicato**
indicheresti	**indichereste**	**avresti indicato**	**avreste indicato**
indicherèbbe	**indicherèbbero**	**avrèbbe indicato**	**avrèbbero indicato**
6 present subjunctive		13 past subjunctive	
ìndichi	**indichiamo**	**àbbia indicato**	**abbiamo indicato**
ìndichi	**indichiate**	**àbbia indicato**	**abbiate indicato**
ìndichi	**ìndichino**	**àbbia indicato**	**àbbiano indicato**
7 imperfect subjunctive		14 past perfect subjunctive	
indicassi	**indicàssimo**	**avessi indicato**	**avéssimo indicato**
indicassi	**indicaste**	**avessi indicato**	**aveste indicato**
indicasse	**indicàssero**	**avesse indicato**	**avéssero indicato**

imperative

—	**indichiamo**
ìndica (non indicare)	**indicate**
ìndichi	**ìndichino**

Words related to this verb
Indicò il tuo amico.   He pointed at your friend.
Indica quel che devo fare.   Point out what I have to do.

to infer, to deduce, to conclude

The Seven Simple Tenses		The Seven Compound Tenses	
Singular	Plural	Singular	Plural
1 present indicative		8 present perfect	
inferisco	inferiamo	ho inferito	abbiamo inferito
inferisci	inferite	hai inferito	avete inferito
inferisce	inferiscono	ha inferito	hanno inferito
2 imperfect indicative		9 past perfect	
inferivo	inferivamo	avevo inferito	avevamo inferito
inferivi	inferivate	avevi inferito	avevate inferito
inferiva	inferìvano	aveva inferito	avévano inferito
3 past absolute		10 past anterior	
inferii	inferimmo	èbbi inferito	avemmo inferito
inferisti	inferiste	avesti inferito	aveste inferito
inferì	inferírono	èbbe inferito	èbbero inferito
4 future indicative		11 future perfect	
inferirò	inferiremo	avrò inferito	avremo inferito
inferirai	inferirete	avrai inferito	avrete inferito
inferirà	inferiranno	avrà inferito	avranno inferito
5 present conditional		12 past conditional	
inferirèi	inferiremmo	avrèi inferito	avremmo inferito
inferiresti	inferireste	avresti inferito	avreste inferito
inferirèbbe	inferirèbbero	avrèbbe inferito	avrèbbero inferito
6 present subjunctive		13 past subjunctive	
inferisca	inferiamo	àbbia inferito	abbiamo inferito
inferisca	inferiate	àbbia inferito	abbiate inferito
inferisca	inferìscano	àbbia inferito	àbbiano inferito
7 imperfect subjunctive		14 past perfect subjunctive	
inferissi	inferissimo	avessi inferito	avéssimo inferito
inferissi	inferiste	avessi inferito	aveste inferito
inferisse	inferissero	avesse inferito	avéssero inferito

	imperative
—	inferiamo
inferisci (non inferire)	inferite
inferisca	inferìscano

Words related to this verb
Tu inferisci che noi non andiamo d'accordo.   You're inferring that we don't get along.
inferire una cosa da un'altra   to infer one thing from another

to inflict

The Seven Simple Tenses		The Seven Compound Tenses	
Singular	Plural	Singular	Plural
1 present indicative		8 present perfect	
infliggo	infliggiamo	ho inflitto	abbiamo inflitto
infliggi	infliggete	hai inflitto	avete inflitto
infligge	infliggono	ha inflitto	hanno inflitto
2 imperfect indicative		9 past perfect	
infliggevo	infliggevamo	avevo inflitto	avevamo inflitto
infliggevi	infliggevate	avevi inflitto	avevate inflitto
infliggeva	infliggévano	aveva inflitto	avévano inflitto
3 past absolute		10 past anterior	
inflissi	infliggemmo	èbbi inflitto	avemmo inflitto
infliggesti	infliggeste	avesti inflitto	aveste inflitto
inflisse	inflíssero	èbbe inflitto	èbbero inflitto
4 future indicative		11 future perfect	
infliggerò	infliggeremo	avrò inflitto	avremo inflitto
infliggerai	infliggerete	avrai inflitto	avrete inflitto
infliggerà	infliggeranno	avrà inflitto	avranno inflitto
5 present conditional		12 past conditional	
infliggerèi	infliggeremmo	avrèi inflitto	avremmo inflitto
infliggeresti	infliggereste	avresti inflitto	avreste inflitto
infliggerèbbe	infliggerèbbero	avrèbbe inflitto	avrèbbero inflitto
6 present subjunctive		13 past subjunctive	
infligga	infliggiamo	àbbia inflitto	abbiamo inflitto
infligga	infliggiate	àbbia inflitto	abbiate inflitto
infligga	infliggano	àbbia inflitto	àbbiano inflitto
7 imperfect subjunctive		14 past perfect subjunctive	
infliggessi	infliggéssimo	avessi inflitto	avéssimo inflitto
infliggessi	infliggeste	avessi inflitto	aveste inflitto
infliggesse	infliggéssero	avesse inflitto	avéssero inflitto

	imperative	
		infliggiamo
	infliggi (non inflíggere)	infliggete
	infligga	infliggano

Words related to this verb
Lui mi inflisse un colpo.   He inflicted a blow on me.
Il giudice inflige una pena severa su di lui.   The judge inflicts a severe penalty on him.

135

insistere   Ger. **insistendo**   Past Part. **insistito**

to insist

The Seven Simple Tenses		The Seven Compound Tenses	
Singular	Plural	Singular	Plural
1 present indicative		8 present perfect	
insisto	**insistiamo**	**ho insistito**	**abbiamo insistito**
insisti	**insistete**	**hai insistito**	**avete insistito**
insiste	**insístono**	**ha insistito**	**hanno insistito**
2 imperfect indicative		9 past perfect	
insistevo	**insistevamo**	**avevo insistito**	**avevamo insistito**
insistevi	**insistevate**	**avevi insistito**	**avevate insistito**
insisteva	**insistévano**	**aveva insistito**	**avévano insistito**
3 past absolute		10 past anterior	
insistei (insistètti)	**insistemmo**	**èbbi insistito**	**avemmo insistito**
insistesti	**insisteste**	**avesti insistito**	**aveste insistito**
insistè (insistètte)	**insistérono**	**èbbe insistito**	**èbbero insistito**
	(insistèttero)		
4 future indicative		11 future perfect	
insisterò	**insisteremo**	**avrò insistito**	**avremo insistito**
insisterai	**insisterete**	**avrai insistito**	**avrete insistito**
insisterà	**insisteranno**	**avrà insistito**	**avranno insistito**
5 present conditional		12 past conditional	
insisterèi	**insisteremmo**	**avrèi insistito**	**avremmo insistito**
insisteresti	**insistereste**	**avresti insistito**	**avreste insistito**
insisterèbbe	**insisterèbbero**	**avrèbbe insistito**	**avrèbbero insistito**
6 present subjunctive		13 past subjunctive	
insista	**insistiamo**	**àbbia insistito**	**abbiamo insistito**
insista	**insistiate**	**àbbia insistito**	**abbiate insistito**
insista	**insístano**	**àbbia insistito**	**àbbiano insistito**
7 imperfect subjunctive		14 past perfect subjunctive	
insistessi	**insistéssimo**	**avessi insistito**	**avéssimo insistito**
insistessi	**insisteste**	**avessi insistito**	**aveste insistito**
insistesse	**insistéssero**	**avesse insistito**	**avéssero insistito**

	imperative	
—		**insistiamo**
insisti (non insistere)		**insistete**
insista		**insístano**

Words related to this verb
Insisti perchè egli venga.   Insist on his coming.
Non insistere su questo fatto!   Do not insist on this fact.

136

to understand; to mean

The Seven Simple Tenses		The Seven Compound Tenses	
Singular	Plural	Singular	Plural
1 present indicative		8 present perfect	
intèndo	**intendiamo**	**ho inteso**	**abbiamo inteso**
intèndi	**intendete**	**hai inteso**	**avete inteso**
intènde	**intèndono**	**ha inteso**	**hanno inteso**
2 imperfect indicative		9 past perfect	
intendevo	**intendevamo**	**avevo inteso**	**avevamo inteso**
intendevi	**intendevate**	**avevi inteso**	**avevate inteso**
intendeva	**intendévano**	**aveva inteso**	**avévano inteso**
3 past absolute		10 past anterior	
intesi	**intendemmo**	**èbbi inteso**	**avemmo inteso**
intendesti	**intendeste**	**avesti inteso**	**aveste inteso**
intese	**intésero**	**èbbe inteso**	**èbbero inteso**
4 future indicative		11 future perfect	
intenderò	**intenderemo**	**avrò inteso**	**avremo inteso**
intenderai	**intenderete**	**avrai inteso**	**avrete inteso**
intenderà	**intenderanno**	**avrà inteso**	**avranno inteso**
5 present conditional		12 past conditional	
intenderèi	**intenderemmo**	**avrèi inteso**	**avremmo inteso**
intenderesti	**intendereste**	**avresti inteso**	**avreste inteso**
intenderèbbe	**intenderèbbero**	**avrèbbe inteso**	**avrèbbero inteso**
6 present subjunctive		13 past subjunctive	
intènda	**intendiamo**	**àbbia inteso**	**abbiamo inteso**
intènda	**intendiate**	**àbbia inteso**	**abbiate inteso**
intènda	**intèndano**	**àbbia inteso**	**àbbiano inteso**
7 imperfect subjunctive		14 past perfect subjunctive	
intendessi	**intendéssimo**	**avessi inteso**	**avéssimo inteso**
intendessi	**intendeste**	**avessi inteso**	**aveste inteso**
intendesse	**intendéssero**	**avesse inteso**	**avéssero inteso**

	imperative	
—		**intendiamo**
intèndi (non intèndere)		**intendete**
intènda		**intèndano**

Words related to this verb
Lui intendeva farlo.   He intended to do it.
Gli feci intendere la mia opinione.   I made him understand my opinion.

interrómpere   Ger. interrompèndo   Past Part. interrotto

to interrupt

The Seven Simple Tenses		The Seven Compound Tenses	
Singular	Plural	Singular	Plural
1 present indicative		8 present perfect	
interrompo	interrompiamo	ho interrotto	abbiamo interrotto
interrompi	interrompete	hai interrotto	avete interrotto
interrompe	interrómpono	ha interrotto	hanno interrotto
2 imperfect indicative		9 past perfect	
interrompevo	interrompevamo	avevo interrotto	avevamo interrotto
interrompevi	interrompevate	avevi interrotto	avevate interrotto
interrompeva	interrompévano	aveva interrotto	avévano interrotto
3 past absolute		10 past anterior	
interruppi	interrompemmo	èbbi interrotto	avemmo interrotto
interrompesti	interrompeste	avesti interrotto	aveste interrotto
interruppe	interrúppero	èbbe interrotto	èbbero interrotto
4 future indicative		11 future perfect	
interromperò	interromperemo	avrò interrotto	avremo interrotto
interromperai	interromperete	avrai interrotto	avrete interrotto
interromperà	interromperanno	avrà interrotto	avranno interrotto
5 present conditional		12 past conditional	
interromperèi	interromperemmo	avrèi interrotto	avremmo interrotto
interromperesti	interrompereste	avresti interrotto	avreste interrotto
interromperèbbe	interromperèbbero	avrèbbe interrotto	avrèbbero interrotto
6 present subjunctive		13 past subjunctive	
interrompa	interrompiamo	àbbia interrotto	abbiamo interrotto
interrompa	interrompiate	àbbia interrotto	abbiate interrotto
interrompa	interrómpano	àbbia interrotto	àbbiano interrotto
7 imperfect subjunctive		14 past perfect subjunctive	
interrompessi	interrompéssimo	avessi interrotto	avéssimo interrotto
interrompessi	interrompeste	avessi interrotto	aveste interrotto
interrompesse	interrompéssero	avesse interrotto	avéssero interrotto

imperative

—	interrompiamo
interrompi (non interrómpere)	interrompete
interrompa	interrómpano

Words related to this verb
Lui interrompe sempre le nostre discussioni.   He always interrupts our discussions.
L'edificio interrompe la vista del mare.   The building interrupts (blocks) the view of the sea.

138

The Seven Simple Tenses		The Seven Compound Tenses	
Singular	Plural	Singular	Plural
1 present indicative		8 present perfect	
intervèngo	**interveniamo**	**sono intervenuto**	**siamo intervenuti**
intervièni	**intervenite**	**sèi intervenuto**	**siete intervenuti**
interviène	**intervèngono**	**è intervenuto**	**sono intervenuti**
2 imperfect indicative		9 past perfect	
intervenivo	**intervenivamo**	**èro intervenuto**	**eravamo intervenuti**
intervenivi	**intervenivate**	**èri intervenuto**	**eravate intervenuti**
interveniva	**intervenívano**	**èra intervenuto**	**èrano intervenuti**
3 past absolute		10 past anterior	
intervenni	**intervenimmo**	**fui intervenuto**	**fummo intervenuti**
intervenisti	**interveniste**	**fosti intervenuto**	**foste intervenuti**
intervenne	**intervénnero**	**fu intervenuto**	**fúrono intervenuti**
4 future indicative		11 future perfect	
interverrò	**interverremo**	**sarò intervenuto**	**saremo intervenuti**
interverrai	**interverrete**	**sarai intervenuto**	**sarete intervenuti**
interverrà	**interverranno**	**sarà intervenuto**	**saranno intervenuti**
5 present conditional		12 past conditional	
interverrèi	**interverremmo**	**sarèi intervenuto**	**saremmo intervenuti**
interverresti	**interverreste**	**saresti intervenuto**	**sareste intervenuti**
interverrèbbe	**interverrèbbero**	**sarèbbe intervenuto**	**sarèbbero intervenuti**
6 present subjunctive		13 past subjunctive	
intervènga	**interveniamo**	**sia intervenuto**	**siamo intervenuti**
intervènga	**interveniate**	**sia intervenuto**	**siate intervenuti**
intervènga	**intervèngano**	**sia intervenuto**	**síano intervenuti**
7 imperfect subjunctive		14 past perfect subjunctive	
intervenissi	**interveníssimo**	**fossi intervenuto**	**fóssimo intervenuti**
intervenissi	**inteveniste**	**fossi intervenuto**	**foste intervenuti**
intervenisse	**intervenissero**	**fosse intervenuto**	**fóssero intervenuti**

	imperative	
—		**interveniamo**
	intervièni (non intervenire)	**intervenite**
	intervènga	**intervèngano**

Words related to this verb

Non voglio intervenire in queste cose.   I don't want to intervene in these matters.

intervenire ad un'adunanza   to attend a meeting

introdurre   Ger. **introducèndo**   Past Part. **introdotto**

to introduce, to insert

The Seven Simple Tenses		The Seven Compound Tenses	
Singular	Plural	Singular	Plural
1 present indicative		8 present perfect	
introduco	introduciamo	ho introdotto	abbiamo introdotto
introduci	introducete	hai introdotto	avete introdotto
introduce	introdúcono	ha introdotto	hanno introdotto
2 imperfect indicative		9 past perfect	
introducevo	introducevamo	avevo introdotto	avevamo introdotto
introducevi	introducevate	avevi introdotto	avevate introdotto
introduceva	introducévano	aveva introdotto	avévano introdotto
3 past absolute		10 past anterior	
introdussi	introducemmo	èbbi introdotto	avemmo introdotto
introducesti	introduceste	avesti introdotto	aveste introdotto
introdusse	introdússero	èbbe introdotto	èbbero introdotto
4 future indicative		11 future perfect	
introdurrò	introdurremo	avrò introdotto	avremo introdotto
introdurrai	introdurrete	avrai introdotto	avrete introdotto
introdurrà	introdurranno	avrà introdotto	avranno introdotto
5 present conditional		12 past conditional	
introdurrèi	introdurremmo	avrèi introdotto	avremmo introdotto
introdurresti	introdurreste	avresti introdotto	avreste introdotto
introdurrèbbe	introdurrèbbero	avrèbbe introdotto	avrèbbero introdotto
6 present subjunctive		13 past subjunctive	
introduca	introduciamo	àbbia introdotto	abbiamo introdotto
introduca	introduciate	àbbia introdotto	abbiate introdotto
introduca	introdúcano	àbbia introdotto	àbbiano introdotto
7 imperfect subjunctive		14 past perfect subjunctive	
introducessi	introducéssimo	avessi introdotto	avéssimo introdotto
introducessi	introduceste	avessi introdotto	aveste introdotto
introducesse	introducéssero	avesse introdotto	avéssero introdotto

imperative

—	introduciamo
introduci (non introdurre)	introducete
introduca	introdúcano

Words related to this verb
Lui introdusse la chiave nella toppa.   He inserted the key in the lock.
L'avvocato introdusse un nuovo argomento.   The lawyer introduced a new argument.

The Seven Simple Tenses		The Seven Compound Tenses	
Singular	Plural	Singular	Plural
1 present indicative		8 present perfect	
invado	invadiamo	ho invaso	abbiamo invaso
invadi	invadete	hai invaso	avete invaso
invade	invàdono	ha invaso	hanno invaso
2 imperfect indicative		9 past perfect	
invadevo	invadevamo	avevo invaso	avevamo invaso
invadevi	invadevate	avevi invaso	avevate invaso
invadeva	invadévano	aveva invaso	avévano invaso
3 past absolute		10 past anterior	
invasi	invademmo	èbbi invaso	avemmo invaso
invadesti	invadeste	avesti invaso	aveste invaso
invase	invàsero	èbbe invaso	èbbero invaso
4 future indicative		11 future perfect	
invaderò	invaderemo	avrò invaso	avremo invaso
invaderai	invaderete	avrai invaso	avrete invaso
invaderà	invaderanno	avrà invaso	avranno invaso
5 present conditional		12 past conditional	
invaderèi	invaderemmo	avrèi invaso	avremmo invaso
invaderesti	invadereste	avresti invaso	avreste invaso
invaderèbbe	invaderèbbero	avrèbbe invaso	avrèbbero invaso
6 present subjunctive		13 past subjunctive	
invada	invadiamo	àbbia invaso	abbiamo invaso
invada	invadiate	àbbia invaso	abbiate invaso
invada	invàdano	àbbia invaso	àbbiano invaso
7 imperfect subjunctive		14 past perfect subjunctive	
invadessi	invadéssimo	avessi invaso	avéssimo invaso
invadessi	invadeste	avessi invaso	aveste invaso
invadesse	invadéssero	avesse invaso	avéssero invaso

	imperative	
—		invadiamo
invadi (non invàdere)		invadete
invada		invàdano

Words related to this verb

Il nemico invase la città.   The enemy invaded the city.
Ogni anno i turisti invadono l'Europa.   Every year the tourists invade Europe.

invitare   Ger. **invitando**   Past Part. **invitato**

to invite

The Seven Simple Tenses		The Seven Compound Tenses	
Singular	Plural	Singular	Plural
1 present indicative		8 present perfect	
invìto	invitiamo	ho invitato	abbiamo invitato
invìti	invitate	hai invitato	avete invitato
invìta	invitano	ha invitato	hanno invitato
2 imperfect indicative		9 past perfect	
invitavo	invitavamo	avevo invitato	avevamo invitato
invitavi	invitavate	avevi invitato	avevate invitato
invitava	invitàvano	aveva invitato	avévano invitato
3 past absolute		10 past anterior	
invitai	invitammo	èbbi invitato	avemmo invitato
invitasti	invitaste	avesti invitato	aveste invitato
invitò	invitàrono	èbbe invitato	èbbero invitato
4 future indicative		11 future perfect	
inviterò	inviteremo	avrò invitato	avremo invitato
inviterai	inviterete	avrai invitato	avrete invitato
inviterà	inviteranno	avrà invitato	avranno invitato
5 present conditional		12 past conditional	
inviterèi	inviteremmo	avrèi invitato	avremmo invitato
inviteresti	invitereste	avresti invitato	avreste invitato
inviterèbbe	inviterèbbero	avrèbbe invitato	avrèbbero invitato
6 present subjunctive		13 past subjunctive	
inviti	invitiamo	àbbia invitato	abbiamo invitato
inviti	invitiate	àbbia invitato	abbiate invitato
inviti	invìtino	àbbia invitato	àbbiano invitato
7 imperfect subjunctive		14 past perfect subjunctive	
invitassi	invitàssimo	avessi invitato	avéssimo invitato
invitassi	invitaste	avessi invitato	aveste invitato
invitasse	invitàssero	avesse invitato	avéssero invitato

imperative	
—	invitiamo
invìta (non invitare)	invitate
invìti	invìtino

Words related to this verb
La invitai a pranzo.   I invited her to dinner.
Perchè non inviti Laura e Michele a cena?   Why don't you invite Laura and Michael for dinner?

to wrap (up), to envelop; to imply

The Seven Simple Tenses		The Seven Compound Tenses	
Singular	Plural	Singular	Plural
1 present indicative		8 present perfect	
invòlgo	involgiamo	ho involto	abbiamo involto
invòlgi	involgete	hai involto	avete involto
invòlge	invòlgono	ha involto	hanno involto
2 imperfect indicative		9 past perfect	
involgevo	involgevamo	avevo involto	avevamo involto
involgevi	involgevate	avevi involto	avevate involto
involgeva	involgévano	aveva involto	avévano involto
3 past absolute		10 past anterior	
invòlsi	involgemmo	èbbi involto	avemmo involto
involgesti	involgeste	avesti involto	aveste involto
invòlse	invòlsero	èbbe involto	èbbero involto
4 future indicative		11 future perfect	
involgerò	involgeremo	avrò involto	avremo involto
involgerai	involgerete	avrai involto	avrete involto
involgerà	involgeranno	avrà involto	avranno involto
5 present conditional		12 past conditional	
involgerèi	involgeremmo	avrèi involto	avremmo involto
involgeresti	involgereste	avresti involto	avreste involto
involgerèbbe	involgerèbbero	avrèbbe involto	avrèbbero involto
6 present subjunctive		13 past subjunctive	
invòlga	involgiamo	àbbia involto	abbiamo involto
invòlga	involgiate	àbbia involto	abbiate involto
invòlga	invòlgano	àbbia involto	àbbiano involto
7 imperfect subjunctive		14 past perfect subjunctive	
involgessi	involgéssimo	avessi involto	avéssimo involto
involgessi	involgeste	avessi involto	aveste involto
involgesse	involgéssero	avesse involto	avéssero involto

imperative	
	involgiamo
invòlgi (non invòlgere)	involgete
invòlga	invòlgano

Words related to this verb
Questa domanda involge molte questioni.   This question implies many problems.
Ho involto i fiori.   I wrapped up the flowers.

to teach, to instruct

The Seven Simple Tenses		The Seven Compound Tenses	
Singular	Plural	Singular	Plural
1 present indicative		8 present perfect	
istruisco	istruiamo	ho istruito	abbiamo istruito
istruisci	istruite	hai istruito	avete istruito
istruisce	istruíscono	ha istruito	hanno istruito
2 imperfect indicative		9 past perfect	
istruivo	istruivamo	avevo istruito	avevamo istruito
istruivi	istruivate	avevi istruito	avevate istruito
istruiva	istruívano	aveva istruito	avévano istruito
3 past absolute		10 past anterior	
istruii	istruimmo	èbbi istruito	avemmo istruito
istruisti	istruiste	avesti istruito	aveste istruito
istruí	istruírono	èbbe istruito	èbbero istruito
4 future indicative		11 future perfect	
istruirò	istruiremo	avrò istruito	avremo istruito
istruirai	istruirete	avrai istruito	avrete istruito
istruirà	istruiranno	avrà istruito	avranno istruito
5 present conditional		12 past conditional	
istruirèi	istruiremmo	avrèi istruito	avremmo istruito
istruiresti	istruireste	avresti istruito	avreste istruito
istruirèbbe	istruirèbbero	avrèbbe istruito	avrèbbero istruito
6 present subjunctive		13 past subjunctive	
istruisca	istruiamo	àbbia istruito	abbiamo istruito
istruisca	istruiate	àbbia istruito	abbiate istruito
istruisca	istruíscano	àbbia istruito	àbbiano istruito
7 imperfect subjunctive		14 past perfect subjunctive	
istruissi	istruíssimo	avessi istruito	avéssimo istruito
istruissi	istruiste	avessi istruito	aveste istruito
istruisse	istruíssero	avesse istruito	avéssero istruito

imperative	
—	istruiamo
istruisci (non istruire)	istruite
istruisca	istruíscano

Words related to this verb
Lo istruisco in italiano.   I instruct him in Italian.
La istruirò su come scrivere quella lettera.   I'll teach her how to write that letter.

to leave; to let

The Seven Simple Tenses		The Seven Compound Tenses	
Singular	Plural	Singular	Plural
1 present indicative		8 present perfect	
lascio	lasciamo	ho lasciato	abbiamo lasciato
lasci	lasciate	hai lasciato	avete lasciato
lascia	làsciano	ha lasciato	hanno lasciato
2 imperfect indicative		9 past perfect	
lasciavo	lasciavamo	avevo lasciato	avevamo lasciato
lasciavi	lasciavate	avevi lasciato	avevate lasciato
lasciava	lasciàvano	aveva lasciato	avévano lasciato
3 past absolute		10 past anterior	
lasciai	lasciammo	èbbi lasciato	avemmo lasciato
lasciasti	lasciaste	avesti lasciato	aveste lasciato
lasciò	lasciàrono	èbbe lasciato	èbbero lasciato
4 future indicative		11 future perfect	
lascerò	lasceremo	avrò lasciato	avremo lasciato
lascerai	lascerete	avrai lasciato	avrete lasciato
lascerà	lasceranno	avrà lasciato	avranno lasciato
5 present conditional		12 past conditional	
lascerèi	lasceremmo	avrèi lasciato	avremmo lasciato
lasceresti	lascereste	avresti lasciato	avreste lasciato
lascerèbbe	lascerèbbero	avrèbbe lasciato	avrèbbero lasciato
6 present subjunctive		13 past subjunctive	
lasci	lasciamo	àbbia lasciato	abbiamo lasciato
lasci	lasciate	àbbia lasciato	abbiate lasciato
lasci	làscino	àbbia lasciato	àbbiano lasciato
7 imperfect subjunctive		14 past perfect subjunctive	
lasciassi	lasciàssimo	avessi lasciato	avéssimo lasciato
lasciassi	lasciaste	avessi lasciato	aveste lasciato
lasciasse	lasciàssero	avesse lasciato	avéssero lasciato

	imperative	
—	lasciamo
lascia (non lasciare)	lasciate
lasci	làscino

Words related to this verb
Lasciami stare!   Leave me alone!
Mi lasciò in città.   He left me in the city.

lavare   Ger. **lavando**   Past Part. **lavato**

to wash, to clean

The Seven Simple Tenses		The Seven Compound Tenses	
Singular	Plural	Singular	Plural
1 present indicative		8 present perfect	
làvo	laviamo	ho lavato	abbiamo lavato
làvi	lavate	hai lavato	avete lavato
làva	lavano	ha lavato	hanno lavato
2 imperfect indicative		9 past perfect	
lavavo	lavavamo	avevo lavato	avevamo lavato
lavavi	lavavate	avevi lavato	avevate lavato
lavava	lavàvano	aveva lavato	avévano lavato
3 past absolute		10 past anterior	
lavai	lavammo	èbbi lavato	avemmo lavato
lavasti	lavaste	avesti lavato	aveste lavato
lavò	lavàrono	èbbe lavato	èbbero lavato
4 future indicative		11 future perfect	
laverò	laveremo	avrò lavato	avremo lavato
laverai	laverete	avrai lavato	avrete lavato
laverà	laveranno	avrà lavato	avranno lavato
5 present conditional		12 past conditional	
laverèi	laveremmo	avrèi lavato	avremmo lavato
laveresti	lavereste	avresti lavato	avreste lavato
laverèbbe	laverèbbero	avrèbbe lavato	avrèbbero lavato
6 present subjunctive		13 past subjunctive	
làvi	laviamo	àbbia lavato	abbiamo lavato
làvi	laviate	àbbia lavato	abbiate lavato
làvi	làvino	àbbia lavato	àbbiano lavato
7 imperfect subjunctive		14 past perfect subjunctive	
lavassi	lavàssimo	avessi lavato	avessimo lavato
lavassi	lavaste	avessi lavato	aveste lavato
lavasse	lavàssero	avesse lavato	avéssero lavato

imperative	
—	laviamo
làva (non lavare)	lavate
làvi	làvino

Words related to this verb
Ho lavato le mani del bambino.   I washed the child's hands.
Lei ha lavato la macchina.   She washed the car.

146

to wash oneself

The Seven Simple Tenses		The Seven Compound Tenses	
Singular	Plural	Singular	Plural
1 present indicative		8 present perfect	
mi làvo	ci laviamo	mi sono lavato	ci siamo lavati
ti làvi	vi lavate	ti sèi lavato	vi sièt lavate
si làva	si làvano	si è lavato	si sono lavati
2 imperfect indicative		9 past perfect	
mi lavavo	ci lavavamo	mi èro lavato	ci eravamo lavati
ti lavavi	vi lavavate	ti èri lavato	vi eravate lavati
si lavava	si lavàvano	si èra lavato	si èrano lavati
3 past absolute		10 past anterior	
mi lavai	ci lavammo	mi fui lavato	ci fummo lavati
ti lavasti	vi lavaste	ti fosti lavato	vi foste lavati
si lavò	si lavàrono	si fu lavato	si fúrono lavati
4 future indicative		11 future perfect	
mi laverò	ci laveremo	mi sarò lavato	ci saremo lavati
ti laverai	vi laverete	ti sarai lavato	vi sarete lavati
si laverà	si laveranno	si sarà lavato	si saranno lavati
5 present conditional		12 past conditional	
mi laverei	ci laveremmo	mi sarei lavato	ci saremmo lavati
ti laveresti	vi lavereste	ti saresti lavato	vi sareste lavati
si laverèbbe	si laverèbbero	si sarèbbe lavato	si sarèbbero lavati
6 present subjunctive		13 past subjunctive	
mi làvi	ci laviamo	mi sia lavato	ci siamo lavati
ti làvi	vi laviate	ti sia lavato	vi siate lavati
si làvi	si làvino	si sia lavato	si síano lavati
7 imperfect subjunctive		14 past perfect subjunctive	
mi lavassi	ci lavàssimo	mi fossi lavato	ci fóssimo lavati
ti lavassi	vi lavaste	ti fossi lavato	vi foste lavati
si lavasse	si lavàssero	si fosse lavato	si fóssero lavati

imperative

—	laviamoci
lavati (non ti lavare)	lavatevi
si làvi	si làvino

Words related to this verb
Mi sono lavato le mani.   I washed my hands.
lavarsi le mani dell'affare   to wash one's hands of the affair

147

lèggere	Ger. leggèndo		Past Part. lètto

to read

The Seven Simple Tenses		The Seven Compound Tenses	
Singular	Plural	Singular	Plural
1 present indicative		8 present perfect	
lèggo	leggiamo	ho lètto	abbiamo lètto
lèggi	leggete	hai lètto	avete lètto
lègge	lèggono	ha lètto	hanno lètto
2 imperfect indicative		9 past perfect	
leggevo	leggevamo	avevo lètto	avevamo lètto
leggevi	leggevate	avevi lètto	avevate lètto
leggeva	leggévano	aveva lètto	avévano lètto
3 past absolute		10 past anterior	
lèssi	leggemmo	èbbi lètto	avemmo lètto
leggesti	leggeste	avesti lètto	aveste lètto
lèsse	lèssero	èbbe lètto	èbbero lètto
4 future indicative		11 future perfect	
leggrò	leggeremo	avrò lètto	avremo lètto
leggerai	leggerete	avrai lètto	avrete lètto
leggerà	leggeranno	avrà lètto	avranno lètto
5 present conditional		12 past conditional	
leggerèi	leggeremmo	avrèi lètto	avremmo lètto
leggeresti	leggereste	avresti lètto	avreste lètto
leggerèbbe	leggerèbbero	avrèbbe lètto	avrèbbero lètto
6 present subjunctive		13 past subjunctive	
lègga	leggiamo	àbbia lètto	abbiamo lètto
lègga	leggiate	àbbia lètto	abbiate lètto
lègga	lèggano	àbbia lètto	àbbiano lètto
7 imperfect subjunctive		14 past perfect subjunctive	
leggessi	leggéssimo	avessi lètto	avéssimo lètto
leggessi	leggeste	avessi lètto	aveste lètto
leggesse	leggéssero	avesse lètto	avéssero lètto

imperative	
—	leggiamo
lèggi (non lèggere)	leggete
lègga	lèggano

Words related to this verb
Ho perso gli occhiali; non posso leggere oggi.   I lost my glasses; I can't read today.
Lui legge bene.   He reads well.

to curse

The Seven Simple Tenses		The Seven Compound Tenses	
Singular	Plural	Singular	Plural
1 present indicative		8 present perfect	
maledico	malediciamo	ho maledetto	abbiamo maledetto
maledici	maledite	hai maledetto	avete maledetto
maledice	maledícono	ha maledetto	hanno maledetto
2 imperfect indicative		9 past perfect	
maledicevo	maledicevamo	avevo maledetto	avevamo maledetto
maledicevi	maledicevate	avevi maledetto	avevate maledetto
malediceva	maledicévano	aveva maledetto	avévano maledetto
(*Or regular:* maledivo, *etc.*)			
3 past absolute		10 past anterior	
maledissi	maledicemmo	èbbi maledetto	avemmo maledetto
maledicesti	malediceste	avesti maledetto	aveste maledetto
maledisse	maledíssero	èbbe maledetto	èbbero maledetto
(*or regular:* maledii, *etc.*)			
4 future indicative		11 future perfect	
maledirò	malediremo	avrò maledetto	avremo maledetto
maledirai	maledirete	avrai maledetto	avrete maledetto
maledirà	malediranno	avrà maledetto	avranno maledetto
5 present conditional		12 past conditional	
maledirèi	malediremmo	avrèi maledetto	avremmo maledetto
malediresti	maledireste	avresti maledetto	avreste maledetto
maledirèbbe	maledirèbbero	avrèbbe maledetto	avrèbbero maledetto
6 present subjunctive		13 past subjunctive	
maledica	malediciamo	àbbia maledetto	abbiamo maledetto
maledica	malediciate	àbbia maledetto	abbiate maledetto
maledica	maledícano	àbbia maledetto	àbbiano maledetto
7 imperfect subjunctive		14 past perfect subjunctive	
maledicessi	maledicéssimo	avessi maledetto	avéssimo maledetto
maledicessi	malediceste	avessi maledetto	aveste maledetto
maledicesse	maledicéssero	avesse maledetto	avéssero maledetto
(*Or regular:* maledissi, *etc.*)			

	imperative	
—		malediciamo
maledici (non maledire)		maledite
maledica		maledícano

Words related to this verb
Lui maledisse la propria azione.   He cursed his own action.
Dio maledisse Caino.   God cursed Cain.

149

maltrattare   Ger. **maltrattando**   Past Part. **maltrattato**

to mistreat, to ill-treat, to abuse

The Seven Simple Tenses		The Seven Compound Tenses	
Singular	Plural	Singular	Plural
1 present indicative		8 present perfect	
maltràtto	maltrattiamo	ho maltrattato	abbiamo maltrattato
maltràtti	maltrattate	hai maltrattato	avete maltrattato
maltràtta	maltrattano	ha maltrattato	hanno maltrattato
2 imperfect indicative		9 past perfect	
maltrattavo	maltrattavamo	avevo maltrattato	avevamo maltrattato
maltrattavi	maltrattavate	avevi maltrattato	avevate maltrattato
maltrattava	maltrattàvano	aveva maltrattato	avévano maltrattato
3 past absolute		10 past anterior	
maltrattai	maltrattammo	èbbi maltrattato	avemmo maltrattato
maltrattasti	maltrattaste	avesti maltrattato	aveste maltrattato
maltrattò	maltrattàrono	èbbe maltrattato	èbbero maltrattato
4 future indicative		11 future perfect	
maltratterò	maltratteremo	avrò maltrattato	avremo maltrattato
maltratterai	maltratterete	avrai maltrattato	avrete maltrattato
maltratterà	maltratteranno	avrà maltrattato	avranno maltrattato
5 present conditional		12 past conditional	
maltratterèi	maltratteremmo	avrèi maltrattato	avremmo maltrattato
maltratteresti	maltrattereste	avresti maltrattato	avreste maltrattato
maltratterèbbe	maltratterèbbero	avrèbbe maltrattato	avrèbbero maltrattato
6 present subjunctive		13 past subjunctive	
maltràtti	maltrattiamo	àbbia maltrattato	abbiamo maltrattato
maltràtti	maltrattiate	àbbia maltrattato	abbiate maltrattato
maltràtti	maltràttino	àbbia maltrattato	àbbiano maltrattato
7 imperfect subjunctive		14 past perfect subjunctive	
maltrattassi	maltrattàssimo	avessi maltrattato	avéssimo maltrattato
maltrattassi	maltrattaste	avessi maltrattato	aveste maltrattato
maltrattasse	maltrattàssero	avesse maltrattato	avéssero maltrattato

imperative		
—		maltrattiamo
maltràtta (non maltrattare)		maltrattate
maltràtti		maltràttino

Words related to this verb
Lui maltratta la moglie.   He mistreats his wife.
maltrattare gli animali   to mistreat animals

to send

The Seven Simple Tenses		The Seven Compound Tenses	
Singular	Plural	Singular	Plural
1 present indicative		8 present perfect	
màndo	mandiamo	ho mandato	abbiamo mandato
màndi	mandate	hai mandato	avete mandato
mànda	mandano	ha mandato	hanno mandato
2 imperfect indicative		9 past perfect	
mandavo	mandavamo	avevo mandato	avevamo mandato
mandavi	mandavate	avevi mandato	avevate mandato
mandava	mandàvano	aveva mandato	avévano mandato
3 past absolute		10 past anterior	
mandai	mandammo	èbbi mandato	avemmo mandato
mandasti	mandaste	aveste mandato	aveste mandato
mandò	mandàrono	èbbe mandato	èbbero mandato
4 future indicative		11 future perfect	
manderò	manderemo	avrò mandato	avremo mandato
manderai	manderete	avrai mandato	avrete mandato
manderà	manderanno	avrà mandato	avranno mandato
5 present conditional		12 past conditional	
manderèi	manderemmo	avrèi mandato	avremmo mandato
manderesti	mandereste	avresti mandato	avreste mandato
manderèbbe	manderèbbero	avrèbbe mandato	avrèbbero mandato
6 present subjunctive		13 past subjunctive	
màndi	mandiamo	àbbia mandato	abbiamo mandato
màndi	mandiate	àbbia mandato	abbiate mandato
màndi	màndino	àbbia mandato	àbbiano mandato
7 imperfect subjunctive		14 past perfect subjunctive	
mandassi	mandàssimo	avessi mandato	avéssimo mandato
mandassi	mandaste	avessi mandato	aveste mandato
mandasse	mandàssero	avesse mandato	avéssero mandato

imperative

—	mandiamo
mànda (non mandare)	mandate
màndi	màndino

Words related to this verb
Mandami la lettera!   Send me the letter!
Io manderò il ragazzo a casa di buon'ora.   I will send the boy home early.

151

mangiare	Ger. **mangiando**	Past Part. **mangiato**

to eat

The Seven Simple Tenses		The Seven Compound Tenses	
Singular	Plural	Singular	Plural
1 present indicative		8 present perfect	
mangio	mangiamo	ho mangiato	abbiamo mangiato
mangi	mangiate	hai mangiato	avete mangiato
mangia	màngiano	ha mangiato	hanno mangiato
2 imperfect indicative		9 past perfect	
mangiavo	mangiavamo	avevo mangiato	avevamo mangiato
mangiavi	mangiavate	avevi mangiato	avevate mangiato
mangiava	mangiàvano	aveva mangiato	avévano mangiato
3 past absolute		10 past anterior	
mangiai	mangiammo	èbbi mangiato	avemmo mangiato
mangiasti	mangiaste	avesti mangiato	aveste mangiato
mangiò	mangiàrono	èbbe mangiato	èbbero mangiato
4 future indicative		11 future perfect	
mangerò	mangeremo	avrò mangiato	avremo mangiato
mangerai	mangerete	avrai mangiato	avrete mangiato
mangerà	mangeranno	avrà mangiato	avranno mangiato
5 present conditional		12 past conditional	
mangerèi	mangeremmo	avrèi mangiato	avremmo mangiato
mangeresti	mangereste	avresti mangiato	avreste mangiato
mangerèbbe	mangerèbbero	avrèbbe mangiato	avrèbbero mangiato
6 present subjunctive		13 past subjunctive	
mangi	mangiamo	àbbia mangiato	abbiamo mangiato
mangi	mangiate	àbbia mangiato	abbiate mangiato
mangi	màngino	àbbia mangiato	àbbiano mangiato
7 imperfect subjunctive		14 past perfect subjunctive	
mangiassi	mangiàssimo	avessi mangiato	avéssimo mangiato
mangiassi	mangiaste	avessi mangiato	aveste mangiato
mangiasse	mangiàssero	avesse mangiato	avéssero mangiato

	imperative	
—		mangiamo
	mangia (non mangiare)	mangiate
	mangi	màngino

Words related to this verb
Io mangio bene ogni giorno.   I eat well every day.
Lui mangiava una volta al giorno.   He used to eat once a day.

to maintain, to keep, to preserve

The Seven Simple Tenses		The Seven Compound Tenses	
Singular	Plural	Singular	Plural
1 present indicative		8 present perfect	
mantèngo	manteniamo	ho mantenuto	abbiamo mantenuto
mantièni	mantenete	hai mantenuto	avete mantenuto
mantiène	mantèngono	ha mantenuto	hanno mantenuto
2 imperfect indicative		9 past perfect	
mantenevo	mantenevamo	avevo mantenuto	avevamo mantenuto
mantenevi	mantenevate	avevi mantenuto	avevate mantenuto
manteneva	mantenévano	aveva mantenuto	avévano mantenuto
3 past absolute		10 past anterior	
mantenni	mantenemmo	èbbi mantenuto	avemmo mantenuto
mantenesti	manteneste	avesti mantenuto	aveste mantenuto
mantenne	manténnero	èbbe mantenuto	èbbero mantenuto
4 future indicative		11 future perfect	
manterrò	manterremo	avrò mantenuto	avremo mantenuto
manterrai	manterrete	avrai mantenuto	avrete mantenuto
manterrà	manterranno	avrà mantenuto	avranno mantenuto
5 present conditional		12 past conditional	
manterrèi	manterremmo	avrèi mantenuto	avremmo mantenuto
manterresti	manterreste	avresti mantenuto	avreste mantenuto
manterrèbbe	manterrèbbero	avrèbbe mantenuto	avrèbbero mantenuto
6 present subjunctive		13 past subjunctive	
mantènga	manteniamo	àbbia mantenuto	abbiamo mantenuto
mantènga	manteniate	àbbia mantenuto	abbiate mantenuto
mantènga	mantèngano	àbbia mantenuto	àbbiano mantenuto
7 imperfect subjunctive		14 past perfect subjunctive	
mantenessi	mantenéssimo	avessi mantenuto	avéssimo mantenuto
mantenessi	manteneste	avessi mantenuto	aveste mantenuto
mantenesse	mantenéssero	avesse mantenuto	avéssero mantenuto

imperative

—	manteniamo
mantièni (non mantenere)	mantenete
mantènga	mantèngano

Words related to this verb
La mia famiglia mantiene le sue tradizioni italiane.   My family maintains its Italian traditions.
Il nuotatore si mantiene agile.   The swimmer keeps fit.

méttere*　　　　　　　　Ger. mettèndo　　　　　　　　Past Part. messo

to put, to place, to set

The Seven Simple Tenses		The Seven Compound Tenses	
Singular	Plural	Singular	Plural
1 present indicative		8 present perfect	
metto	mettiamo	ho messo	abbiamo messo
metti	mettete	hai messo	avete messo
mette	méttono	ha messo	hanno messo
2 imperfect indicative		9 past perfect	
mettevo	mettevamo	avevo messo	avevamo messo
mettevi	mettevate	avevi messo	avevate messo
metteva	mettévano	aveva messo	avévano messo
3 past absolute		10 past anterior	
misi	mettemmo	èbbi messo	avemmo messo
mettesti	metteste	avesti messo	aveste messo
mise	mísero	èbbe messo	èbbero messo
4 future indicative		11 future perfect	
metterò	metteremo	avrò messo	avremo messo
metterai	metterete	avrai messo	avrete messo
metterà	metteranno	avrà messo	avranno messo
5 present conditional		12 past conditional	
metterèi	metteremmo	avrèi messo	avremmo messo
metteresti	mettereste	avresti messo	avreste messo
metterèbbe	metterèbbero	avrèbbe messo	avrèbbero messo
6 present subjunctive		13 past subjunctive	
metta	mettiamo	àbbia messo	abbiamo messo
metta	mettiate	àbbia messo	abbiate messo
metta	méttano	àbbia messo	àbbiano messo
7 imperfect subjunctive		14 past perfect subjunctive	
mettessi	mettéssimo	avessi messo	avéssimo messo
mettessi	metteste	avessi messo	aveste messo
mettesse	mettéssero	avesse messo	avéssero messo

imperative

—	mettiamo
metti (non méttere)	mettete
metta	méttano

---

* Like *méttere* are *ammèttere, commèttere, compromèttere, dimèttere, omèttere, permèttere, promèttere, rimèttere, scommèttere, smèttere, sommèttere, sottomèttere, trasmèttere*, etc.

Words related to this verb

Non mettere il libro sulla tavola.　　Don't put the book on the table.
Non mettere quel coltello sul tavolo della cucina. È molto tagliente.　　Don't put that knife on the kitchen table. It is very sharp.

The Seven Simple Tenses		The Seven Compound Tenses	
Singular	Plural	Singular	Plural
1 present indicative		8 present perfect	
mòrdo	mordiamo	ho mòrso	abbiamo mòrso
mòrdi	mordete	hai mòrso	avete mòrso
mòrde	mòrdono	ha mòrso	hanno mòrso
2 imperfect indicative		9 past perfect	
mordevo	mordevamo	avevo mòrso	avevamo mòrso
mordevi	mordevate	avevi mòrso	avevate mòrso
mordeva	mordévano	aveva mòrso	avévano mòrso
3 past absolute		10 past anterior	
mòrsi	mordemmo	èbbi mòrso	avemmo mòrso
mordesti	mordeste	avesti mòrso	aveste mòrso
mòrse	mòrsero	èbbe mòrso	èbbero mòrso
4 future indicative		11 future perfect	
morderò	morderemo	avrò mòrso	avremo mòrso
morderai	morderete	avrai mòrso	avrete mòrso
morderà	morderanno	avrà mòrso	avranno mòrso
5 present conditional		12 past conditional	
morderèi	morderemmo	avrèi mòrso	avremmo mòrso
morderesti	mordereste	avresti mòrso	avreste mòrso
morderèbbe	morderèbbero	avrèbbe mòrso	avrèbbero mòrso
6 present subjunctive		13 past subjunctive	
mòrda	mordiamo	àbbia mòrso	abbiamo mòrso
mòrda	mordiate	àbbia mòrso	abbiate mòrso
mòrda	mòrdano	àbbia mòrso	àbbiano mòrso
7 imperfect subjunctive		14 past perfect subjunctive	
mordessi	mordéssimo	avessi mòrso	avéssimo mòrso
mordessi	mordeste	avessi mòrso	aveste mòrso
mordesse	mordéssero	avesse mòrso	avéssero mòrso

	imperative	
—		mordiamo
mòrdi (non mòrdere)		mordete
mòrda		mòrdano

Words related to this verb
Il mio gatto non morde.   My cat does not bite.
Il cane mi morse.   The dog bit me.

morire   Ger. **morèndo**   Past Part. **mòrto**

to die

The Seven Simple Tenses		The Seven Compound Tenses	
Singular	Plural	Singular	Plural
1 present indicative		8 present perfect	
muòio	moriamo	sono mòrto	siamo mòrti
muòri	morite	sèi mòrto	sìete mòrti
muòre	muòiono	è mòrto	sono mòrti
2 imperfect indicative		9 past perfect	
morivo	morivamo	èro mòrto	eravamo mòrti
morivi	morivate	èri mòrto	eravate mòrti
moriva	morívano	èra mòrto	èrano mòrti
3 past absolute		10 past anterior	
morii	morimmo	fui mòrto	fummo mòrti
moristi	moriste	fosti mòrto	foste mòrti
morí	morírono	fu mòrto	fúrono mòrti
4 future indicative		11 future perfect	
morrò (morirò)	morremo (moriremo)	sarò mòrto	saremo mòrti
morrai (morirai)	morrete (morirete)	sarai mòrto	sarete mòrti
morrà (morirà)	morranno (moriranno)	sarà mòrto	saranno mòrti
5 present conditional		12 past conditional	
morrèi (morirèi)	morremmo (moriremmo)	sarèi mòrto	saremmo mòrti
morresti	morreste (morireste)	saresti mòrto	sareste mòrti
(moriresti)		sarèbbe mòrto	sarèbbero mòrti
morrèbbe	morrèbbero		
(morirèbbe)	(morirèbbero)		
6 present subjunctive		13 past subjunctive	
muòia	moriamo	sia mòrto	siamo mòrti
muòia	moriate	sia mòrto	siate mòrti
muòia	muòiano	sia mòrto	síano mòrti
7 imperfect subjunctive		14 past perfect subjunctive	
morissi	moríssimo	fossi mòrto	fóssimo mòrti
morissi	moriste	fossi mòrto	foste mòrti
morisse	moríssero	fosse mòrto	fóssero mòrti

imperative	
—	moriamo
muòri (non morire)	morite
muòia	muòiano

Words related to this verb
Lei muore di paura quando rimane sola.   She dies of fright when she remains alone.
Michelangelo morì molti anni fa.   Michelangelo died many years ago.

156

to show

The Seven Simple Tenses		The Seven Compound Tenses	
Singular	Plural	Singular	Plural
1 present indicative		8 present perfect	
mòstro	**mostriamo**	**ho mostrato**	**abbiamo mostrato**
mòstri	**mostrate**	**hai mostrato**	**avete mostrato**
mòstra	**mostrano**	**ha mostrato**	**hanno mostrato**
2 imperfect indicative		9 past perfect	
mostravo	**mostravamo**	**avevo mostrato**	**avevamo mostrato**
mostravi	**mostravate**	**avevi mostrato**	**avevate mostrato**
mostrava	**mostràvano**	**aveva mostrato**	**avévano mostrato**
3 past absolute		10 past anterior	
mostrai	**mostrammo**	**èbbi mostrato**	**avemmo mostrato**
mostrasti	**mostraste**	**avesti mostrato**	**aveste mostrato**
mostrò	**mostràrono**	**èbbe mostrato**	**èbbero mostrato**
4 future indicative		11 future perfect	
mostrerò	**mostreremo**	**avrò mostrato**	**avremo mostrato**
mostrerai	**mostrerete**	**avrai mostrato**	**avrete mostrato**
mostrerà	**mostreranno**	**avrà mostrato**	**avranno mostrato**
5 present conditional		12 past conditional	
mostrerèi	**mostreremmo**	**avrèi mostrato**	**avremmo mostrato**
mostreresti	**mostrereste**	**avresti mostrato**	**avreste mostrato**
mostrerèbbe	**mostrerèbbero**	**avrèbbe mostrato**	**avrèbbero mostrato**
6 present subjunctive		13 past subjunctive	
mostri	**mostriamo**	**àbbia mostrato**	**abbiamo mostrato**
mostri	**mostriate**	**àbbia mostrato**	**abbiate mostrato**
mostri	**mòstrino**	**àbbia mostrato**	**àbbiano mostrato**
7 imperfect subjunctive		14 past perfect subjunctive	
mostrassi	**mostràssimo**	**avessi mostrato**	**avéssimo mostrato**
mostrassi	**mostraste**	**avessi mostrato**	**aveste mostrato**
mostrasse	**mostràssero**	**avesse mostrato**	**avéssero mostrato**

imperative

—	**mostriamo**
mòstra (non **mostrare**)	**mostrate**
mòstri	**mòstrino**

Words related to this verb
Mi mostra il libro.   He shows me the book.
mostra d'arte   art exhibition

157

muòvere* Ger. movèndo (muovèndo) Past Part. mòsso

to move, to stir

The Seven Simple Tenses		The Seven Compound Tenses	
Singular	Plural	Singular	Plural
1 present indicative		8 present perfect	
muòvo	moviamo (muoviamo)	ho mòsso	abbiamo mòsso
muòvi	movete (muovete)	hai mòsso	avete mòsso
muòve	muòvono	ha mòsso	hanno mòsso
2 imperfect indicative		9 past perfect	
movevo	movevamo	avevo mòsso	avevamo mòsso
(muovevo)	(muovevamo)	avevi mòsso	avevate mòsso
movevi (muovevi)	movevate (muovevate)	aveva mòsso	avévano mòsso
moveva (muoveva)	movévano (muovévano)		
3 past absolute		10 past anterior	
mòssi	movemmo (muovemmo)	èbbi mòsso	avemmo mòsso
movesti (muovesti)	moveste (muoveste)	avesti mòsso	aveste mòsso
mòsse	mòssero	èbbe mòsso	èbbero mòsso
4 future indicative		11 future perfect	
moverò (muoverò)	moveremo (muoveremo)	avrò mòsso	avremo mòsso
moverai	moverete	avrai mòsso	avrete mòsso
(muoverai)	(muoverete)	avrà mòsso	avranno mòsso
moverà (muoverà)	moveranno		
	(muoveranno)		
5 present conditional		12 past conditional	
moverèi	moveremmo	avrèi mòsso	avremmo mòsso
(muoverèi)	(muoveremmo)	avresti mòsso	avreste mòsso
moveresti	movereste	avrèbbe	avrèbbero
(muoveresti)	(muovereste)	mòsso	mòsso
moverèbbe	moverèbbero		
(muoverèbbe)	(muoverèbbero)		
6 present subjunctive		13 past subjunctive	
muòva	moviamo (muoviamo)	àbbia mòsso	abbiamo mòsso
muòva	moviate (muoviate)	àbbia mòsso	abbiate mòsso
muòva	muòvano	àbbia mòsso	àbbiano mòsso
7 imperfect subjunctive		14 past perfect subjunctive	
movessi	movéssimo	avessi mòsso	avéssimo mòsso
(muovessi)	(muovéssimo)	avessi mòsso	aveste mòsso
movessi (muovessi)	moveste (muoveste)	avesse mòsso	avéssero mòsso
movesse	movéssero		
(muovesse)	(muovéssero)		

imperative	
—	moviamo (muoviamo)
muòvi (non muòvere)	movete (muovete)
muòva	muòvano

* Like *muòvere* are *commuòvere*, *promuòvere*, *rimuòvere*, *smuòvere*, and *sommuòvere*.

The Seven Simple Tenses		The Seven Compound Tenses	
Singular	Plural	Singular	Plural
1 present indicative		8 present perfect	
nasco	nasciamo	sono nato	siamo nati
nasci	nascete	sèi nato	sième nati
nasce	nàscono	è nato	sono nati
2 imperfect indicative		9 past perfect	
nascevo	nascevamo	èro nato	eravamo nati
nascevi	nascevate	èri nato	eravate nati
nasceva	nascévano	èra nato	èrano nati
3 past absolute		10 past anterior	
nacqui	nascemmo	fui nato	fummo nati
nascesti	nasceste	fosti nato	foste nati
nacque	nàcquero	fu nato	fúrono nati
4 future indicative		11 future perfect	
nascerò	nasceremo	sarò nato	saremo nati
nascerai	nascerete	sarai nato	sarete nati
nascerà	nasceranno	sarà nato	saranno nati
5 present conditional		12 past conditional	
nascerèi	nasceremmo	sarèi nato	saremmo nati
nasceresti	nascereste	saresti nato	sareste nati
nascerèbbe	nascerèbbero	sarèbbe nato	sarèbbero nati
6 present subjunctive		13 past subjunctive	
nasca	nasciamo	sia nato	siamo nati
nasca	nasciate	sia nato	siate nati
nasca	nàscano	sia nato	síano nati
7 imperfect subjunctive		14 past perfect subjunctive	
nascessi	nascéssimo	fossi nato	fóssimo nati
nascessi	nasceste	fossi nato	foste nati
nascesse	nascéssero	fosse nato	fóssero nati

	imperative	
—		nasciamo
nasci (non nàscere)		nascete
nasca		nàscano

* Like *nàscere* is *rinàscere*.

Words related to this verb
Dante nacque nel milleduecentosessantacinque.   Dante was born in 1265.
Lei non è nata ieri.   She wasn't born yesterday.

nascóndere   Ger. **nascondèndo**   Past Part. **nascosto**

to hide

The Seven Simple Tenses		The Seven Compound Tenses	
Singular	Plural	Singular	Plural
1 present indicative		8 present perfect	
nascondo	**nascondiamo**	**ho nascosto**	**abbiamo nascosto**
nascondi	**nascondete**	**hai nascosto**	**avete nascosto**
nasconde	**nascóndono**	**ha nascosto**	**hanno nascosto**
2 imperfect indicative		9 past perfect	
nascondevo	**nascondevamo**	**avevo nascosto**	**avevamo nascosto**
nascondevi	**nascondevate**	**avevi nascosto**	**avevate nascosto**
nascondeva	**nascondévano**	**aveva nascosto**	**avévano nascosto**
3 past absolute		10 past anterior	
nascosi	**nascondemmo**	**èbbi nascosto**	**avemmo nascosto**
nascondesti	**nascondeste**	**avesti nascosto**	**aveste nascosto**
nascose	**nascósero**	**èbbe nascosto**	**èbbero nascosto**
4 future indicative		11 future perfect	
nasconderò	**nasconderemo**	**avrò nascosto**	**avremo nascosto**
nasconderai	**nasconderete**	**avrai nascosto**	**avrete nascosto**
nasconderà	**nasconderanno**	**avrà nascosto**	**avranno nascosto**
5 present conditional		12 past conditional	
nasconderèi	**nasconderemmo**	**avrèi nascosto**	**avremmo nascosto**
nasconderesti	**nascondereste**	**avresti nascosto**	**avreste nascosto**
nasconderèbbe	**nasconderèbbero**	**avrèbbe nascosto**	**avrèbbero nascosto**
6 present subjunctive		13 past subjunctive	
nasconda	**nascondiamo**	**àbbia nascosto**	**abbiamo nascosto**
nasconda	**nascondiate**	**àbbia nascosto**	**abbiate nascosto**
nasconda	**nascóndano**	**àbbia nascosto**	**àbbiano nascosto**
7 imperfect subjunctive		14 past perfect subjunctive	
nascondessi	**nascondéssimo**	**avessi nascosto**	**avéssimo nascosto**
nascondessi	**nascondeste**	**avessi nascosto**	**aveste nascosto**
nascondesse	**nascondéssero**	**avesse nascosto**	**avéssero nascosto**

imperative

—	**nascondiamo**
nascondi (non **nascóndere**)	**nascondete**
nasconda	**nascóndano**

Words related to this verb
Io mi nascosi nell'armadio quando ero ragazzo. I hid in the closet when I was a child.
Dove hai nascosto il suo libro? Where have you hidden his book?

to harm, to hurt, to injure

The Seven Simple Tenses		The Seven Compound Tenses	
Singular	Plural	Singular	Plural
1 present indicative		8 present perfect	
nòccio (nuòco)	nociamo (nuociamo)	ho nociuto (nuociuto)	abbiamo nociuto
nuòci	nocete (nuocete)	hai nociuto	avete nociuto
nuòce	nòcciono (nuòcono)	ha nociuto	hanno nociuto
2 imperfect indicative		9 past perfect	
nocevo	nocevamo	avevo nociuto	avevamo nociuto
(nuocevo)	(nuocevamo)	avevi nociuto	avevate nociuto
nocevi (nuocevi)	nocevate (nuocevate)	aveva nociuto	avévano nociuto
noceva	nocévano		
(nuoceva)	(nuocévano)		
3 past absolute		10 past anterior	
nòcqui	nocemmo	èbbi nociuto	avemmo nociuto
	(nuocemmo)	avesti nociuto	aveste nociuto
nocesti	noceste (nuoceste)	èbbe nociuto	èbbero nociuto
(nuocesti)			
nòcque	nòcquero		
4 future indicative		11 future perfect	
nocerò	noceremo	avrò nociuto	avremo nociuto
(nuocerò)	(nuoceremo)	avrai nociuto	avrete nociuto
nocerai	nocerete (nuocerete)	avrà nociuto	avranno nociuto
(nuocerai)			
nocerà	noceranno		
(nuocerà)	(nuoceranno)		
5 present conditional		12 past conditional	
nocerèi	noceremmo	avrèi nociuto	avremmo nociuto
(nuocerèi)	(nuoceremmo)	avresti nociuto	avreste nociuto
noceresti	nocereste	avrèbbe nociuto	avrèbbero
(nuoceresti)	(nuocereste)		nociuto
nocerèbbe	nocerèbbero		
(nuocerèbbe)	(nuocerèbbero)		
6 present subjunctive		13 past subjunctive	
nòccia (nuòca)	nociamo (nuociamo)	àbbia nociuto	abbiamo nociuto
nòccia (nuòca)	nociate (nuociate)	àbbia nociuto	abbiate nociuto
nòccia (nuòca)	nòcciano (nuòcano)	àbbia nociuto	àbbiano nociuto
7 imperfect subjunctive		14 past perfect subjunctive	
nocessi	nocéssimo	avessi nociuto	avéssimo nociuto
(nuocessi)	(nuocéssimo)	avessi nociuto	aveste nociuto
nocessi	noceste (nuoceste)	avesse nociuto	avéssero nociuto
(nuocessi)			
nocesse	nocéssero		
(nuocesse)	(nuocéssero)		

	imperative	
		nociamo (nuociamo)
nuòci (non nuòcere)		nocete (nuocete)
nòccia (nuòca)		nòcciano (nuòcano)

occupare   Ger. occupando   Past Part. occupato

to occupy

The Seven Simple Tenses		The Seven Compound Tenses	
Singular	Plural	Singular	Plural
1　present indicative		8　present perfect	
òccupo	occupiamo	ho occupato	abbiamo occupato
òccupi	occupate	hai occupato	avete occupato
òccupa	òccupano	ha occupato	hanno occupato
2　imperfect indicative		9　past perfect	
occupavo	occupavamo	avevo occupato	avevamo occupato
occupavi	occupavate	avevi occupato	avevate occupato
occupava	occupàvano	aveva occupato	avévano occupato
3　past absolute		10　past anterior	
occupai	occupammo	èbbi occupato	avemmo occupato
occupasti	occupaste	avesti occupato	aveste occupato
occupò	occupàrono	èbbe occupato	èbbero occupato
4　future indicative		11　future perfect	
occuperò	occuperemo	avrò occupato	avremo occupato
occuperai	occuperete	avrai occupato	avrete occupato
occuperà	occuperanno	avrà occupato	avranno occupato
5　present conditional		12　past conditional	
occuperèi	occuperemmo	avrèi occupato	avremmo occupato
occuperesti	occupereste	avresti occupato	avreste occupato
occuperèbbe	occuperèbbero	avrèbbe occupato	avrèbbero occupato
6　present subjunctive		13　past subjunctive	
òccupi	occupiamo	àbbia occupato	abbiamo occupato
òccupi	occupiate	àbbia occupato	abbiate occupato
òccupi	òccupino	àbbia occupato	àbbiano occupato
7　imperfect subjunctive		14　past perfect subjunctive	
occupassi	occupàssimo	avessi occupato	avéssimo occupato
occupassi	occupaste	avessi occupato	aveste occupato
occupasse	occupàssero	avesse occupato	avéssero occupato

	imperative	
—		occupiamo
òccupa (non occupare)		occupate
òccupi		òccupino

Words related to this verb
Lui occupa questo posto.   He occupies this place.
Questi libri occupano molto spazio.   These books take up a lot of space.

The Seven Simple Tenses		The Seven Compound Tenses	
Singular	Plural	Singular	Plural
1 present indicative		8 present perfect	
offèndo	offendiamo	ho offeso	abbiamo offeso
offèndi	offendete	hai offeso	avete offeso
offènde	offèndono	ha offeso	hanno offeso
2 imperfect indicative		9 past perfect	
offendevo	offendevamo	avevo offeso	avevamo offeso
offendevi	offendevate	avevi offeso	avevate offeso
offendeva	offendévano	aveva offeso	avévano offeso
3 past absolute		10 past anterior	
offesi	offendemmo	èbbi offeso	avemmo offeso
offendesti	offendeste	avesti offeso	aveste offeso
offese	offésero	èbbe offeso	èbbero offeso
4 future indicative		11 future perfect	
offenderò	offenderemo	avrò offeso	avremo offeso
offenderai	offenderete	avrai offeso	avrete offeso
offenderà	offenderanno	avrà offeso	avranno offeso
5 present conditional		12 past conditional	
offenderèi	offenderemmo	avrèi offeso	avremmo offeso
offenderesti	offendereste	avresti offeso	avreste offeso
offenderèbbe	offenderèbbero	avrèbbe offeso	avrèbbero offeso
6 present subjunctive		13 past subjunctive	
offènda	offendiamo	àbbia offeso	abbiamo offeso
offènda	offendiate	àbbia offeso	abbiate offeso
offènda	offèndano	àbbia offeso	àbbiano offeso
7 imperfect subjunctive		14 past perfect subjunctive	
offendessi	offendéssimo	avessi offeso	avéssimo offeso
offendessi	offendeste	avessi offeso	aveste offeso
offendesse	offendéssero	avesse offeso	avéssero offeso

imperative	
—	offendiamo
offèndi (non offèndere)	offendete
offènda	offèndano

Words related to this verb
Lui mi ha offeso. He offended me.
Lui mi offende con la sua condotta. He offends me with his conduct.

offrire
Ger. offrèndo   Past Part. offèrto

to offer

The Seven Simple Tenses		The Seven Compound Tenses	
Singular	Plural	Singular	Plural
1 present indicative		**8 present perfect**	
òffro	offriamo	ho offèrto	abbiamo offèrto
òffri	offrite	hai offèrto	avete offèrto
òffre	òffrono	ha offèrto	hanno offèrto
2 imperfect indicative		**9 past perfect**	
offrivo	offrivamo	avevo offèrto	avevamo offèrto
offrivi	offrivate	avevi offèrto	avevate offèrto
offriva	offrívano	aveva offèrto	avévano offèrto
3 past absolute		**10 past anterior**	
offèrsi	offrimmo	èbbi offèrto	avemmo offèrto
offristi	offriste	avesti offèrto	aveste offèrto
offèrse	offèrsero	èbbe offèrto	èbbero offèrto
(Or regular: offrii, *etc.)*			
4 future indicative		**11 future perfect**	
offrirò	offriremo	avrò offèrto	avremo offèrto
offrirai	offrirete	avrai offèrto	avrete offèrto
offrirà	offriranno	avrà offèrto	avranno offèrto
5 present conditional		**12 past conditional**	
offrirèi	offriremmo	avrei offerto	avremmo offèrto
offriresti	offrireste	avresti offerto	avreste offèrto
offrirèbbe	offrirèbbero	avrèbbe offèrto	avrèbbero offèrto
6 present subjunctive		**13 past subjunctive**	
òffra	offriamo	àbbia offèrto	abbiamo offèrto
òffra	offriate	àbbia offèrto	abbiate offèrto
òffra	òffrano	àbbia offèrto	àbbiano offèrto
7 imperfect subjunctive		**14 past perfect subjunctive**	
offrissi	offríssimo	avessi offèrto	avéssimo offèrto
offrissi	offriste	avessi offèrto	aveste offèrto
offrisse	offríssero	avesse offèrto	avéssero offèrto

	imperative	
—		offriamo
òffri (non offrire)		offrite
òffra		òffrano

Words related to this verb
Lei mi offre da bere. She offers me a drink.
Lui mi offrì la sua amicizia. He offered me his friendship.

The Seven Simple Tenses		The Seven Compound Tenses	
Singular	Plural	Singular	Plural
1 present indicative		8 present perfect	
ometto	omettiamo	ho omesso	abbiamo omesso
ometti	omettete	hai omesso	avete omesso
omette	ométtono	ha omesso	hanno omesso
2 imperfect indicative		9 past perfect	
omettevo	omettevamo	avevo omesso	avevamo omesso
omettevi	omettevate	avevi omesso	avevate omesso
ometteva	omettévano	aveva omesso	avévano omesso
3 past absolute		10 past anterior	
omisi	omettemmo	èbbi omesso	avemmo omesso
omettesti	ometteste	avesti omesso	aveste omesso
omise	omísero	èbbe omesso	èbbero omesso
4 future indicative		11 future perfect	
ometterò	ometteremo	avrò omesso	avremo omesso
ometterai	ometterete	avrai omesso	avrete omesso
ometterà	ometteranno	avrà omesso	avranno omesso
5 present conditional		12 past conditional	
ometterèi	ometterèmmo	avrèi omesso	avremmo omesso
ometteresti	omettereste	avresti omesso	avreste omesso
ometterèbbe	ometterèbbero	avrèbbe omesso	avrèbbero omesso
6 present subjunctive		13 past subjunctive	
ometta	omettiamo	àbbia omesso	abbiamo omesso
ometta	omettiate	àbbia omesso	abbiate omesso
ometta	ométtano	àbbia omesso	àbbiano omesso
7 imperfect subjunctive		14 past perfect subjunctive	
omettessi	omettéssimo	avessi omesso	avéssimo omesso
omettessi	ometteste	avessi omesso	aveste omesso
omettesse	omettéssero	avesse omesso	avéssero omesso

imperative	
—	omettiamo
ometti (non ométtere)	omettete
ometta	ométtano

Words related to this verb
Io non scrivo bene; ometto molte parole.   I don't write well; I leave out many words.
Lui non ha omesso niente.   He has not omitted anything.

to oppose

The Seven Simple Tenses		The Seven Compound Tenses	
Singular	Plural	Singular	Plural
1 present indicative		8 present perfect	
oppongo	**opponiamo**	**ho opposto**	**abbiamo opposto**
opponi	**opponete**	**hai opposto**	**avete opposto**
oppone	**oppóngono**	**ha opposto**	**hanno opposto**
2 imperfect indicative		9 past perfect	
opponevo	**opponevamo**	**avevo opposto**	**avevamo opposto**
opponevi	**opponevate**	**avevi opposto**	**avevate opposto**
opponeva	**opponévano**	**aveva opposto**	**avévano opposto**
3 past absolute		10 past anterior	
opposi	**opponemmo**	**èbbi opposto**	**avemmo opposto**
opponesti	**opponeste**	**avesti opposto**	**aveste opposto**
oppose	**oppósero**	**èbbe opposto**	**èbbero opposto**
4 future indicative		11 future perfect	
opporrò	**opporremo**	**avrò opposto**	**avremo opposto**
opporrai	**opporrete**	**avrai opposto**	**avrete opposto**
opporrà	**opporranno**	**avrà opposto**	**avranno opposto**
5 present conditional		12 past conditional	
opporrèi	**opporremmo**	**avrèi opposto**	**avremmo opposto**
opporresti	**opporreste**	**avresti opposto**	**avreste opposto**
opporrèbbe	**opporrèbbero**	**avrèbbe opposto**	**avrèbbero opposto**
6 present subjunctive		13 past subjunctive	
opponga	**opponiamo**	**àbbia opposto**	**abbiamo opposto**
opponga	**opponiate**	**àbbia opposto**	**abbiate opposto**
opponga	**oppóngano**	**àbbia opposto**	**àbbiano opposto**
7 imperfect subjunctive		14 past perfect subjunctive	
opponessi	**opponéssimo**	**avessi opposto**	**avéssimo opposto**
opponessi	**opponeste**	**avessi opposto**	**aveste opposto**
opponesse	**opponéssero**	**avesse opposto**	**avéssero opposto**

imperative	
—	**opponiamo**
opponi (non opporre)	**opponete**
opponga	**oppóngano**

Words related to this verb
Io oppongo il nemico con la bontà.   I oppose the enemy with goodness.
Loro si oppongono alla tua decisione.   They oppose your decision.

Ger. **opprimendo**   Past Part. **oppresso**   **opprimere***

to oppress, to weigh down, to overwhelm

The Seven Simple Tenses		The Seven Compound Tenses	
Singular	Plural	Singular	Plural
1 present indicative		8 present perfect	
opprìmo	**opprimiamo**	**ho oppresso**	**abbiamo oppresso**
opprìmi	**opprimete**	**hai oppresso**	**avete oppresso**
opprìme	**opprìmono**	**ha oppresso**	**hanno oppresso**
2 imperfect indicative		9 past perfect	
opprimevo	**opprimevamo**	**avevo oppresso**	**avevamo oppresso**
opprimevi	**opprimevate**	**avevi oppresso**	**avevate oppresso**
opprimeva	**opprimévano**	**aveva oppresso**	**avévano oppresso**
3 past absolute		10 past anterior	
oppressi	**oprimemmo**	**èbbi oppresso**	**avemmo oppresso**
opprimesti	**opprimeste**	**avesti oppresso**	**aveste oppresso**
oppresse	**oppressero**	**èbbe oppresso**	**èbbero oppresso**
4 future indicative		11 future perfect	
opprimerò	**opprimeremo**	**avrò oppresso**	**avremo oppresso**
opprimerai	**opprimerete**	**avrai oppresso**	**avrete oppresso**
opprimerà	**opprimeranno**	**avrà oppresso**	**avranno oppresso**
5 present conditional		12 past conditional	
opprimerèi	**opprimerèmmo**	**avrèi oppresso**	**avremmo oppresso**
opprimeresti	**opprimereste**	**avresti oppresso**	**avreste oppresso**
opprimerèbbe	**opprimerèbbero**	**avrèbbe oppresso**	**avrèbbero oppresso**
6 present subjunctive		13 past subjunctive	
opprìma	**opprimiamo**	**àbbia oppresso**	**abbiamo oppresso**
opprìma	**opprimiate**	**àbbia oppresso**	**abbiate oppresso**
opprìma	**opprìmano**	**àbbia oppresso**	**àbbiano oppresso**
7 imperfect subjunctive		14 past perfect subjunctive	
opprimessi	**oppriméssimo**	**avessi oppresso**	**avéssimo oppresso**
opprimessi	**opprimeste**	**avessi oppresso**	**aveste oppresso**
opprimesse	**oppriméssero**	**avesse oppresso**	**avéssero oppresso**

imperative

—	**opprimiamo**
opprìmi (non opprimere)	**opprimete**
opprìma	**opprìmano**

* like *opprimere* are *comprimere* and *reprimere*

Words related to this verb

opprimere la gente   to oppress people
Quel cibo opprime lo stomaco   That food weighs heavily on the stomach.
opprimere una persona di domande   to overwhelm a person with questions

osservare   Ger. osservando   Past Part. osservato

to observe, to watch

The Seven Simple Tenses		The Seven Compound Tenses	
Singular	Plural	Singular	Plural
1 present indicative		8 present perfect	
osservo	osserviamo	ho osservato	abbiamo osservato
osservi	osservate	hai osservato	avete osservato
osserva	osservano	ha osservato	hanno osservato
2 imperfect indicative		9 past perfect	
osservavo	osservavamo	avevo osservato	avevamo osservato
osservavi	osservavate	avevi osservato	avevate osservato
osservava	osservàvano	aveva osservato	avévano osservato
3 past absolute		10 past anterior	
osservai	osservammo	èbbi osservato	avemmo osservato
osservasti	osservaste	avesti osservato	aveste osservato
osservò	osservàrono	èbbe osservato	èbbero osservato
4 future indicative		11 future perfect	
osserverò	osserveremo	avrò osservato	avremo osservato
osserverai	osserverete	avrai osservato	avrete osservato
osserverà	osserveranno	avrà osservato	avranno osservato
5 present conditional		12 past conditional	
osserverèi	osserveremmo	avrèi osservato	avremmo osservato
osserveresti	osservereste	avresti osservato	avreste osservato
osserverèbbe	osserverèbbero	avrèbbe osservato	avrèbbero osservato
6 present subjunctive		13 past subjunctive	
osservi	osserviamo	àbbia osservato	abbiamo osservato
osservi	osserviate	àbbia osservato	abbiate osservato
osservi	ossèrvino	àbbia osservato	àbbiano osservato
7 imperfect subjunctive		14 past perfect subjunctive	
osservassi	osservàssimo	avessi osservato	avessimo osservato
osservassi	osservaste	avessi osservato	aveste osservato
osservasse	osservàssero	avesse osservato	avéssero osservato

	imperative	
—		osserviamo
osserva (non osservare)		osservate
osservi		ossèrvino

Words related to this verb
Io osservai tutto l'incidente.   I observed the whole accident.
Lo osserva ogni giorno.   She watches him every day.

to obtain, to get

The Seven Simple Tenses		The Seven Compound Tenses	
Singular	Plural	Singular	Plural
1 present indicative		8 present perfect	
ottèngo	otteniamo	ho ottenuto	abbiamo ottenuto
ottièni	ottenete	hai ottenuto	avete ottenuto
ottiène	ottèngono	ha ottenuto	hanno ottenuto
2 imperfect indicative		9 past perfect	
ottenevo	ottenevamo	avevo ottenuto	avevamo ottenuto
ottenevi	ottenevate	avevi ottenuto	avevate ottenuto
otteneva	ottenévano	aveva ottenuto	avévano ottenuto
3 past absolute		10 past anterior	
ottenni	ottenemmo	èbbi ottenuto	avemmo ottenuto
ottenesti	otteneste	avesti ottenuto	aveste ottenuto
ottenne	otténnero	èbbe ottenuto	èbbero ottenuto
4 future indicative		11 future perfect	
otterrò	otterremo	avrò ottenuto	avremo ottenuto
otterrai	otterrete	avrai ottenuto	avrete ottenuto
otterrà	otterranno	avrà ottenuto	avranno ottenuto
5 present conditional		12 past conditional	
otterrèi	otterremmo	avrèi ottenuto	avremmo ottenuto
otterresti	otterreste	avresti ottenuto	avreste ottenuto
otterrèbbe	otterrèbbero	avrèbbe ottenuto	avrèbbero ottenuto
6 present subjunctive		13 past subjunctive	
ottènga	otteniamo	àbbia ottenuto	abbiamo ottenuto
ottènga	otteniate	àbbia ottenuto	abbiate ottenuto
ottènga	ottèngano	àbbia ottenuto	àbbiano ottenuto
7 imperfect subjunctive		14 past perfect subjunctive	
ottenessi	ottenéssimo	avessi ottenuto	avéssimo ottenuto
ottenessi	otteneste	avessi ottenuto	aveste ottenuto
ottenesse	ottenéssero	avesse ottenuto	avéssero ottenuto

imperative

—	otteniamo
ottièni (non ottenere)	ottenete
ottènga	ottèngano

Words related to this verb

Giovanni deve ottenere il permesso dal padre.   John must get permission from his father.

Come hai ottenuto il libro?   How did you obtain the book?

pagare	Ger. **pagando**	Past Part. **pagato**

to pay

|

Singular	Plural	Singular	Plural
1 present indicative		8 present perfect	
pago	**paghiamo**	**ho pagato**	**abbiamo pagato**
paghi	**pagate**	**hai pagato**	**avete pagato**
paga	**pagano**	**ha pagato**	**hanno pagato**
2 imperfect indicative		9 past perfect	
pagavo	**pagavamo**	**avevo pagato**	**avevamo pagato**
pagavi	**pagavate**	**avevi pagato**	**avevate pagato**
pagava	**pagavano**	**aveva pagato**	**avévano pagato**
3 past absolute		10 past anterior	
pagai	**pagammo**	**èbbi pagato**	**avemmo pagato**
pagasti	**pagaste**	**avesti pagato**	**aveste pagato**
pagò	**pagarono**	**èbbe pagato**	**èbbero pagato**
4 future indicative		11 future perfect	
pagherò	**pagheremo**	**avrò pagato**	**avremo pagato**
pagherai	**pagherete**	**avrai pagato**	**avrete pagato**
pagherà	**pagheranno**	**avrà pagato**	**avranno pagato**
5 present conditional		12 past conditional	
pagherèi	**pagheremmo**	**avrèi pagato**	**avremmo pagato**
pagheresti	**paghereste**	**avresti pagato**	**avreste pagato**
pagherèbbe	**pagherèbbero**	**avrèbbe pagato**	**avrèbbero pagato**
6 present subjunctive		13 past subjunctive	
paghi	**paghiamo**	**àbbia pagato**	**abbiamo pagato**
paghi	**paghiate**	**àbbia pagato**	**abbiate pagato**
paghi	**paghino**	**àbbia pagato**	**àbbiano pagato**
7 imperfect subjunctive		14 past perfect subjunctive	
pagassi	**pagassimo**	**avessi pagato**	**avéssimo pagato**
pagassi	**pagaste**	**avessi pagato**	**aveste pagato**
pagasse	**pagassero**	**avesse pagato**	**avéssero pagato**

imperative

—	**paghiamo**
paga (non pagare)	**pagate**
paghi	**paghino**

Words related to this verb
Pago il conto. I pay the bill.
pagare i debiti to pay one's debts
pagare in natura to pay in kind

to appear, to seem

The Seven Simple Tenses		The Seven Compound Tenses	
Singular	Plural	Singular	Plural
1 present indicative		8 present perfect	
paio	paiamo (pariamo)	sono parso	siamo parsi
pari	parete	sèi parso	siète parso (i)
pare	pàiono	è parso	sono parsi
2 imperfect indicative		9 past perfect	
parevo	parevamo	èro parso	eravamo parsi
parevi	parevate	èri parso	eravate parso (i)
pareva	parévano	èra parso	èrano parsi
3 past absolute		10 past anterior	
parvi	paremmo	fui parso	fummo parsi
paresti	pareste	fosti parso	foste parso (i)
parve	pàrvero	fu parso	fúrono parsi
4 future indicative		11 future perfect	
parrò	parremo	sarò parso	saremo parsi
parrai	parrete	sarai parso	sarete parso (i)
parrà	parranno	sarà parso	saranno parsi
5 present conditional		12 past conditional	
parrèi	parremmo	sarèi parso	saremmo parsi
parresti	parreste	saresti parso	sareste parso (i)
parrèbbe	parrèbbero	sarèbbe parso	sarèbbero parsi
6 present subjunctive		13 past subjunctive	
paia	paiamo (pariamo)	sia parso	siamo parsi
paia	paiate (pariate)	sia parso	siate parso (i)
paia	pàiano	sia parso	síano parsi
7 imperfect subjunctive		14 past perfect subjunctive	
paressi	paréssimo	fossi parso	fóssimo parsi
paressi	pareste	fossi parso	foste parso (i)
paresse	paréssero	fosse parso	fóssero parsi

imperative

—	paiamo (pariamo)
pari (non parere)	parete
paia	pàiano

* The compounds of *parere* are conjugated with *-ire*: e.g., *apparire*, *comparire*, *scomparire*. As for *sparire*, it is regular in its present tenses: i.e., *sparisco, sparisca*, etc. The imperative of *parere* is seldom if ever used: cf. "to seem" in English.

Words related to this verb
Lei pare malata.   She seems ill.
Non è quel che pare.   It is not what it appears to be.

parlare Ger. **parlando** Past Part. **parlato**

to speak, to talk

The Seven Simple Tenses		The Seven Compound Tenses	
Singular	Plural	Singular	Plural
1 present indicative		8 present perfect	
pàrlo	parliamo	ho parlato	abbiamo parlato
pàrli	parlate	hai parlato	avete parlato
pàrla	pàrlano	ha parlato	hanno parlato
2 imperfect indicative		9 past perfect	
parlavo	parlavamo	avevo parlato	avevamo parlato
parlavi	parlavate	avevi parlato	avevate parlato
parlava	parlavano	aveva parlato	avévano parlato
3 past absolute		10 past anterior	
parlai	parlammo	èbbi parlato	avemmo parlato
parlasti	parlaste	avesti parlato	aveste parlato
parlò	parlarono	èbbe parlato	èbbero parlato
4 future indicative		11 future perfect	
parlerò	parleremo	avrò parlato	avremo parlato
parlerai	parlerete	avrai parlato	avrete parlato
parlerà	parleranno	avrà parlato	avranno parlato
5 present conditional		12 past conditional	
parlerèi	parleremmo	avrèi parlato	avremmo parlato
parleresti	parlereste	avresti parlato	avreste parlato
parlerèbbe	parlerèbbero	avrèbbe parlato	avrèbbero parlato
6 present subjunctive		13 past subjunctive	
pàrli	parliamo	àbbia parlato	abbiamo parlato
pàrli	parliate	àbbia parlato	abbiate parlato
pàrli	pàrlino	àbbia parlato	àbbiano parlato
7 imperfect subjunctive		14 past perfect subjunctive	
parlassi	parlàssimo	avessi parlato	avessimo parlato
parlassi	parlaste	avessi parlato	aveste parlato
parlasse	parlàssero	avesse parlato	avéssero parlato

	imperative	
—		parliamo
pàrla (non parlare)		parlate
pàrli		pàrlino

Words related to this verb
Il bambino non parla ancora. The baby does not talk yet.
Con chi parlo? With whom am I speaking?

to leave, to go away, to set out

The Seven Simple Tenses		The Seven Compound Tenses	
Singular	Plural	Singular	Plural
1　present indicative		8　present perfect	
pàrto	**partiamo**	**sono partito**	**siamo partiti**
pàrti	**partite**	**sèi partito**	**sième partiti**
pàrte	**pàrtono**	**è partito**	**sono partiti**
2　imperfect indicative		9　past perfect	
partivo	**partivamo**	**èro partito**	**eravamo partiti**
partivi	**partivate**	**èri partito**	**eravate partiti**
partiva	**partivano**	**èra partito**	**èrano partiti**
3　past absolute		10　past anterior	
partii	**partimmo**	**fui partito**	**fummo partiti**
partisti	**partiste**	**fosti partito**	**foste partiti**
partì	**partìrono**	**fu partito**	**fúrono partiti**
4　future indicative		11　future perfect	
partirò	**partiremo**	**sarò partito**	**saremo partiti**
partirai	**partirete**	**sarai partito**	**sarete partiti**
partirà	**partiranno**	**sarà partito**	**saranno partiti**
5　present conditional		12　past conditional	
partirèi	**partiremmo**	**sarèi partito**	**saremmo partiti**
partiresti	**partireste**	**saresti partito**	**sareste partiti**
partirèbbe	**partirèbbero**	**sarèbbe partito**	**sarèbbero partiti**
6　present subjunctive		13　past subjunctive	
pàrta	**partiamo**	**sia partito**	**siamo partiti**
pàrta	**partiate**	**sia partito**	**siate partiti**
pàrta	**pàrtano**	**sia partito**	**síano partiti**
7　imperfect subjunctive		14　past perfect subjunctive	
partissi	**partìssimo**	**fossi partito**	**fóssimo partiti**
partissi	**partiste**	**fossi partito**	**foste partiti**
partisse	**partìssero**	**fosse partito**	**fóssero partiti**

imperative	
—	**partiamo**
pàrti (non partire)	**partite**
pàrta	**pàrtano**

Words related to this verb
Il treno parte alle otto.　The train leaves at eight.
a partire da　beginning with . . .
partire a piedi　to leave on foot

passeggiare   Ger. **passeggiando**   Past Part. **passeggiato**

to walk, to take a walk, to stroll

The Seven Simple Tenses		The Seven Compound Tenses	
Singular	Plural	Singular	Plural
1 present indicative		8 present perfect	
passeggio	passeggiamo	ho passeggiato	abbiamo passeggiato
passeggi	passeggiate	hai passeggiato	avete passeggiato
passeggia	passeggiano	ha passeggiato	hanno passeggiato
2 imperfect indicative		9 past perfect	
passeggiavo	passeggiavamo	avevo passeggiato	avevamo passeggiato
passeggiavi	passeggiavate	avevi passeggiato	avevate passeggiato
passeggiava	passeggiàvano	aveva passeggiato	avévano passeggiato
3 past absolute		10 past anterior	
passeggiai	passeggiammo	èbbi passeggiato	avemmo passeggiato
passeggiasti	passeggiaste	avesti passeggiato	aveste passeggiato
passeggiò	passeggiàrono	èbbe passeggiato	èbbero passeggiato
4 future indicative		11 future perfect	
passeggerò	passeggeremo	avrò passeggiato	avremo passeggiato
passeggerai	passeggerete	avrai passeggiato	avrete passeggiato
passeggerà	passeggeranno	avrà passeggiato	avranno passeggiato
5 present conditional		12 past conditional	
passeggerèi	passeggeremmo	avrèi passeggiato	avremmo passeggiato
passeggeresti	passeggereste	avresti passeggiato	avreste passeggiato
passeggerèbbe	passeggerèbbero	avrèbbe passeggiato	avrèbbero passeggiato
6 present subjunctive		13 past subjunctive	
passeggi	passeggiamo	àbbia passeggiato	abbiamo passeggiato
passeggi	passeggiate	àbbia passeggiato	abbiate passeggiato
passeggi	passeggino	àbbia passeggiato	àbbiano passeggiato
7 imperfect subjunctive		14 past perfect subjunctive	
passeggiassi	passeggiàssimo	avessi passeggiato	avéssimo passeggiato
passeggiassi	passeggiaste	avessi passeggiato	aveste passeggiato
passeggiasse	passeggiàssero	avesse passeggiato	avéssero passeggiato

imperative	
—	passeggiamo
passeggia (non passeggiare)	passeggiate
passeggi	passeggino

Words related to this verb
Lui passeggia per il giardino.   He strolls through the garden.
Passeggiammo per un'ora.   We strolled for an hour.

to hang

The Seven Simple Tenses		The Seven Compound Tenses	
Singular	Plural	Singular	Plural
1 present indicative		8 present perfect	
pèndo	pendiamo	ho penduto	abbiamo penduto
pèndi	pendete	hai penduto	avete penduto
pènde	pèndono	ha penduto	hanno penduto
2 imperfect indicative		9 past perfect	
pendevo	pendevamo	avevo penduto	avevamo penduto
pendevi	pendevate	avevi penduto	avevate penduto
pendeva	pendévano	aveva penduto	avévano penduto
3 past absolute		10 past anterior	
pendei (pendètti)	pendemmo	èbbi penduto	avemmo penduto
pendesti	pendeste	avesti penduto	aveste penduto
pendé (pendètte)	pendérono (pendèttero)	èbbe penduto	èbbero penduto
4 future indicative		11 future perfect	
penderò	penderemo	avrò penduto	avremo penduto
penderai	penderete	avrai penduto	avrete penduto
penderà	penderanno	avrà penduto	avranno penduto
5 present conditional		12 past conditional	
penderèi	penderemmo	avrèi penduto	avremmo penduto
penderesti	pendereste	avresti penduto	avreste penduto
penderèbbe	penderèbbero	avrèbbe penduto	avrèbbero penduto
6 present subjunctive		13 past subjunctive	
pènda	pendiamo	àbbia penduto	abbiamo penduto
pènda	pendiate	àbbia penduto	abbiate penduto
pènda	pèndano	àbbia penduto	àbbiano penduto
7 imperfect subjunctive		14 past perfect subjunctive	
pendessi	pendéssimo	avessi penduto	avéssimo penduto
pendessi	pendeste	avessi penduto	aveste penduto
pendesse	pendéssero	avesse penduto	avéssero penduto

	imperative	
—		pendiamo
pèndi (non pèndere)		pendete
pènda		pèndano

Words related to this verb
Molte mele pendono dall'albero.   Many apples hang from the tree.
La lampada pendeva dal soffitto.   The lamp was hanging from the ceiling.

pensare	Ger. **pensando**	Past Part. **pensato**

to think

The Seven Simple Tenses		The Seven Compound Tenses	
Singular	Plural	Singular	Plural
1 present indicative		8 present perfect	
pènso	**pensiamo**	ho pensato	abbiamo pensato
pènsi	**pensate**	hai pensato	avete pensato
pènsa	**pènsano**	ha pensato	hanno pensato
2 imperfect indicative		9 past perfect	
pensavo	pensavamo	avevo pensato	avevamo pensato
pensavi	pensavate	avevi pensato	avevate pensato
pensava	pensàvano	aveva pensato	avévano pensato
3 past absolute		10 past anterior	
pensai	pensammo	èbbi pensato	avemmo pensato
pensasti	pensaste	avesti pensato	aveste pensato
pensò	pensàrono	èbbe pensato	èbbero pensato
4 future indicative		11 future perfect	
penserò	penseremo	avrò pensato	avremo pensato
penserai	penserete	avrai pensato	avrete pensato
penserà	penseranno	avrà pensato	avranno pensato
5 present conditional		12 past conditional	
penserèi	penseremmo	avrèi pensato	avremmo pensato
penseresti	pensereste	avresti pensato	avreste pensato
penserèbbe	penserèbbero	avrèbbe pensato	avrèbbero pensato
6 present subjunctive		13 past subjunctive	
pensi	pensiamo	àbbia pensato	abbiamo pensato
pensi	pensiate	àbbia pensato	abbiate pensato
pensi	pènsino	àbbia pensato	àbbiano pensato
7 imperfect subjunctive		14 past perfect subjunctive	
pensassi	pensàssimo	avessi pensato	avéssimo pensato
pensassi	pensaste	avessi pensato	aveste pensato
pensasse	pensàssero	avesse pensato	avéssero pensato

	imperative	
—		pensiamo
pènsa (non pensare)		pensate
pènsi		**pènsino**

Words related to this verb
Penso; dunque sono.   I think; therefore I am.
Penso di no.   I think not.

Ger. **percotèndo (percuotèndo)** Past Part. **percòsso** **percuotere**

to strike, to hit, to beat

The Seven Simple Tenses		The Seven Compound Tenses	
Singular	Plural	Singular	Plural
1 present indicative		8 present perfect	
percuòto	**perc(u)otiamo**	**ho**	**abbiamo**
percuòti	**perc(u)otete**	**hai**	**avete**
percuòte	**percuòtono**	**ha**	**hanno percòsso**
2 imperfect indicative		9 past perfect	
perc(u)otevo	**perc(u)otevamo**	**avevo**	**avevamo**
perc(u)otevi	**perc(u)otevate**	**avevi**	**avevate**
perc(u)oteva	**perc(u)otévano**	**aveva**	**avévano percòsso**
3 past absolute		10 past anterior	
percòssi	**perc(u)otemmo**	**èbbi**	**avemmo**
perc(u)otesti	**perc(u)oteste**	**avesti**	**aveste**
percòsse	**percòssero**	**èbbe**	**èbbero percòsso**
4 future indicative		11 future perfect	
perc(u)oterò	**perc(u)oteremo**	**avrò**	**avremo**
perc(u)oterai	**perc(u)oterete**	**avrai**	**avrete**
perc(u)oterà	**percoteranno**	**avrà**	**avranno percòsso**
5 present conditional		12 past conditional	
perc(u)oterèi	**perc(u)oteremmo**	**avrèi**	**avremmo**
perc(u)oteresti	**perc(u)otereste**	**avresti**	**avreste**
perc(u)oterèbbe	**perc(u)oterèbbero**	**avrèbbe**	**avrèbbero percòsso**
6 present subjunctive		13 past subjunctive	
percuòta	**perc(u)otiamo**	**àbbia**	**abbiamo**
percuòta	**perc(u)otiate**	**àbbia**	**abbiate**
percuòta	**percuòtano**	**àbbia**	**àbbiano percòsso**
7 imperfect subjunctive		14 past perfect subjunctive	
perc(u)otessi	**perc(u)otéssimo**	**avessi percòsso**	**avéssimo percòsso**
perc(u)otessi	**perc(u)oteste**	**avessi percòsso**	**aveste percòsso**
perc(u)otesse	**perc(u)otéssero**	**avesse percòsso**	**avéssero percòsso**

imperative	
—	**perc(u)otiamo**
percuòti (non percuotere)	**perc(u)otiano**
percuòta	**percuòtano**

Words related to this verb
Il fulmine percosse la casa.   Lightning struck the house.
Non è bene percuotere i bambini.   It is not good to hit children.

pèrdere*   Ger. perdèndo   Past Part. perduto (pèrso)

to lose, to waste

The Seven Simple Tenses		The Seven Compound Tenses	
Singular	Plural	Singular	Plural
1 present indicative		8 present perfect	
pèrdo	perdiamo	ho perduto (pèrso)	abbiamo perduto
pèrdi	perdete	hai perduto	avete perduto
pèrde	pèrdono	ha perduto	hanno perduto
2 imperfect indicative		9 past perfect	
perdevo	perdevamo	avevo perduto	avevamo perduto
perdevi	perdevate	avevi perduto	avevate perduto
perdeva	perdévano	aveva perduto	avévano perduto
3 past absolute		10 past anterior	
pèrsi	perdemmo	èbbi perduto	avemmo perduto
perdesti	perdeste	avesti perduto	aveste perduto
pèrse	pèrsero	èbbe perduto	èbbero perduto
(Or regular: perdei (perdètti), *etc.)*			
4 future indicative		11 future perfect	
perderò	perderemo	avrò perduto	avremo perduto
perderai	perderete	avrai perduto	avrete perduto
perderà	perderanno	avrà perduto	avranno perduto
5 present conditional		12 past conditional	
perderèi	perderemmo	avrèi perduto	avremmo perduto
perderesti	perdereste	avresti perduto	avreste perduto
perderèbbe	perderèbbero	avrèbbe perduto	avrèbbero perduto
6 present subjunctive		13 past subjunctive	
pèrda	perdiamo	àbbia perduto	abbiamo perduto
pèrda	perdiate	àbbia perduto	abbiate perduto
pèrda	pèrdano	àbbia perduto	àbbiano perduto
7 imperfect subjunctive		14 past perfect subjunctive	
perdessi	perdéssimo	avessi perduto	avéssimo perduto
perdessi	perdeste	avessi perduto	aveste perduto
perdesse	perdéssero	avesse perduto	avéssero perduto

	imperative	
—	perdiamo	
pèrdi (non pèrdere)	perdete	
pèrda	pèrdano	

*The Past Absolute of *dispèrdere* is *dispèrsi*, and its Past Participle is *dispèrso*.

Words related to this verb
Spero che la madre non perda il bimbo.   I hope the mother will not lose her child.
Io ho perso tutti i soldi!   I have lost all the money!

to permit, to allow

The Seven Simple Tenses		The Seven Compound Tenses	
Singular	Plural	Singular	Plural
1 present indicative		8 present perfect	
permetto	**permettiamo**	**ho permesso**	**abbiamo permesso**
permetti	**permettete**	**hai permesso**	**avete permesso**
permette	**perméttono**	**ha permesso**	**hanno permesso**
2 imperfect indicative		9 past perfect	
permettevo	**permettevamo**	**avevo permesso**	**avevamo permesso**
permettevi	**permettevate**	**avevi permesso**	**avevate permesso**
permetteva	**permettévano**	**aveva permesso**	**avévano permesso**
3 past absolute		10 past anterior	
permisi	**permettemmo**	**èbbi permesso**	**avemmo permesso**
permettesti	**permetteste**	**avesti permesso**	**aveste permesso**
permise	**permísero**	**èbbe permesso**	**èbbero permesso**
4 future indicative		11 future perfect	
permetterò	**permetteremo**	**avrò permesso**	**avremo permesso**
permetterai	**permetterete**	**avrai permesso**	**avrete permesso**
permetterà	**permetteranno**	**avrà permesso**	**avranno permesso**
5 present conditional		12 past conditional	
permetterèi	**permetteremmo**	**avrèi permesso**	**avremmo permesso**
permetteresti	**permettereste**	**avresti permesso**	**avreste permesso**
permetterèbbe	**permetterèbbero**	**avrèbbe permesso**	**avrèbbero permesso**
6 present subjunctive		13 past subjunctive	
permetta	**permettiamo**	**àbbia permesso**	**abbiamo permesso**
permetta	**permettiate**	**àbbia permesso**	**abbiate permesso**
permetta	**perméttano**	**àbbia permesso**	**àbbiano permesso**
7 imperfect subjunctive		14 past perfect subjunctive	
permettessi	**permettéssimo**	**avessi permesso**	**avéssimo permesso**
permettessi	**permetteste**	**avessi permesso**	**aveste permesso**
permettesse	**permettéssero**	**avesse permesso**	**avéssero permesso**

imperative

—	**permettiamo**
permetti (non perméttere)	**permettete**
permetta	**perméttano**

Words related to this verb
Mi permetti di entrare?   Will you permit me to enter?
Lei non permette queste sciocchezze.   She does not permit this nonsense.

persuadere*		Ger. **persuadèndo**	Past Part. **persuaso**

to persuade

The Seven Simple Tenses		The Seven Compound Tenses	

Singular	Plural	Singular	Plural
1 present indicative		8 present perfect	
persuado	**persuadiamo**	**ho persuaso**	**abbiamo persuaso**
persuadi	**persuadete**	**hai persuaso**	**avete persuaso**
persuade	**persuàdono**	**ha persuaso**	**hanno persuaso**
2 imperfect indicative		9 past perfect	
persuadevo	**persuadevamo**	**avevo persuaso**	**avevamo persuaso**
persuadevi	**persuadevate**	**avevi persuaso**	**avevate persuaso**
persuadeva	**persuadévano**	**aveva persuaso**	**avévano persuaso**
3 past absolute		10 past anterior	
persuasi	**persuademmo**	**èbbi persuaso**	**avemmo persuaso**
persuadesti	**persuadeste**	**avesti persuaso**	**aveste persuaso**
persuase	**persuàsero**	**èbbe persuaso**	**èbbero persuaso**
4 future indicative		11 future perfect	
persuaderò	**persuaderemo**	**avrò persuaso**	**avremo persuaso**
persuaderai	**persuaderete**	**avrai persuaso**	**avrete persuaso**
persuaderà	**persuaderanno**	**avrà persuaso**	**avranno persuaso**
5 present conditional		12 past conditional	
persuaderèi	**persuaderemmo**	**avrèi persuaso**	**avremmo persuaso**
persuaderesti	**persuadereste**	**avresti persuaso**	**avreste persuaso**
persuaderèbbe	**persuaderèbbero**	**avrèbbe persuaso**	**avrèbbero persuaso**
6 present subjunctive		13 past subjunctive	
persuada	**persuadiamo**	**àbbia persuaso**	**abbiamo persuaso**
persuada	**persuadiate**	**àbbia persuaso**	**abbiate persuaso**
persuada	**persuàdano**	**àbbia persuaso**	**àbbiano persuaso**
7 imperfect subjunctive		14 past perfect subjunctive	
persuadessi	**persuadéssimo**	**avessi persuaso**	**avéssimo persuaso**
persuadessi	**persuadeste**	**avessi persuaso**	**aveste persuaso**
persuadesse	**persuadéssero**	**avesse persuaso**	**avéssero persuaso**

imperative

—	**persuadiamo**
persuadi (non **persuadere**)	**persuadete**
persuada	**persuàdano**

* Like *persuadere* is *dissuadere*.

Words related to this verb
Io lo persuado di venire con me. I persuade him to come with me.
Persuadi a Maria di venire al concerto. Persuade Mary to come to the concert.

Ger. piacèndo   Past Part. piaciuto   piacere*

to please, to like

The Seven Simple Tenses		The Seven Compound Tenses	
Singular	Plural	Singular	Plural
1 present indicative		8 present perfect	
piaccio	piacciamo (piaciamo)	sono piaciuto	siamo piaciuti
piaci	piacete	sèi piaciuto	sièti piaciuti
piace	piàcciono	è piaciuto	sono piaciuti
2 imperfect indicative		9 past perfect	
piacevo	piacevamo	èro piaciuto	eravamo piaciuti
piacevi	piacevate	èri piaciuto	eravate piaciuti
piaceva	piacévano	èra piaciuto	èrano piaciuti
3 past absolute		10 past anterior	
piacqui	piacemmo	fui piaciuto	fummo piaciuti
piacesti	piaceste	fosti piaciuto	foste piaciuti
piacque	piàcquero	fu piaciuto	fúrono piaciuti
4 future indicative		11 future perfect	
piacerò	piaceremo	sarò piaciuto	saremo piaciuti
piacerai	piacerete	sarai piaciuto	sarete piaciuti
piacerà	piaceranno	sarà piaciuto	saranno piaciuti
5 present conditional		12 past conditional	
piacerèi	piaceremmo	sarèi piaciuto	saremmo piaciuti
piaceresti	piacereste	saresti piaciuto	sareste piaciuti
piacerèbbe	piacerèbbero	sarèbbe piaciuto	sarèbbero piaciuti
6 present subjunctive		13 past subjunctive	
piaccia	piacciamo (piaciamo)	sia piaciuto	siamo piaciuti
piaccia	piacciate (piaciate)	sia piaciuto	piaciuti
piaccia	piàcciano	sia piaciuto	síano piaciuti
7 imperfect subjunctive		14 past perfect subjunctive	
piacessi	piacéssimo	fossi piaciuto	fóssimo piaciuti
piacessi	piaceste	fossi piaciuto	foste piaciuti
piacesse	piacéssero	fosse piaciuto	fóssero piaciuti

imperative

—	piacciamo (piaciamo)
piaci (non piacere)	piacete
piaccia	piàcciano

* Like *piacere* are *compiacere* (conjugated with *avere*), *dispiacere*, and *spiacere*.

Words related to this verb
Ti piace leggere?   Do you like to read?
Non mi è piaciuto quel pranzo.   I did not like that meal.

181

to weep, to cry

The Seven Simple Tenses		The Seven Compound Tenses	
Singular	Plural	Singular	Plural
1 present indicative		8 present perfect	
piango	piangiamo	ho pianto	abbiamo pianto
piangi	piangete	hai pianto	avete pianto
piange	piàngono	ha pianto	hanno pianto
2 imperfect indicative		9 past perfect	
piangevo	piangevamo	avevo pianto	avevamo pianto
piangevi	piangevate	avevi pianto	avevate pianto
piangeva	piangévano	aveva pianto	avévano pianto
3 past absolute		10 past anterior	
piansi	piangemmo	èbbi pianto	avemmo pianto
piangesti	piangeste	avesti pianto	aveste pianto
pianse	piànsero	èbbe pianto	èbbero pianto
4 future indicative		11 future perfect	
piangerò	piangeremo	avrò pianto	avremo pianto
piangerai	piangerete	avrai pianto	avrete pianto
piangerà	piangeranno	avrà pianto	avranno pianto
5 present conditional		12 past conditional	
piangerèi	piangeremmo	avrèi pianto	avremmo pianto
piangeresti	piangereste	avresti pianto	avreste pianto
piangerèbbe	piangerèbbero	avrèbbe pianto	avrèbbero pianto
6 present subjunctive		13 past subjunctive	
pianga	piangiamo	àbbia pianto	abbiamo pianto
pianga	piangiate	àbbia pianto	abbiate pianto
pianga	piàngano	àbbia pianto	àbbiano pianto
7 imperfect subjunctive		14 past perfect subjunctive	
piangessi	piangéssimo	avessi pianto	avéssimo pianto
piangessi	piangeste	avessi pianto	aveste pianto
piangesse	piangéssero	avesse pianto	avéssero pianto

imperative	
—	piangiamo
piangi (non piàngere)	piangete
pianga	piàngano

Words related to this verb
Mio figlio ha pianto tutta la notte.   My son cried all night.
Lei non piange mai.   She never cries.

182

to rain

The Seven Simple Tenses		The Seven Compound Tenses	
Singular	Plural	Singular	Plural
1 present indicative		8 present perfect	
piòve	**piòvono**	**è* piovuto**	**sono piovuti**
2 imperfect indicative		9 past perfect	
pioveva	**piovévano**	**èra piovuto**	**èrano piovuti**
3 past absolute		10 past anterior	
piòvve	**piòvvero**	**fu piovuto**	**fúrono piovuti**
4 future indicative		11 future perfect	
pioverà	**pioveranno**	**sarà piovuto**	**saranno piovuti**
5 present conditional		12 past conditional	
pioverèbbe	**pioverèbbero**	**sarèbbe piovuto**	**sarèbbero piovuti**
6 present subjunctive		13 past subjunctive	
piòva	**piòvano**	**sia piovuto**	**síano piovuti**
7 imperfect subjunctive		14 past perfect subjunctive	
piovesse	**piovéssero**	**fosse piovuto**	**fóssero piovuti**

imperative

* *Piòvere* may be conjugated with *avere*.

Words related to this verb
Nel deserto non piove spesso.   It does not rain often in the desert.
Quest'anno è piovuto molto.   This year it has rained a great deal.

to hand, to offer, to hold out

The Seven Simple Tenses		The Seven Compound Tenses	
Singular	Plural	Singular	Plural
1 present indicative		8 present perfect	
pòrgo	**porgiamo**	**ho pòrto**	**abbiamo pòrto**
pòrgi	**porgete**	**hai pòrto**	**avete pòrto**
pòrge	**pòrgono**	**ha pòrto**	**hanno pòrto**
2 imperfect indicative		9 past perfect	
porgevo	**porgevamo**	**avevo pòrto**	**avevamo pòrto**
porgevi	**porgevate**	**avevi pòrto**	**avevate pòrto**
porgeva	**porgévano**	**aveva pòrto**	**avévano pòrto**
3 past absolute		10 past anterior	
pòrsi	**porgemmo**	**èbbi pòrto**	**avemmo pòrto**
porgesti	**porgeste**	**avesti pòrto**	**aveste pòrto**
pòrse	**pòrsero**	**èbbe pòrto**	**èbbero pòrto**
4 future indicative		11 future perfect	
porgerò	**porgeremo**	**avrò pòrto**	**avremo pòrto**
porgerai	**porgerete**	**avrai pòrto**	**avrete pòrto**
porgerà	**porgeranno**	**avrà pòrto**	**avranno pòrto**
5 present conditional		12 past conditional	
porgerèi	**porgeremmo**	**avrèi pòrto**	**avremmo pòrto**
porgeresti	**porgereste**	**avresti pòrto**	**avreste pòrto**
porgerèbbe	**porgerèbbero**	**avrèbbe pòrto**	**avrèbbero pòrto**
6 present subjunctive		13 past subjunctive	
pòrga	**porgiamo**	**àbbia pòrto**	**abbiamo pòrto**
pòrga	**porgiate**	**àbbia pòrto**	**abbiate pòrto**
pòrga	**pòrgano**	**àbbia pòrto**	**àbbiano pòrto**
7 imperfect subjunctive		14 past perfect subjunctive	
porgessi	**porgéssimo**	**avessi pòrto**	**avéssimo pòrto**
porgessi	**porgeste**	**avessi pòrto**	**aveste pòrto**
porgesse	**porgéssero**	**avesse pòrto**	**avéssero pòrto**

	imperative	
—		**porgiamo**
pòrgi (non pòrgere)		**porgete**
pòrga		**pòrgano**

Words related to this verb

Lui mi porse il bicchiere.   He handed me the glass.
Mi porse la mano.   He offered me his hand.

to put, to place, to set

The Seven Simple Tenses		The Seven Compound Tenses	
Singular	Plural	Singular	Plural
1 present indicative		8 present perfect	
pongo	**poniamo**	**ho posto**	**abbiamo posto**
poni	**ponete**	**hai posto**	**avete posto**
pone	**póngono**	**ha posto**	**hanno posto**
2 imperfect indicative		9 past perfect	
ponevo	**ponevamo**	**avevo posto**	**avevamo posto**
ponevi	**ponevate**	**avevi posto**	**avevate posto**
poneva	**ponévano**	**aveva posto**	**avévano posto**
3 past absolute		10 past anterior	
posi	**ponemmo**	**èbbi posto**	**avemmo posto**
ponesti	**poneste**	**avesti posto**	**aveste posto**
pose	**pósero**	**èbbe posto**	**èbbero posto**
4 future indicative		11 future perfect	
porrò	**porremo**	**avrò posto**	**avremo posto**
porrai	**porrete**	**avrai posto**	**avrete posto**
porrà	**porranno**	**avrà posto**	**avranno posto**
5 present conditional		12 past conditional	
porrèi	**porremmo**	**avrèi posto**	**avremmo posto**
porresti	**porreste**	**avresti posto**	**avreste posto**
porrèbbe	**porrèbbero**	**avrèbbe posto**	**avrèbbero posto**
6 present subjunctive		13 past subjunctive	
ponga	**poniamo**	**àbbia posto**	**abbiamo posto**
ponga	**poniate**	**àbbia posto**	**abbiate posto**
ponga	**póngano**	**àbbia posto**	**àbbiano posto**
7 imperfect subjunctive		14 past perfect subjunctive	
ponessi	**ponéssimo**	**avessi posto**	**avéssimo posto**
ponessi	**poneste**	**avessi posto**	**aveste posto**
ponesse	**ponéssero**	**avesse posto**	**avéssero posto**

imperative

	poniamo
poni (non **porre**)	**ponete**
ponga	**póngano**

* Like *porre* are *comporre*, *disporre*, *esporre*, *frapporre*, *imporre*, *opporre*, *posporre*, *proporre*, *riporre*, *scomporre*, *supporre*, *trasporre*, etc.

Words related to this verb
Lui ha posto il libro sullo scaffale.   He put the book on the shelf.
Mi hai posto(a) in una cattiva situazione.   You have placed me in a bad situation.

portare   Ger. **portando**   Past Part. **portato**

to bring, to carry; to wear

The Seven Simple Tenses		The Seven Compound Tenses	
Singular	Plural	Singular	Plural
1 present indicative		8 present perfect	
pòrto	portiamo	ho portato	abbiamo portato
pòrti	portate	hai portata	avete portato
pòrta	pòrtano	ha portato	hanno portato
2 imperfect indicative		9 past perfect	
portavo	portavamo	avevo portato	avevamo portato
portavi	portavate	avevi portato	avevate portato
portava	portàvano	aveva portato	avévano portato
3 past absolute		10 past anterior	
portai	portammo	èbbi portato	avemmo portato
portasti	portaste	avesti portato	aveste portato
portò	portàrono	èbbe portato	èbbero portato
4 future indicative		11 future perfect	
porterò	porteremo	avrò portato	avremo portato
porterai	porterete	avrai portato	avrete portato
porterà	porteranno	avrà portato	avranno portato
5 present conditional		12 past conditional	
porterèi	porteremmo	avrèi portato	avremmo portato
porteresti	portereste	avresti portato	avreste portato
porterèbbe	porterèbbero	avrèbbe portato	avrèbbero portato
6 present subjunctive		13 past subjunctive	
pòrti	portiamo	àbbia portato	abbiamo portato
pòrti	portiate	àbbia portato	abbiate portato
pòrti	pòrtino	àbbia portato	àbbiano portato
7 imperfect subjunctive		14 past perfect subjunctive	
portassi	portàssimo	avessi portato	avéssimo portato
portassi	portaste	avessi portato	aveste portato
portasse	portàssero	avesse portato	avéssero portato

	imperative	
—		portiamo
pòrta (non portare)		portate
pòrti		pòrtino

Words related to this verb

Io porto un abito nuovo.   I am wearing a new suit.
Tu porti molti libri oggi.   You are carrying many books today.

to possess

The Seven Simple Tenses		The Seven Compound Tenses	
Singular	Plural	Singular	Plural
1 present indicative		8 present perfect	
possièdo (possèggo)	possediamo	ho posseduto	abbiamo posseduto
possièdi	possedete	hai posseduto	avete posseduto
possiède	possièdono	ha posseduto	hanno posseduto
	(possèggono)		
2 imperfect indicative		9 past perfect	
possedevo	possedevamo	avevo posseduto	avevamo posseduto
possedevi	possedevate	avevi posseduto	avevate posseduto
possedeva	possedévano	aveva posseduto	avévano posseduto
3 past absolute		10 past anterior	
possedètti	possedemmo	èbbi posseduto	avemmo posseduto
possedesti	possedeste	avesti posseduto	aveste posseduto
possedètte	possedèttero	èbbe posseduto	èbbero posseduto
4 future indicative		11 future perfect	
possederò	possederemo	avrò posseduto	avremo posseduto
possederai	possederete	avrai posseduto	avrete posseduto
possederà	possederanno	avrà posseduto	avranno posseduto
5 present conditional		12 past conditional	
possederèi	possederemmo	avrèi posseduto	avremmo posseduto
possederesti	possedereste	avresti posseduto	avreste posseduto
possederèbbe	possederèbbero	avrèbbe posseduto	avrèbbero posseduto
6 present subjunctive		13 past subjunctive	
possièda (possègga)	possediamo	àbbia posseduto	abbiamo posseduto
possièda (possègga)	possediate	àbbia posseduto	abbiate posseduto
possièda (possègga)	possièdano	àbbia posseduto	àbbiano posseduto
	(possèggano)		
7 imperfect subjunctive		14 past perfect subjunctive	
possedessi	possedéssimo	avessi posseduto	avéssimo posseduto
possedessi	possedeste	avessi posseduto	aveste posseduto
possedesse	possedéssero	avesse posseduto	avéssero posseduto

	imperative	
—	possediamo	
possièdi (non possedere)	possedete	
possièda (possègga)	possièdano (possèggano)	

Words related to this verb
Possiede una buona memoria.   He has a good memory.
Non possediamo molto denaro.   We do not possess much money.

potere	Ger. potèndo	Past Part. potuto

to be able, can, may

The Seven Simple Tenses		The Seven Compound Tenses	
Singular	Plural	Singular	Plural
1 present indicative		8 present perfect	
pòsso	possiamo	ho* potuto	abbiamo potuto
puòi	potete	hai potuto	avete potuto
può	pòssono	ha potuto	hanno potuto
2 imperfect indicative		9 past perfect	
potevo	potevamo	avevo potuto	avevamo potuto
potevi	potevate	avevi potuto	avevate potuto
poteva	potévano	aveva potuto	avévano potuto
3 past absolute		10 past anterior	
potei	potemmo	èbbi potuto	avemmo potuto
potesti	poteste	avesti potuto	aveste potuto
poté	potérono	èbbe potuto	èbbero potuto
4 future indicative		11 future perfect	
potró	potremo	avrò potuto	avremo potuto
potrai	potrete	avrai potuto	avrete potuto
potrà	potranno	avrà potuto	avranno potuto
5 present conditional		12 past conditional	
potrèi	potremmo	avrèi potuto	avremmo potuto
potresti	potreste	avresti potuto	avreste potuto
potrèbbe	potrèbbero	avrèbbe potuto	avrèbbero potuto
6 present subjunctive		13 past subjunctive	
pòssa	possiamo	àbbia potuto	abbiamo potuto
pòssa	possiate	àbbia potuto	abbiate potuto
pòssa	pòssano	àbbia potuto	àbbiano potuto
7 imperfect subjunctive		14 past perfect subjunctive	
potessi	potéssimo	avessi potuto	avéssimo potuto
potessi	poteste	avessi potuto	aveste potuto
potesse	potéssero	avesse potuto	avéssero potuto
		imperative	

* Potere takes èssere when the following infinitive requires it.

Words related to this verb
Non posso venire oggi. I cannot come today.
Puoi scrivere tu se vuoi. You can write if you want to.

to predict

The Seven Simple Tenses		The Seven Compound Tenses	
Singular	Plural	Singular	Plural
1 present indicative		8 present perfect	
predico	prediciamo	ho predetto	abbiamo predetto
predici	predite	hai predetto	avete predetto
predice	predicono	ha predetto	hanno predetto
2 imperfect indicative		9 past perfect	
predicevo	predicevamo	avevo predetto	avevamo predetto
predicevi	predicevate	avevi predetto	avevate predetto
prediceva	predicévano	aveva predetto	avévano predetto
3 past absolute		10 past anterior	
predissi	predicemmo	èbbi predetto	avemmo predetto
predicesti	prediceste	avesti predetto	aveste predetto
predisse	predíssero	èbbe predetto	èbbero predetto
4 future indicative		11 future perfect	
predirò	prediremo	avrò predetto	avremo predetto
predirai	predirete	avrai predetto	avrete predetto
predirà	prediranno	avrà predetto	avranno predetto
5 present conditional		12 past conditional	
predirèi	prediremmo	avrèi predetto	avremmo predetto
prediresti	predireste	avresti predetto	avreste predetto
predirèbbe	predirèbbero	avrèbbe predetto	avrèbbero predetto
6 present subjunctive		13 past subjunctive	
predica	prediciamo	àbbia predetto	abbiamo predetto
predica	prediciate	àbbia predetto	abbiate predetto
predica	predícano	àbbia predetto	àbbiano predetto
7 imperfect subjunctive		14 past perfect subjunctive	
predicessi	predicéssimo	avessi predetto	avéssimo predetto
predicessi	prediceste	avessi predetto	aveste predetto
predicesse	predicéssero	avesse predetto	avéssero predetto

	imperative	
—		prediciamo
predici (non predire)		predite
predica		predícano

Words related to this verb
Lei predice il futuro.   She predicts the future.
Lui predice che io vincerò.   He predicts that I will win.

prèmere*   Ger. **premèndo**   Past Part. **premuto**

to press, to squeeze; to be urgent

The Seven Simple Tenses		The Seven Compound Tenses	
Singular	Plural	Singular	Plural
1 present indicative		8 present perfect	
prèmo	**premiamo**	**ho premuto**	**abbiamo premuto**
prèmi	**premete**	**hai premuto**	**avete premuto**
prème	**prèmono**	**ha premuto**	**hanno premuto**
2 imperfect indicative		9 past perfect	
premevo	**premevamo**	**avevo premuto**	**avevamo premuto**
premevi	**premevate**	**avevi premuto**	**avevate premuto**
premeva	**premévano**	**aveva premuto**	**avévano premuto**
3 past absolute		10 past anterior	
premei (premètti)	**prememmo**	**èbbi premuto**	**avemmo premuto**
premesti	**premeste**	**avesti premuto**	**aveste premuto**
premé (premètte)	**premérono**	**èbbe premuto**	**èbbero premuto**
	(premèttero)		
4 future indicative		11 future perfect	
premerò	**premeremo**	**avrò premuto**	**avremo premuto**
premerai	**premerete**	**avrai premuto**	**avrete premuto**
premerà	**premeranno**	**avrà premuto**	**avranno premuto**
5 present conditional		12 past conditional	
premerèi	**premeremmo**	**avrèi premuto**	**avremmo premuto**
premeresti	**premereste**	**avresti premuto**	**avreste premuto**
premerèbbe	**premerèbbero**	**avrèbbe premuto**	**avrèbbero premuto**
6 present subjunctive		13 past subjunctive	
prèma	**premiamo**	**àbbia premuto**	**abbiamo premuto**
prèma	**premiate**	**àbbia premuto**	**abbiate premuto**
prèma	**prèmano**	**àbbia premuto**	**àbbiano premuto**
7 imperfect subjunctive		14 past perfect subjunctive	
premessi	**preméssimo**	**avessi premuto**	**avéssimo premuto**
premessi	**premeste**	**avessi premuto**	**aveste premuto**
premesse	**preméssero**	**avesse premuto**	**avéssero premuto**

imperative	
—	**premiamo**
prèmi (non prèmere)	**premete**
prèma	**prèmano**

* The compounds of *prèmere* are *comprímere*, *deprímere*, *esprímere*, *imprímere*, *opprímere*, *reprímere*, *sopprímere*, all irregular in the Past Absolute and Past Participle, and the regular *sprèmere*.

Words related to this verb
Lui mi preme la mano.   He squeezes my hand.
Io premo il bottone.   I press the button.
Questo problema preme a molta gente.   This problem is urgent for many people.

Ger. prendèndo   Past Part. preso   prèndere*

to take

The Seven Simple Tenses		The Seven Compound Tenses	
Singular	Plural	Singular	Plural
1 present indicative		8 present perfect	
prèndo	prendiamo	ho preso	abbiamo preso
prèndi	prendete	hai preso	avete preso
prènde	prèndono	ha preso	hanno preso
2 imperfect indicative		9 past perfect	
prendevo	prendevamo	avevo preso	avevamo preso
prendevi	prendevate	avevi preso	avevate preso
prendeva	prendévano	aveva preso	avévano preso
3 past absolute		10 past anterior	
presi	prendemmo	èbbi preso	avemmo preso
prendesti	prendeste	avesti preso	aveste preso
prese	présero	èbbe preso	èbbero preso
4 future indicative		11 future perfect	
prenderò	prenderemo	avrò preso	avremo preso
prenderai	prenderete	avrai preso	avrete preso
prenderà	prenderanno	avrà preso	avranno preso
5 present conditional		12 past conditional	
prenderèi	prenderemmo	avrèi preso	avremmo preso
prenderesti	prendereste	avresti preso	avreste preso
prenderèbbe	prenderèbbero	avrèbbe preso	avrèbbero preso
6 present subjunctive		13 past subjunctive	
prènda	prendiamo	àbbia preso	abbiamo preso
prènda	prendiate	àbbia preso	abbiate preso
prènda	prèndano	àbbia preso	àbbiano preso
7 imperfect subjunctive		14 past perfect subjunctive	
prendessi	prendéssimo	avessi preso	avéssimo preso
prendessi	prendeste	avessi preso	aveste preso
prendesse	prendéssero	avesse preso	avéssero preso

imperative

—	prendiamo
prèndi (non prèndere)	prendete
prènda	prèndano

* Like *prèndere* are *apprèndere, comprèndere, intraprèndere, riprèndere, sorprèndere,* etc.

Words related to this verb
Non prendo più il caffè.   I don't take coffee any more.
Lui prende la medicina.   He takes the medicine.

preparare   Ger. **preparando**   Past Part. **preparato**

to prepare

The Seven Simple Tenses		The Seven Compound Tenses	
Singular	Plural	Singular	Plural
1 present indicative		8 present perfect	
prepàro	**prepariamo**	**ho preparato**	**abbiamo preparato**
prepàri	**preparate**	**hai preparato**	**avete preparato**
prepàra	**prepàrano**	**ha preparato**	**hanno preparato**
2 imperfect indicative		9 past perfect	
preparavo	**preparavamo**	**avevo preparato**	**avevamo preparato**
preparavi	**preparavate**	**avevi preparato**	**avevate preparato**
preparava	**preparavano**	**aveva preparato**	**avévano preparato**
3 past absolute		10 past anterior	
preparai	**preparammo**	**èbbi preparato**	**avemmo preparato**
preparasti	**preparaste**	**avesti preparato**	**aveste preparato**
preparò	**preparàrono**	**èbbe preparato**	**èbbero preparato**
4 future indicative		11 future perfect	
preparerò	**prepareremo**	**avrò preparato**	**avremo preparato**
preparerai	**preparerete**	**avrai preparato**	**avrete preparato**
preparerà	**prepareranno**	**avrà preparato**	**avranno preparato**
5 present conditional		12 past conditional	
preparerèi	**prepareremmo**	**avrèi preparato**	**avremmo preparato**
prepareresti	**preparereste**	**avresti preparato**	**avreste preparato**
preparerèbbe	**preparerèbbero**	**avrèbbe preparato**	**avrèbbero preparato**
6 present subjunctive		13 past subjunctive	
prepàri	**prepariamo**	**àbbia preparato**	**abbiamo preparato**
prepàri	**prepariate**	**àbbia preparato**	**abbiate preparato**
prepàri	**prepàrino**	**àbbia preparato**	**àbbiano preparato**
7 imperfect subjunctive		14 past perfect subjunctive	
preparassi	**preparàssimo**	**avessi preparato**	**avéssimo preparato**
preparassi	**preparaste**	**avessi preparato**	**aveste preparato**
preparasse	**preparàssero**	**avesse preparato**	**avéssero preparato**

	imperative	
—		**prepariamo**
prepàra (non **preparare**)		**preparate**
prepàri		**prepàrino**

Words related to this verb
Lo preparai a una cattiva notizia.   I prepared him for bad news.
La studentessa deve preparare la lezione.   The student must prepare the lesson.

to present, to introduce

The Seven Simple Tenses		The Seven Compound Tenses	
Singular	Plural	Singular	Plural
1 present indicative		8 present perfect	
presento	**presentiamo**	**ho presentato**	**abbiamo presentato**
presenti	**presentate**	**hai presentato**	**avete presentato**
presenta	**presentano**	**ha presentato**	**hanno presentato**
2 imperfect indicative		9 past perfect	
presentavo	**presentavamo**	**avevo presentato**	**avevamo presentato**
presentavi	**presentavate**	**avevi presentato**	**avevate presentato**
presentava	**presentàvano**	**aveva presentato**	**avévano presentato**
3 past absolute		10 past anterior	
presentai	**presentammo**	**èbbi presentato**	**avemmo presentato**
presentasti	**presentaste**	**avesti presentato**	**aveste presentato**
presentò	**presentàrono**	**èbbe presentato**	**èbbero presentato**
4 future indicative		11 future perfect	
presenterò	**presenteremo**	**avrò presentato**	**avremo presentato**
presenterai	**presenterete**	**avrai presentato**	**avrete presentato**
presenterà	**presenteranno**	**avrà presentato**	**avranno presentato**
5 present conditional		12 past conditional	
presenterèi	**presenteremmo**	**avrèi presentato**	**avremmo presentato**
presenteresti	**presentereste**	**avresti presentato**	**avreste presentato**
presenterèbbe	**presenterèbbero**	**avrèbbe presentato**	**avrèbbero presentato**
6 present subjunctive		13 past subjunctive	
presenti	**presentiamo**	**àbbia presentato**	**abbiamo presentato**
presenti	**presentiate**	**àbbia presentato**	**abbiate presentato**
presenti	**presentino**	**àbbia presentato**	**àbbiano presentato**
7 imperfect subjunctive		14 past perfect subjunctive	
presentassi	**presentàssimo**	**avessi presentato**	**avéssimo presentato**
presentassi	**presentaste**	**avessi presentato**	**aveste presentato**
presentasse	**presentàssero**	**avesse presentato**	**avéssero presentato**

	imperative	
—		**presentiamo**
presenta (non **presentare**)		**presentate**
presenti		**presentino**

Words related to this verb

Ti ho presentato Maria ieri.   I introduced Mary to you yesterday.
Presentammo i compiti al maestro.   We presented the assignments to the teacher.

prestare   Ger. **prestando**   Past Part. **prestato**

to lend

The Seven Simple Tenses		The Seven Compound Tenses	
Singular	Plural	Singular	Plural
1 present indicative		8 present perfect	
prèsto	**prestiamo**	**ho prestato**	**abbiamo prestato**
prèsti	**prestate**	**hai prestato**	**avete prestato**
prèsta	**prèstano**	**ha prestato**	**hanno prestato**
2 imperfect indicative		9 past perfect	
prestavo	**prestavamo**	**avevo prestato**	**avevamo prestato**
prestavi	**prestavate**	**avevi prestato**	**avevate prestato**
prestava	**prestàvano**	**aveva prestato**	**avévano prestato**
3 past absolute		10 past anterior	
prestai	**prestammo**	**èbbi prestato**	**avemmo prestato**
prestasti	**prestaste**	**avesti prestato**	**aveste prestato**
prestò	**prestàrono**	**èbbe prestato**	**èbbero prestato**
4 future indicative		11 future perfect	
presterò	**presteremo**	**avrò prestato**	**avremo prestato**
presterai	**presterete**	**avrai prestato**	**avrete prestato**
presterà	**presteranno**	**avrà prestato**	**avranno prestato**
5 present conditional		12 past conditional	
presterèi	**presteremmo**	**avrèi prestato**	**avremmo prestato**
presteresti	**prestereste**	**avresti prestato**	**avreste prestato**
presterèbbe	**presterèbbero**	**avrèbbe prestato**	**avrèbbero prestato**
6 present subjunctive		13 past subjunctive	
prèsti	**prestiamo**	**àbbia prestato**	**abbiamo prestato**
prèsti	**prestiate**	**àbbia prestato**	**abbiate prestato**
prèsti	**prèstino**	**àbbia prestato**	**àbbiano prestato**
7 imperfect subjunctive		14 past perfect subjunctive	
prestassi	**prestàssimo**	**avessi prestato**	**avéssimo prestato**
prestassi	**prestaste**	**avessi prestato**	**aveste prestato**
prestasse	**prestàssero**	**avesse prestato**	**avéssero prestato**

	imperative	
—		**prestiamo**
prèsta (non prestare)		**prestate**
prèsti		**prèstino**

Words related to this verb
Io non presto soldi a nessuno.   I do not lend money to anyone.
Prestami il libro, per piacere.   Lend me the book, please.

to claim, to contend, to pretend; to demand

The Seven Simple Tenses		The Seven Compound Tenses	
Singular	Plural	Singular	Plural

1 present indicative		8 present perfect	
pretèndo	pretendiamo	ho preteso	abbiamo preteso
pretèndi	pretendete	hai preteso	avete preteso
pretènde	pretèndono	ha preteso	hanno preteso

2 imperfect indicative		9 past perfect	
pretendevo	pretendevamo	avevo preteso	avevamo preteso
pretendevi	pretendevate	avevi preteso	avevate preteso
pretendeva	pretendévano	aveva preteso	avévano preteso

3 past absolute		10 past anterior	
pretesi	pretendemmo	èbbi preteso	avemmo preteso
pretendesti	pretendeste	avesti preteso	aveste preteso
pretese	pretésero	èbbe preteso	èbbero preteso

4 future indicative		11 future perfect	
pretenderò	pretenderemo	avrò preteso	avremo preteso
pretenderai	pretenderete	avrai preteso	avrete preteso
pretenderà	pretenderanno	avrà preteso	avranno preteso

5 present conditional		12 past conditional	
pretenderèi	pretenderemmo	avrèi preteso	avremmo preteso
pretenderesti	pretendereste	avresti preteso	avreste preteso
pretenderèbbe	pretenderèbbero	avrèbbe preteso	avrèbbero preteso

6 present subjunctive		13 past subjunctive	
pretènda	pretendiamo	àbbia preteso	abbiamo preteso
pretènda	pretendiate	àbbia preteso	abbiate preteso
pretènda	pretèndano	àbbia preteso	àbbiano preteso

7 imperfect subjunctive		14 past perfect subjunctive	
pretendessi	pretendéssimo	avessi preteso	avéssimo preteso
pretendessi	pretendeste	avessi preteso	aveste preteso
pretendesse	pretendéssero	avesse preteso	avéssero preteso

imperative	
—	pretendiamo
pretèndi (non pretèndere)	pretendete
pretènda	pretèndano

Words related to this verb
Lui pretende essere malato.   He is pretending to be ill.
L'uomo pretende mille dollari da me.   The man demands one thousand dollars from me.

to prevail

The Seven Simple Tenses		The Seven Compound Tenses	
Singular	Plural	Singular	Plural
1 present indicative		8 present perfect	
prevalgo	**prevaliamo**	**ho* prevalso**	**abbiamo prevalso**
prevali	**prevalete**	**hai prevalso**	**avete prevalso**
prevale	**prevàlgono**	**ha prevalso**	**hanno prevalso**
2 imperfect indicative		9 past perfect	
prevalevo	**prevalevamo**	**avevo prevalso**	**avevamo prevalso**
prevalevi	**prevalevate**	**avevi prevalso**	**avevate prevalso**
prevaleva	**prevalévano**	**aveva prevalso**	**avévano prevalso**
3 past absolute		10 past anterior	
prevalsi	**prevalemmo**	**èbbi prevalso**	**avemmo prevalso**
prevalesti	**prevaleste**	**avesti prevalso**	**aveste prevalso**
prevalse	**prevàlsero**	**èbbe prevalso**	**èbbero prevalso**
4 future indicative		11 future perfect	
prevarrò	**prevarremo**	**avrò prevalso**	**avremo prevalso**
prevarrai	**prevarrete**	**avrai prevalso**	**avrete prevalso**
prevarrà	**prevarranno**	**avrà prevalso**	**avranno prevalso**
5 present conditional		12 past conditional	
prevarrèi	**prevarremmo**	**avrèi prevalso**	**avremmo prevalso**
prevarresti	**prevarreste**	**avresti prevalso**	**avreste prevalso**
prevarrèbbe	**prevarrèbbero**	**avrèbbe prevalso**	**avrèbbero prevalso**
6 present subjunctive		13 past subjunctive	
prevalga	**prevaliamo**	**àbbia prevalso**	**abbiamo prevalso**
prevalga	**prevaliate**	**àbbia prevalso**	**abbiate prevalso**
prevalga	**prevàlgano**	**àbbia prevalso**	**àbbiano prevalso**
7 imperfect subjunctive		14 past perfect subjunctive	
prevalessi	**prevaléssimo**	**avessi prevalso**	**avéssimo prevalso**
prevalessi	**prevaleste**	**avessi prevalso**	**aveste prevalso**
prevalesse	**prevaléssero**	**avesse prevalso**	**avéssero prevalso**

	imperative	
—		**prevaliamo**
prevali (non prevalere)		**prevalete**
prevalga		**prevàlgano**

* *Prevalere* may be conjugated with *èssere*.

Words related to this verb

La sua opinione prevalse.   His opinion prevailed.
Lui prevale su di tutti.   He prevails over everyone.

Ger. **prevedèndo**   Past Part. **preveduto (previsto)**   **prevedere**

to foresee

The Seven Simple Tenses		The Seven Compound Tenses	
Singular	Plural	Singular	Plural
1 present indicative		8 present perfect	
prevedo	**prevediamo**	**ho preveduto**	**abbiamo preveduto**
(preveggo)		**(previsto)**	
prevedi	**prevedete**	**hai preveduto**	**avete preveduto**
prevede	**prevédono**	**ha preveduto**	**hanno preveduto**
	(prevéggono)		
2 imperfect indicative		9 past perfect	
prevedevo	**prevedevamo**	**avevo preveduto**	**avevamo preveduto**
prevedevi	**prevedevate**	**avevi preveduto**	**avevate preveduto**
prevedeva	**prevedévano**	**aveva preveduto**	**avévano preveduto**
3 past absolute		10 past anterior	
previdi	**prevedemmo**	**èbbi preveduto**	**avemmo preveduto**
prevedesti	**prevedeste**	**avesti preveduto**	**aveste preveduto**
previde	**prevídero**	**èbbe preveduto**	**èbbero preveduto**
4 future indicative		11 future perfect	
prevederò	**prevederemo**	**avrò preveduto**	**avremo preveduto**
prevederai	**prevederete**	**avrai preveduto**	**avrete preveduto**
prevederà	**prevederanno**	**avrà preveduto**	**avranno preveduto**
5 present conditional		12 past conditional	
prevederèi	**prevederemmo**	**avrèi preveduto**	**avremmo preveduto**
prevederesti	**prevedereste**	**avresti preveduto**	**avreste preveduto**
prevederèbbe	**prevederèbbero**	**avrèbbe preveduto**	**avrèbbero preveduto**
6 present subjunctive		13 past subjunctive	
preveda	**prevediamo**	**àbbia preveduto**	**abbiamo preveduto**
(prevegga)		**àbbia preveduto**	**abbiate preveduto**
preveda	**prevediate**	**àbbia preveduto**	**àbbiano preveduto**
(prevegga)			
preveda	**prevédano**		
(prevegga)	**(prevéggano)**		
7 imperfect subjunctive		14 past perfect subjunctive	
prevedessi	**prevedéssimo**	**avessi preveduto**	**avéssimo preveduto**
prevedessi	**prevedeste**	**avessi preveduto**	**aveste preveduto**
prevedesse	**prevedéssero**	**avesse preveduto**	**avéssero preveduto**

	imperative	
		prevediamo
prevedi (non prevedere)		**prevedete**
preveda (prevegga)		**prevédano (prevéggano)**

Words related to this verb
La zingara previde la catastrofe.   The Gypsy foresaw the catastrophe.
Io prevedo tutte le possibilità.   I foresee all the possibilities.

197

prevenire   Ger. **prevenèndo**   Past Part. **prevenuto**

to precede, to anticipate

The Seven Simple Tenses		The Seven Compound Tenses	
Singular	Plural	Singular	Plural
1 present indicative		**8 present perfect**	
prevèngo	preveniamo	ho prevenuto	abbiamo prevenuto
previèni	prevenite	hai prevenuto	avete prevenuto
previène	prevèngono	ha prevenuto	hanno prevenuto
2 imperfect indicative		**9 past perfect**	
prevenivo	prevenivamo	avevo prevenuto	avevamo prevenuto
prevenivi	prevenivate	avevi prevenuto	avevate prevenuto
preveniva	prevenívano	aveva prevenuto	avévano prevenuto
3 past absolute		**10 past anterior**	
prevenni	prevenimmo	èbbi prevenuto	avemmo prevenuto
prevenisti	preveniste	avesti prevenuto	aveste prevenuto
prevenne	prevénnero	èbbe prevenuto	èbbero prevenuto
4 future indicative		**11 future perfect**	
preverrò	preverremo	avrò prevenuto	avremo prevenuto
preverrai	preverrete	avrai prevenuto	avrete prevenuto
preverrà	preverranno	avrà prevenuto	avranno prevenuto
5 present conditional		**12 past conditional**	
preverrèi	preverremmo	avrèi prevenuto	avremmo prevenuto
preverresti	preverreste	avresti prevenuto	avreste prevenuto
preverrèbbe	preverrèbbero	avrèbbe prevenuto	avrèbbero prevenuto
6 present subjunctive		**13 past subjunctive**	
prevènga	preveniamo	àbbia prevenuto	abbiamo prevenuto
prevènga	preveniate	àbbia prevenuto	abbiate prevenuto
prevènga	prevèngano	àbbia prevenuto	àbbiano prevenuto
7 imperfect subjunctive		**14 past perfect subjunctive**	
prevenissi	preveníssimo	avessi prevenuto	avéssimo prevenuto
prevenissi	preveniste	avessi prevenuto	aveste prevenuto
prevenisse	preveníssero	avesse prevenuto	avéssero prevenuto

	imperative	
—		preveniamo
	previèni (non prevenire)	prevenite
	prevènga	prevèngano

Words related to this verb
prevenire una domanda   to anticipate a question
prevenire un pericolo   to prevent a danger

The Seven Simple Tenses		The Seven Compound Tenses	
Singular	Plural	Singular	Plural
1 present indicative		8 present perfect	
produco	produciamo	ho prodotto	abbiamo prodotto
produci	producete	hai prodotto	avete prodotto
produce	prodúcono	ha prodotto	hanno prodotto
2 imperfect indicative		9 past perfect	
producevo	producevamo	avevo prodotto	avevamo prodotto
producevi	producevate	avevi prodotto	avevate prodotto
produceva	producévano	aveva prodotto	avévano prodotto
3 past absolute		10 past anterior	
produssi	producemmo	èbbi prodotto	avemmo prodotto
producesti	produceste	avesti prodotto	aveste prodotto
produsse	prodússero	èbbe prodotto	èbbero prodotto
4 future indicative		11 future perfect	
produrrò	produrremo	avrò prodotto	avremo prodotto
produrrai	produrrete	avrai prodotto	avrete prodotto
produrrà	produrranno	avrà prodotto	avranno prodotto
5 present conditional		12 past conditional	
produrrèi	produrremmo	avrèi prodotto	avremmo prodotto
produrresti	produrreste	avresti prodotto	avreste prodotto
produrrèbbe	produrrèbbero	avrèbbe prodotto	avrèbbero prodotto
6 present subjunctive		13 past subjunctive	
produca	produciamo	àbbia prodotto	abbiamo prodotto
produca	produciate	àbbia prodotto	abbiate prodotto
produca	prodúcano	àbbia prodotto	àbbiano prodotto
7 imperfect subjunctive		14 past perfect subjunctive	
producessi	producéssimo	avessi prodotto	avéssimo prodotto
producessi	produceste	avessi prodotto	aveste prodotto
producesse	producéssero	avesse prodotto	avéssero prodotto

	imperative	
—		produciamo
	produci (non produrre)	producete
	produca	prodúcano

Words related to this verb
L'artigiano produce oggetti di buona qualità.   The artisan produces objects of good quality.
Cosa producevano in questa fabbrica?   What did they produce in this factory?

prométtere	Ger. promettèndo	Past Part. promesso

to promise

The Seven Simple Tenses		The Seven Compound Tenses	
Singular	Plural	Singular	Plural
1 present indicative		8 present perfect	
prometto	promettiamo	ho promesso	abbiamo promesso
prometti	promettete	hai promesso	avete promesso
promette	prométtono	ha promesso	hanno promesso
2 imperfect indicative		9 past perfect	
promettevo	promettevamo	avevo promesso	avevamo promesso
promettevi	promettevate	avevi promesso	avevate promesso
prometteva	promettévano	aveva promesso	avévano promesso
3 past absolute		10 past anterior	
promisi	promettemmo	èbbi promesso	avemmo promesso
promettesti	prometteste	avesti promesso	aveste promesso
promise	promísero	èbbe promesso	èbbero promesso
4 future indicative		11 future perfect	
prometterò	prometteremo	avrò promesso	avremo promesso
prometterai	prometterete	avrai promesso	avrete promesso
prometterà	prometteranno	avrà promesso	avranno promesso
5 present conditional		12 past conditional	
prometterèi	prometteremmo	avrèi promesso	avremmo promesso
prometteresti	promettereste	avresti promesso	avreste promesso
prometterèbbe	prometterèbbero	avrèbbe promesso	avrèbbero promesso
6 present subjunctive		13 past subjunctive	
prometta	promettiamo	àbbia promesso	abbiamo promesso
prometta	promettiate	àbbia promesso	abbiate promesso
prometta	prométtano	àbbia promesso	àbbiano promesso
7 imperfect subjunctive		14 past perfect subjunctive	
promettessi	promettéssimo	avessi promesso	avéssimo promesso
promettessi	prometteste	avessi promesso	aveste promesso
promettesse	promettéssero	avesse promesso	avéssero promesso

imperative		
—		promettiamo
	prometti (non prométtere)	promettete
	prometta	prométtano

Words related to this verb

Ha promesso di venire presto.   She promised to come early.
Il governo promette molte cose.   The government promises many things.

Ger. **promovèndo (promuovèndo)**   Past Part. **promòsso   promuòvere**

to promote

The Seven Simple Tenses		The Seven Compound Tenses	
Singular	Plural	Singular	Plural
1 present indicative		8 present perfect	
promuòvo	**prom(u)oviamo**	**ho promòsso**	**abbiamo promòsso**
promuòvi	**prom(u)ovete**	**hai promòsso**	**avete promòsso**
promuòve	**promuòvono**	**ha promòsso**	**hanno promòsso**
2 imperfect indicative		9 past perfect	
prom(u)ovevo	**prom(u)ovevamo**	**avevo promòsso**	**avevamo promòsso**
prom(u)ovevi	**prom(u)ovevate**	**avevi promòsso**	**avevate promòsso**
prom(u)oveva	**prom(u)ovévano**	**aveva promòsso**	**avévano promòsso**
3 past absolute		10 past anterior	
promòssi	**prom(u)ovemmo**	**èbbi promòsso**	**avemmo promòsso**
prom(u)ovesti	**prom(u)oveste**	**avesti promòsso**	**aveste promòsso**
promòsse	**promòssero**	**èbbe promòsso**	**èbbero promòsso**
4 future indicative		11 future perfect	
prom(u)overò	**prom(u)overemo**	**avrò promòsso**	**avremo promòsso**
prom(u)overai	**prom(u)overete**	**avrai promòsso**	**avrete promòsso**
prom(u)overà	**prom(u)overanno**	**avrà promòsso**	**avranno promòsso**
5 present conditional		12 past conditional	
prom(u)overèi	**prom(u)overemmo**	**avrèi promòsso**	**avremmo promòsso**
prom(u)overesti	**prom(u)overeste**	**avresti promòsso**	**avreste promòsso**
prom(u)overèbbe	**prom(u)overèbbero**	**avrèbbe promòsso**	**avrèbbero promòsso**
6 present subjunctive		13 past subjunctive	
promuòva	**prom(u)oviamo**	**àbbia promòsso**	**abbiamo promòsso**
promuòva	**prom(u)oviate**	**àbbia promòsso**	**abbiate promòsso**
promuòva	**promuòvano**	**àbbia promòsso**	**àbbiano promòsso**
7 imperfect subjunctive		14 past perfect subjunctive	
prom(u)ovessi	**prom(u)ovéssimo**	**avessi promòsso**	**avéssimo promòsso**
prom(u)ovessi	**prom(u)oveste**	**avessi promòsso**	**aveste promòsso**
prom(u)ovesse	**prom(u)ovéssero**	**avesse promòsso**	**avéssero promòsso**

imperative

—	**prom(u)oviamo**
promuòvi (non promuòvere)	**prom(u)ovete**
promuòva	**promuòvano**

pronunziare   Ger. **pronunziando**   Past Part. **pronunziato**

to pronounce

The Seven Simple Tenses		The Seven Compound Tenses	
Singular	Plural	Singular	Plural
1　present indicative		8　present perfect	
pronùnzio	pronunziamo	ho pronunziato	abbiamo pronunziato
pronùnzi	pronunziate	hai pronunziato	avete pronunziato
pronùnzia	pronùnziano	ha pronunziato	hanno pronunziato
2　imperfect indicative		9　past perfect	
pronunziavo	pronunziavamo	avevo pronunziato	avevamo pronunziato
pronunziavi	pronunziavate	avevi pronunziato	avevate pronunziato
pronunziava	pronunziàvano	aveva pronunziato	avévano pronunziato
3　past absolute		10　past anterior	
pronunziai	pronunziammo	èbbi pronunziato	avemmo pronunziato
pronunziasti	pronunziaste	avesti pronunziato	aveste pronunziato
pronunziò	pronunziàrono	èbbe pronunziato	èbbero pronunziato
4　future indicative		11　future perfect	
pronunzierò	pronunzieremo	avrò pronunziato	avremo pronunziato
pronunzierai	pronunzierete	avrai pronunziato	avrete pronunziato
pronunzierà	pronunzieranno	avrà pronunziato	avranno pronunziato
5　present conditional		12　past conditional	
pronunzierèi	pronunzieremmo	avrèi pronunziato	avremmo pronunziato
pronunzieresti	pronunziereste	avresti pronunziato	avreste pronunziato
pronunzi-　erèbbe	pronunzi-　erèbbero	avrèbbe　pronunziato	avrèbbero　pronunziato
6　present subjunctive		13　past subjunctive	
pronùnzi	pronunziamo	àbbia pronunziato	abbiamo pronunziato
pronùnzi	pronunziate	àbbia pronunziato	abbiate pronunziato
pronùnzi	pronùnzino	àbbia pronunziato	àbbiano pronunziato
7　imperfect subjunctive		14　past perfect subjunctive	
pronunziassi	pronunziassimo	avessi pronunziato	avéssimo pronunziato
pronunziassi	pronunziaste	avessi pronunziato	aveste pronunziato
pronunziasse	pronunziàssero	avesse pronunziato	avéssero pronunziato

	imperative	
—		pronunziamo
pronùnzia (non pronunziare)		pronunziate
pronùnzi		pronùnzino

Words related to this verb
Ho pronunziato bene la parola.   I pronounced the word well.
La pronunzia buona è importante.   Good pronunciation is important.

to propose

The Seven Simple Tenses		The Seven Compound Tenses	
Singular	Plural	Singular	Plural
1 present indicative		8 present perfect	
propongo	**proponiamo**	**ho proposto**	**abbiamo proposto**
proponi	**proponete**	**hai proposto**	**avete proposto**
propone	**propóngono**	**ha proposto**	**hanno proposto**
2 imperfect indicative		9 past perfect	
proponevo	**proponevamo**	**avevo proposto**	**avevamo proposto**
proponevi	**proponevate**	**avevi proposto**	**avevate proposto**
proponeva	**proponévano**	**aveva proposto**	**avévano proposto**
3 past absolute		10 past anterior	
proposi	**proponemmo**	**èbbi proposto**	**avemmo proposto**
proponesti	**proponeste**	**avesti proposto**	**aveste proposto**
propose	**propósero**	**èbbe proposto**	**èbbero proposto**
4 future indicative		11 future perfect	
proporrò	**proporremo**	**avrò proposto**	**avremo proposto**
proporrai	**proporrete**	**avrai proposto**	**avrete proposto**
proporrà	**proporranno**	**avrà proposto**	**avranno proposto**
5 present conditional		12 past conditional	
proporrèi	**proporremmo**	**avrèi proposto**	**avremmo proposto**
proporresti	**proporreste**	**avresti proposto**	**avreste proposto**
proporrèbbe	**proporrèbbero**	**avrèbbe proposto**	**avrèbbero proposto**
6 present subjunctive		13 past subjunctive	
proponga	**proponiamo**	**àbbia proposto**	**abbiamo proposto**
proponga	**proponiate**	**àbbia proposto**	**abbiate proposto**
proponga	**propóngano**	**àbbia proposto**	**àbbiano proposto**
7 imperfect subjunctive		14 past perfect subjunctive	
proponessi	**proponéssimo**	**avessi proposto**	**avéssimo proposto**
proponessi	**proponeste**	**avessi proposto**	**aveste proposto**
proponesse	**proponéssero**	**avesse proposto**	**avéssero proposto**

	imperative	
—		**proponiamo**
proponi (non proporre)		**proponete**
proponga		**propóngano**

Words related to this verb
Lui propone molte cose, ma non fa niente.   He proposes many things but does
nothing.
Ho proposto una cosa che non gli piace.   I proposed something he doesn't like.

protèggere   Ger. **proteggèndo**   Past Part. **protètto**

to protect

The Seven Simple Tenses		The Seven Compound Tenses	
Singular	Plural	Singular	Plural
1 present indicative		8 present perfect	
protèggo	**proteggiamo**	**ho protètto**	**abbiamo protètto**
protèggi	**proteggete**	**hai protètto**	**avete protètto**
protègge	**protèggono**	**ha protètto**	**hanno protètto**
2 imperfect indicative		9 past perfect	
proteggevo	**proteggevamo**	**avevo protètto**	**avevamo protètto**
proteggevi	**proteggevate**	**avevi protètto**	**avevate protètto**
proteggeva	**proteggévano**	**aveva protètto**	**avévano protètto**
3 past absolute		10 past anterior	
protèssi	**proteggemmo**	**èbbi protètto**	**avemmo protètto**
proteggesti	**proteggeste**	**avesti protètto**	**aveste protètto**
protèsse	**protèssero**	**èbbe protètto**	**èbbero protètto**
4 future indicative		11 future perfect	
proteggerò	**proteggeremo**	**avrò protètto**	**avremo protètto**
proteggerai	**proteggerete**	**avrai protètto**	**avrete protètto**
proteggerà	**proteggeranno**	**avrà protètto**	**avranno protètto**
5 present conditional		12 past conditional	
proteggerèi	**proteggeremmo**	**avrèi protètto**	**avremmo protètto**
proteggeresti	**proteggereste**	**avresti protètto**	**avreste protètto**
proteggerèbbe	**proteggerèbbero**	**avrèbbe protètto**	**avrèbbero protètto**
6 present subjunctive		13 past subjunctive	
protègga	**proteggiamo**	**àbbia protètto**	**abbiamo protètto**
protègga	**proteggiate**	**àbbia protètto**	**abbiate protètto**
protègga	**protèggano**	**àbbia protètto**	**àbbiano protètto**
7 imperfect subjunctive		14 past perfect subjunctive	
proteggessi	**proteggéssimo**	**avessi protètto**	**avéssimo protètto**
proteggessi	**proteggeste**	**avessi protètto**	**aveste protètto**
proteggesse	**proteggéssero**	**avesse protètto**	**avéssero protètto**

imperative

—	**proteggiamo**
protèggi (non **protèggere**)	**proteggete**
protègga	**protèggano**

Words related to this verb
Io protego tutti i miei oggetti di valore.   I protect all my valuable objects.
La madre protege il figlio.   The mother protects her child.

The Seven Simple Tenses		The Seven Compound Tenses	
Singular	Plural	Singular	Plural
1 present indicative		8 present perfect	
provvedo	**provvediamo**	**ho provveduto**	**abbiamo provveduto**
(**provveggo**)		(**provvisto**)	
provvedi	**provvedete**	**hai provveduto**	**avete provveduto**
provvede	**provvédono**	**ha provveduto**	**hanno provveduto**
	(**provvéggono**)		
2 imperfect indicative		9 past perfect	
provvedevo	**provvedevamo**	**avevo provveduto**	**avevamo provveduto**
provvedevi	**provvedevate**	**avevi provveduto**	**avevate provveduto**
provvedeva	**provvedévano**	**aveva provveduto**	**avévano provveduto**
3 past absolute		10 past anterior	
provvidi	**provvedemmo**	**èbbi provveduto**	**avemmo provveduto**
provvedesti	**provvedeste**	**avesti provveduto**	**aveste provveduto**
provvide	**provvídero**	**èbbe provveduto**	**èbbero provveduto**
4 future indicative		11 future perfect	
provvederò	**provvederemo**	**avrò provveduto**	**avremo provveduto**
provvederai	**provvederete**	**avrai provveduto**	**avrete provveduto**
provvederà	**provvederanno**	**avrà provveduto**	**avranno provveduto**
5 present conditional		12 past conditional	
provvederèi	**provvederemmo**	**avrèi provveduto**	**avremmo provveduto**
provvederesti	**provvedereste**	**avresti provveduto**	**avreste provveduto**
provvederèbbe	**provvederèbbero**	**avrèbbe**	**avrèbbero**
		provveduto	**provveduto**
6 present subjunctive		13 past subjunctive	
provveda	**provvediamo**	**àbbia provveduto**	**abbiamo provveduto**
(**provvegga**)		**àbbia provveduto**	**abbiate provveduto**
provveda	**provvediate**	**àbbia provveduto**	**àbbiano provveduto**
(**provvegga**)			
provveda	**provvédano**		
(**provvegga**)	(**provvéggano**)		
7 imperfect subjunctive		14 past perfect subjunctive	
provvedessi	**provvedéssimo**	**avessi provveduto**	**avéssimo provveduto**
provvedessi	**provvedeste**	**avessi provveduto**	**aveste provveduto**
provvedesse	**provvedéssero**	**avesse provveduto**	**avéssero provveduto**

	imperative	
—		**provvediamo**
provvedi (non provvedere)		**provvedete**
provveda (provvegga)		**provvédano (provvéggano)**

Words related to this verb
Anna ci provvide con buone cose da mangiare.   Ann provided us with good things to eat.
Il padre e la madre provvedono per la famiglia.   The father and mother provide for the family.

pulire

Ger. **pulendo**   Past Part. **pulito**

to clean

The Seven Simple Tenses		The Seven Compound Tenses	
Singular	Plural	Singular	Plural
1 present indicative		8 present perfect	
pulìsco	**puliamo**	**ho pulito**	**abbiamo pulito**
pulìsci	**pulite**	**hai pulito**	**avete pulito**
pulìsce	**pulìscono**	**ha pulito**	**hanno pulito**
2 imperfect indicative		9 past perfect	
pulivo	**pulivamo**	**avevo pulito**	**avevamo pulito**
pulivi	**pulivate**	**avevi pulito**	**avevate pulito**
puliva	**pulivano**	**aveva pulito**	**avévano pulito**
3 past absolute		10 past anterior	
pulìi	**pulimmo**	**èbbi pulito**	**avemmo pulito**
pulisti	**puliste**	**avesti pulito**	**aveste pulito**
pulì	**pulìrono**	**èbbe pulito**	**èbbero pulito**
4 future indicative		11 future perfect	
pulirò	**puliremo**	**avrò pulito**	**avremo pulito**
pulirai	**pulirete**	**avrai pulito**	**avrete pulito**
pulirà	**puliranno**	**avrà pulito**	**avranno pulito**
5 present conditional		12 past conditional	
pulirèi	**puliremmo**	**avrèi pulito**	**avremmo pulito**
puliresti	**pulireste**	**avresti pulito**	**avreste pulito**
pulirèbbe	**pulirèbbero**	**avrèbbe pulito**	**avrèbbero pulito**
6 present subjunctive		13 past subjunctive	
pulisca	**puliamo**	**àbbia pulito**	**abbiamo pulito**
pulisca	**puliate**	**àbbia pulito**	**abbiate pulito**
pulisca	**pulìscano**	**àbbia pulito**	**àbbiano pulito**
7 imperfect subjunctive		14 past perfect subjunctive	
pulissi	**pulìssimo**	**avessi pulito**	**avéssimo pulito**
pulissi	**puliste**	**avessi pulito**	**aveste pulito**
pulisse	**pulìssero**	**avesse pulito**	**avéssero pulito**

	imperative	
	pulìsci (non pulire)	**puliamo pulite**
	pulìsca	**pulìscano**

Words related to this verb
Devo pulire la casa.   I must clean the house.
Faccio pulire quest'abito.   I am having this dress cleaned.

to prick, to pinch, to sting

The Seven Simple Tenses		The Seven Compound Tenses	
Singular	Plural	Singular	Plural
1 present indicative		8 present perfect	
pungo	**pungiamo**	**ho punto**	**abbiamo punto**
pungi	**pungete**	**hai punto**	**avete punto**
punge	**púngono**	**ha punto**	**hanno punto**
2 imperfect indicative		9 past perfect	
pungevo	**pungevamo**	**avevo punto**	**avevamo punto**
pungevi	**pungevate**	**avevi punto**	**avevate punto**
pungeva	**pungévano**	**aveva punto**	**avévano punto**
3 past absolute		10 past anterior	
punsi	**pungemmo**	**èbbi punto**	**avemmo punto**
pungesti	**pungeste**	**avesti punto**	**aveste punto**
punse	**púnsero**	**èbbe punto**	**èbbero punto**
4 future indicative		11 future perfect	
pungerò	**pungeremo**	**avrò punto**	**avremo punto**
pungerai	**pungerete**	**avrai punto**	**avrete punto**
pungerà	**pungeranno**	**avrà punto**	**avranno punto**
5 present conditional		12 past conditional	
pungerèi	**pungeremmo**	**avrèi punto**	**avremmo punto**
pungeresti	**pungereste**	**avresti punto**	**avreste punto**
pungerèbbe	**pungerèbbero**	**avrèbbe punto**	**avrèbbero punto**
6 present subjunctive		13 past subjunctive	
punga	**pungiamo**	**àbbia punto**	**abbiamo punto**
punga	**pungiate**	**àbbia punto**	**abbiate punto**
punga	**púngano**	**àbbia punto**	**àbbiano punto**
7 imperfect subjunctive		14 past perfect subjunctive	
pungessi	**pungéssimo**	**avessi punto**	**avéssimo punto**
pungessi	**pungeste**	**avessi punto**	**aveste punto**
pungesse	**pungéssero**	**avesse punto**	**avéssero punto**

	imperative	
—		**pungiamo**
pungi (non púngere)		**pungete**
punga		**púngano**

Words related to this verb
Quella zanzara mi ha punto tre volte.   That mosquito has stung me three times.
Il freddo mi punge la faccia.   The cold stings my face.

raccomandare

Ger. **raccomandando** Past Part. **raccomandato**

to recommend

The Seven Simple Tenses		The Seven Compound Tenses	
Singular	Plural	Singular	Plural
1 present indicative		**8 present perfect**	
raccomando	raccomandiamo	ho	abbiamo
raccomandi	raccomandate	hai	avete
raccomanda	raccomandano	ha	hanno raccomandato
2 imperfect indicative		**9 past perfect**	
raccomandavo	raccomandavamo	avevo	avevamo
raccomandavi	raccomandavate	avevi	avevate
raccomandava	raccomandàvano	aveva	avévano raccomandato
3 past absolute		**10 past anterior**	
raccomandai	raccomandammo	èbbi	avemmo
raccomandasti	raccomandaste	avesti	aveste
raccomandò	raccomandàrono	èbbe	èbbero raccomandato
4 future indicative		**11 future perfect**	
raccomanderò	raccomanderemo	avrò	avremo
raccomanderai	raccomanderete	avrai	avrete
raccomenderà	raccomanderanno	avrà	avranno raccomandato
5 present conditional		**12 past conditional**	
raccomanderèi	raccomanderemmo	avrèi	avremmo
raccomanderesti	raccomandereste	avresti	avreste
raccomanderèbbe	raccomanderèbbero	avrèbbe	avrèbbero raccomandato
6 present subjunctive		**13 past subjunctive**	
raccomandi	raccomandiamo	àbbia raccomandato	abbiamo raccomandato
raccomandi	raccomandiate	àbbia raccomandato	abbiate raccomandato
raccomandi	raccomandino	àbbia raccomandato	àbbiano raccomandato
7 imperfect subjunctive		**14 past perfect subjunctive**	
raccomandassi	raccomandàssimo	avessi raccomandato	avéssimo raccomandato
raccomandassi	raccomandaste	avessi raccomandato	aveste raccomandato
raccomandasse	raccomandàssero	avesse raccomandato	avéssero raccomandato

imperative

—	raccomandiamo
raccomanda (non raccomandare)	raccomandate
raccomandi	raccomandino

208

to shave, to graze, to raze

The Seven Simple Tenses		The Seven Compound Tenses	
Singular	Plural	Singular	Plural
1 present indicative		**8 present perfect**	
rado	radiamo	ho raso	abbiamo raso
radi	radete	hai raso	avete raso
rade	ràdono	ha raso	hanno raso
2 imperfect indicative		**9 past perfect**	
radevo	radevamo	avevo raso	avevamo raso
radevi	radevate	avevi raso	avevate raso
radeva	radévano	aveva raso	avévano raso
3 past absolute		**10 past anterior**	
rasi	rademmo	èbbi raso	avemmo raso
radesti	radeste	avesti raso	aveste raso
rase	ràsero	èbbe raso	èbbero raso
4 future indicative		**11 future perfect**	
raderò	raderemo	avrò raso	avremo raso
raderai	raderete	avrai raso	avrete raso
raderà	raderanno	avrà raso	avranno raso
5 present conditional		**12 past conditional**	
raderèi	raderemmo	avrèi raso	avremmo raso
raderesti	radereste	avresti raso	avreste raso
raderèbbe	raderèbbero	avrèbbe raso	avrèbbero raso
6 present subjunctive		**13 past subjunctive**	
rada	radiamo	àbbia raso	abbiamo raso
rada	radiate	àbbia raso	abbiate raso
rada	ràdano	àbbia raso	àbbiano raso
7 imperfect subjunctive		**14 past perfect subjunctive**	
radessi	radéssimo	avessi raso	avéssimo raso
radessi	radeste	avessi raso	aveste raso
radesse	radéssero	avesse raso	avéssero raso

imperative	
—	radiamo
radi (non ràdere)	radete
rada	ràdano

Words related to this verb

Io mi rado ogni mattina.   I shave every morning.
Il barbiere mi ha raso male.   The barber shaved me badly.
Un ciclone rase tutte le case al suolo.   A tornado razed all the houses to the ground.

raggiúngere   Ger. **raggiungèndo**   Past Part. **raggiunto**

to reach, to catch up to, to get to

The Seven Simple Tenses		The Seven Compound Tenses	
Singular	Plural	Singular	Plural
1 present indicative		8 present perfect	
raggiùngo	raggiungiamo	ho raggiunto	abbiamo raggiunto
raggiùngi	raggiungete	hai raggiunto	avete raggiunto
raggiùnge	raggiúngono	ha raggiunto	hanno raggiunto
2 imperfect indicative		9 past perfect	
raggiungevo	raggiungevamo	avevo raggiunto	avevamo raggiunto
raggiungevi	raggiungevate	avevi raggiunto	avevate raggiunto
raggiungeva	raggiungévano	aveva raggiunto	avévano raggiunto
3 past absolute		10 past anterior	
raggiunsi	raggiungemmo	èbbi raggiunto	avemmo raggiunto
raggiungesti	raggiungeste	avesti raggiunto	aveste raggiunto
raggiunse	raggiúnsero	èbbe raggiunto	èbbero raggiunto
4 future indicative		11 future perfect	
raggiungerò	raggiungeremo	avrò raggiunto	avremo raggiunto
raggiungerai	raggiungerete	avrai raggiunto	avrete raggiunto
raggiungerà	raggiungeranno	avrà raggiunto	avranno raggiunto
5 present conditional		12 past conditional	
raggiungerèi	raggiungeremmo	avrèi raggiunto	avremmo raggiunto
raggiungeresti	raggiungereste	avresti raggiunto	avreste raggiunto
raggiungerèbbe	raggiungerèbbero	avrèbbe raggiunto	avrèbbero raggiunto
6 present subjunctive		13 past subjunctive	
raggiunga	raggiungiamo	àbbia raggiunto	abbiamo raggiunto
raggiunga	raggiungiate	àbbia raggiunto	abbiate raggiunto
raggiunga	raggiúngano	àbbia raggiunto	àbbiano raggiunto
7 imperfect subjunctive		14 past perfect subjunctive	
raggiungessi	raggiungéssimo	avessi raggiunto	avéssimo raggiunto
raggiungessi	raggiungeste	avessi raggiunto	aveste raggiunto
raggiungesse	raggiungéssero	avesse raggiunto	avéssero raggiunto

	imperative	
—		raggiungiamo
raggiùngi (non raggiungere)		raggiungete
raggiùnga		raggiúngano

Words related to this verb

Li raggiungerò.   I will catch up to them.
raggiungere buoni risultati   to achieve good results

to draw up, to edit

The Seven Simple Tenses		The Seven Compound Tenses	
Singular	Plural	Singular	Plural
1 present indicative		8 present perfect	
redigo	**redigiamo**	**ho redatto**	**abbiamo redatto**
redigi	**redigete**	**hai redatto**	**avete redatto**
redige	**redígono**	**ha redatto**	**hanno redatto**
2 imperfect indicative		9 past perfect	
redigevo	**redigevamo**	**avevo redatto**	**avevamo redatto**
redigevi	**redigevate**	**avevi redatto**	**avevate redatto**
redigeva	**redigévano**	**aveva redatto**	**avévano redatto**
3 past absolute		10 past anterior	
redassi	**redigemmo**	**èbbi redatto**	**avemmo redatto**
redigesti	**redigeste**	**avesti redatto**	**aveste redatto**
redasse	**redàssero**	**èbbe redatto**	**èbbero redatto**
4 future indicative		11 future perfect	
redigerò	**redigeremo**	**avrò redatto**	**avremo redatto**
redigerai	**redigerete**	**avrai redatto**	**avrete redatto**
redigerà	**redigeranno**	**avrà redatto**	**avranno redatto**
5 present conditional		12 past conditional	
redigerèi	**redigeremmo**	**avrèi redatto**	**avremmo redatto**
redigeresti	**redigereste**	**avresti redatto**	**avreste redatto**
redigerèbbe	**redigerèbbero**	**avrèbbe redatto**	**avrèbbero redatto**
6 present subjunctive		13 past subjunctive	
rediga	**redigiamo**	**àbbia redatto**	**abbiamo redatto**
rediga	**redigiate**	**àbbia redatto**	**abbiate redatto**
rediga	**redígano**	**àbbia redatto**	**àbbiano redatto**
7 imperfect subjunctive		14 past perfect subjunctive	
redigessi	**redigéssimo**	**avessi redatto**	**avéssimo redatto**
redigessi	**redigeste**	**avessi redatto**	**aveste redatto**
redigesse	**redigéssero**	**avesse redatto**	**avéssero redatto**

	imperative	
		redigiamo
	redigi (non redígere)	**redigete**
	rediga	**redígano**

Words related to this verb
Il redattore redige l'articolo.   The editor edits the article.
Questo libro deve essere redatto prudentemente.   This book must be edited carefully.

règgere*	Ger. reggèndo	Past Part. rètto

to support, to bear

The Seven Simple Tenses		The Seven Compound Tenses	
Singular	Plural	Singular	Plural
1 present indicative		8 present perfect	
règgo	reggiamo	ho rètto	abbiamo rètto
règgi	reggete	hai rètto	avete rètto
règge	règgono	ha rètto	hanno rètto
2 imperfect indicative		9 past perfect	
reggevo	reggevamo	avevo rètto	avevamo rètto
reggevi	reggevate	avevi rètto	avevate rètto
reggeva	reggévano	aveva rètto	avévano rètto
3 past absolute		10 past anterior	
rèssi	reggemmo	èbbi rètto	avemmo rètto
reggesti	reggeste	avesti rètto	aveste rètto
rèsse	rèssero	èbbe rètto	èbbero rètto
4 future indicative		11 future perfect	
reggerò	reggeremo	avrò rètto	avremo rètto
reggerai	reggerete	avrai rètto	avrete rètto
reggerà	reggeranno	avrà rètto	avranno rètto
5 present conditional		12 past conditional	
reggerèi	reggeremmo	avrèi rètto	avremmo rètto
reggeresti	reggereste	avresti rètto	avreste rètto
reggerèbbe	reggerèbbero	avrèbbe rètto	avrèbbero rètto
6 present subjunctive		13 past subjunctive	
règga	reggiamo	àbbia rètto	abbiamo rètto
règga	reggiate	àbbia rètto	abbiate rètto
règga	règgano	àbbia rètto	àbbiano rètto
7 imperfect subjunctive		14 past perfect subjunctive	
reggessi	reggéssimo	avessi rètto	avéssimo rètto
reggessi	reggeste	avessi rètto	aveste rètto
reggesse	reggéssero	avesse rètto	avéssero rètto

imperative	
—	reggiamo
règgi (non règgere)	reggete
règga	règgano

* Like *règgere* are *corrèggere* and *sorrèggere*.

Words related to this verb
Io non reggo il dolore bene. I don't bear pain well.
L'arco è retto da due colonne. The arch is supported by two columns.

212

to render, to give back

The Seven Simple Tenses		The Seven Compound Tenses	
Singular	Plural	Singular	Plural
1 present indicative		8 present perfect	
rèndo	rendiamo	ho reso (renduto)	abbiamo reso
rèndi	rendete	hai reso	avete reso
rènde	rèndono	ha reso	hanno reso
2 imperfect indicative		9 past perfect	
rendevo	rendevamo	avevo reso	avevamo reso
rendevi	rendevate	avevi reso	avevate reso
rendeva	rendévano	aveva reso	avévano reso
3 past absolute		10 past anterior	
resi (rendei)	rendemmo	èbbi reso	avemmo reso
rendesti	rendeste	avesti reso	aveste reso
rese	résero	èbbe reso	èbbero reso
(rendé,	(rendérono,		
rendètte)	rendèttero)		
4 future indicative		11 future perfect	
renderò	renderemo	avrò reso	avremo reso
renderai	renderete	avrai reso	avrete reso
renderà	renderanno	avrà reso	avranno reso
5 present conditional		12 past conditional	
renderèi	renderemmo	avrèi reso	avremmo reso
renderesti	rendereste	avresti reso	avreste reso
renderèbbe	renderèbbero	avrèbbe reso	avrèbbero reso
6 present subjunctive		13 past subjunctive	
rènda	rendiamo	àbbia reso	abbiamo reso
rènda	rendiate	àbbia reso	abbiate reso
rènda	rèndano	àbbia reso	àbbiano reso
7 imperfect subjunctive		14 past perfect subjunctive	
rendessi	rendéssimo	avessi reso	avéssimo reso
rendessi	rendeste	avessi reso	aveste reso
rendesse	rendéssero	avesse reso	avéssero reso

imperative

	—	rendiamo
	rèndi (non rèndere)	rendete
	rènda	rèndano

Words related to this verb
Se tu mi presti il denaro, io te lo rendo.   If you lend me the money, I will give it
back to you.
Ti renderò il libro domani.   I'll give you back the book tomorrow.

resistere   Ger. **resistendo**   Past Part. **resistito**

to resist

The Seven Simple Tenses		The Seven Compound Tenses	
Singular	Plural	Singular	Plural
1 present indicative		8 present perfect	
resisto	**resistiamo**	**ho resistito**	**abbiamo resistito**
resisti	**resistete**	**hai resistito**	**avete resistito**
resiste	**resístono**	**ha resistito**	**hanno resistito**
2 imperfect indicative		9 past perfect	
resistevo	**resistevamo**	**avevo resistito**	**avevamo resistito**
resistevi	**resistevate**	**avevi resistito**	**avevate resistito**
resisteva	**resistévano**	**aveva resistito**	**avévano resistito**
3 past absolute		10 past anterior	
resistèi	**resistemmo**	**èbbi resistito**	**avemmo resistito**
resistesti	**resisteste**	**avesti resistito**	**aveste resistito**
resistè	**resistérono**	**èbbe resistito**	**èbbero resistito**
4 future indicative		11 future perfect	
resisterò	**resisteremo**	**avrò resistito**	**avremo resistito**
resisterai	**resisterete**	**avrai resistito**	**avrete resistito**
resisterà	**resisteranno**	**avrà resistito**	**avranno resistito**
5 present conditional		12 past conditional	
resisterèi	**resisteremmo**	**avrèi resistito**	**avremmo resistito**
resisteresti	**resistereste**	**avresti resistito**	**avreste resistito**
resisterèbbe	**resisterèbbero**	**avrèbbe resistito**	**avrèbbero resistito**
6 present subjunctive		13 past subjunctive	
resista	**resistiamo**	**àbbia resistito**	**abbiamo resistito**
resista	**resistiate**	**àbbia resistito**	**abbiate resistito**
resista	**resístano**	**àbbia resistito**	**àbbiano resistito**
7 imperfect subjunctive		14 past perfect subjunctive	
resistessi	**resistéssimo**	**avessi resistito**	**avéssimo resistito**
resistessi	**resisteste**	**avessi resistito**	**aveste resistito**
resistesse	**resistéssero**	**avesse resistito**	**avéssero resistito**

imperative

—	**resistiamo**
resisti (non resistere)	**resistete**
resista	**resístano**

Words related to this verb
Cerchiamo di resistere alle tentazioni. We try to resist temptations.
Resisto al dolore. I endure pain.

to resume, to summarize; to rehire

The Seven Simple Tenses		The Seven Compound Tenses	
Singular	Plural	Singular	Plural
1 present indicative		8 present perfect	
riassumo	**riassumiamo**	**ho riassunto**	**abbiamo riassunto**
riassumi	**riassumete**	**hai riassunto**	**avete riassunto**
riassume	**riassúmono**	**ha riassunto**	**hanno riassunto**
2 imperfect indicative		9 past perfect	
riassumevo	**riassumevamo**	**avevo riassunto**	**avevamo riassunto**
riassumevi	**riassumevate**	**avevi riassunto**	**avevate riassunto**
riassumeva	**riassumévano**	**aveva riassunto**	**avévano riassunto**
3 past absolute		10 past anterior	
riassunsi	**riassumemmo**	**èbbi riassunto**	**avemmo riassunto**
riassumesti	**riassumeste**	**avesti riassunto**	**aveste riassunto**
riassunse	**riassúnsero**	**èbbe riassunto**	**èbbero riassunto**
4 future indicative		11 future perfect	
riassumerò	**riassumeremo**	**avrò riassunto**	**avremo riassunto**
riassumerai	**riassumerete**	**avrai riassunto**	**avrete riassunto**
riassumerà	**riassumeranno**	**avrà riassunto**	**avranno riassunto**
5 present conditional		12 past conditional	
riassumerèi	**riassumeremmo**	**avrèi riassunto**	**avremmo riassunto**
riassumeresti	**riassumereste**	**avresti riassunto**	**avreste riassunto**
riassumerèbbe	**riassumerèbbero**	**avrèbbe riassunto**	**avrèbbero riassunto**
6 present subjunctive		13 past subjunctive	
riassuma	**riassumiamo**	**àbbia riassunto**	**abbiamo riassunto**
riassuma	**riassumiate**	**àbbia riassunto**	**abbiate riassunto**
riassuma	**riassúmano**	**àbbia riassunto**	**àbbiano riassunto**
7 imperfect subjunctive		14 past perfect subjunctive	
riassumessi	**riassuméssimo**	**avessi riassunto**	**avéssimo riassunto**
riassumessi	**riassumeste**	**avessi riassunto**	**aveste riassunto**
riassumesse	**riassuméssero**	**avesse riassunto**	**avéssero riassunto**

	imperative	
—		**riassumiamo**
riassumi (non riassúmere)		**riassumete**
riassuma		**riassúmano**

Words related to this verb

Devo riassumere la storia per la classe.   I have to summarize the story for the class.
L'uomo fu riassunto dopo tre settimane.   The man was rehired after three weeks.

rídere* Ger. ridèndo Past Part. riso

to laugh

The Seven Simple Tenses		The Seven Compound Tenses	
Singular	Plural	Singular	Plural
1 present indicative		8 present perfect	
rido	ridiamo	ho riso	abbiamo riso
ridi	ridete	hai riso	avete riso
ride	rídono	ha riso	hanno riso
2 imperfect indicative		9 past perfect	
ridevo	ridévamo	avevo riso	avevamo riso
ridevi	ridevate	avevi riso	avevate riso
rideva	ridévano	aveva riso	avévano riso
3 past absolute		10 past anterior	
risi	ridemmo	èbbi riso	avemmo riso
ridesti	rideste	avesti riso	aveste riso
rise	rísero	èbbe riso	èbbero riso
4 future indicative		11 future perfect	
riderò	rideremo	avrò riso	avremo riso
riderai	riderete	avrai riso	avrete riso
riderà	rideranno	avrà riso	avranno riso
5 present conditional		12 past conditional	
riderèi	rideremmo	avrèi riso	avremmo riso
rideresti	ridereste	avresti riso	avreste riso
riderèbbe	riderèbbero	avrèbbe riso	avrèbbero riso
6 present subjunctive		13 past subjunctive	
rida	ridiamo	àbbia riso	abbiamo riso
rida	ridiate	àbbia riso	abbiate riso
rida	rídano	àbbia riso	àbbiano riso
7 imperfect subjunctive		14 past perfect subjunctive	
ridessi	ridéssimo	avessi riso	avéssimo riso
ridessi	rideste	avessi riso	aveste riso
ridesse	ridéssero	avesse riso	avéssero riso

imperative

—	ridiamo
ridi (non rídere)	ridete
rida	rídano

*Like rídere are arrídere, derídere, irrídere, and sorrídere.

Words related to this verb
Ho riso molto oggi. I laughed a lot today.
Loro non ridono molto. They don't laugh much.

216

to say again, to repeat

The Seven Simple Tenses		The Seven Compound Tenses	
Singular	Plural	Singular	Plural
1 present indicative		**8 present perfect**	
ridico	ridiciamo	ho ridetto	abbiamo ridetto
ridici	ridite	hai ridetto	avete ridetto
ridice	ridícono	ha ridetto	hanno ridetto
2 imperfect indicative		**9 past perfect**	
ridicevo	ridicevamo	avevo ridetto	avevamo ridetto
ridicevi	ridicevate	avevi ridetto	avevate ridetto
ridiceva	ridicévano	aveva ridetto	avévano ridetto
3 past absolute		**10 past anterior**	
ridissi	ridicemmo	èbbi ridetto	avemmo ridetto
ridicesti	ridiceste	avesti ridetto	aveste ridetto
ridisse	ridíssero	èbbe ridetto	èbbero ridetto
4 future indicative		**11 future perfect**	
ridirò	ridiremo	avrò ridetto	avremo ridetto
ridirai	ridirete	avrai ridetto	avrete ridetto
ridirà	ridiranno	avrà ridetto	avranno ridetto
5 present conditional		**12 past conditional**	
ridirèi	ridiremmo	avrèi ridetto	avremmo ridetto
ridiresti	ridireste	avresti ridetto	avreste ridetto
ridirèbbe	ridirèbbero	avrèbbe ridetto	avrèbbero ridetto
6 present subjunctive		**13 past subjunctive**	
ridica	ridiciamo	àbbia ridetto	abbiamo ridetto
ridica	ridiciate	àbbia ridetto	abbiate ridetto
ridica	ridícano	àbbia ridetto	àbbiano ridetto
7 imperfect subjunctive		**14 past perfect subjunctive**	
ridicessi	ridicéssimo	avessi ridetto	avéssimo ridetto
ridicessi	ridiceste	avessi ridetto	aveste ridetto
ridicesse	ridicéssero	avesse ridetto	avéssero ridetto

imperative	
—	ridiciamo
ridici (non ridire)	ridite
ridica	ridícano

Words related to this verb
Io ho ridetto la storia per ogni persona.   I repeated the story for each person.

ridurre   Ger. riducèndo   Past Part. ridotto

to reduce

The Seven Simple Tenses		The Seven Compound Tenses	
Singular	Plural	Singular	Plural
1 present indicative		8 present perfect	
riduco	riduciamo	ho ridotto	abbiamo ridotto
riduci	riducete	hai ridotto	avete ridotto
riduce	ridúcono	ha ridotto	hanno ridotto
2 imperfect indicative		9 past perfect	
riducevo	riducevamo	avevo ridotto	avevamo ridotto
riducevi	riducevate	avevi ridotto	avevate ridotto
riduceva	riducévano	aveva ridotto	avévano ridotto
3 past absolute		10 past anterior	
ridussi	riducemmo	èbbi ridotto	avemmo ridotto
riducesti	riduceste	avesti ridotto	aveste ridotto
ridusse	ridússero	èbbe ridotto	èbbero ridotto
4 future indicative		11 future perfect	
ridurrò	ridurremo	avrò ridotto	avremo ridotto
ridurrai	ridurrete	avrai ridotto	avrete ridotto
ridurrà	ridurranno	avrà ridotto	avranno ridotto
5 present conditional		12 past conditional	
ridurrèi	ridurremmo	avrèi ridotto	avremmo ridotto
ridurresti	ridurreste	avresti ridotto	avreste ridotto
ridurrèbbe	ridurrèbbero	avrèbbe ridotto	avrèbbero ridotto
6 present subjunctive		13 past subjunctive	
riduca	riduciamo	àbbia ridotto	abbiamo ridotto
riduca	riduciate	àbbia ridotto	abbiate ridotto
riduca	ridúcano	àbbia ridotto	àbbiano ridotto
7 imperfect subjunctive		14 past perfect subjunctive	
riducessi	riducéssimo	avessi ridotto	avéssimo ridotto
riducessi	riduceste	avessi ridotto	aveste ridotto
riducesse	riducéssero	avesse ridotto	avéssero ridotto

	imperative	
—		riduciamo
riduci (non ridurre)		riducete
riduca		ridúcano

Words related to this verb

Il fuoco ridusse la casa in cenere.   The fire reduced the house to ashes.
Non ridurti a questo.   Don't reduce yourself to this (don't lower yourself).

to do again, to make again

The Seven Simple Tenses		The Seven Compound Tenses	
Singular	Plural	Singular	Plural
1 present indicative		8 present perfect	
rifaccio (rifò)	rifacciamo	ho rifatto	abbiamo rifatto
rifai	rifate	hai rifatto	avete rifatto
rifà	rifanno	ha rifatto	hanno rifatto
2 imperfect indicative		9 past perfect	
rifacevo	rifacevamo	avevo rifatto	avevamo rifatto
rifacevi	rifacevate	avevi rifatto	avevate rifatto
rifaceva	rifacévano	aveva rifatto	avévano rifatto
3 past absolute		10 past anterior	
rifeci	rifacemmo	èbbi rifatto	avemmo rifatto
rifacesti	rifaceste	avesti rifatto	aveste rifatto
rifece	rifécero	èbbe rifatto	èbbero rifatto
4 future indicative		11 future perfect	
rifarò	rifaremo	avrò rifatto	avremo rifatto
rifarai	rifarete	avrai rifatto	avrete rifatto
rifarà	rifaranno	avrà rifatto	avranno rifatto
5 present conditional		12 past conditional	
rifarèi	rifaremmo	avrèi rifatto	avremmo rifatto
rifaresti	rifareste	avresti rifatto	avreste rifatto
rifarèbbe	rifarèbbero	avrèbbe rifatto	avrèbbero rifatto
6 present subjunctive		13 past subjunctive	
rifaccia	rifacciamo	àbbia rifatto	abbiamo rifatto
rifaccia	rifacciate	àbbia rifatto	abbiate rifatto
rifaccia	rifàcciano	àbbia rifatto	àbbiano rifatto
7 imperfect subjunctive		14 past perfect subjunctive	
rifacessi	rifacéssimo	avessi rifatto	avéssimo riffato
rifacessi	rifaceste	avessi rifatto	aveste rifatto
rifacesse	rifaccésero	avesse rifatto	avéssero rifatto

	imperative	
—	rifacciamo
rifai (non rifare)	rifate
rifaccia	rifàcciano

Words related to this verb
Non rifare il letto.   Don't make the bed.
È tutto da rifare.   It must all be done again.

riflettere   Ger. **riflettendo**   Past Part. **riflettuto (riflesso)**

to reflect

The Seven Simple Tenses		The Seven Compound Tenses	
Singular	Plural	Singular	Plural
1 present indicative		8 present perfect	
rifletto	**riflettiamo**	**ho riflettuto (riflesso)**	**abbiamo riflettuto**
rifletti	**riflettete**	**hai riflettuto**	**avete riflettuto**
riflette	**riflettono**	**ha riflettuto**	**hanno riflettuto**
2 imperfect indicative		9 past perfect	
riflettevo	**riflettevamo**	**avevo riflettuto**	**avevamo riflettuto**
riflettevi	**riflettevate**	**avevi riflettuto**	**avevate riflettuto**
rifletteva	**riflettévano**	**aveva riflettuto**	**avévano riflettuto**
3 past absolute		10 past anterior	
riflettèi	**riflettemmo**	**èbbi riflettuto**	**avemmo riflettuto**
riflettesti	**rifletteste**	**avesti riflettuto**	**aveste riflettuto**
riflettè	**riflettérono**	**èbbe riflettuto**	**èbbero riflettuto**
4 future indicative		11 future perfect	
rifletterò	**rifletteremo**	**avrò rifflettuto**	**avremo riflettuto**
rifletterai	**rifletterete**	**avrai riflettuto**	**avrete riflettuto**
rifletterà	**rifletteranno**	**avrà riflettuto**	**avranno riflettuto**
5 present conditional		12 past conditional	
rifletterèi	**rifletteremmo**	**avrèi riflettuto**	**avremmo riflettuto**
rifletteresti	**riflettereste**	**avresti riflettuto**	**avreste riflettuto**
rifletterèbbe	**rifletterèbbero**	**avrèbbe riflettuto**	**avrèbbero riflettuto**
6 present subjunctive		13 past subjunctive	
rifletta	**riflettiamo**	**àbbia riflettuto**	**abbiamo riflettuto**
rifletta	**riflettiate**	**àbbia riflettuto**	**abbiate riflettuto**
rifletta	**riflettano**	**àbbia riflettuto**	**àbbiano riflettuto**
7 imperfect subjunctive		14 past perfect subjunctive	
riflettessi	**riflettéssimo**	**avessi riflettuto**	**avéssimo riflettuto**
riflettessi	**rifletteste**	**avessi riflettuto**	**aveste riflettuto**
riflettesse	**riflettéssero**	**avesse riflettuto**	**avéssero riflettuto**

	imperative	
—		**riflettiamo**
rifletti (non riflettere)		**riflettete**
rifletta		**riflettano**

Words related to this verb
Lo specchio riflette l'immagine.   The mirror reflects the image.
Il voto riflette il suo lavoro.   The grade reflects his work.

Ger. **rimanèndo** Past Part. **rimasto** **rimanere**

to remain, to stay

The Seven Simple Tenses		The Seven Compound Tenses	
Singular	Plural	Singular	Plural
1 present indicative		8 present perfect	
rimango	rimaniamo	sono rimasto	siamo rimasti
rimani	rimanete	sèi rimasto	siète rimasti
rimane	rimàngono	è rimasto	sono rimasti
2 imperfect indicative		9 past perfect	
rimanevo	rimanevamo	èro rimasto	eravamo rimasti
rimanevi	rimanevate	èri rimasto	eravate rimasti
rimaneva	rimanévano	èra rimasto	èrano rimasti
3 past absolute		10 past anterior	
rimasi	rimanemmo	fui rimasto	fummo rimasti
rimanesti	rimaneste	fosti rimasto	foste rimasti
rimase	rimàsero	fu rimasto	fúrono rimasti
4 future indicative		11 future perfect	
rimarrò	rimarremo	sarò rimasto	saremo rimasti
rimarrai	rimarrete	sarai rimasto	sarete rimasti
rimarrà	rimarranno	sarà rimasto	saranno rimasti
5 present conditional		12 past conditional	
rimarrèi	rimarremmo	sarèi rimasto	saremmo rimasti
rimarresti	rimarreste	saresti rimasto	sareste rimasti
rimarrèbbe	rimarrèbbero	sarèbbe rimasto	sarèbbero rimasti
6 present subjunctive		13 past subjunctive	
rimanga	rimaniamo	sia rimasto	siamo rimasti
rimanga	rimaniate	sia rimasto	siate rimasti
rimanga	rimàngano	sia rimasto	síano rimasti
7 imperfect subjunctive		14 past perfect subjunctive	
rimanessi	rimanéssimo	fossi rimasto	fóssimo rimasti
rimanessi	rimaneste	fossi rimasto	foste rimasti
rimanesse	rimanéssero	fosse rimasto	fóssero rimasti

imperative

—	rimaniamo
rimani (non rimanere)	rimanete
rimanga	rimàngano

Words related to this verb
Roberto è rimasto a casa perchè era malato. Robert stayed home because he was ill.
Solo questo è rimasto. Only this is left.

rincréscere   Ger. rincrescèndo   Past Part. rincresciuto

to be sorry for, to regret

The Seven Simple Tenses		The Seven Compound Tenses	
Singular	Plural	Singular	Plural
1 present indicative		8 present perfect	
rincresco	rincresciamo	sono rincresciuto	siamo rincresciuti
rincresci	rincrescete	sèi rincresciuto	siète rincresciuti
rincresce	rincréscono	è rincresciuto	sono rincresciuti
2 imperfect indicative		9 past perfect	
rincrescevo	rincrescevamo	èro rincresciuto	eravamo rincresciuti
rincrescevi	rincrescevate	èri rincresciuto	eravate rincresciuti
rincresceva	rincrescévano	èra rincresciuto	èrano rincresciuti
3 past absolute		10 past anterior	
rincrebbi	rincrescemmo	fui rincresciuto	fummo rincresciuti
rincrescesti	rincresceste	fosti rincresciuto	foste rincresciuti
rincrebbe	rincrébbero	fu rincresciuto	fúrono rincresciuti
4 future indicative		11 future perfect	
rincrescerò	rincresceremo	sarò rincresciuto	saremo rincresciuti
rincrescerai	rincrescerete	sarai rincresciuto	sarete rincresciuti
rincrescerà	rincresceranno	sarà rincresciuto	saranno rincresciuti
5 present conditional		12 past conditional	
rincrescerèi	rincresceremmo	sarèi rincresciuto	saremmo rincresciuti
rincresceresti	rincrescereste	saresti rincresciuto	sareste rincresciuti
rincrescerèbbe	rincrescerèbbero	sarèbbe rincresciuto	sarèbbero rincresciuti
6 present subjunctive		13 past subjunctive	
rincresca	rincresciamo	sia rincresciuto	siamo rincresciuti
rincresca	rincresciate	sia rincresciuto	siate rincresciuti
rincresca	rincréscano	sia rincresciuto	síano rincresciuti
7 imperfect subjunctive		14 past perfect subjunctive	
rincrescessi	rincrescéssimo	fossi rincresciuto	fóssimo rincresciuti
rincrescessi	rincresceste	fossi rincresciuto	foste rincresciuti
rincrescesse	rincrescéssero	fosse rincresciuto	fóssero rincresciuti

	imperative	
—		rincresciamo
rincresci (non rincréscere)		rincrescete
rincresca		rincréscano

Words related to this verb
Mi rincresce che non l'ho visto.   I'm sorry that I did not see him.
Ti rincresce aprire la finestra?   Would you mind opening the window?

to thank

The Seven Simple Tenses		The Seven Compound Tenses	
Singular	Plural	Singular	Plural
1 present indicative		8 present perfect	
ringràzio	ringraziamo	ho ringraziato	abbiamo ringraziato
ringràzi	ringraziate	hai ringraziato	avete ringraziato
ringràzia	ringraziano	ha ringraziato	hanno ringraziato
2 imperfect indicative		9 past perfect	
ringraziavo	ringraziavamo	avevo ringraziato	avevamo ringraziato
ringraziavi	ringraziavate	avevi ringraziato	avevate ringraziato
ringraziava	ringraziàvano	aveva ringraziato	avévano ringraziato
3 past absolute		10 past anterior	
ringraziai	ringraziammo	èbbi ringraziato	avemmo ringraziato
ringraziasti	ringraziaste	avesti ringraziato	aveste ringraziato
ringraziò	ringraziàrono	èbbe ringraziato	èbbero ringraziato
4 future indicative		11 future perfect	
ringrazierò	ringrazieremo	avrò ringraziato	avremo ringraziato
ringrazierai	ringrazierete	avrai ringraziato	avrete ringraziato
ringrazierà	ringrazieranno	avrà ringraziato	avranno ringraziato
5 present conditional		12 past conditional	
ringrazierèi	ringrazieremmo	avrèi ringraziato	avremmo ringraziato
ringrazieresti	ringraziereste	avresti ringraziato	avreste ringraziato
ringrazierèbbe	ringrazierèbbero	avrèbbe ringraziato	avrèbbero ringraziato
6 present subjunctive		13 past subjunctive	
ringràzi	ringraziamo	àbbia ringraziato	abbiamo ringraziato
ringràzi	ringraziate	àbbia ringraziato	abbiate ringraziato
ringràzi	ringràzino	àbbia ringraziato	àbbiano ringraziato
7 imperfect subjunctive		14 past perfect subjunctive	
ringraziassi	ringraziàssimo	avessi ringraziato	avéssimo ringraziato
ringraziassi	ringraziaste	avessi ringraziato	aveste ringraziato
ringraziasse	ringraziàssero	avesse ringraizato	avéssero ringraziato

imperative		
—	ringraziamo	
ringràzia (non ringraziare)	ringraziate	
ringràzi	ringràzino	

Words related to this verb
ringraziare di cuore   to thank heartily
Sia ringraziato il cielo!   Thank heavens!

riscaldare

Ger. **riscaldando**   Past Part. **riscaldato**

to heat, to warm up

The Seven Simple Tenses		The Seven Compound Tenses	
Singular	Plural	Singular	Plural
1 present indicative		8 present perfect	
riscàldo	riscaldiamo	ho riscaldato	abbiamo riscaldato
riscàldi	riscaldate	hai riscaldato	avete riscaldato
riscàlda	riscaldano	ha riscaldato	hanno riscaldato
2 imperfect indicative		9 past perfect	
riscaldavo	riscaldavamo	avevo riscaldato	avevamo riscaldato
riscaldavi	riscaldavate	avevi riscaldato	avevate riscaldato
riscaldava	riscaldàvano	aveva riscaldato	avévano riscaldato
3 past absolute		10 past anterior	
riscaldai	riscaldammo	èbbi riscaldato	avemmo riscaldato
riscaldasti	riscaldaste	avesti riscaldato	aveste riscaldato
riscaldò	riscaldàrono	èbbe riscaldato	èbbero riscaldato
4 future indicative		11 future perfect	
riscalderò	riscalderemo	avrò riscaldato	avremo riscaldato
riscalderai	riscalderete	avrai riscaldato	avrete riscaldato
riscalderà	riscalderanno	avrà riscaldato	avranno riscaldato
5 present conditional		12 past conditional	
riscalderèi	riscalderemmo	avrèi riscaldato	avremmo riscaldato
riscalderesti	riscaldereste	avresti riscaldato	avreste riscaldato
riscalderèbbe	riscalderèbbero	avrèbbe riscaldato	avrèbbero riscaldato
6 present subjunctive		13 past subjunctive	
riscàldi	riscaldiamo	àbbia riscaldato	abbiamo riscaldato
riscàldi	riscaldiate	àbbia riscaldato	abbiate riscaldato
riscàldi	riscàldino	àbbia riscaldato	àbbiano riscaldato
7 imperfect subjunctive		14 past perfect subjunctive	
riscaldassi	riscaldàssimo	avessi riscaldato	avéssimo riscaldato
riscaldassi	riscaldaste	avessi riscaldato	aveste riscaldato
riscaldasse	riscaldàssero	avesse riscaldato	avéssero riscaldato

	imperative	
—	riscaldiamo	
riscàlda (non riscaldare)	riscaldate	
riscàldi	riscàldino	

Words related to this verb

Il cameriere riscalda il caffè.   The waiter is warming up the coffee.
Il sole riscalda l'aria.   The sun warms up the air.

to resolve

The Seven Simple Tenses		The Seven Compound Tenses	
Singular	Plural	Singular	Plural
1 present indicative		8 present perfect	
risòlvo	risolviamo	ho risolto	abbiamo risolto
risòlvi	risolvete	hai risolto	avete risolto
risòlve	risòlvono	ha risolto	hanno risolto
2 imperfect indicative		9 past perfect	
risolvevo	risolvevamo	avevo risolto	avevamo risolto
risolvevi	risolvevate	avevi risolto	avevate risolto
risolveva	risolvévano	aveva risolto	avévano risolto
3 past absolute		10 past anterior	
risolsi	risolvemmo	èbbi risolto	avemmo risolto
risolvesti	risolveste	avesti risolto	aveste risolto
risolse	risólsero	èbbe risolto	èbbero risolto
4 future indicative		11 future perfect	
risolverò	risolveremo	avrò risolto	avremo risolto
risolverai	risolverete	avrai risolto	avrete risolto
risolverà	risolveranno	avrà risolto	avranno risolto
5 present conditional		12 past conditional	
risolverèi	risolveremmo	avrèi risolto	avremmo risolto
risolveresti	risolvereste	avresti risolto	avreste risolto
risolverèbbe	risolverèbbero	avrèbbe risolto	avrèbbero risolto
6 present subjunctive		13 past subjunctive	
risòlva	risolviamo	àbbia risolto	abbiamo risolto
risòlva	risolviate	àbbia risolto	abbiate risolto
risòlva	risòlvano	àbbia risolto	àbbiano risolto
7 imperfect subjunctive		14 past perfect subjunctive	
risolvessi	risolvéssimo	avessi risolto	avéssimo risolto
risolvessi	risolveste	avessi risolto	aveste risolto
risolvesse	risolvéssero	avesse risolto	avéssero risolto

imperative	
—	risolviamo
risòlvi (non risolvere)	risolvete
risòlva	risòlvano

Words related to this verb
risolvere un dubbio   to resolve a doubt
risolvere una questione   to settle a question

rispóndere   Ger. rispondèndo   Past Part. rispòsto

to answer, to reply

The Seven Simple Tenses		The Seven Compound Tenses	
Singular	Plural	Singular	Plural
1 present indicative		8 present perfect	
rispondo	rispondiamo	ho rispòsto	abbiamo rispòsto
rispondi	rispondete	hai rispòsto	avete rispòsto
risponde	rispóndono	ha rispòsto	hanno rispòsto
2 imperfect indicative		9 past perfect	
rispondevo	rispondevamo	avevo rispòsto	avevamo rispòsto
rispondevi	rispondevate	avevi rispòsto	avevate rispòsto
rispondeva	rispondévano	aveva rispòsto	avévano rispòsto
3 past absolute		10 past anterior	
risposi	rispondemmo	èbbi rispòsto	avemmo rispòsto
rispondesti	rispondeste	avesti rispòsto	aveste rispòsto
rispose	rispósero	èbbe rispòsto	èbbero rispòsto
4 future indicative		11 future perfect	
risponderò	risponderemo	avrò rispòsto	avremo rispòsto
risponderai	risponderete	avrai rispòsto	avrete rispòsto
risponderà	risponderanno	avrà rispòsto	avranno rispòsto
5 present conditional		12 past conditional	
risponderèi	risponderemmo	avrèi rispòsto	avremmo rispòsto
risponderesti	rispondereste	avresti rispòsto	avreste rispòsto
risponderèbbe	risponderèbbero	avrèbbe rispòsto	avrèbbero rispòsto
6 present subjunctive		13 past subjunctive	
risponda	rispondiamo	àbbia rispòsto	abbiamo rispòsto
risponda	rispondiate	àbbia rispòsto	abbiate rispòsto
risponda	rispóndano	àbbia rispòsto	àbbiano rispòsto
7 imperfect subjunctive		14 past perfect subjunctive	
rispondessi	rispondéssimo	avessi rispòsto	avéssimo rispòsto
rispondessi	rispondeste	avessi rispòsto	aveste rispòsto
rispondesse	rispondéssero	avesse rispòsto	avéssero rispòsto

imperative	
—	rispondiamo
rispondi (non rispóndere)	rispondete
risponda	rispóndano

Words related to this verb

Perchè Pietro non risponde alle mie lettere? Why doesn't Peter answer my letters?
Lui rispose bruscamente. He replied brusquely.

to hold, to detain, to stop, to retain

The Seven Simple Tenses		The Seven Compound Tenses	
Singular	Plural	Singular	Plural
1 present indicative		8 present perfect	
ritèngo	**riteniamo**	**ho ritenuto**	**abbiamo ritenuto**
ritièni	**ritenete**	**hai ritenuto**	**avete ritenuto**
ritiène	**ritèngono**	**ha ritenuto**	**hanno ritenuto**
2 imperfect indicative		9 past perfect	
ritenevo	**ritenevamo**	**avevo ritenuto**	**avevamo ritenuto**
ritenevi	**ritenevate**	**avevi ritenuto**	**avevate ritenuto**
riteneva	**ritenévano**	**aveva ritenuto**	**avévano ritenuto**
3 past absolute		10 past anterior	
ritenni	**ritenemmo**	**èbbi ritenuto**	**avemmo ritenuto**
ritenesti	**riteneste**	**avesti ritenuto**	**aveste ritenuto**
ritenne	**riténnero**	**èbbe ritenuto**	**èbbero ritenuto**
4 future indicative		11 future perfect	
riterrò	**riterremo**	**avrò ritenuto**	**avremo ritenuto**
riterrai	**riterrete**	**avrai ritenuto**	**avrete ritenuto**
riterrà	**riterranno**	**avrà ritenuto**	**avranno ritenuto**
5 present conditional		12 past conditional	
riterrèi	**riterremmo**	**avrèi ritenuto**	**avremmo ritenuto**
riterresti	**riterreste**	**avresti ritenuto**	**avreste ritenuto**
riterrèbbe	**riterrèbbero**	**avrèbbe ritenuto**	**avrèbbero ritenuto**
6 present subjunctive		13 past subjunctive	
ritènga	**riteniamo**	**àbbia ritenuto**	**abbiamo ritenuto**
ritènga	**riteniate**	**àbbia ritenuto**	**abbiate ritenuto**
ritènga	**ritèngano**	**àbbia ritenuto**	**àbbiano ritenuto**
7 imperfect subjunctive		14 past perfect subjunctive	
ritenessi	**ritenéssimo**	**avessi ritenuto**	**avéssimo ritenuto**
ritenessi	**riteneste**	**avessi ritenuto**	**aveste ritenuto**
ritenesse	**ritenéssero**	**avesse ritenuto**	**avéssero ritenuto**

	imperative	
—	**riteniamo**	
ritièni (non ritenere)	**ritenete**	
ritènga	**ritèngano**	

Words related to this verb
ritenere le lacrime   to hold back one's tears
ritenere il posto   to keep one's place
ritenere il nemico   to hold the enemy back

ritornare	Ger. ritornando	Past Part. ritornato

to return, to come back, to go back

The Seven Simple Tenses		The Seven Compound Tenses	
Singular	Plural	Singular	Plural
1 present indicative		8 present perfect	
ritòrno	ritorniamo	sono ritornato	siamo ritornati
ritòrni	ritornate	sèi ritornato	sième ritornati
ritòrna	ritòrnano	è ritornato	sono ritornati
2 imperfect indicative		9 past perfect	
ritornavo	ritornavamo	èro ritornato	eravamo ritornati
ritornavi	ritornavate	èri ritornato	eravate ritornati
ritornava	ritornàvano	èra ritornato	èrano ritornati
3 past absolute		10 past anterior	
ritornai	ritornammo	fui ritornato	fummo ritornati
ritornasti	ritornaste	fosti ritornato	foste ritornati
ritornò	ritornàrono	fu ritornato	fúrono ritornati
4 future indicative		11 future perfect	
ritornerò	ritorneremo	sarò ritornato	saremo ritornati
ritornerai	ritornerete	sarai ritornato	sarete ritornati
ritornerà	ritorneranno	sarà ritornato	saranno ritornati
5 present conditional		12 past conditional	
ritornerèi	ritorneremmo	sarèi ritornato	saremmo ritornati
ritorneresti	ritornereste	saresti ritornato	sareste ritornati
ritornerèbbe	ritornerèbbero	sarèbbe ritornato	sarèbbero ritornati
6 present subjunctive		13 past subjunctive	
ritòrni	ritorniamo	sia ritornato	siamo ritornati
ritòrni	ritorniate	sia ritornato	siate ritornati
ritòrni	ritòrnino	sia ritornato	síano ritornati
7 imperfect subjunctive		14 past perfect subjunctive	
ritornassi	ritornàssimo	fossi ritornato	fóssimo ritornati
ritornassi	ritornaste	fossi ritornato	foste ritornati
ritornasse	ritornàssero	fosse ritornato	fóssero ritornati

imperative	
—	ritorniamo
ritòrna (non ritornare)	ritornate
ritòrni	ritòrnino

Words related to this verb
Non ritornerò più. I will never come back
ritornare ad una vecchia abitudine to go back to an old habit

to withdraw; to portray

The Seven Simple Tenses		The Seven Compound Tenses	
Singular	Plural	Singular	Plural
1 present indicative		8 present perfect	
ritraggo	ritraiamo (ritragghiamo)	ho ritratto	abbiamo ritratto
ritrai	ritraete	hai ritratto	avete ritratto
ritrae	ritràggono	ha ritratto	hanno ritratto
2 imperfect indicative		9 past perfect	
ritraevo	ritraevamo	avevo ritratto	avevamo ritratto
ritraevi	ritraevate	avevi ritratto	avevate ritratto
ritraeva	ritraévano	aveva ritratto	avévano ritratto
3 past absolute		10 past anterior	
ritrassi	ritraemmo	èbbi ritratto	avemmo ritratto
ritraesti	ritraeste	avesti ritratto	aveste ritratto
ritrasse	ritràssero	èbbe ritratto	èbbero ritratto
4 future indicative		11 future perfect	
ritrarrò	ritrarremo	avrò ritratto	avremo ritratto
ritrarrai	ritrarrete	avrai ritratto	avrete ritratto
ritrarrà	ritrarranno	avrà ritratto	avranno ritratto
5 present conditional		12 past conditional	
ritrarrèi	ritrarremmo	avrèi ritratto	avremmo ritratto
ritrarresti	ritrarreste	avresti ritratto	avreste ritratto
ritrarrèbbe	ritrarrèbbero	avrèbbe ritratto	avrèbbero ritratto
6 present subjunctive		13 past subjunctive	
ritragga	ritraiamo (ritragghiamo)	àbbia ritratto	abbiamo ritratto
ritragga	ritraiate (ritragghiate)	àbbia ritratto	abbiate ritratto
ritragga	ritràggano	àbbia ritratto	àbbiano ritratto
7 imperfect subjunctive		14 past perfect subjunctive	
ritraessi	ritraéssimo	avessi ritratto	avéssimo ritratto
ritraessi	ritraeste	avessi ritratto	aveste ritratto
ritraesse	ritraéssero	avesse ritratto	avéssero ritratto

	imperative	
		ritraiamo (ritragghiamo)
	ritrai (non ritrarre)	ritraete
	ritragga	ritràggano

Words related to this verb
All'improvviso, lui ritrasse la mano.   All of a sudden, he withdrew his hand.
L'artista ritrae la scena bene.   The artist portrays the scene well

riuscire   Ger. **riuscèndo**   Past Part. **riuscito**

to succeed, to go out again

The Seven Simple Tenses		The Seven Compound Tenses	
Singular	Plural	Singular	Plural
1 present indicative		8 present perfect	
rièsco	riusciamo	sono riuscito	siamo riusciti
rièsci	riuscite	sèi riuscito	siète riusciti
rièsce	rièscono	è riuscito	sono riusciti
2 imperfect indicative		9 past perfect	
riuscivo	riuscivamo	èro riuscito	eravamo riusciti
riuscivi	riuscivate	èri riuscito	eravate riusciti
riusciva	riuscívano	èra riuscito	èrano riusciti
3 past absolute		10 past anterior	
riuscii	riuscimmo	fui riuscito	fummo riusciti
riuscisti	riusciste	fosti riuscito	foste riusciti
riuscí	riuscírono	fu riuscito	fúrono riusciti
4 future indicative		11 future perfect	
riuscirò	riusciremo	sarò riuscito	saremo riusciti
riuscirai	riuscirete	sarai riuscito	sarete riusciti
riuscirà	riusciranno	sarà riuscito	saranno riusciti
5 present conditional		12 past conditional	
riuscirèi	riusciremmo	sarèi riuscito	saremmo riusciti
riusciresti	riuscireste	saresti riuscito	sareste riusciti
riuscirèbbe	riuscirèbbero	sarèbbe riuscito	sarèbbero riusciti
6 present subjunctive		13 past subjunctive	
rièsca	riusciamo	sia riuscito	siamo riusciti
rièsca	riusciate	sia riuscito	siate riusciti
rièsca	rièscano	sia riuscito	síano riusciti
7 imperfect subjunctive		14 past perfect subjunctive	
riuscissi	riuscíssimo	fossi riuscito	fóssimo riusciti
riuscissi	riusciste	fossi riuscito	foste riusciti
riuscisse	riuscíssero	fosse riuscito	fóssero riusciti

	imperative	
—		riusciamo
rièsci (non riuscire)		riuscite
rièsca		rièscano

Words related to this verb

Se non si prova, non si riesce.   If one doesn't try, one doesn't succeed.
Dopo mangiato, Maria è riuscita.   After eating, Mary went out again.

to turn around; to apply

The Seven Simple Tenses		The Seven Compound Tenses	
Singular	Plural	Singular	Plural
1 present indicative		8 present perfect	
mi rivòlgo	ci rivolgiamo	mi sono rivòlto	ci siamo rivòlti
ti rivòlgi	vi rivolgete	ti sèi rivòlto	vi siète rivòlti
si rivòlge	si rivòlgono	si è rivòlto	si sono rivòlti
2 imperfect indicative		9 past perfect	
mi rivolgevo	ci rivolgevamo	mi èro rivòlto	ci eravamo rivòlti
ti rivolgevi	vi rivolgevate	ti èri rivòlto	vi eravate rivòlti
si rivolgeva	si rivolgévano	si èra rivòlto	si èrano rivòlti
3 past absolute		10 past anterior	
mi rivòlsi	ci rivolgemmo	mi fui rivòlto	ci fummo rivòlti
ti rivolgesti	vi rivolgeste	ti fosti rivòlto	vi foste rivòlti
si rivòlse	si rivòlsero	si fu rivòlto	si fúrono rivòlti
4 future indicative		11 future perfect	
mi rivolgerò	ci rivolgeremo	mi sarò rivòlto	ci saremo rivòlti
ti rivolgerai	vi rivolgerete	ti sarai rivòlto	vi sarete rivòlti
si rivolgerà	si rivolgeranno	si sarà rivòlto	si saranno rivòlti
5 present conditional		12 past conditional	
mi rivolgerèi	ci rivolgeremmo	mi sarèi rivòlto	ci saremmo rivòlti
ti rivolgeresti	vi rivolgereste	ti saresti rivòlto	vi sareste rivòlti
si rivolgerèbbe	si rivolgerèbbero	si sarèbbe rivòlto	si sarèbbero rivòlti
6 present subjunctive		13 past subjunctive	
mi rivòlga	ci rivolgiamo	mi sia rivòlto	ci siamo rivòlti
ti rivòlga	vi rivolgiate	ti sia rivòlto	vi siate rivòlti
si rivòlga	si rivòlgano	si sia rivòlto	si síano rivòlti
7 imperfect subjunctive		14 past perfect subjunctive	
mi rivolgessi	ci rivolgéssimo	mi fossi rivòlto	ci fóssimo rivòlti
ti rivolgessi	vi rivolgeste	ti fossi rivòlto	vi foste rivòlti
si rivolgesse	si rivolgéssero	si fosse rivòlto	si fóssero rivòlti

imperative	
—	rivòlgiamoci
rivòlgiti (non ti rivòlgere)	rivolgétevi
si rivòlga	si rivòlgano

Words related to this verb

Io mi rivolsi alla persona che parlava.   I turned to the person who was speaking.
A chi rivolgi queste parole?   To whom are you addressing these words?

ródere* Ger. rodèndo Past Part. roso

to gnaw

The Seven Simple Tenses		The Seven Compound Tenses	
Singular	Plural	Singular	Plural
1 present indicative		8 present perfect	
rodo	rodiamo	ho roso	abbiamo roso
rodi	rodete	hai roso	avete roso
rode	ródono	ha roso	hanno roso
2 imperfect indicative		9 past perfect	
rodevo	rodevamo	avevo roso	avevamo roso
rodevi	rodevate	avevi roso	avevate roso
rodeva	rodévano	aveva roso	avévano roso
3 past absolute		10 past anterior	
rosi	rodemmo	èbbi roso	avemmo roso
rodesti	rodeste	avesti roso	aveste roso
rose	rósero	èbbe roso	èbbero roso
4 future indicative		11 future perfect	
roderò	roderemo	avrò roso	avremo roso
roderai	roderete	avrai roso	avrete roso
roderà	roderanno	avrà roso	avranno roso
5 present conditional		12 past conditional	
roderèi	roderemmo	avrèi roso	avremmo roso
roderesti	rodereste	avresti roso	avreste roso
roderèbbe	roderèbbero	avrèbbe roso	avrèbbero roso
6 present subjunctive		13 past subjunctive	
roda	rodiamo	àbbia roso	abbiamo roso
roda	rodiate	àbbia roso	abbiate roso
roda	ródano	àbbia roso	àbbiano roso
7 imperfect subjunctive		14 past perfect subjunctive	
rodessi	rodéssimo	avessi roso	avéssimo roso
rodessi	rodeste	avessi roso	aveste roso
rodesse	rodéssero	avesse roso	avéssero roso

	imperative
—	rodiamo
rodi (non ródere)	rodete
roda	ródano

* Like *ródere* are *corródere* and *eródere*.

Words related to this verb
Al cane piace rodere l'osso. The dog likes to gnaw on the bone.
É un osso duro da rodere! It's a hard nut to crack!

to break

The Seven Simple Tenses		The Seven Compound Tenses	
Singular	Plural	Singular	Plural
1 present indicative		8 present perfect	
rompo	rompiamo	ho rotto	abbiamo rotto
rompi	rompete	hai rotto	avete rotto
rompe	rómpono	ha rotto	hanno rotto
2 imperfect indicative		9 past perfect	
rompevo	rompevamo	avevo rotto	avevamo rotto
rompevi	rompevate	avevi rotto	avevate rotto
rompeva	rompévano	aveva rotto	avévano rotto
3 past absolute		10 past anterior	
ruppi	rompemmo	èbbi rotto	avemmo rotto
rompesti	rompeste	avesti rotto	aveste rotto
ruppe	rúppero	èbbe rotto	èbbero rotto
4 future indicative		11 future perfect	
romperò	romperemo	avrò rotto	avremo rotto
romperai	romperete	avrai rotto	avrete rotto
romperà	romperanno	avrà rotto	avranno rotto
5 present conditional		12 past conditional	
romperèi	romperemmo	avrèi rotto	avremmo rotto
romperesti	rompereste	avresti rotto	avreste rotto
romperèbbe	romperèbbero	avrèbbe rotto	avrèbbero rotto
6 present subjunctive		13 past subjunctive	
rompa	rompiamo	àbbia rotto	abbiamo rotto
rompa	rompiate	àbbia rotto	abbiate rotto
rompa	rómpano	àbbia rotto	àbbiano rotto
7 imperfect subjunctive		14 past perfect subjunctive	
rompessi	rompéssimo	avessi rotto	avéssimo rotto
rompessi	rompeste	avessi rotto	aveste rotto
rompesse	rompéssero	avesse rotto	avéssero rotto

imperative	
—	rómpiamo
rompi (non rómpere)	rompete
rompa	rómpano

* Like *rómpere* are *corrómpere*, *interrómpere*, *prorómpere*, etc.

Words related to this verb
Lui non rompe mai niente   He never breaks anything.
Io ho rotto la tazza.   I have broken the cup.
Chi ha rotto il vetro?   Who broke the glass?

salire*   Ger. **salèndo**   Past Part. **salito**

to go up, to come up, to mount

The Seven Simple Tenses		The Seven Compound Tenses	
Singular	Plural	Singular	Plural
1 present indicative		8 present perfect	
salgo	saliamo	sono salito	siamo saliti
sali	salite	sèi salito	sièlte saliti
sale	sàlgono	è salito	sono saliti
2 imperfect indicative		9 past perfect	
salivo	salivamo	èro salito	eravamo saliti
salivi	salivate	èri salito	eravate saliti
saliva	salívano	èra salito	érano saliti
3 past absolute		10 past anterior	
salii	salimmo	fui salito	fummo saliti
salisti	saliste	fosti salito	foste saliti
salí	salírono	fu salito	fúrono saliti
4 future indicative		11 future perfect	
salirò	saliremo	sarò salito	saremo saliti
salirai	salirete	sarai salito	sarete saliti
salirà	saliranno	sarà salito	saranno saliti
5 present conditional		12 past conditional	
salirèi	saliremmo	sarèi salito	saremmo saliti
saliresti	salireste	saresti salito	sareste saliti
salirèbbe	salirèbbero	sarèbbe salito	sarèbbero saliti
6 present subjunctive		13 past subjunctive	
salga	saliamo	sia salito	siamo saliti
salga	saliate	sia salito	siate saliti
salga	sàlgano	sia salito	síano saliti
7 imperfect subjunctive		14 past perfect subjunctive	
salissi	salíssimo	fossi salito	fóssimo saliti
salissi	saliste	fossi salito	foste saliti
salisse	salíssero	fosse salito	fóssero saliti

	imperative	
—		saliamo
sali (non salire)		salite
salga		sàlgano

*Like *salire* are *assalire* (conj. with *avere*) and *risalire*.

Words related to this verb
Io salgo le scale ogni giorno.   I go up the stairs every day.
Lui è salito al sommo del monte.   He climbed to the top of the mountain.

to jump, to leap

The Seven Simple Tenses		The Seven Compound Tenses	
Singular	Plural	Singular	Plural
1 present indicative		8 present perfect	
sàlto	saltiamo	ho saltato	abbiamo saltato
sàlti	saltate	hai saltato	avete saltato
sàlta	sàltano	ha saltato	hanno saltato
2 imperfect indicative		9 past perfect	
saltavo	saltavamo	avevo saltato	avevamo saltato
saltavi	saltavate	avevi saltato	avevate saltato
saltava	saltàvano	aveva saltato	avévano saltato
3 past absolute		10 past anterior	
saltai	saltammo	èbbi saltato	avemmo saltato
saltasti	saltaste	avesti saltato	aveste saltato
saltò	saltàrono	èbbe saltato	èbbero saltato
4 future indicative		11 future perfect	
salterò	salteremo	avrò saltato	avremo saltato
salterai	salterete	avrai saltato	avrete saltato
salterà	salteranno	avrà saltato	avranno saltato
5 present conditional		12 past conditional	
salterèi	salteremmo	avrèi saltato	avremmo saltato
slateresti	saltereste	avresti saltato	avreste saltato
salterèbbe	salterèbbero	avrèbbe saltato	avrèbbero saltato
6 present subjunctive		13 past subjunctive	
sàlti	saltiamo	àbbia saltato	abbiamo saltato
sàlti	saltiate	àbbia saltato	abbiate saltato
sàlti	sàltino	àbbia saltato	àbbiano saltato
7 imperfect subjunctive		14 past perfect subjunctive	
saltassi	saltàssimo	avessi saltato	avéssimo saltato
saltassi	saltaste	avessi saltato	aveste saltato
saltasse	saltàssero	avesse saltato	avéssero saltato

imperative	
—	saltiamo
sàlta (non saltare)	saltate
sàlti	sàltino

Words related to this verb
Egli saltò due metri.   He jumped two meters.
Il cane mi saltò addosso.   The dog jumped on me.

235

sapere	Ger. sapèndo	Past Part. saputo

to know; to learn (in the Past Abs. and compound tenses)

The Seven Simple Tenses		The Seven Compound Tenses	
Singular	Plural	Singular	Plural
1 present indicative		8 present perfect	
so	sappiamo	ho* saputo	abbiamo saputo
sai	sapete	hai saputo	avete saputo
sa	sanno	ha saputo	hanno saputo
2 imperfect indicative		9 past perfect	
sapevo	sapevamo	avevo saputo	avevamo saputo
sapevi	sapevate	avevi saputo	avevate saputo
sapeva	sapévano	aveva saputo	avévano saputo
3 past absolute		10 past anterior	
sèppi	sapemmo	èbbi saputo	avemmo saputo
sapesti	sapeste	avesti saputo	aveste saputo
sèppe	sèppero	èbbe saputo	èbbero saputo
4 future indicative		11 future perfect	
saprò	sapremo	avrò saputo	avremo saputo
saprai	saprete	avrai saputo	avrete saputo
saprà	sapranno	avrà saputo	avranno saputo
5 present conditional		12 past conditional	
saprèi	sapremmo	avrèi saputo	avremmo saputo
sapresti	sapreste	avresti saputo	avreste saputo
saprèbbe	saprèbbero	avrèbbe saputo	avrèbbero saputo
6 present subjunctive		13 past subjunctive	
sàppia	sappiamo	àbbia saputo	abbiamo saputo
sàppia	sappiate	àbbia saputo	abbiate saputo
sàppia	sàppiano	àbbia saputo	àbbiano saputo
7 imperfect subjunctive		14 past perfect subjunctive	
sapessi	sapéssimo	avessi saputo	avéssimo saputo
sapessi	sapeste	avessi saputo	aveste saputo
sapesse	sapéssero	avesse saputo	avéssero saputo

imperative	
—	sappiamo
sappi (non sapere)	sappiate
sàppia	sàppiano

* *Sapere* takes *èssere* when the following infinitive requires it.

Words related to this verb
Io so parlare italiano.   I know how to speak Italian.
Giovanni seppe del fatto due mesi dopo.   John learned of the fact two months later.

to choose, to select

The Seven Simple Tenses		The Seven Compound Tenses	
Singular	Plural	Singular	Plural
1 present indicative		8 present perfect	
scelgo	scegliamo	ho scelto	abbiamo scelto
scegli	scegliete	hai scelto	avete scelto
sceglie	scélgono	ha scelto	hanno scelto
2 imperfect indicative		9 past perfect	
sceglievo	sceglievamo	avevo scelto	avevamo scelto
sceglievi	sceglievate	avevi scelto	avevate scelto
sceglieva	sceglievano	aveva scelto	avévano scelto
3 past absolute		10 past anterior	
scelsi	scegliemmo	èbbi scelto	avemmo scelto
scegliesti	sceglieste	avesti scelto	aveste scelto
scelse	scélsero	èbbe scelto	èbbero scelto
4 future indicative		11 future perfect	
sceglierò	sceglieremo	avrò scelto	avremo scelto
sceglierai	sceglierete	avrai scelto	avrete scelto
sceglierà	sceglieranno	avrà scelto	avranno scelto
5 present conditional		12 past conditional	
sceglierèi	sceglieremmo	avrèi scelto	avremmo scelto
sceglieresti	scegliereste	avresti scelto	avreste scelto
sceglierèbbe	sceglierèbbero	avrèbbe scelto	avrèbbero scelto
6 present subjunctive		13 past subjunctive	
scegla	scègliamo	àbbia scelto	abbiamo scelto
scegla	scegliate	àbbia scelto	abbiate scelto
scegla	scélgano	àbbia scelto	àbbiano scelto
7 imperfect subjunctive		14 past perfect subjunctive	
scegliessi	scegliéssimo	avessi scelto	avéssimo scelto
scegliessi	sceglieste	avessi scelto	aveste scelto
scegliesse	scegliéssero	avesse scelto	avéssero scelto

imperative	
—	scegliamo
scegli (non scégliere)	scegliete
scelga	scélgano

* Like *scégliere* is *sciògliere*, meaning *to untie*, *loosen*.

Words related to this verb
Lui ha scelto una donna intelligente come moglie.   He chose an intelligent woman for a wife.
Lei sceglie un vestito azzurro da indossare   She chooses a blue suit to wear.

scéndere* Ger. scendèndo Past Part. sceso

to descend; to go down, to come down

The Seven Simple Tenses		The Seven Compound Tenses	
Singular	Plural	Singular	Plural
1 present indicative		8 present perfect	
scendo	scendiamo	sono sceso	siamo scesi
scendi	scendete	sèi sceso	siète scesi
scende	scéndono	è sceso	sono scesi
2 imperfect indicative		9 past perfect	
scendevo	scendevamo	èro sceso	eravamo scesi
scendevi	scendevate	èri sceso	eravate scesi
scendeva	scendévano	èra sceso	érano scesi
3 past absolute		10 past anterior	
scesi	scendemmo	fui sceso	fummo scesi
scendesti	scendeste	fosti sceso	foste scesi
scese	scésero	fu sceso	fúrono scesi
4 future indicative		11 future perfect	
scenderò	scenderemo	sarò sceso	saremo scesi
scenderai	scenderete	sarai sceso	sarete scesi
scenderà	scenderanno	sarà sceso	saranno scesi
5 present conditional		12 past conditional	
scenderèi	scenderemmo	sarèi sceso	saremmo scesi
scenderesti	scendereste	saresti sceso	sareste scesi
scenderèbbe	scenderèbbero	sarèbbe sceso	sarèbbero scesi
6 present subjunctive		13 past subjunctive	
scenda	scendiamo	sia sceso	siamo scesi
scenda	scendiate	sia sceso	siate scesi
scenda	scéndano	sia sceso	síano scesi
7 imperfect subjunctive		14 past perfect subjunctive	
scendessi	scendéssimo	fossi sceso	fóssimo scesi
scendessi	scendeste	fossi sceso	foste scesi
scendesse	scendéssero	fosse sceso	fóssero scesi

	imperative	
—		scendiamo
scendi (non scéndere)		scendete
scenda		scéndano

*Like *scéndere* are *ascéndere*, *condiscéndere* (conjugated with *avere*), *discéndere*, etc.

Words related to this verb
Sono stanco(a). Non voglio scendere le scale un'altra volta. I'm tired. I don't want to go down the stairs again.
Se scendi, possiamo giocare. If you come down, we can play.

to disappear; to cut a sorry figure

The Seven Simple Tenses		The Seven Compound Tenses	
Singular	Plural	Singular	Plural
1 present indicative		**8 present perfect**	
scompaio	scompariamo	sono scomparso	siamo scomparsi
scompari	scomparite	sèi scomparso	siète scomparsi
scompare	scompàiono	è scomparso	sono scomparsi
(*Or regular:* scomparisco, *etc.*)			
2 imperfect indicative		**9 past perfect**	
scomparivo	scomparivamo	èro scomparso	eravamo scomparsi
scomparivi	scomparivate	èri scomparso	eravate scomparsi
scompariva	scomparívano	èra scomparso	èrano scomparsi
3 past absolute		**10 past anterior**	
scomparvi	scomparimmo	fui scomparso	fummo scomparsi
scomparisti	scompariste	fosti scomparso	foste scomparsi
scomparve	scompàrvero	fu scomparso	fúrono scomparsi
(*Or regular:* scomparii, *etc.*)			
4 future indicative		**11 future perfect**	
scomparirò	scompariremo	sarò scomparso	saremo scomparsi
scomparirai	scomparirete	sarai scomparso	sarete scomparsi
scomparirà	scompariranno	sarà scomparso	saranno scomparsi
5 present conditional		**12 past conditional**	
scomparirèi	scompariremmo	sarèi scomparso	saremmo scomparsi
scompariresti	scomparireste	saresti scomparso	sareste scomparsi
scomparirèbbe	scomparirèbbero	sarèbbe scomparso	sarèbbero scomparsi
6 present subjunctive		**13 past subjunctive**	
scompaia	scompariamo	sia scomparso	siamo scomparsi
scompaia	scompariate	sia scomparso	siate scomparsi
scompaia	scompàiano	sia scomparso	síano scomparsi
(*Or regular:* scomparisca, *etc.*)			
7 imperfect subjunctive		**14 past perfect subjunctive**	
scomparissi	scomparíssimo	fossi scomparso	fóssimo scomparsi
scomparissi	scompariste	fossi scomparso	foste scomparsi
scomparissse	scomparíssero	fosse scomparso	fóssero scomparsi

imperative

—	scompariamo
scompari (scomparisci) (non scomparire)	scomparite
scompaia (scomparisca)	scompàiano (scomparíscano)

* *Scomparire* meaning *to cut a sorry figure*, requires the regular tenses.

Words related to this verb
Lei è scomparsa.   She disappeared.
Lui scomparisce quando esce con gli amici.   He cuts a sorry figure when he goes out with his friends.

sconfíggere Ger. **sconfiggèndo** Past Part. **sconfitto**

to defeat

The Seven Simple Tenses		The Seven Compound Tenses	
Singular	Plural	Singular	Plural
1 present indicative		8 present perfect	
sconfiggo	**sconfiggiamo**	**ho sconfitto**	**abbiamo sconfitto**
sconfiggi	**sconfiggete**	**hai sconfitto**	**avete sconfitto**
sconfigge	**sconfíggono**	**ha sconfitto**	**hanno sconfitto**
2 imperfect indicative		9 past perfect	
sconfiggevo	**sconfiggevamo**	**avevo sconfitto**	**avevamo sconfitto**
sconfiggevi	**sconfiggevate**	**avevi sconfitto**	**avevate sconfitto**
sconfiggeva	**sconfiggévano**	**aveva sconfitto**	**avévano sconfitto**
3 past absolute		10 past anterior	
sconfissi	**sconfiggemmo**	**èbbi sconfitto**	**avemmo sconfitto**
sconfiggesti	**sconfiggeste**	**avesti sconfitto**	**aveste sconfitto**
sconfisse	**sconfíssero**	**èbbe sconfitto**	**èbbero sconfitto**
4 future indicative		11 future perfect	
sconfiggerò	**sconfiggeremo**	**avrò sconfitto**	**avremo sconfitto**
sconfiggerai	**sconfiggerete**	**avrai sconfitto**	**avrete sconfitto**
sconfiggerà	**sconfiggeranno**	**avrà sconfitto**	**avranno sconfitto**
5 present conditional		12 past conditional	
sconfiggerèi	**sconfiggeremmo**	**avrèi sconfitto**	**avremmo sconfitto**
sconfiggeresti	**sconfiggereste**	**avresti sconfitto**	**avreste sconfitto**
sconfiggerèbbe	**sconfiggerèbbero**	**avrèbbe sconfitto**	**avrèbbero sconfitto**
6 present subjunctive		13 past subjunctive	
sconfigga	**sconfiggiamo**	**àbbia sconfitto**	**abbiamo sconfitto**
sconfigga	**sconfiggiate**	**àbbia sconfitto**	**abbiate sconfitto**
sconfigga	**sconfíggano**	**àbbia sconfitto**	**àbbiano sconfitto**
7 imperfect subjunctive		14 past perfect subjunctive	
sconfiggessi	**sconfiggéssimo**	**avessi sconfitto**	**avéssimo sconfitto**
sconfiggessi	**sconfiggeste**	**avessi sconfitto**	**aveste sconfitto**
sconfiggesse	**sconfiggéssero**	**avesse sconfitto**	**avéssero sconfitto**

imperative	
—	**sconfiggiamo**
sconfiggi (non sconfíggere)	**sconfiggete**
sconfigga	**sconfiggano**

Words related to this verb
Lei mi sconfigge sempre quando giochiamo al tennis.   She always defeats me
when we play tennis.
Lui sconfisse il rivale.   He defeated his rival.

to uncover, to discover

The Seven Simple Tenses		The Seven Compound Tenses	
Singular	Plural	Singular	Plural
1 present indicative		8 present perfect	
scòpro	scopriamo	ho scopèrto	abbiamo scopèrto
scòpri	scoprite	hai scopèrto	avete scopèrto
scòpre	scòprono	ha scopèrto	hanno scopèrto
2 imperfect indicative		9 past perfect	
scoprivo	scoprivamo	avevo scopèrto	avevamo scopèrto
scoprivi	scoprivate	avevi scopèrto	avevate scopèrto
scopriva	scoprívano	aveva scopèrto	avévano scopèrto
3 past absolute		10 past anterior	
scopèrsi	scoprimmo	èbbi scopèrto	avemmo scopèrto
scopristi	scopriste	avesti scopèrto	aveste scopèrto
scopèrse	scopèrsero	èbbe scopèrto	èbbero scopèrto
(*Or regular;* scoprii, *etc.*)			
4 future indicative		11 future perfect	
scoprirò	scopriremo	avrò scopèrto	avremo scopèrto
scoprirai	scoprirete	avrai scopèrto	avrete scopèrto
scoprirà	scopriranno	avrà scopèrto	avranno scopèrto
5 present conditional		12 past conditional	
scoprirèi	scopriremmo	avrèi scopèrto	avremmo scopèrto
scopriresti	scoprireste	avresti scopèrto	avreste scopèrto
scoprirèbbe	scoprirèbbero	avrèbbe scopèrto	avrèbbero scopèrto
6 present subjunctive		13 past subjunctive	
scòpra	scopriamo	àbbia scopèrto	abbiamo scopèrto
scòpra	scopriate	àbbia scopèrto	abbiate scopèrto
scòpra	scòprano	àbbia scopèrto	àbbiano scopèrto
7 imperfect subjunctive		14 past perfect subjunctive	
scoprissi	scopríssimo	avessi scopèrto	avéssimo scopèrto
scoprissi	scopriste	avessi scopèrto	aveste scopèrto
scoprisse	scopríssero	avesse scopèrto	avéssero scopèrto

	imperative	
—	scopriamo	
scòpri (non scoprire)	scoprite	
scòpra	scòprano	

Words related to this verb

Ho scoperto una scatola piena di oro.   I discovered a box full of gold.
Colombo scoperse (scoprì) l'America.   Columbus discovered America.

241

scrívere*   Ger. scrivèndo   Past Part. scritto

to write

The Seven Simple Tenses		The Seven Compound Tenses	
Singular	Plural	Singular	Plural
1 present indicative		8 present perfect	
scrivo	scriviamo	ho scritto	abbiamo scritto
scrivi	scrivete	hai scritto	avete scritto
scrive	scrívono	ha scritto	hanno scritto
2 imperfect indicative		9 past perfect	
scrivevo	scrivevamo	avevo scritto	avevamo scritto
scrivevi	scrivevate	avevi scritto	avevate scritto
scriveva	scrivévano	aveva scritto	avévano scritto
3 past absolute		10 past anterior	
scrissi	scrivemmo	èbbi scritto	avemmo scritto
scrivesti	scriveste	avesti scritto	aveste scritto
scrisse	scríssero	èbbe scritto	èbbero scritto
4 future indicative		11 future perfect	
scriverò	scriveremo	avrò scritto	avremo scritto
scriverai	scriverete	avrai scritto	avrete scritto
scriverà	scriveranno	avrà scritto	avranno scritto
5 present conditional		12 past conditional	
scriverèi	scriveremmo	avrèi scritto	avremmo scritto
scriveresti	scrivereste	avresti scritto	avreste scritto
scriverèbbe	scriverèbbero	avrèbbe scritto	avrèbbero scritto
6 present subjunctive		13 past subjunctive	
scriva	scriviamo	àbbia scritto	abbiamo scritto
scriva	scriviate	àbbia scritto	abbiate scritto
scriva	scrívano	àbbia scritto	àbbiano scritto
7 imperfect subjunctive		14 past perfect subjunctive	
scrivessi	scrivéssimo	avessi scritto	avéssimo scritto
scrivessi	scriveste	avessi scritto	aveste scritto
scrivesse	scrivéssero	avesse scritto	avéssero scritto

imperative

—	scriviamo
scrivi (non scrívere)	scrivete
scriva	scrívano

* Like *scrívere* are *descrívere, prescrívere, proscrívere, soiioscrívere, trascrívere*, etc.

Words related to this verb
Lei ha scritto una bella poesia.   She has written a beautiful poem.
Io le scrissi una lettera.   I wrote her a letter.

scuòtere*

to shake

The Seven Simple Tenses		The Seven Compound Tenses	
Singular	Plural	Singular	Plural
1 present indicative		8 present perfect	
scuòto	scotiamo (scuotiamo)	ho scòsso	abbiamo scòsso
scuòti	scotete (scuotete)	hai scòsso	avete scòsso
scuòte	scuòtono	ha scòsso	hanno scòsso
2 imperfect indicative		9 past perfect	
scotevo (scuotevo)	scotevamo (scuotevamo)	avevo scòsso	avevamo scòsso
scotevi (scuotevi)	scotevate (scuotevate)	avevi scòsso	avevate scòsso
scoteva (scuoteva)	scotévano (scuotévano)	aveva scòsso	avévano scòsso
3 past absolute		10 past anterior	
scòssi	scotemmo (scuotemmo)	èbbi scòsso	avemmo scòsso
scotesti (scuotesti)	scoteste (scuoeste)	avesti scòsso	aveste scòsso
scòsse	scòssero	èbbe scòsso	èbbero scòsso
4 future indicative		11 future perfect	
scoterò (scuoterò)	scoteremo (scuoteremo)	avrò scòsso	avremo scòsso
scoterai (scuoterai)	scoterete (scuoterete)	avrai scòsso	avrete scòsso
scoterà (scuoterà)	scoteranno (scuoteranno)	avrà scòsso	avranno scòsso
5 present conditional		12 past conditional	
scoterèi (scuoterèi)	scoteremmo	avrèi scòsso	avremmo scòsso
	(scuoteremmo)	avresti scòsso	avreste scòsso
scoteresti	scotereste (scuotereste)	avrèbbe scòsso	avrèbbero scòsso
(scuoteresti)			
scoterèbbe	scoterèbbero		
(scuoterèbbe)	(scuoterèbbero)		
6 present subjunctive		13 past subjunctive	
scuòta	scotiamo (scuotiamo)	àbbia scòsso	abbiamo scòsso
scuòta	scotiate (scuotiate)	àbbia scòsso	abbiate scòsso
scuòta	scuòtano	àbbia scòsso	àbbiano scòsso
7 imperfect subjunctive		14 past perfect subjunctive	
scotessi (scuotessi)	scotéssimo (scuotéssimo)	avessi scòsso	avéssimo scòsso
scotessi (scuotessi)	scoteste (scuoteste)	avessi scòsso	aveste scòsso
scotesse (scuotesse)	scotéssero (scuotéssero)	avesse scòsso	avéssero scòsso

imperative	
—	scotiamo (scuotiamo)
scuòti (non scuòtere)	scotete (scuotete)
scuòta	scuòtano

*Like *scuòtere* are *percuòtere* and *riscuòtere*.

Words related to this verb
Il cane si scuote quando esce dall'acqua.   The dog shakes himself when he comes
out of the water.

scusare   Ger. **scusando**   Past Part. **scusato**

to excuse

The Seven Simple Tenses		The Seven Compound Tenses	
Singular	Plural	Singular	Plural
1 present indicative		8 present perfect	
scùso	scusiamo	ho scusato	abbiamo scusato
scùsi	scusate	hai scusato	avete scusato
scùsa	scusano	ha scusato	hanno scusato
2 imperfect indicative		9 past perfect	
scusavo	scusavamo	avevo scusato	avevamo scusato
scusavi	scusavate	avevi scusato	avevate scusato
scusava	scusàvano	aveva scusato	avévano scusato
3 past absolute		10 past anterior	
scusai	scusammo	èbbi scusato	avemmo scusato
scusasti	scusaste	avesti scusato	aveste scusato
scusò	scusàrono	èbbe scusato	èbbero scusato
4 future indicative		11 future perfect	
scuserò	scuseremo	avrò scusato	avremo scusato
scuserai	scuserete	avrai scusato	avrete scusato
scuserà	scuseranno	avrà scusato	avranno scusato
5 present conditional		12 past conditional	
scuserèi	scuseremmo	avrèi scusato	avremmo scusato
scuseresti	scusereste	avresti scusato	avreste scusato
scuserèbbe	scuserèbbero	avrèbbe scusato	avrèbbero scusato
6 present subjunctive		13 past subjunctive	
scùsi	scusiamo	àbbia scusato	abbiamo scusato
scùsi	scusiate	àbbia scusato	abbiate scusato
scùsi	scùsino	àbbia scusato	àbbiano scusato
7 imperfect subjunctive		14 past perfect subjunctive	
scusassi	scussàssimo	avessi scusato	avéssimo scusato
scusassi	scusaste	avessi scusato	aveste scusato
scusasse	scusàssero	avesse scusato	avéssero scusato

	imperative	
—		scusiamo
scùsa (non scusare)		scusate
scùsi		scùsino

Words related to this verb
Scusa la mia domanda.   Excuse my question.
Scusa! Scusi! Scusate!   Excuse me! Sorry! Pardon me!

to sit

The Seven Simple Tenses		The Seven Compound Tenses	
Singular	Plural	Singular	Plural
1 present indicative		8 present perfect	
sièdo (sèggo)	sediamo	ho seduto	abbiamo seduto
sièdi	sedete	hai seduto	avete seduto
sième	sièdono (sèggono)	ha seduto	hanno seduto
2 imperfect indicative		9 past perfect	
sedevo	sedevamo	avevo seduto	avevamo seduto
sedevi	sedevate	avevi seduto	avevate seduto
sedeva	sedévano	aveva seduto	avévano seduto
3 past absolute		10 past anterior	
sedei (sedètti)	sedemmo	èbbi seduto	avemmo seduto
sedesti	sedeste	avesti seduto	aveste seduto
sedé (sedètte)	sedérono (sedèttero)	èbbe seduto	èbbero seduto
4 future indicative		11 future perfect	
sederò	sederemo	avrò seduto	avremo seduto
sederai	sederete	avrai seduto	avrete seduto
sederà	sederanno	avrà seduto	avranno seduto
5 present conditional		12 past conditional	
sederèi	sederemmo	avrei seduto	avremmo seduto
sederesti	sedereste	avresti seduto	avreste seduto
sederèbbe	sederèbbero	avrèbbe seduto	avrèbbero seduto
6 present subjunctive		13 past subjunctive	
sièda (sègga)	sediamo	àbbia seduto	abbiamo seduto
sièda (sègga)	sediate	àbbia seduto	abbiate seduto
sièda (sègga)	sièdano (sèggano)	àbbia seduto	àbbiano seduto
7 imperfect subjunctive		14 past perfect subjunctive	
sedessi	sedéssimo	avessi seduto	avéssimo seduto
sedessi	sedeste	avessi seduto	aveste seduto
sedesse	sedéssero	avesse seduto	avéssero seduto

	imperative	
—		sediamo
sièdi (non sedere)		sedete
sièda (sègga)		sièdano (sèggano)

*Like *sedere* is *possedere*.

Words related to this verb
Lui sedeva vicino alla finestra. He was sitting near the window.
Noi ci sediamo sempre insieme a scuola. We always sit together in school.

seguire	Ger. seguendo	Past Part. seguito

to follow

The Seven Simple Tenses		The Seven Compound Tenses	
Singular	Plural	Singular	Plural
1 present indicative		8 present perfect	
sèguo	seguiamo	ho seguito	abbiamo seguito
sègui	seguite	hai seguito	avete seguito
sègue	seguono	ha seguito	hanno seguito
2 imperfect indicative		9 past perfect	
seguivo	seguivamo	avevo seguito	avevamo seguito
seguivi	seguivate	avevi seguito	avevate seguito
seguiva	seguivano	aveva seguito	avévano seguito
3 past absolute		10 past anterior	
seguii	seguimmo	èbbi seguito	avemmo seguito
seguisti	seguiste	avesti seguito	aveste seguito
seguì	seguirono	èbbe seguito	èbbero seguito
4 future indicative		11 future perfect	
seguirò	seguiremo	avrò seguito	avremo seguito
seguirai	seguirete	avrai seguito	avrete seguito
seguirà	seguiranno	avrà seguito	avranno seguito
5 present conditional		12 past conditional	
seguirèi	seguiremmo	avrèi seguito	avremmo seguito
seguiresti	seguireste	avresti seguito	avreste seguito
seguirèbbe	seguirèbbero	avrèbbe seguito	avrèbbero seguito
6 present subjunctive		13 past subjunctive	
sègua	seguiamo	àbbia seguito	abbiamo seguito
sègua	seguiate	àbbia seguito	abbiate seguito
sègua	sèguano	àbbia seguito	àbbiano seguito
7 imperfect subjunctive		14 past perfect subjunctive	
seguissi	seguíssimo	avessi seguito	avéssimo seguito
seguissi	seguiste	avessi seguito	aveste seguito
seguisse	seguíssero	avesse seguito	avéssero seguito

imperative	
—	seguiamo
sègui (non seguire)	seguite
sègua	sèguano

Words related to this verb
Segui quella macchina!   Follow that car!
Seguiamo questa strada.   Lets's follow this road.

The Seven Simple Tenses		The Seven Compound Tenses	
Singular	Plural	Singular	Plural
1 present indicative		8 present perfect	
sèrvo	serviamo	ho servito	abbiamo servito
sèrvi	servite	hai servito	avete servito
sèrve	servono	ha servito	hanno servito
2 imperfect indicative		9 past perfect	
servivo	servivamo	avevo servito	avevamo servito
servivi	servivate	avevi servito	avevate servito
serviva	servivano	aveva servito	avévano servito
3 past absolute		10 past anterior	
servii	servimmo	èbbi servito	avemmo servito
servisti	serviste	avesti servito	aveste servito
servì	servírono	èbbe servito	èbbero servito
4 future indicative		11 future perfect	
servirò	serviremo	avro servito	avremo servito
scrvirai	servirete	avrai servito	avrete servito
servirà	serviranno	avrà servito	avranno servito
5 present conditional		12 past conditional	
servirèi	serviremmo	avrèi servito	avremmo servito
serviresti	servireste	avresti servito	avreste servito
servirèbbe	servirèbbero	avrèbbe servito	avrèbbero servito
6 present subjunctive		13 past subjunctive	
sèrva	serviamo	àbbia servito	abbiamo servito
sèrva	serviate	àbbia servito	abbiate servito
sèrva	sèrvano	àbbia servito	àbbiano servito
7 imperfect subjunctive		14 past perfect subjunctive	
servissi	servìssimo	avessi servito	avéssimo servito
servissi	serviste	avessi servito	aveste servito
servisse	servìssero	avesse servito	avéssero servito

	imperative	
—	serviamo	
sèrvi (non servire)	servite	
sèrva	sèrvano	

Words related to this verb
La cameriera ha servito il caffè. The waitress served the coffee.
servire la patria to serve one's country

soddisfare Ger. **soddisfacèndo** Past Part. **soddisfatto**

to satisfy

The Seven Simple Tenses		The Seven Compound Tenses	
Singular	Plural	Singular	Plural
1 present indicative		8 present perfect	
soddisfaccio	**soddisfacciamo**	**ho soddisfatto**	**abbiamo soddisfatto**
(**soddisfò**)		**hai soddisfatto**	**avete soddisfatto**
soddisfai	**soddisfate**	**ha soddisfatto**	**hanno soddisfatto**
soddisfà	**soddisfanno**		
(*Or regular:* soddisfo, *etc.*)			
2 imperfect indicative		9 past perfect	
soddisfacevo	**soddisfacevamo**	**avevo soddisfatto**	**avevamo soddisfatto**
soddisfacevi	**soddisfacevate**	**avevi soddisfatto**	**avevate soddisfatto**
soddisfaceva	**soddisfacévano**	**aveva soddisfatto**	**avévano soddisfatto**
3 past absolute		10 past anterior	
soddisfeci	**soddisfacemmo**	**èbbi soddisfatto**	**avemmo soddisfatto**
soddisfacesti	**soddisfaceste**	**avesti soddisfatto**	**aveste soddisfatto**
soddisfece	**soddisfécero**	**èbbe soddisfatto**	**èbbero soddisfatto**
4 future indicative		11 future perfect	
soddisfarò	**soddisfaremo**	**avrò soddisfatto**	**avremo soddisfatto**
soddisfarai	**soddisfarete**	**avrai soddisfatto**	**avrete soddisfatto**
soddisfarà	**soddisfaranno**	**avrà soddisfatto**	**avranno soddisfatto**
(*Or regular:* soddisferò, *etc.*)			
5 present conditional		12 past conditional	
soddisfarèi	**soddisfaremmo**	**avrèi soddisfatto**	**avremmo soddisfatto**
soddisfaresti	**soddisfareste**	**avresti soddisfatto**	**avreste soddisfatto**
soddisfarèbbe	**soddisfarèbbero**	**avrèbbe soddisfatto**	**avrèbbero soddisfatto**
(*Or regular:* soddisferèi, *etc.*)			
6 present subjunctive		13 past subjunctive	
soddisfaccia	**soddisfacciamo**	**àbbia soddisfatto**	**abbiamo soddisfatto**
soddisfaccia	**soddisfacciate**	**àbbia soddisfatto**	**abbiate soddisfatto**
soddisfaccia	**soddisfàcciano**	**àbbia soddisfatto**	**àbbiano soddisfatto**
(*Or regular:* soddisfi, *etc.*)			
7 imperfect subjunctive		14 past perfect subjunctive	
soddisfacessi	**soddisfacéssimo**	**avessi soddisfatto**	**avéssimo soddisfatto**
soddisfacessi	**soddisfaceste**	**avessi soddisfatto**	**aveste soddisfatto**
soddisfacesse	**soddisfacéssero**	**avesse soddisfatto**	**avéssero soddisfatto**

imperative	
—	**soddisfacciamo** (**soddisfiamo**)
soddisfa' (**non soddisfare**)	**soddisfate**
soddisfaccia (**soddisfi**)	**soddisfàcciano** (**soddísfino**)

Words related to this verb
Lui non è mai soddisfatto. He is never satisfied.
Questo lavoro non mi soddisfa. This work does not satisfy me.

to suffer, to bear, to endure

The Seven Simple Tenses		The Seven Compound Tenses	
Singular	Plural	Singular	Plural
1 present indicative		8 present perfect	
sòffro	soffriamo	ho soffèrto	abbiamo soffèrto
sòffri	soffrite	hai soffèrto	avete soffèrto
sòffre	sòffrono	ha soffèrto	hanno soffèrto
2 imperfect indicative		9 past perfect	
soffrivo	soffrivamo	avevo soffèrto	avevamo soffèrto
soffrivi	soffrivate	avevi soffèrto	avevate soffèrto
soffriva	soffrívano	aveva soffèrto	avévano soffèrto
3 past absolute		10 past anterior	
soffèrsi	soffrimmo	èbbi soffèrto	avemmo soffèrto
soffristi	soffriste	avesti soffèrto	aveste soffèrto
soffèrse	soffèresero	èbbe soffèrto	èbbero soffèrto
(Or regular: soffrii, etc.)			
4 future indicative		11 future perfect	
soffrirò	soffriremo	avrò soffèrto	avremo soffèrto
soffrirai	soffrirete	avrai soffèrto	avrete soffèrto
soffrirà	soffriranno	avrà soffèrto	avranno soffèrto
5 present conditional		12 past conditional	
soffrirèi	soffriremmo	avrèi soffèrto	avremmo soffèrto
soffriresti	soffrireste	avresti soffèrto	avreste soffèrto
soffrirèbbe	soffrirèbbero	avrèbbe soffèrto	avrèbbero soffèrto
6 present subjunctive		13 past subjunctive	
sòffra	soffriamo	àbbia soffèrto	abbiamo soffèrto
sòffra	soffriate	àbbia soffèrto	abbiate soffèrto
sòffra	sòffrano	àbbia soffèrto	àbbiano soffèrto
7 imperfect subjunctive		14 past perfect subjunctive	
soffrissi	soffríssimo	avessi soffèrto	avéssimo soffèrto
soffrissi	soffriste	avessi soffèrto	aveste soffèrto
soffrisse	soffríssero	avesse soffèrto	avéssero soffèrto

imperative	
—	soffriamo
sòffri (non soffrire)	soffrite
sòffra	sòffrano

Words related to this verb
Il mio cane soffre molto il calso durante l'estate.   My dog suffers a lot from the heat during the summer.
Non posso soffrire quella persona.   I cannot bear (put up with) that person.

sognare	Ger. sognando	Past Part. sognato

to dream

The Seven Simple Tenses		The Seven Compound Tenses	
Singular	Plural	Singular	Plural
1 present indicative		**8 present perfect**	
sògno	sogniamo	ho sognato	abbiamo sognato
sògni	sognate	hai sognato	avete sognato
sògna	sògnano	ha sognato	hanno sognato
2 imperfect indicative		**9 past perfect**	
sognavo	sognavamo	avevo sognato	avevamo sognato
sognavi	sognavate	avevi sognato	avevate sognato
sognava	sognàvano	aveva sognato	avévano sognato
3 past absolute		**10 past anterior**	
sognai	sognammo	èbbi sognato	avemmo sognato
sognasti	sognaste	avesti sognato	aveste sognato
sognò	sognàrono	èbbe sognato	èbbero sognato
4 future indicative		**11 future perfect**	
sognerò	sogneremo	avrò sognato	avremo sognato
sognerai	sognerete	avrai sognato	avrete sognato
sognerà	sogneranno	avrà sognato	avranno sognato
5 present conditional		**12 past conditional**	
sognerèi	sogneremmo	avrèi sognato	avremmo sognato
sogneresti	sognereste	avresti sognato	avreste sognato
sognerèbbe	sognerèbbero	avrèbbe sognato	avrèbbero sognato
6 present subjunctive		**13 past subjunctive**	
sògni	sogniamo	àbbia sognato	abbiamo sognato
sògni	sogniate	àbbia sognato	abbiate sognato
sògni	sògnino	àbbia sognato	àbbiano sognato
7 imperfect subjunctive		**14 past perfect subjunctive**	
sognassi	sognàssimo	avessi sognato	avéssimo sognato
sognassi	sognaste	avessi sognato	aveste sognato
sognasse	sognàssero	avesse sognato	avéssero sognato

imperative	
—	sogniamo
sògna (non sognare)	sognate
sògni	sògnino

Words related to this verb
sogni d'oro   sweet dreams
essere nel paese dei sogni   to be in dreamland

The Seven Simple Tenses		The Seven Compound Tenses	
Singular	Plural	Singular	Plural
1 present indicative		8 present perfect	
sorgo	sorgiamo	sono sorto	siamo sorti
sorgi	sorgete	sèi sorto	sière sorto(i)
sorge	sórgono	è sorto	sono sorti
2 imperfect indicative		9 past perfect	
sorgevo	sorgevamo	èro sorto	eravamo sorti
sorgevi	sorgevate	èri sorto	eravate sorto(i)
sorgeva	sorgévano	èra sorto	èrano sorti
3 past absolute		10 past anterior	
sorsi	sorgemmo	fui sorto	fummo sorti
sorgesti	sorgeste	fosti sorto	foste sorto(i)
sorse	sórsero	fu sorto	fúrono sorti
4 future indicative		11 future perfect	
sorgerò	sorgeremo	sarò sorto	saremo sorti
sorgerai	sorgerete	sarai sorto	sarete sorto(i)
sorgerà	sorgeranno	sarà sorto	saranno sorti
5 present conditional		12 past conditional	
sorgerèi	sorgeremmo	sarèi sorto	saremmo sorti
sorgeresti	sorgereste	saresti sorto	sareste sorto(i)
sorgerèbbe	sorgerèbbero	sarèbbe sorto	sarèbbero sorti
6 present subjunctive		13 past subjunctive	
sorga	sorgiamo	sia sorto	siamo sorti
sorga	sorgiate	sia sorto	siate sorto(i)
sorga	sórgano	sia sorto	síano sorti
7 imperfect subjunctive		14 past perfect subjunctive	
sorgessi	sorgéssimo	fossi sorto	fóssimo sorti
sorgessi	sorgeste	fossi sorto	foste sorto(l)
sorgesse	sorgéssero	fosse sorto	fóssero sorti

	imperative	
—		sorgiamo
sorgi (non sórgere)		sorgete
sorga		sórgano

*Like *sórgere* are *insórgere* and *risórgere*.

Words related to this verb
A che ora sorge il sole oggi?   At what time does the sun rise today?
Quando il re entrò, tutti sorsero in piedi.   When the king entered, everyone rose to their feet.

sorprèndere

Ger. sorprendèndo **Past Part. sorpreso**

to surprise

The Seven Simple Tenses		The Seven Compound Tenses	
Singular	Plural	Singular	Plural
1 present indicative		8 present perfect	
sorprèndo	sorprendiamo	ho sorpreso	abbiamo sorpreso
sorprèndi	sorprendete	hai sorpreso	avete sorpreso
sorprènde	sorprèndono	ha sorpreso	hanno sorpreso
2 imperfect indicative		9 past perfect	
sorprendevo	sorprendevamo	avevo sorpreso	avevamo sorpreso
sorprendevi	sorprendevate	avevi sorpreso	avevate sorpreso
sorprendeva	sorprendévano	aveva sorpreso	avévano sorpreso
3 past absolute		10 past anterior	
sorpresi	sorprendemmo	èbbi sorpreso	avemmo sorpreso
sorprendesti	sorprendeste	avesti sorpreso	aveste sorpreso
sorprese	sorprésero	èbbe sorpreso	èbbero sorpreso
4 future indicative		11 future perfect	
sorprenderò	sorprenderemo	avrò sorpreso	avremo sorpreso
sorprenderai	sorprenderete	avrai sorpreso	avrete sorpreso
sorprenderà	sorprenderanno	avrà sorpreso	avranno sorpreso
5 present conditional		12 past conditional	
sorprenderèi	sorprenderemmo	avrèi sorpreso	avremmo sorpreso
sorprenderesti	sorprendereste	avresti sorpreso	avreste sorpreso
sorprenderèbbe	sorprenederèbbero	avrèbbe sorpreso	avrèbbero sorpreso
6 present subjunctive		13 past subjunctive	
sorprènda	sorprendiamo	àbbia sorpreso	abbiamo sorpreso
sorprènda	sorprendiate	àbbia sorpreso	abbiate sorpreso
sorprènda	sorprèndano	àbbia sorpreso	àbbiano sorpreso
7 imperfect subjunctive		14 past perfect subjunctive	
sorprendessi	sorprendéssimo	avessi sorpreso	avéssimo sorpreso
sorprendessi	sorprendeste	avessi sorpreso	aveste sorpreso
sorprendesse	sorprendéssero	avesse sorpreso	avéssero sorpreso

	imperative	
—		sorprendiamo
	sorprèndi (non sorprèndere)	sorprendete
	sorprènda	sorprèndano

Words related to this verb

Questo ragazzo mi sorprende ogni giorno.   This child surprises me every day.
Lo sorpresi mentre fumava.   I surprised him while he was smoking.

to smile

The Seven Simple Tenses		The Seven Compound Tenses	
Singular	Plural	Singular	Plural
1 present indicative		8 present perfect	
sorrido	sorridiamo	ho sorriso	abbiamo sorriso
sorridi	sorridete	hai sorriso	avete sorriso
sorride	sorrídono	ha sorriso	hanno sorriso
2 imperfect indicative		9 past perfect	
sorridevo	sorridevamo	avevo sorriso	avevamo sorriso
sorridevi	sorridevate	avevi sorriso	avevate sorriso
sorrideva	sorridévano	aveva sorriso	avévano sorriso
3 past absolute		10 past anterior	
sorrisi	sorridemmo	èbbi sorriso	avemmo sorriso
sorridesti	sorrideste	avesti sorriso	aveste sorriso
sorrise	sorrísero	èbbe sorriso	èbbero sorriso
4 future indicative		11 future perfect	
sorriderò	sorrideremo	avrò sorriso	avremo sorriso
sorriderai	sorriderete	avrai sorriso	avrete sorriso
sorriderà	sorrideranno	avrà sorriso	avranno sorriso
5 present conditional		12 past conditional	
sorriderèi	sorrideremmo	avrèi sorriso	avremmo sorriso
sorrideresti	sorridereste	avresti sorriso	avreste sorriso
sorriderèbbe	sorriderèbbero	avrèbbe sorriso	avrèbbero sorriso
6 present subjunctive		13 past subjunctive	
sorrida	sorridiamo	àbbia sorriso	abbiamo sorriso
sorrida	sorridiate	àbbia sorriso	abbiate sorriso
sorrida	sorrídano	àbbia sorriso	àbiano sorriso
7 imperfect subjunctive		14 past perfect subjunctive	
sorridessi	sorridéssimo	avessi sorriso	avéssimo sorriso
sorridessi	sorrideste	avessi sorriso	aveste sorriso
sorridesse	sorridéssero	avesse sorriso	avéssero sorriso

	imperative	
—	sorridiamo	
sorridi (non sorrídere)	sorridete	
sorrida	sorrídano	

Words related to this verb
Quel bambino sorride sempre.   That baby is always smiling.
Lei mi sorride quando mi vede.   She smiles at me when she sees me.

sospendere   Ger. **sospendendo**   Past Part. **sospeso**

to suspend, to hang up

The Seven Simple Tenses		The Seven Compound Tenses	
Singular	Plural	Singular	Plural
1 present indicative		8 present perfect	
sospèndo	sospendiamo	ho sospeso	abbiamo sospeso
sospèndi	sospendete	hai sospeso	avete sospeso
sospènde	sospèndono	ha sospeso	hanno sospeso
2 imperfect indicative		9 past perfect	
sospendevo	sospendevamo	avevo sospeso	avevamo sospeso
sospendevi	sospendevate	avevi sospeso	avevate sospeso
sospendeva	sospendévano	aveva sospeso	avévano sospeso
3 past absolute		10 past anterior	
sospendei	sospendemmo	èbbi sospeso	avemmo sospeso
sospendesti	sospendeste	avesti sospeso	aveste sospeso
sospendè	sospendérono	èbbe sospeso	èbbero sospeso
4 future indicative		11 future perfect	
sospenderò	sospenderemo	avrò sospeso	avremo sospeso
sospenderai	sospenderete	avrai sospeso	avrete sospeso
sospenderà	sospenderanno	avrà sospeso	avranno sospeso
5 present conditional		12 past conditional	
sospenderèi	sospenderemmo	avrèi sospeso	avremmo sospeso
sospenderesti	sospendereste	avresti sospeso	avreste sospeso
sospenderèbbe	sospenderèbbero	avrèbbe sospeso	avrèbbero sospeso
6 present subjunctive		13 past subjunctive	
sospènda	sospendiamo	àbbia sospeso	abbiamo sospeso
sospènda	sospendiate	àbbia sospeso	abbiate sospeso
sospènda	sospèndano	àbbia sospeso	àbbiano sospeso
7 imperfect subjunctive		14 past perfect subjunctive	
sospendessi	sospendéssimo	avessi sospeso	avéssimo sospeso
sospendessi	sospendeste	avessi sospeso	aveste sospeso
sospendesse	sospendéssero	avesse sospeso	avéssero sospeso

imperative	
—	sospendiamo
sospèndi (non sospendere)	sospendete
sospènda	sospèndano

Words related to this verb
sospendere una partenza   to suspend a departure
sospendere una sentenza   to suspend a sentence
sospendere un quadro   to hang a painting

to sustain, to uphold, to support

The Seven Simple Tenses		The Seven Compound Tenses	
Singular	Plural	Singular	Plural
1 present indicative		8 present perfect	
sostèngo	sosteniamo	ho sostenuto	abbiamo sostenuto
sostièni	sostenete	hai sostenuto	avete sostenuto
sostiène	sostèngono	ha sostenuto	hanno sostenuto
2 imperfect indicative		9 past perfect	
sostenevo	sostenevamo	avevo sostenuto	avevamo sostenuto
sostenevi	sostenevate	avevi sostenuto	avevate sostenuto
sosteneva	sostenévano	aveva sostenuto	avévano sostenuto
3 past absolute		10 past anterior	
sostenni	sostenemmo	èbbi sostenuto	avemmo sostenuto
sostenesti	sosteneste	avesti sostenuto	aveste sostenuto
sostenne	sosténnero	èbbe sostenuto	èbbero sostenuto
4 future indicative		11 future perfect	
sosterrò	sosterremo	avrò sostenuto	avremo sostenuto
sosterrai	sosterrete	avrai sostenuto	avrete sostenuo
sosterrà	sosterranno	avrà sostenuto	avranno sostenuto
5 present conditional		12 past conditional	
sosterrèi	sosterremmo	avrèi sostenuto	avremmo sostenuto
sosterresti	sosterreste	avresti sostenuto	avreste sostenuto
sosterrèbbe	sosterrèbbero	avrèbbe sostenuto	avrèbbero sostenuto
6 present subjunctive		13 past subjunctive	
sostènga	sosteniamo	àbbia sostenuto	abbiamo sostenuto
sostènga	sosteniate	àbbia sostenuto	abbiate sostenuto
sostènga	sostèngano	àbbia sostenuto	àbbiano sostenuto
7 imperfect subjunctive		14 past perfect subjunctive	
sostenessi	sostenéssimo	avessi sostenuto	avéssimo sostenuto
sostenessi	sosteneste	avessi sostenuto	aveste sostenuto
sostenesse	sostenéssero	avesse sostenuto	avéssero sostenuto

imperative

—	sosteniamo
sostièni (non sostenere)	sostenete
sostènga	sostèngano

Words related to this verb
Una sola corda lo sostenne quando cadde.   A single rope supported him when he fell.
Questa teoria è sostenuta dai fatti.   This theory is supported by facts.

sottométtere   Ger. **sottomettèndo**   Past Part. **sottomesso**

to submit, to subject, to subdue

The Seven Simple Tenses		The Seven Compound Tenses	
Singular	Plural	Singular	Plural
1 present indicative		8 present perfect	
sottometto	**sottomettiamo**	**ho sottomesso**	**abbiamo sottomesso**
sottometti	**sottomettete**	**hai sottomesso**	**avete sottomesso**
sottomette	**sottométtono**	**ha sottomesso**	**hanno sottomesso**
2 imperfect indicative		9 past perfect	
sottomettevo	**sottomettevamo**	**avevo sottomesso**	**avevamo sottomesso**
sottomettevi	**sottomettevate**	**avevi sottomesso**	**avevate sottomesso**
sottometteva	**sottomettévano**	**aveva sottomesso**	**avévano sottomesso**
3 past absolute		10 past anterior	
sottomisi	**sottomettemmo**	**èbbi sottomesso**	**avemmo sottomesso**
sottomettesti	**sottometteste**	**avesti sottomesso**	**aveste sottomesso**
sottomise	**sottomísero**	**èbbe sottomesso**	**èbbero sottomesso**
4 future indicative		11 future perfect	
sottometterò	**sottometteremo**	**avrò sottomesso**	**avremo sottomesso**
sottometterai	**sottometterete**	**avrai sottomesso**	**avreste sottomesso**
sottometterà	**sottometteranno**	**avrà sottomesso**	**avranno sottomesso**
5 present conditional		12 past conditional	
sottometterèi	**sottometteremmo**	**avrèi sottomesso**	**avremmo sottomesso**
sottometteresti	**sottomettereste**	**avresti sottomesso**	**avreste sottomesso**
sottometterèbbe	**sottometterèbbero**	**avrèbbe sottomesso**	**avrèbbero sottomesso**
6 present subjunctive		13 past subjunctive	
sottometta	**sottomettiamo**	**àbbia sottomesso**	**abbiamo sottomesso**
sottometta	**sottomettiate**	**àbbia sottomesso**	**abbiate sottomesso**
sottometta	**sottométtano**	**àbbia sottomesso**	**àbbiano sottomesso**
7 imperfect subjunctive		14 past perfect subjunctive	
sottomettessi	**sottomettéssimo**	**avessi sottomesso**	**avéssimo sottomesso**
sottomettessi	**sottometteste**	**avessi sottomesso**	**aveste sottomesso**
sottomettesse	**sottomettéssero**	**avesse sottomesso**	**avéssero sottomesso**

	imperative	
	—	**sottomettiamo**
	sottometti (non sottomettere)	**sottomettete**
	sottometta	**sottométtano**

Words related to this verb
Ho sottomesso il caso alla corte.   I submitted the case to the court.
sottomettere una nazione   to subject a nation

to subtract, to withdraw

The Seven Simple Tenses		The Seven Compound Tenses	
Singular	Plural	Singular	Plural
1 present indicative		8 present perfect	
sottraggo	sottraiamo	ho sottratto	abbiamo sottratto
sottrai	sottraete	hai sottratto	avete sottratto
sottrae	sottràggono	ha sottratto	hanno sottratto
2 imperfect indicative		9 past perfect	
sottraevo	sottraevamo	avevo sottratto	avevamo sottratto
sottraevi	sottraevate	avevi sottratto	avevate sottratto
sottraeva	sottraévano	aveva sottratto	avévano sottratto
3 past absolute		10 past anterior	
sottrassi	sottraemmo	èbbi sottratto	avemmo sottratto
sottraesti	sottraeste	avesti sottratto	aveste sottratto
sottrasse	sottràssero	èbbe sottratto	èbbero sottratto
4 future indicative		11 future perfect	
sottrarrò	sottrarremo	avrò sottratto	avremo sottratto
sottrarrai	sottrarrete	avrai sottratto	avrete sottratto
sottrarrà	sottrarranno	avrà sottratto	avranno sottratto
5 present conditional		12 past conditional	
sottrarrèi	sottrarremo	avrèi sottratto	avremmo sottratto
sottrarresti	sottrarreste	avresti sottratto	avreste sottratto
sottrarrèbbe	sottrarrèbbero	avrèbbe sottratto	avrèbbero sottratto
6 present subjunctive		13 past subjunctive	
sottragga	sottraiamo	àbbia sottratto	abbiamo sottratto
sottragga	sottraiate	àbbia sottratto	abbiate sottratto
sottragga	sottràggano	àbbia sottratto	àbbiano sottratto
7 imperfect subjunctive		14 past perfect subjunctive	
sottraessi	sottraéssimo	avessi sottratto	avéssimo sottratto
sottraessi	sottraeste	avessi sottratto	aveste sottratto
sottraesse	sottraéssero	avesse sottratto	avéssero sottratto

imperative	
—	sottraiamo
sottrai (non sottrarre)	sottraete
sottragga	sottràggano

Words related to this verb
Sottrai cinque da dieci.   Subtract five from ten.
Lui sottrae i soldi dalla banca.   He withdraws the money from the bank.

spàndere   Ger. spandèndo   Past Part. spanto (spanduto)

to spread

The Seven Simple Tenses		The Seven Compound Tenses	
Singular	Plural	Singular	Plural
1 present indicative		8 present perfect	
spando	spandiamo	ho spanto (spanduto)	abbiamo spanto
spandi	spandete	hai spanto	avete spanto
spande	spàndono	ha spanto	hanno spanto
2 imperfect indicative		9 past perfect	
spandevo	spandevamo	avevo spanto	avevamo spanto
spandevi	spandevate	avevi spanto	avevate spanto
spandeva	spandévano	aveva spanto	avévano spanto
3 past absolute		10 past anterior	
spandei (spandètti, spansi)	spandemmo	èbbi spanto	avemmo spanto
spandesti	spandeste	avesti spanto	aveste spanto
spandé (spandètte, spanse)	spandérono (spandèttero, spànsero)	èbbe spanto	èbbero spanto
4 future indicative		11 future perfect	
spanderò	spanderemo	avrò spanto	avremo spanto
spanderai	spanderete	avrai spanto	avrete spanto
spanderà	spanderanno	avrà spanto	avranno spanto
5 present conditional		12 past conditional	
spanderèi	spanderemmo	avrèi spanto	avremmo spanto
spanderesti	spandereste	avresti spanto	avreste spanto
spanderèbbe	spanderèbbero	avrèbbe spanto	avrèbbero spanto
6 present subjunctive		13 past subjunctive	
spanda	spandiamo	àbbia spanto	abbiamo spanto
spanda	spandiate	àbbia spanto	abbiate spanto
spanda	spàndano	àbbia spanto	àbbiano spanto
7 imperfect subjunctive		14 past perfect subjunctive	
spandessi	spandéssimo	avessi spanto	avéssimo spanto
spandessi	spandeste	avessi spanto	aveste spanto
spandesse	spandéssero	avesse spanto	avéssero spanto

imperative	
—	spandiamo
spandi (non spàndere)	spandete
spanda	spàndano

Words related to this verb
Chi spande queste bugie?   Who is spreading these lies?
La pianta spande i rami.   The plant spreads its branches.

to spread, to shed

The Seven Simple Tenses		The Seven Compound Tenses	
Singular	Plural	Singular	Plural
1 present indicative		**8 present perfect**	
spargo	spargiamo	ho sparso	abbiamo sparso
spargi	spargete	hai sparso	avete sparso
sparge	spàrgono	ha sparso	hanno sparso
2 imperfect indicative		**9 past perfect**	
spargevo	spargevamo	avevo sparso	avevamo sparso
spargevi	spargevate	avevi sparso	avevate sparso
spargeva	spargévano	aveva sparso	avévano sparso
3 past absolute		**10 past anterior**	
sparsi	spargemmo	èbbi sparso	avemmo sparso
spargesti	spargeste	avesti sparso	aveste sparso
sparse	spàrsero	èbbe sparso	èbbero sparso
4 future indicative		**11 future perfect**	
spargerò	spargeremo	avrò sparso	avremo sparso
spargerai	spargerete	avrai sparso	avrete sparso
spargerà	spargeranno	avrà sparso	avranno sparso
5 present conditional		**12 past conditional**	
spargerèi	spargeremmo	avrèi sparso	avremmo sparso
spargeresti	spargereste	avresti sparso	avreste sparso
spargerèbbe	spargerèbbero	avrèbbe sparso	avrèbbero sparso
6 present subjunctive		**13 past subjunctive**	
sparga	spargiamo	àbbia sparso	abbiamo sparso
sparga	spargiate	àbbia sparso	abbiate sparso
sparga	spàrgano	àbbia sparso	àbbiano sparso
7 imperfect subjunctive		**14 past perfect subjunctive**	
spargessi	spargéssimo	avessi sparso	avéssimo sparso
spargessi	spargeste	avessi sparso	aveste sparso
spargesse	spargéssero	avesse sparso	avéssero sparso

imperative

	spargiamo
spargi (non spàrgere)	spargete
sparga	spàrgano

Words related to this verb
Ho sparso molte lacrime per te.   I have shed many tears because of you.
Lui sparge le notizie per il vicinato.   He spreads the news through the
neighborhood.

spégnere (spéngere)   Ger. **spegnèndo (spengèndo)**   Past Part. **spento**

to extinguish, to put out

The Seven Simple Tenses		The Seven Compound Tenses	
Singular	Plural	Singular	Plural
1 present indicative		8 present perfect	
spengo	spegniamo (spengiamo)	ho spento	abbiamo spento
spegni (spengi)	spegnete (spengete)	hai spento	avete spento
spegne (spenge)	spéngono	ha spento	hanno spento
2 imperfect indicative		9 past perfect	
spegnevo	spegnevamo	avevo spento	avevamo spento
(spengevo)	(spengevamo)	avevi spento	avevate spento
spegnevi	spegnevate (spengevate)	aveva spento	avévano spento
(spengevi)			
spegneva	spegnévano (spengévano)		
(spengeva)			
3 past absolute		10 past anterior	
spensi	spegnemmo (spengemmo)	èbbi spento	avemmo spento
spegnesti	spegneste (spengeste)	avesti spento	aveste spento
(spengesti)		èbbe spento	èbbero spento
spense	spénsero		
4 future indicative		11 future perfect	
spegnerò	spegneremo	avrò spento	avremo spento
(spengerò)	(spengeremo)	avrai spento	avrete spento
spegnerai	spegnerete (spengerete)	avrà spento	avranno spento
(spengerai)			
spegnerà	spegneranno		
(spengerà)	(spengeranno)		
5 present conditional		12 past conditional	
spegnerèi	spegneremmo	avrèi spento	avremmo spento
(spengerèi)	(spengeremmo)	avresti spento	avreste spento
spegneresti	spegnereste (spengereste)	avrèbbe spento	avrèbbero spento
(spengeresti)			
spegnerèbbe	spegnerèbbero		
(spengerèbbe)	(spengerèbbero)		
6 present subjunctive		13 past subjunctive	
spenga	spegniamo (spengiamo)	àbbia spento	abbiamo spento
spenga	spegniate (spengiate)	àbbia spento	abbiate spento
spenga	spéngano	àbbia spento	àbbiano spento
7 imperfect subjunctive		14 past perfect subjunctive	
spegnessi	spegnéssimo	avessi spento	avéssimo spento
(spengessi)	(spengéssimo)	avessi spento	aveste spento
spegnessi	spegneste (spengeste)	avesse spento	avéssero spento
(spengessi)			
spegnesse	spegnéssero (spengéssero)		
(spengesse)			

imperative

—	spegniamo (spengiamo)
spegni (spengi) (non spégnere, non spéngere)	spegnete (spengete)
spenga	spéngano

Ger. spendèndo   Past Part. speso   **spèndere**

to spend, to expend

The Seven Simple Tenses		The Seven Compound Tenses	
Singular	Plural	Singular	Plural
1 present indicative		8 present perfect	
spèndo	spendiamo	ho speso	abbiamo speso
spèndi	spendete	hai speso	avete speso
spènde	spèndono	ha speso	hanno speso
2 imperfect indicative		9 past perfect	
spendevo	spendevamo	avevo speso	avevamo speso
spendevi	spendevate	avevi speso	avevate speso
spendeva	spendévano	aveva speso	avévano speso
3 past absolute		10 past anterior	
spesi	spendemmo	èbbi speso	avemmo speso
spendesti	spendeste	avesti speso	aveste speso
spese	spésero	èbbe speso	èbbero speso
4 future indicative		11 future perfect	
spenderò	spenderemo	avrò speso	avremo speso
spenderai	spenderete	avrai speso	avrete speso
spenderà	spenderanno	avrà speso	avranno speso
5 present conditional		12 past conditional	
spenderèi	spenderemmo	avrèi speso	avremmo speso
spenderesti	spendereste	avresti speso	avreste speso
spenderèbbe	spenderèbbero	avrèbbe speso	avrèbbero speso
6 present subjunctive		13 past subjunctive	
spènda	spendiamo	àbbia speso	abbiamo speso
spènda	spendiate	àbbia speso	abbiate speso
spènda	spèndano	àbbia speso	àbbiano speso
7 imperfect subjunctive		14 past perfect subjunctive	
spendessi	spendéssimo	avessi speso	avéssimo speso
spendessi	spendeste	avessi speso	aveste speso
spendesse	spendéssero	avesse speso	avéssero speso

imperative

	spendiamo
spèndi (non spèndere)	spendete
spènda	spèndano

Words related to this verb
Lui spende molto denaro ogni giorno.   He spends a lot of money every day.
Luca spende molto denaro in attrezzature sportive.   Luke spends a lot of money on gym equipment.

to explain

The Seven Simple Tenses		The Seven Compound Tenses	
Singular	Plural	Singular	Plural
1 present indicative		8 present perfect	
spiègo	spieghiamo	ho spiegato	abbiamo spiegato
spièghi	spiegate	hai spiegato	avete spiegato
spièga	spiègano	ha spiegato	hanno spiegato
2 imperfect indicative		9 past perfect	
spiegavo	spiegavamo	avevo spiegato	avevamo spiegato
spiegavi	spiegavate	avevi spiegato	avevate spiegato
spiegava	spiegàvano	aveva spiegato	avévano spiegato
3 past absolute		10 past anterior	
spiegai	spiegammo	èbbi spiegato	avemmo spiegato
spiegasti	spiegaste	avesti spiegato	aveste spiegato
spiegò	spiegàrono	èbbe spiegato	èbbero spiegato
4 future indicative		11 future perfect	
spiegherò	spiegheremo	avrò spiegato	avremo spiegato
spiegherai	spiegherete	avrai spiegato	avrete spiegato
spiegherà	spiegheranno	avrà spiegato	avranno spiegato
5 present conditional		12 past conditional	
spiegherèi	spiegheremmo	avrèi spiegato	avremmo spiegato
spiegheresti	spieghereste	avresti spiegato	avreste spiegato
spiegherèbbe	spiegherèbbero	avrèbbe spiegato	avrèbbero spiegato
6 present subjunctive		13 past subjunctive	
spièghi	spieghiamo	àbbia spiegato	abbiamo spiegato
spièghi	spieghiate	àbbia spiegato	abbiate spiegato
spièghi	spièghino	àbbia spiegato	àbbiano spiegato
7 imperfect subjunctive		14 past perfect subjunctive	
spiegassi	spiegàssimo	avessi spiegato	avéssimo spiegato
spiegassi	spiegaste	avessi spiegato	aveste spiegato
spiegasse	spiegàssero	avesse spiegato	avéssero spiegato

	imperative	
—		spieghiamo
	spièga (non spiegare)	spiegate
	spièghi	spièghino

Words related to this verb
Tu non spieghi bene le regole.   You don't explain the rules well.
Spiegami questa parola.   Explain this word to me.

to push, to shove

The Seven Simple Tenses		The Seven Compound Tenses	
Singular	Plural	Singular	Plural
1 present indicative		8 present perfect	
spingo	spingiamo	ho spinto	abbiamo spinto
spingi	spingete	hai spinto	avete spinto
spinge	spíngono	ha spinto	hanno spinto
2 imperfect indicative		9 past perfect	
spingevo	spingevamo	avevo spinto	avevamo spinto
spingevi	spingevate	avevi spinto	avevate spinto
spingeva	spingévano	aveva spinto	avévano spinto
3 past absolute		10 past anterior	
spinsi	spingemmo	èbbi spinto	avemmo spinto
spingesti	spingeste	avesti spinto	aveste spinto
spinse	spínsero	èbbe spinto	èbbero spinto
4 future indicative		11 future perfect	
spingerò	spingeremo	avrò spinto	avremo spinto
spingerai	spingerete	avrai spinto	avrete spinto
spingerà	spingeranno	avrà spinto	avranno spinto
5 present conditional		12 past conditional	
spingerèi	spingeremmo	avrèi spinto	avremmo spinto
spingeresti	spingereste	avresti spinto	avreste spinto
spingerèbbe	spingerèbbero	avrèbbe spinto	avrèbbero spinto
6 present subjunctive		13 past subjunctive	
spinga	spingiamo	àbbia spinto	abbiamo spinto
spinga	spingiate	àbbia spinto	abbiate spinto
spinga	spíngano	àbbia spinto	àbbiano spinto
7 imperfect subjunctive		14 past perfect subjunctive	
spingessi	spingéssimo	avessi spinto	avéssimo spinto
spingessi	spingeste	avessi spinto	aveste spinto
spingesse	spingéssero	avesse spinto	avéssero spinto

imperative

—	spingiamo
spingi (non spíngere)	spingete
spinga	spíngano

* Like *spingere* are *respingere* and *sospingere*.

Words related to this verb
Lui mi spinge a fare meglio.   He pushes me to do better.
Se la spingo, la faccio cadere.   If I push her, I will make her fall.

sposare	Ger. sposando	Past Part. sposato

to marry

The Seven Simple Tenses		The Seven Compound Tenses	
Singular	Plural	Singular	Plural
1 present indicative		8 present perfect	
spòso	sposiamo	ho sposato	abbiamo sposato
spòsi	sposate	hai sposato	avete sposato
spòsa	sposano	ha sposato	hanno sposato
2 imperfect indicative		9 past perfect	
sposavo	sposavamo	avevo sposato	avevamo sposato
sposavi	sposavate	avevi sposato	avevate sopsato
sposava	sposàvano	aveva sposato	avévano sposato
3 past absolute		10 past anterior	
sposai	sposammo	èbbi sposato	avemmo sposato
sposasti	sposaste	avesti sposato	aveste sposato
sposò	sposàrono	èbbe sposato	èbbero sposato
4 future indicative		11 future perfect	
sposerò	sposeremo	avrò sposato	avremo sposato
sposerai	sposerete	avrai sposato	avrete sposato
sposerà	sposeranno	avrà sposato	avranno sposato
5 present conditional		12 past conditional	
sposerèi	sposeremmo	avrèi sposato	avremmo sposato
sposeresti	sposereste	avresti sposato	avreste sposato
sposerèbbe	sposerèbbero	avrèbbe sposato	avrèbbero sposato
6 present subjunctive		13 past subjunctive	
spòsi	sposiamo	àbbia sposato	abbiamo sposato
spòsi	sposiate	àbbia sposato	abbiate sposato
spòsi	spòsino	àbbia sposato	àbbiano sposato
7 imperfect subjunctive		14 past perfect subjunctive	
sposassi	sposàssimo	avessi sposato	avéssimo sposato
sposassi	sposaste	avessi sposato	aveste sposato
sposasse	sposàssero	avesse sposato	avéssero sposato

	imperative	
—		sposiamo
spòsa (non sposare)		sposate
spòsi		spòsino

Words related to this verb

Sposò una bella donna.   He married a beautiful woman.
sposare una causa   to embrace a cause

to establish

The Seven Simple Tenses		The Seven Simple Tenses	
Singular	Plural	Singular	Plural

1   present indicative
		8 present perfect	
stabilisco	stabiliamo	ho stabilito	abbiamo stabilito
stabilisci	stabilite	hai stabilito	avete stabilito
stabilisce	stabiliscono	ha stabilito	hanno stabilito

2   imperfect indicative
		9 past perfect	
stabilivo	stabilivamo	avevo stabilito	avevamo stabilito
stabilivi	stabilivate	avevi stabilito	avevate stabilito
stabiliva	stabilivano	aveva stabilito	avévano stabilito

3   past absolute
		10 past anterior	
stabilii	stabilimmo	èbbi stabilito	avemmo stabilito
stabilisti	stabiliste	avesti stabilito	aveste stabilito
stabilì	stabilìrono	èbbe stabilito	èbbero stabilito

4   future indicative
		11 future perfect	
stabilirò	stabiliremo	avrò stabilito	avremo stabilito
stabilirai	stabilirete	avrai stabilito	avrete stabilito
stabilirà	stabiliranno	avrà stabilito	avranno stabilito

5   present conditional
		12 past conditional	
stabilirèi	stabiliremmo	avrèi stabilito	avreinmo stabilito
stabiliresti	stabilireste	avresti stabilito	avreste stabllito
stabilirèbbe	stabilirèbbero	avrèbbe stabilito	avrèbbero stabilito

6   present subjunctive
		13 past subjunctive	
stabilisca	stabiliamo	àbbia stabilito	abbiamo stabilito
stabilisca	stabiliate	àbbia stabilito	abbiate stabilito
stabilisca	stabiliscano	àbbia stabilito	àbbiano stabilito

7   imperfect subjunctive
		14 past perfect subjunctive	
stabilissi	stabilìssimo	avessi stabilito	avéssimo stabilito
stabilissi	stabiliste	avessi stabilito	aveste stabilito
stabilisse	stabilìssero	avesse stabilito	avéssero stabilito

imperative

—	stablliamo
stabilisci (non stabilire)	stabilite
stabilisca	stabilìscano

Words related to this verb
Lui stabilisce le regole.   He establishes the rules.
stabilire un fatto   to establish a fact

stare*   Ger. **stando**   Past Part. **stato**

to stay; to stand

The Seven Simple Tenses		The Seven Simple Tenses	
Singular	Plural	Singular	Plural
1 present indicative		8 present perfect	
sto	stiamo	sono stato	siamo stati
stai	state	sèi stato	siète stato (i)
sta	stanno	è stato	sono stati
2 imperfect indicative		9 past perfect	
stavo	stavamo	èro stato	eravamo stati
stavi	stavate	èri stato	eravate stato (i)
stava	stàvano	èra stato	èrano stati
3 past absolute		10 past anterior	
stètti	stemmo	fui stato	fummo stati
stesti	steste	fosti stato	foste stato (i)
stètte	stèttero	fu stato	fúrono stati
4 future indicative		11 future perfect	
starò	staremo	sarò stato	saremo stati
starai	starete	sarai stato	sarete stato (i)
starà	staranno	sarà stato	saranno stati
5 present conditional		12 past conditional	
starèi	staremmo	sarèi stato	saremmo stati
staresti	stareste	saresti stato	sareste stato (i)
starèbbe	starèbbero	sarèbbe stato	sarèbbero stati
6 present subjunctive		13 past subjunctive	
stia	stiamo	sia stato	siamo stati
stia	stiate	sia stato	siate stato (i)
stia	stíano	sia stato	síano stati
7 imperfect subjunctive		14 past perfect subjunctive	
stessi	stéssimo	fossi stato	fóssimo stati
stessi	steste	fossi stato	foste stato (i)
stesse	stéssero	fosse stato	fóssero stati

	imperative	
—		stiamo
sta' (non stare)		state
stia		stíano

* Like *stare* are *ristare*, *soprastare*, and *sottostare*. *Stare* is also used to ask and answer questions regarding health.

Words related to this verb
Come sta Giovanni oggi?   How is John feeling today?
Dove stai? Non ti posso vedere.   Where are you? I can't see you?

to spread, to extend, to draw up

The Seven Simple Tenses		The Seven Compound Tenses	
Singular	Plural	Singular	Plural
1 present indicative		8 present perfect	
stèndo	stendiamo	ho steso	abbiamo steso
stèndi	stendete	hai steso	avete steso
stènde	stèndono	ha steso	hanno steso
2 imperfect indicative		9 past perfect	
stendevo	stendevamo	avevo steso	avevamo steso
stendevi	stendevate	avevi steso	avevate steso
stendeva	stendévano	aveva steso	avévano steso
3 past absolute		10 past anterior	
stesi	stendemmo	èbbi steso	avemmo steso
stendesti	stendeste	avesti steso	aveste steso
stose	stésero	èbbe steso	èbbero steso
4 future indicative		11 future perfect	
stenderò	stenderemo	avrò steso	avremo steso
stenderai	stenderete	avrai steso	avrete steso
stenderà	stenderanno	avrà steso	avranno steso
5 present conditional		12 past conditional	
stenderèi	stenderemmo	avrèi steso	avremmo steso
stenderesti	stendereste	avresti steso	avreste steso
stenderèbbe	stenderèbbero	avrèbbe steso	avrèbbero steso
6 present subjunctive		13 past subjunctive	
stènda	stendiamo	àbbia steso	abbiamo steso
stènda	stendiate	àbbia steso	abbiate steso
stènda	stèndano	àbbia steso	àbbiano steso
7 imperfect subjunctive		14 past perfect subjunctive	
stendessi	stendéssimo	avessi steso	avéssimo steso
stendessi	stendeste	avessi steso	aveste steso
stendesse	stendéssero	avesse steso	avéssero steso

	imperative	
—		stendiamo
stèndi (non stèndere)		stendete
stènda		stèndano

Words related to this verb
Lui si stese sull'erba. He spread out (stretched out) on the grass.
Chi ha steso il giornale sul tavolo? Who spread out the newspaper on the table?

stríngere*   Ger. **stringèndo**   Past Part. **stretto**

to press, to squeeze

The Seven Simple Tenses		The Seven Compound Tenses	
Singular	Plural	Singular	Plural
1 present indicative		8 present perfect	
stringo	**stringiamo**	**ho stretto**	**abbiamo stretto**
stringi	**stringete**	**hai stretto**	**avete stretto**
stringe	**stríngono**	**ha stretto**	**hanno stretto**
2 imperfect indicative		9 past perfect	
stringevo	**stringevamo**	**avevo stretto**	**avevamo stretto**
stringevi	**stringevate**	**avevi stretto**	**avevate stretto**
stringeva	**stringévano**	**aveva stretto**	**avévano stretto**
3 past absolute		10 past anterior	
strinsi	**stringemmo**	**èbbi stretto**	**avemmo stretto**
stringesti	**stringeste**	**avesti stretto**	**aveste stretto**
strinse	**strínsero**	**èbbe stretto**	**èbbero stretto**
4 future indicative		11 future perfect	
stringerò	**stringeremo**	**avrò stretto**	**avremo stretto**
stringerai	**stringerete**	**avrai stretto**	**avrete stretto**
stringerà	**stringeranno**	**avrà stretto**	**avranno stretto**
5 present conditional		12 past conditional	
stringerèi	**stringeremmo**	**avrèi stretto**	**avremmo stretto**
stringeresti	**stringereste**	**avresti stretto**	**avreste stretto**
stringerèbbe	**stringerèbbero**	**avrèbbe stretto**	**avrèbbero stretto**
6 present subjunctive		13 past subjunctive	
stringa	**stringiamo**	**àbbia stretto**	**abbiamo stretto**
stringa	**stringiate**	**àbbia stretto**	**abbiate stretto**
stringa	**stríngano**	**àbbia stretto**	**àbbiano stretto**
7 imperfect subjunctive		14 past perfect subjunctive	
stringessi	**stringéssimo**	**avessi stretto**	**avéssimo stretto**
stringessi	**stringeste**	**avessi stretto**	**aveste stretto**
stringesse	**stringéssero**	**avesse stretto**	**avéssero stretto**

imperative	
—	**stringiamo**
stringi (non stríngere)	**stringiamo**
stringa	**stríngano**

* Like *stringere* are *costringere* and *restringere*.

Words related to this verb
Non stringere il gattino cosi!   Don't squeeze the kitten like that!
Lui mi strinse la mano.   He shook my hand.

The Seven Simple Tenses		The Seven Compound Tenses	
Singular	Plural	Singular	Plural
1 present indicative		8 present perfect	
stùdio	studiamo	ho studiato	abbiamo studiato
stùdi	studiate	hai studiato	avete studiato
stùdia	stùdiano	ha studiato	hanno studiato
2 imperfect indicative		9 past perfect	
studiavo	studiavamo	avevo studiato	avevamo studiato
studiavi	studiavate	avevi studiato	avevate studiato
studiava	studiàvano	aveva studiato	avévano studiato
3 past absolute		10 past anterior	
studiai	studiammo	èbbi studiato	avemmo studiato
studiasti	studiaste	avesti studiato	aveste studiato
studiò	studiàrono	èbbe studiato	èbbero studiato
4 future indicative		11 future perfect	
studierò	studieremo	avrò studiato	avremo studiato
studierai	studierete	avrai studiato	avrete studiato
studierà	studieranno	avrà studiato	avranno studiato
5 present conditional		12 past conditional	
studierèi	studieremmo	avrèi studiato	avremmo studiato
studieresti	studiereste	avresti studiato	avreste studiato
studierèbbe	studierèbbero	avrèbbe studiato	avrèbbero studiato
6 present subjunctive		13 past subjunctive	
stùdi	studiamo	àbbia studiato	abbiamo studiato
stùdi	studiate	àbbia studiato	abbiate studiato
stùdi	stùdino	àbbia studiato	àbbiano studiato
7 imperfect subjunctive		14 past perfect subjunctive	
studiassi	studiàssimo	avessi studiato	avéssimo studiato
studiassi	studiaste	avessi studiato	aveste studiato
studiasse	studiàssero	avesse studiato	avéssero studiato

imperative	
—	studiamo
stùdia (non studiare)	studiate
stùdi	stùdino

Words related to this verb
Io studio molto a scuola.   I study a lot at school.
studiare il violino   to study the violin
Non voglio studiare.   I don't want to study.

succèdere* Ger. succedèndo Past Part. succèsso

to happen, to occur

The Seven Simple Tenses		The Seven Compound Tenses	
Singular	Plural	Singular	Plural
1 present indicative		8 present perfect	
succède	**succèdono**	**è succèsso**	**sono succèssi**
2 imperfect indicative		9 past perfect	
succedeva	**succedévano**	**èra succèsso**	**èrano succèssi**
3 past absolute		10 past anterior	
succèsse	**succèssero**	**fu succèsso**	**fúrono succèssi**
4 future indicative		11 future perfect	
succederà	**succederanno**	**sarà succèsso**	**saranno succèssi**
5 present conditional		12 past conditional	
succederèbbe	**succederèbbero**	**sarèbbe succèsso**	**sarebbero succèssi**
6 present subjunctive		13 past subjunctive	
succèda	**succèdano**	**sia succèsso**	**síano succèssi**
7 imperfect subjunctive		14 past perfect subjunctive	
succedesse	**succedéssero**	**fosse succèsso**	**fóssero succèssi**
		imperative	

* *Succèdere*, meaning *to succeed* (*come after*), is regular and is also conjugated with *èssere*.

Words related to this verb
Cosa è successo? What happened?
Questo succede ogni giorno. This happens every day.

270

Ger. suonando   Past Part. suonato   suonare (sonare)

to play, to ring, to sound

The Seven Simple Tenses		The Seven Compound Tenses	
Singular	Plural	Singular	Plural
1 present indicative		8 present perfect	
suòno	suoniamo	ho suonato	abbiamo suonato
suòni	suonate	hai suonato	avete suonato
suòna	suònano	ha suonato	hanno suonato
2 imperfect indicative		9 past perfect	
suonavo	suonavamo	avevo suonato	avevamo suonato
suonavi	suonavate	avevi suonato	avevate suonato
suonava	suonàvano	aveva suonato	avévano suonato
3 past absolute		10 past anterior	
suonai	suonammo	èbbi suonato	avemmo suonato
suonasti	suonaste	avesti suonato	aveste suonato
suonò	suonàrono	èbbe suonato	èbbero suonato
4 future indicative		11 future perfect	
suonerò	suoneremo	avrò suonato	avremo suonato
suonerai	suonerete	avrai suonato	avrete suonato
suonerà	suoneranno	avrà suonato	avranno suonato
5 present conditional		12 past conditional	
suonerèi	suoneremmo	avrèi suonato	avremmo suonato
suoneresti	suonereste	avresti suonato	avreste suonato
suonerèbbe	suonerèbbero	avrèbbe suonato	avrèbbero suonato
6 present subjunctive		13 past subjunctive	
suòni	suoniamo	àbbia suonato	abbiamo suonato
suòni	suoniate	àbbia suonato	abbiate suonato
suòni	suònino	àbbia suonato	àbbiano suonato
7 imperfect subjunctive		14 past perfect subjunctive	
suonassi	suonàssimo	avessi suonato	avéssimo suonato
suonassi	suonaste	avessi suonato	aveste suonato
suonasse	suonàssero	avesse suonato	avéssero suonato

	imperative	
—		suoniamo
suòna (non suonare)		suonate
suòni		suònino

Words related to this verb
Lui suona il violino.   He plays the violin.
Io suono il campanello.   I ring the bell.
suonare a orecchio   to play by ear

supporre (supponere)   Ger. supponèndo   Past Part. supposto

to suppose, to assume, to guess

The Seven Simple Tenses		The Seven Compound Tenses	
Singular	Plural	Singular	Plural
1 present indicative		**8 present perfect**	
suppongo	supponiamo	ho supposto	abbiamo supposto
supponi	supponete	hai supposto	avete supposto
suppone	suppóngono	ha supposto	hanno supposto
2 imperfect indicative		**9 past perfect**	
supponevo	supponevamo	avevo supposto	avevamo supposto
supponevi	supponevate	avevi supposto	avevate supposto
supponeva	supponévano	aveva supposto	avévano supposto
3 past absolute		**10 past anterior**	
supposi	supponemmo	èbbi supposto	avemmo supposto
supponesti	supponeste	avesti supposto	aveste supposto
suppose	suppósero	èbbe supposto	èbbero supposto
4 future indicative		**11 future perfect**	
supporrò	supporremo	avrò supposto	avremo supposto
supporrai	supporrete	avrai supposto	avrete supposto
supporrà	supporranno	avrà supposto	avranno supposto
5 present conditional		**12 past conditional**	
supporrèi	supporremmo	avrèi supposto	avremmo supposto
supporresti	supporreste	avresti supposto	avreste supposto
supporrèbbe	supporrèbbero	avrèbbe supposto	avrèbbero supposto
6 present subjunctive		**13 past subjunctive**	
supponga	supponiamo	àbbia supposto	abbiamo supposto
supponga	supponiate	àbbia supposto	abbiate supposto
supponga	suppóngano	àbbia supposto	àbbiano supposto
7 imperfect subjunctive		**14 past perfect subjunctive**	
supponessi	supponéssimo	avessi supposto	avéssimo supposto
supponessi	supponeste	avessi supposto	aveste supposto
supponesse	supponéssero	avesse supposto	avéssero supposto

	imperative	
—		supponiamo
supponi (non supporre)		supponete
supponga		suppóngano

Words related to this verb
Suppongo che egli venga.   I suppose he will come.
Supponiamo che verrà.   We suppose she will come.

to disappear, to vanish

The Seven Simple Tenses		The Seven Compound Tenses	
Singular	Plural	Singular	Plural
1 present indicative		8 present perfect	
svanìsco	svaniamo	ho savnito	siamo svaniti
svanìsci	svanite	sei svanito	siete svaniti
svanìsce	svanìscono	è svanito	sono svaniti
2 imperfect indicative		9 past perfect	
svanivo	svanivamo	èro svanito	eravamo svaniti
svanivi	svanivate	èri svanito	eravate svaniti
svaniva	svanívano	èra svanito	èrano svaniti
3 past absolute		10 past anterior	
svanii	svanimmo	fui svanito	fummo svaniti
svanisti	svaniste	fosti svanito	foste svaniti
svanì	svanírono	fu svanito	fúrono svaniti
4 future indicative		11 future perfect	
svanirò	svaniremo	sarò svanito	saremo svaniti
svanirai	svanirete	sarai svanito	sarete svaniti
svanirà	svaniranno	sarà svanito	saranno svaniti
5 present conditional		12 past conditional	
svanirèi	svaniremmo	sarèi svanito	saremmo svaniti
svaniresti	svanireste	saresti svanito	sareste svaniti
svanirèbbe	svanirèbbero	sarèbbe svanito	sarèbbero svaniti
6 present subjunctive		13 past subjunctive	
svanìsca	svaniamo	sia svanito	siamo svaniti
svanìsca	svaniate	sia svanito	siate svaniti
svanìsca	svanìscano	sia svanito	síano svaniti
7 imperfect subjunctive		14 past perfect subjunctive	
svanissi	svaníssimo	fossi svanito	fóssimo svaniti
svanissi	svaniste	fossi svanito	foste svaniti
svanisse	svaníssero	fosse svanito	fóssero svaniti

	imperative	
—	svaniamo
svanìsci (non svanire)	svanite
svanìsca	svanìscano

Words related to this verb
Il mago svanì.   The magician disappeared.
Le mie speranze svanirono.   My hopes vanished.

svenire   Ger. svenèndo   Past Part. svenuto

to faint, to swoon

The Seven Simple Tenses		The Seven Compound Tenses	
Singular	Plural	Singular	Plural
1 present indicative		8 present perfect	
svèngo	sveniamo	sono svenuto	siamo svenuti
svièni	svenite	sèi svenuto	sième svenuti
svième	svèngono	è svenuto	sono svenuti
2 imperfect indicative		9 past perfect	
svenivo	svenivamo	èro svenuto	eravamo svenuti
svenivi	svenivate	èri svenuto	eravate svenuti
sveniva	svenívano	èra svenuto	èrano svenuti
3 past absolute		10 past anterior	
svenni	svenimmo	fui svenuto	fummo svenuti
svenisti	sveniste	fosti svenuto	foste svenuti
svenne	svénnero	fu svenuto	fúrono svenuti
4 future indicative		11 future perfect	
svenirò	sveniremo	sarò svenuto	saremo svenuti
svenirai	svenirete	sarai svenuto	sarete svenuti
svenirà	sveniranno	sarà svenuto	saranno svenuti
5 present conditional		12 past conditional	
svenirèi	sveniremmo	sarèi svenuto	saremmo svenuti
sveniresti	svenireste	saresti svenuto	sareste svenuti
svenirèbbe	svenirèbbero	sarèbbe svenuto	sarèbbero svenuti
6 present subjunctive		13 past subjunctive	
svènga	sveniamo	sia svenuto	siamo svenuti
svènga	sveniate	sia svenuto	siate svenuti
svènga	svèngano	sia svenuto	síano svenuti
7 imperfect subjunctive		14 past perfect subjunctive	
svenissi	sveníssimo	fossi svenuto	fóssimo svenuti
svenissi	sveniste	fossi svenuto	foste svenuti
svenisse	sveníssero	fosse svenuto	fóssero svenuti

	imperative	
—		sveniamo
svièni (non svenire)		svenite
svènga		svèngano

Words related to this verb
Lei sviene spesso.   She faints often.
Lui sviene dalla gioia.   He swoons with joy.
Loro sono svenuti dalla paura.   They fainted from fear.

Ger. svolgèndo   Past Part. svòlto   **svòlgere**

to unfold, to develop

The Seven Simple Tenses		The Seven Compound Tenses	
Singular	Plural	Singular	Plural
1 present indicative		8 present perfect	
svòlgo	svolgiamo	ho svòlto	abbiamo svòlto
svòlgi	svolgete	hai svòlto	avete svòlto
svòlge	svòlgono	ha svòlto	hanno svòlto
2 imperfect indicative		9 past perfect	
svolgevo	svolgevamo	avevo svòlto	avevamo svòlto
svolgevi	svolgevate	avevi svòlto	avevate svòlto
svolgeva	svolgévano	aveva svòlto	avévano svòlto
3 past absolute		10 past anterior	
svòlsi	svolgemmo	èbbi svòlto	avemmo svòlto
svolgesti	svolgeste	avesti svòlto	aveste svòlto
svòlse	svòlsero	èbbe svòlto	èbbero svòlto
4 future indicative		11 future perfect	
svolgerò	svolgeremo	avrò svòlto	avremo svòlto
svolgerai	svolgerete	avrai svòlto	avrete svòlto
svolgerà	svolgeranno	avrà svòlto	avranno svòlto
5 present conditional		12 past conditional	
svolgerèi	svolgeremmo	avrèi svòlto	avremmo svòlto
svolgeresti	svolgereste	avresti svòlto	avreste svòlto
svolgerèbbe	svolgerèbbero	avrèbbe svòlto	avrèbbero svòlto
6 present subjunctive		13 past subjunctive	
svòlga	svolgiamo	àbbia svòlto	abbiamo svòlto
svòlga	svolgiate	àbbia svòlto	abbiate svòlto
svòlga	svòlgano	àbbia svòlto	àbbiano svòlto
7 imperfect subjunctive		14 past perfect subjunctive	
svolgessi	svolgéssimo	avessi svòlto	avéssimo svòlto
svolgessi	svolgeste	avessi svòlto	aveste svòlto
svolgesse	svolgéssero	avesse svòlto	avéssero svòlto

imperative

—	svolgiamo
svòlgi (non svòlgere)	svolgete
svòlga	svòlgano

Words related to this verb
Come hai svolto la storia?   How did you develop the story?
Svolse la storia in un articolo.   He developed the story into an article.

tacere	Ger. tacèndo	Past Part. taciuto

to be silent, to pass over in silence

The Seven Simple Tenses		The Seven Compound Tenses	
Singular	Plural	Singular	Plural
1 present indicative		8 present perfect	
taccio	tacciamo (taciamo)	ho taciuto	abbiamo taciuto
taci	tacete	hai taciuto	avete taciuto
tace	tàcciono	ha taciuto	hanno taciuto
2 imperfect indicative		9 past perfect	
tacevo	tacevamo	avevo taciuto	avevamo taciuto
tacevi	tacevate	avevi taciuto	avevate taciuto
taceva	tacévano	aveva taciuto	avévano taciuto
3 past absolute		10 past anterior	
tacqui	tacemmo	èbbi taciuto	avemmo taciuto
tacesti	taceste	avesti taciuto	aveste taciuto
tacque	tàcquero	èbbe taciuto	èbbero taciuto
4 future indicative		11 future perfect	
tacerò	taceremo	avrò taciuto	avremo taciuto
tacerai	tacerete	avrai taciuto	avrete taciuto
tacerà	taceranno	avrà taciuto	avranno taciuto
5 present conditional		12 past conditional	
tacerèi	taceremmo	avrèi taciuto	avremmo taciuto
taceresti	tacereste	avresti taciuto	avreste taciuto
tacerèbbe	tacerèbbero	avrèbbe taciuto	avrèbbero taciuto
6 present subjunctive		13 past subjunctive	
taccia	tacciamo (taciamo)	àbbia taciuto	abbiamo taciuto
taccia	tacciate (taciate)	àbbia taciuto	abbiate taciuto
taccia	tàcciano	àbbia taciuto	àbbiano taciuto
7 imperfect subjunctive		14 past perfect subjunctive	
tacessi	tacéssimo	avessi taciuto	avéssimo taciuto
tacessi	taceste	avessi taciuto	aveste taciuto
tacesse	tacéssero	avesse taciuto	avéssero taciuto

	imperative	
	—	tacciamo (taciamo)
	taci (non tacere)	tacete
	taccia	tàcciano

Words related to this verb

Taci, non ti voglio sentire! Be quiet, I don't want to hear you!
I ragazzi tacciono quando il professore entra. The students quiet down (keep quiet) when the professor enters.

to stretch out, to hold out, to tend

The Seven Simple Tenses		The Seven Compound Tenses	
Singular	Plural	Singular	Plural
1 present indicative		8 present perfect	
tèndo	tendiamo	ho teso	abbiamo teso
tèndi	tendete	hai teso	avete teso
tènde	tèndono	ha teso	hanno teso
2 imperfect indicative		9 past perfect	
tendevo	tendevamo	avevo teso	avevamo teso
tendevi	tendevate	avevi teso	avevate teso
tendeva	tendévano	aveva teso	avévano teso
3 past absolute		10 past anterior	
tesi	tendemmo	èbbi teso	avemmo teso
tendesti	tendeste	avesti teso	aveste teso
tese	tésero	èbbe teso	èbero teso
4 future indicative		11 future perfect	
tenderò	tenderemo	avrò teso	avremo teso
tenderai	tenderete	avrai teso	avrete teso
tenderà	tenderanno	avrà teso	avranno teso
5 present conditional		12 past conditional	
tenderèi	tenderemmo	avrèi teso	avremmo teso
tenderesti	tendereste	avresti teso	avreste teso
tenderèbbe	tenderèbbero	avrèbbe teso	avrèbbero teso
6 present subjunctive		13 past subjunctive	
tènda	tendiamo	àbbia teso	abbiamo teso
tènda	tendiate	àbbia teso	abbiate teso
tènda	tèndano	àbbia teso	àbbiano teso
7 imperfect subjunctive		14 past perfect subjunctive	
tendessi	tendéssimo	avessi teso	avéssimo teso
tendessi	tendeste	avessi teso	aveste teso
tendesse	tendéssero	avesse teso	avéssero teso

imperative

—	tendiamo
tèndi (non tèndere)	tendete
tènda	tèndano

* Like tèndere are attèndere, contèndere, estèndere, intèndere, pretèndere, protèndere, stèndere, etc.

Words related to this verb
Lui tese la cordicella e prese il coniglio. He stretched out the cord and caught the rabbit.
Lui mi tende la mano in atto di amicizia. He holds out his hand to me as an act of friendship.

tenere*   Ger. tenèndo   Past Part. tenuto

to keep, to hold

The Seven Simple Tenses		The Seven Compound Tenses	
Singular	Plural	Singular	Plural
1 present indicative		8 present perfect	
tèngo	teniamo	ho tenuto	abbiamo tenuto
tièni	tenete	hai tenuto	avete tenuto
tiène	tèngono	ha tenuto	hanno tenuto
2 imperfect indicative		9 past perfect	
tenevo	tenevamo	avevo tenuto	avevamo tenuto
tenevi	tenevate	avevi tenuto	avevate tenuto
teneva	tenévano	aveva tenuto	avévano tenuto
3 past absolute		10 past anterior	
tenni	tenemmo	èbbi tenuto	avemmo tenuto
tenesti	teneste	avesti tenuto	aveste tenuto
tenne	ténnero	èbbe tenuto	èbbero tenuto
4 future indicative		11 future perfect	
terrò	terremo	avrò tenuto	avremo tenuto
terrai	terrete	avrai tenuto	avrete tenuto
terrà	terranno	avrà tenuto	avranno tenuto
5 present conditional		12 past conditional	
terrèi	terremmo	avrèi tenuto	avremmo tenuto
terresti	terreste	avresti tenuto	avreste tenuto
terrèbbe	terrèbbero	avrèbbe tenuto	avrèbbero tenuto
6 present subjunctive		13 past subjunctive	
tènga	teniamo	àbbia tenuto	abbiamo tenuto
tènga	teniate	àbbia tenuto	abbiate tenuto
tènga	tèngano	àbbia tenuto	àbbiano tenuto
7 imperfect subjunctive		14 past perfect subjunctive	
tenessi	tenéssimo	avessi tenuto	avéssimo tenuto
tenessi	teneste	avessi tenuto	aveste tenuto
tenesse	tenéssero	avesse tenuto	avéssero tenuto

imperative	
—	teniamo
tièni (non tenere)	tenete
tènga	tèngano

* Like *tenere* are *appartenere*, *astenersi*, *contenere*, *mantenere*, *ottenere*, *ritenere*, *sostenere*, *trattenere*, etc.

Words related to this verb
Il professore li ha tenuti in classe per tre ore.   The professor kept them in class for three hours.
Due colonne tengono su l'arco.   Two columns hold up the arch.

278

Ger. tingèndo   Past Part. tinto   **tíngere**

to dye

The Seven Simple Tenses		The Seven Compound Tenses	
Singular	Plural	Singular	Plural
1 present indicative		8 present perfect	
tingo	tingiamo	ho tinto	abbiamo tinto
tingi	tingete	hai tinto	avete tinto
tinge	tíngono	ha tinto	hanno tinto
2 imperfect indicative		9 past perfect	
tingevo	tingevamo	avevo tinto	avevamo tinto
tingevi	tingevate	avevi tinto	avevate tinto
tingeva	tingévano	aveva tinto	avévano tinto
3 past absolute		10 past anterior	
tinsi	tingemmo	èbbi tinto	avemmo tinto
tingesti	tingeste	avesti tinto	aveste tinto
tinse	tínsero	èbbe tinto	èbbero tinto
4 future indicative		11 future perfect	
tingerò	tingeremo	avrò tinto	avremo tinto
tingerai	tingerete	avrai tinto	avrete tinto
tingerà	tingeranno	avrà tinto	avranno tinto
5 present conditional		12 past conditional	
tingerèi	tingeremmo	avrèi tinto	avremmo tinto
tingeresti	tingereste	avresti tinto	avreste tinto
tingerèbbe	tingerèbbero	avrèbbe tinto	avrèbbero tinto
6 present subjunctive		13 past subjunctive	
tinga	tingiamo	àbbia tinto	abbiamo tinto
tinga	tingiate	àbbia tinto	abbiate tinto
tinga	tíngano	àbbia tinto	àbbiano tinto
7 imperfect subjunctive		14 past perfect subjunctive	
tingessi	tingéssimo	avessi tinto	avéssimo tinto
tingessi	tingeste	avessi tinto	aveste tinto
tingesse	tingéssero	avesse tinto	avéssero tinto

imperative	
—	tingiamo
tingi (non tíngere)	tingete
tinga	tíngano

Words related to this verb
Non mi piacciono i capelli tinti.   I don't like dyed hair.
Chi ha tinto questa camicia?   Who dyed this shirt?

tògliere   Ger. toglièndo   Past Part. tòlto

to take away, to remove

The Seven Simple Tenses		The Seven Compound Tenses	
Singular	Plural	Singular	Plural
1 present indicative		8 present perfect	
tòlgo	togliamo	ho tòlto	abbiamo tòlto
tògli	togliete	hai tòlto	avete tòlto
tòglie	tòlgono	ha tòlto	hanno tòlto
2 imperfect indicative		9 past perfect	
toglievo	toglievamo	avevo tòlto	avevamo tòlto
toglievi	toglievate	avevi tòlto	avevate tòlto
toglieva	togliévano	aveva tòlto	avévano tòlto
3 past absolute		10 past anterior	
tòlsi	togliemmo	èbbi tòlto	avemmo tòlto
togliesti	toglieste	avesti tòlto	aveste tòlto
tòlse	tòlsero	èbbe tòlto	èbbero tòlto
4 future indicative		11 future perfect	
toglierò	toglieremo	avrò tòlto	avremo tòlto
toglierai	toglierete	avrai tòlto	avrete tòlto
toglierà	toglieranno	avrà tòlto	avranno tòlto
5 present conditional		12 past conditional	
toglierèi	toglieremmo	avrèi tòlto	avremmo tòlto
toglieresti	togliereste	avresti tòlto	avreste tòlto
toglierèbbe	toglierèbbero	avrèbbe tòlto	avrèbbero tòlto
6 present subjunctive		13 past subjunctive	
tòlga	togliamo	àbbia tòlto	abbiamo tòlto
tòlga	togliate	àbbia tòlto	abbiate tòlto
tòlga	tòlgano	àbbia tòlto	àbbiano tòlto
7 imperfect subjunctive		14 past perfect subjunctive	
togliessi	togliéssimo	avessi tòlto	avéssimo tòlto
togliessi	toglieste	avessi tòlto	aveste tòlto
togliesse	togliéssero	avesse tòlto	avéssero tòlto

imperative		
—	togliamo	
tògli (non tògliere)	togliete	
tòlga	tòlgano	

Words related to this verb
Chi ha tolto i libri dallo scaffale?   Who took the books from the shelf?
Toglilo di qui!   Take it away from here!

Ger. torcèndo   Past Part. tòrto   tòrcere*

to twist, to wring

The Seven Simple Tenses		The Seven Compound Tenses	
Singular	Plural	Singular	Plural
1 present indicative		8 present perfect	
tòrco	torciamo	ho tòrto	abbiamo tòrto
tòrci	torcete	hai tòrto	avete tòrto
tòrce	tòrcono	ha tòrto	hanno tòrto
2 imperfect indicative		9 past perfect	
torcevo	torcevamo	avevo tòrto	avevamo tòrto
torcevi	torcevate	avevi tòrto	avevate tòrto
torceva	torcévano	aveva tòrto	avévano tòrto
3 past absolute		10 past anterior	
tòrsi	torcemmo	èbbi tòrto	avemmo tòrto
torcesti	torceste	avesti tòrto	aveste tòrto
tòrse	tòrsero	èbbe tòrto	èbbero tòrto
4 future indicative		11 future perfect	
torcerò	torceremo	avrò tòrto	avremo tòrto
torcerai	torcerete	avrai tòrto	avrete tòrto
torcerà	torceranno	avrà tòrto	avranno tòrto
5 present conditional		12 past conditional	
torcerèi	torceremmo	avrèi tòrto	avremmo tòrto
torceresti	torcereste	avresti tòrto	avreste tòrto
torcerèbbe	torcerèbbero	avrèbbe tòrto	avrèbbero tòrto
6 present subjunctive		13 past subjunctive	
tòrca	torciamo	àbbia tòrto	abbiamo tòrto
tòrca	torciate	àbbia tòrto	abbiate tòrto
tòrca	tòrcano	àbbia tòrto	àbbiano tòrto
7 imperfect subjunctive		14 past perfect subjunctive	
torcessi	torcéssimo	avessi tòrto	avéssimo tòrto
torcessi	torceste	avessi tòrto	aveste tòrto
torcesse	torcéssero	avesse tòrto	avéssero tòrto

	imperative	
—		torciamo
tòrci (non tòrcere)		torcete
tòrca		tòrcano

* Like *tòrcere* are *contòrcere*, *estòrcere*, *ritòrcere*, and *scontòrcersi*.

Words related to this verb
Lui mi torse il braccio.   He twisted my arm.
Se ti prendo, ti torco il collo!   If I catch you, I'll wring your neck!

tradurre	Ger. traducèndo	Past Part. tradotto

to translate

The Seven Simple Tenses		The Seven Compound Tenses	
Singular	Plural	Singular	Plural
1 present indicative		8 present perfect	
traduco	traduciamo	ho tradotto	abbiamo tradotto
traduci	traducete	hai tradotto	avete tradotto
traduce	tradúcono	ha tradotto	hanno tradotto
2 imperfect indicative		9 past perfect	
traducevo	traducevamo	avevo tradotto	avevamo tradotto
traducevi	traducevate	avevi tradotto	avevate tradotto
traduceva	traducévano	aveva tradotto	avévano tradotto
3 past absolute		10 past anterior	
tradussi	traducemmo	èbbi tradotto	avemmo tradotto
traducesti	traduceste	avesti tradotto	aveste tradotto
tradusse	tradússero	èbbe tradotto	èbbero tradotto
4 future indicative		11 future perfect	
tradurrò	tradurremo	avrò tradotto	avremo tradotto
tradurrai	tradurrete	avrai tradotto	avrete tradotto
tradurrà	tradurranno	avrà tradotto	avranno tradotto
5 present conditional		12 past conditional	
tradurrèi	tradurremmo	avrèi tradotto	avremmo tradotto
tradurresti	tradurreste	avresti tradotto	avreste tradotto
tradurrèbbe	tradurrèbbero	avrèbbe tradotto	avrèbbero tradotto
6 present subjunctive		13 past subjunctive	
traduca	traduciamo	àbbia tradotto	abbiamo tradotto
traduca	traduciate	àbbia tradotto	abbiate tradotto
traduca	tradúcano	àbbia tradotto	àbbiano tradotto
7 imperfect subjunctive		14 past perfect subjunctive	
traducessi	traducéssimo	avessi tradotto	avéssimo tradotto
traducessi	traduceste	avessi tradotto	aveste tradotto
traducesse	traducéssero	avesse tradotto	avéssero tradotto

	imperative	
—	traduciamo
traduci (non tradurre)	traducete
traduca	tradúcano

Words related to this verb
Lui traduce bene dall'italiano.   He translates well from Italian.
Io le traducevo le lettere.   I used to translate her letters.

Ger. **traèndo**	Past Part. **tratto**	**trarre***

to draw, to pull

The Seven Simple Tenses		The Seven Compound Tenses	
Singular	Plural	Singular	Plural
1 present indicative		8 present perfect	
traggo	**traiamo (tragghiamo)**	**ho tratto**	**abbiamo tratto**
trai	**traete**	**hai tratto**	**avete tratto**
trae	**tràggono**	**ha tratto**	**hanno tratto**
2 imperfect indicative		9 past perfect	
traevo	**traevamo**	**avevo tratto**	**avevamo tratto**
traevi	**traevate**	**avevi tratto**	**avevate tratto**
traeva	**traévano**	**aveva tratto**	**avévano tratto**
3 past absolute		10 past anterior	
trassi	**traemmo**	**èbbi tratto**	**avemmo tratto**
traesti	**traeste**	**avesti tratto**	**aveste tratto**
tràsse	**tràssero**	**èbbe tratto**	**èbbero tratto**
4 future indicative		11 future perfect	
trarrò	**trarremo**	**avrò tratto**	**avremo tratto**
trarrai	**trarrete**	**avrai tratto**	**avrete tratto**
trarrà	**trarranno**	**avrà tratto**	**avranno tratto**
5 present conditional		12 past conditional	
trarrèi	**trarremmo**	**avrèi tratto**	**avremmo tratto**
trarresti	**trarreste**	**avresti tratto**	**avreste tratto**
trarrèbbe	**trarrèbbero**	**avrèbbe tratto**	**avrèbbero tratto**
6 present subjunctive		13 past subjunctive	
tragga	**traiamo (tragghiamo)**	**àbbia tratto**	**abbiamo tratto**
tragga	**traiate (tragghiate)**	**àbbia tratto**	**abbiate tratto**
tragga	**tràggano**	**àbbia tratto**	**àbbiano tratto**
7 imperfect subjunctive		14 past perfect subjunctive	
traessi	**traéssimo**	**avessi tratto**	**avéssimo tratto**
traessi	**traeste**	**avessi tratto**	**aveste tratto**
traesse	**traéssero**	**avesse tratto**	**avéssero tratto**

imperative

—	**traiamo (tragghiamo)**
trai (non trarre)	**traete**
tragga	**tràggano**

* Like *trarre* are *astrarre*, *attrarre*, *contrarre*, *detrarre*, *distrarre*, *estrarre*, *protrarre*, *ritrarre*, and *sottrarre*.

Words related to this verb
Lui ci trasse a sè.   He drew us to him.
Loro trassero conclusioni affrettate sull'incidente di macchina.   They drew hurried conclusions about the car accident.

trattenere	Ger. trattenèndo	Past Part. trattenuto

to keep back, to restrain, to entertain, to detain

The Seven Simple Tenses		The Seven Compound Tenses	
Singular	Plural	Singular	Plural
1 present indicative		8 present perfect	
trattèngo	tratteniamo	ho trattenuto	abbiamo trattenuto
trattièni	trattenete	hai trattenuto	avete trattenuto
trattiène	trattèngono	ha trattenuto	hanno trattenuto
2 imperfect indicative		9 past perfect	
trattenevo	trattenevamo	avevo trattenuto	avevamo trattenuto
trattenevi	trattenevate	avevi trattenuto	avevate trattenuto
tratteneva	trattenévano	aveva trattenuto	avévano trattenuto
3 past absolute		10 past anterior	
trattenni	trattenemmo	èbbi trattenuto	avemmo trattenuto
trattenesti	tratteneste	avesti trattenuto	aveste trattenuto
trattenne	tratténnero	èbbe trattenuto	èbbero trattenuto
4 future indicative		11 future perfect	
tratterrò	tratterremo	avrò trattenuto	avremo trattenuto
tratterrai	tratterrete	avrai trattenuto	avrete trattenuto
tratterrà	tratterranno	avrà trattenuto	avranno trattenuto
5 present conditional		12 past conditional	
tratterrèi	tratterremmo	avrèi trattenuto	avremmo trattenuto
tratterresti	tratterreste	avresti trattenuto	avreste trattenuto
tratterrèbbe	tratterrèbbero	avrèbbe trattenuto	avrèbbero trattenuto
6 present subjunctive		13 past subjunctive	
trattènga	tratteniamo	àbbia trattenuto	abbiamo trattenuto
trattènga	tratteniate	àbbia trattenuto	abbiate trattenuto
trattènga	trattèngano	àbbia trattenuto	àbbiano trattenuto
7 imperfect subjunctive		14 past perfect subjunctive	
trattenessi	trattenéssimo	avessi trattenuto	avéssimo trattenuto
trattenessi	tratteneste	avessi trattenuto	aveste trattenuto
trattenesse	trattenéssero	avesse trattenuto	avéssero trattenuto

	imperative	
—		tratteniamo
trattièni (non trattenere)		trattenete
trattènga		trattèngano

Words related to this verb

Ogni volta che mi vede mi trattiene.   Every time he sees me he detains me.
Io lo trattengo dal battersi.   I keep him from fighting.

to find

The Seven Simple Tenses		The Seven Compound Tenses	
Singular	Plural	Singular	Plural
1 present indicative		8 present perfect	
tròvo	troviamo	ho trovato	abbiamo trovato
tròvi	trovate	hai trovato	avete trovato
tròva	trovano	ha trovato	hanno trovato
2 imperfect indicative		9 past perfect	
trovavo	trovavamo	avevo trovato	avevamo trovato
trovavi	trovavate	avevi trovato	avevate trovato
trovava	trovàvano	aveva trovato	avévano trovato
3 past absolute		10 past anterior	
trovai	trovammo	èbbi trovato	avemmo trovato
trovasti	trovaste	avesti trovato	aveste trovato
trovò	trovàrono	èbbe trovato	èbbero trovato
4 future indicative		11 future perfect	
troverò	troveremo	avrò trovato	avremo trovato
troverai	troverete	avrai trovato	avrete trovato
troverà	troveranno	avrà trovato	avranno trovato
5 present conditional		12 past conditional	
troverèi	troveremmo	avrèi trovato	avremmo trovato
troveresti	trovereste	avresti trovato	avreste trovato
troverèbbe	troverèbbero	avrèbbe trovato	avrèbbero trovato
6 present subjunctive		13 past subjunctive	
tròvi	troviamo	àbbia trovato	abbiamo trovato
tròvi	troviate	àbbia trovato	abbiate trovato
tròvi	tròvino	àbbia trovato	àbbiano trovato
7 imperfect subjunctive		14 past perfect subjunctive	
trovassi	trovàssimo	avessi trovato	avéssimo trovato
trovassi	trovaste	avessi trovato	aveste trovato
trovasse	trovàssero	avesse trovato	avéssero trovato

imperative

—	troviamo
tròva (non trovare)	trovate
tròvi	tròvino

Words related to this verb
Ho trovato il libro.   I have found the book.
Lo trovai a letto.   I found him in bed.

uccídere		Ger. uccidèndo	Past Part. ucciso

to kill

The Seven Simple Tenses		The Seven Compound Tenses	
Singular	Plural	Singular	Plural
1 present indicative		8 present perfect	
uccido	uccidiamo	ho ucciso	abbiamo ucciso
uccidi	uccidete	hai ucciso	avete ucciso
uccide	uccídono	ha ucciso	hanno ucciso
2 imperfect indicative		9 past perfect	
uccidevo	uccidevamo	avevo ucciso	avevamo ucciso
uccidevi	uccidevate	avevi ucciso	avevate ucciso
uccideva	uccidévano	aveva ucciso	avévano ucciso
3 past absolute		10 past anterior	
uccisi	uccidemmo	èbbi ucciso	avemmo ucciso
uccidesti	uccideste	avesti ucciso	aveste ucciso
uccise	uccísero	èbbe ucciso	èbbero ucciso
4 future indicative		11 future perfect	
ucciderò	uccideremo	avrò ucciso	avremo ucciso
ucciderai	ucciderete	avrai ucciso	avrete ucciso
ucciderà	uccideranno	avrà ucciso	avranno ucciso
5 present conditional		12 past conditional	
ucciderèi	uccideremmo	avrèi ucciso	avremmo ucciso
uccideresti	uccidereste	avresti ucciso	avreste ucciso
ucciderèbbe	ucciderèbbero	avrèbbe ucciso	avrèbbero ucciso
6 present subjunctive		13 past subjunctive	
uccida	uccidiamo	àbbia ucciso	abbiamo ucciso
uccida	uccidiate	àbbia ucciso	abbiate ucciso
uccida	uccídano	àbbia ucciso	àbbiano ucciso
7 imperfect subjunctive		14 past perfect subjunctive	
uccidessi	uccidéssimo	avessi ucciso	avéssimo ucciso
uccidessi	uccideste	avessi ucciso	aveste ucciso
uccidesse	uccidéssero	avesse ucciso	avéssero ucciso

	imperative	
—		uccidiamo
uccidi (non uccídere)		uccidete
uccida		uccídano

Words related to this verb
Lui uccise la zanzara. He killed the mosquito.
Io no ho ucciso nessuno. I have not killed anyone.

The Seven Simple Tenses		The Seven Compound Tenses	
Singular	Plural	Singular	Plural
1 present indicative		8 present perfect	
òdo	udiamo	ho udito	abbiamo udito
òdi	udite	hai udito	avete udito
òde	òdono	ha udito	hanno udito
2 imperfect indicative		9 past perfect	
udivo	udivamo	avevo udito	avevamo udito
udivi	udivate	avevi udito	avevate udito
udiva	udívano	aveva udito	avévano udito
3 past absolute		10 past anterior	
udii	udimmo	èbbi udito	avemmo udito
udisti	udiste	avesti udito	aveste udito
udí	udírono	èbbe udito	èbbero udito
4 future indicative		11 future perfect	
udrò	udremo	avrò udito	avremo udito
udrai	udrete	avrai udito	avrete udito
udrà	udranno	avrà udito	avranno udito
5 present conditional		12 past conditional	
udrèi	udremmo	avrèi udito	avremmo udito
udresti	udreste	avresti udito	avreste udito
udrèbbe	udrèbbero	avrèbbe udito	avrèbbero udito
6 present subjunctive		13 past subjunctive	
òda	udiamo	àbbia udito	abbiamo udito
òda	udiate	àbbia udito	abbiate udito
òda	òdano	àbbia udito	àbbiano udito
7 imperfect subjunctive		14 past perfect subjunctive	
udissi	udíssimo	avessi udito	avéssimo udito
udissi	udiste	avessi udito	aveste udito
udisse	udíssero	avesse udito	avéssero udito

imperative		
—		udiamo
	òdi (non udìre)	udite
	òda	òdano

Words related to this verb
Io odo un rumore.   I hear a noise.
Dalla mia camera io udivo il mare.   From my room I could hear the sea.

to grease, to smear

The Seven Simple Tenses		The Seven Compound Tenses	
Singular	Plural	Singular	Plural
1 present indicative		8 present perfect	
ungo	ungiamo	ho unto	abbiamo unto
ungi	ungete	hai unto	avete unto
unge	úngono	ha unto	hanno unto
2 imperfect indicative		9 past perfect	
ungevo	ungevamo	avevo unto	avevamo unto
ungevi	ungevate	avevi unto	avevate unto
ungeva	ungévano	aveva unto	avévano unto
3 past absolute		10 past anterior	
unsi	ungemmo	èbbi unto	avemmo unto
ungesti	ungeste	avesti unto	aveste unto
unse	únsero	èbbe unto	èbbero unto
4 future indicative		11 future perfect	
ungerò	ungeremo	avrò unto	avremo unto
ungerai	ungerete	avrai unto	avrete unto
ungerà	ungeranno	avrà unto	avranno unto
5 present conditional		12 past conditional	
ungerèi	ungeremmo	avrèi unto	avremmo unto
ungeresti	ungereste	avresti unto	avreste unto
ungerèbbe	ungerèbbero	avrèbbe unto	avrèbbero unto
6 present subjunctive		13 past subjunctive	
unga	ungiamo	àbbia unto	abbiamo unto
unga	ungiate	àbbia unto	abbiate unto
unga	úngano	àbbia unto	àbbiano unto
7 imperfect subjunctive		14 past perfect subjunctive	
ungessi	ungéssimo	avessi unto	avéssimo unto
ungessi	ungeste	avessi unto	aveste unto
ungesse	ungéssero	avesse unto	avéssero unto

	imperative	
—		ungiamo
ungi (non úngere)		ungete
unga		úngano

Words related to this verb
Mi sono unto di olio.   I smeared myself with oil.
Il meccanico unge le rotelle.   The mechanic greases the wheels.

288

to go out, to come out

The Seven Simple Tenses		The Seven Compound Tenses	
Singular	Plural	Singular	Plural
1 present indicative		8 present perfect	
èsco	usciamo	sono uscito	siamo usciti
èsci	uscite	sèi uscito	siète usciti
èsce	èscono	è uscito	sono usciti
2 imperfect indicative		9 past perfect	
uscivo	uscivamo	èro uscito	eravamo usciti
uscivi	uscivate	èri uscito	eravate usciti
usciva	uscívano	èra uscito	èrano usciti
3 past absolute		10 past anterior	
uscii	uscimmo	fui uscito	fummo usciti
uscisti	usciste	fosti uscito	foste usciti
uscí	uscírono	fu uscito	fúrono usciti
4 future indicative		11 future perfect	
uscirò	usciremo	sarò uscito	saremo usciti
uscirai	uscirete	sarai uscito	sarete usciti
uscirà	usciranno	sarà uscito	saranno usciti
5 present conditional		12 past conditional	
uscirèi	usciremmo	sarèi uscito	saremmo uscitl
usciresti	uscireste	saresti uscito	sareste usciti
uscirèbbe	uscirèbbero	sarèbbe uscito	sarèbbero usciti
6 present subjunctive		13 past subjunctive	
èsca	usciamo	sia uscito	siamo usciti
èsca	usciate	sia uscito	siate usciti
èsca	èscano	sia uscito	síano usciti
7 imperfect subjunctive		14 past perfect subjunctive	
uscissi	uscíssimo	fossi uscito	fóssimo usciti
uscissi	usciste	fossi uscito	foste usciti
uscisse	uscíssero	fosse uscito	fóssero usciti

imperative

—	usciamo
èsci (non uscire)	uscite
èsca	èscano

*Like *uscire* is *riuscire*.

Words related to this verb
Io non esco mai di notte. I never go out at night.
Perchè non esci un poco? Why don't you go out for a while?

valere*　　　　　　　　Ger. valèndo　　　Past Part. valso (valuto)

to be worth, to be of value

The Seven Simple Tenses		The Seven Compound Tenses	
Singular	Plural	Singular	Plural
1 present indicative		8 present perfect	
valgo	valiamo	sono valso (valuto)	siamo valsi
vali	valete	sèi valso	siète valsi
vale	vàlgono	è valso	sono valsi
2 imperfect indicative		9 past perfect	
valevo	valevamo	èro valso	eravamo valsi
valevi	valevate	èri valso	eravate valsi
valeva	valévano	èra valso	èrano valsi
3 past absolute		10 past anterior	
valsi	valemmo	fui valso	fummo valsi
valesti	valeste	fosti valso	foste valsi
valse	vàlsero	fu valso	fúrono valsi
4 future indicative		11 future perfect	
varrò	varremo	sarò valso	saremo valsi
varrai	varrete	sarai valso	sarete valsi
varrà	varranno	sarà valso	saranno valsi
5 present conditional		12 past conditional	
varrèi	varremmo	sarèi valso	saremmo valsi
varresti	varreste	saresti valso	sareste valsi
varrèbbe	varrèbbero	sarèbbe valso	sarèbbero valsi
6 present subjunctive		13 past subjunctive	
valga	valiamo	sia valso	siamo valsi
valga	valiate	sia valso	siate valsi
valga	vàlgano	sia valso	síano valsi
7 imperfect subjunctive		14 past perfect subjunctive	
valessi	valéssimo	fossi valso	fóssimo valsi
valessi	valeste	fossi valso	foste valsi
valesse	valéssero	fosse valso	fóssero valsi

	imperative	
—		valiamo
vali (non valere)		valete
valga		vàlgano

* Like *valere* are *equivalere* and *prevalere*. *Valere* is rarely conjugated with *avere*.

Words related to this verb
Quanto vale questa collana? How much is this necklace worth?
Questa storia non vale niente. This story is not worth anything.

to see

The Seven Simple Tenses		The Seven Compound Tenses	
Singular	Plural	Singular	Plural
1 present indicative		8 present perfect	
vedo (veggo)	vediamo	ho veduto (visto)	abbiamo veduto
vedi	vedete	hai veduto	avete veduto
vede	védono (véggono)	ha veduto	hanno veduto
2 imperfect indicative		9 past perfect	
vedevo	vedevamo	avevo veduto	avevamo veduto
vedevi	vedevate	avevi veduto	avevate veduto
vedeva	vedévano	aveva veduto	avévano veduto
3 past absolute		10 past anterior	
vidi	vedemmo	èbbi veduto	avemmo veduto
vedesti	vedeste	avesti veduto	aveste veduto
vide	vídero	èbbe veduto	èbbero veduto
4 future indicative		11 future perfect	
vedrò	vedremo	avrò veduto	avremo veduto
vedrai	vedrete	avrai veduto	avrete veduto
vedrà	vedranno	avrà veduto	avranno veduto
5 present conditional		12 past conditional	
vedrèi	vedremmo	avrèi veduto	avremmo veduto
vedresti	vedreste	avresti veduto	avreste veduto
vedrèbbe	vedrèbbero	avrèbbe veduto	avrèbbero veduto
6 present subjunctive		13 past subjunctive	
veda (vegga)	vediamo	àbbia veduto	abbiamo veduto
veda (vegga)	vediate	àbbia veduto	abbiate veduto
veda (vegga)	védano (véggano)	àbbia veduto	àbbiano veduto
7 imperfect subjunctive		14 past perfect subjunctive	
vedessi	vedéssimo	avessi veduto	avéssimo veduto
vedessi	vedeste	avessi veduto	aveste veduto
vedesse	vedéssero	avesse veduto	avéssero veduto

imperative

		vediamo
	vedi (non vedere)	vedete
	veda (vegga)	védano (véggano)

*Like *vedere* are *antivedere, avvedersi, intravvedere, rivedere,* and *travedere.*

Words related to this verb
Cosa vedi dalla finestra? What do you see from the window?
Io vedo la ragazza. I see the girl.

vendere   Ger. **vendendo**   Past Part. **venduto**

to sell

The Seven Simple Tenses		The Seven Compound Tenses	
Singular	Plural	Singular	Plural
1 present indicative		8 present perfect	
vendo	**vendiamo**	**ho venduto**	**abbiamo venduto**
vendi	**vendete**	**hai venduto**	**avete venduto**
vende	**vendono**	**ha venduto**	**hanno venduto**
2 imperfect indicative		9 past perfect	
vendevo	**vendevamo**	**avevo venduto**	**avevamo venduto**
vendevi	**vendevate**	**avevi venduto**	**avevate venduto**
vendeva	**vendèvano**	**aveva venduto**	**avévano venduto**
3 past absolute		10 past anterior	
vendei	**vendemmo**	**èbbi venduto**	**avemmo venduto**
vendesti	**vendeste**	**avesti venduto**	**aveste venduto**
vendè	**vendèrono**	**èbbe venduto**	**èbbero venduto**
4 future indicative		11 future perfect	
venderò	**venderemo**	**avrò venduto**	**avremo venduto**
venderai	**venderete**	**avrai venduto**	**avrete venduto**
venderà	**venderanno**	**avrà venduto**	**avranno venduto**
5 present conditional		12 past conditional	
venderèi	**venderemmo**	**avrèi venduto**	**avremmo venduto**
venderesti	**vendereste**	**avresti venduto**	**avreste venduto**
venderèbbe	**venderèbbero**	**avrèbbe venduto**	**avrèbbero venduto**
6 present subjunctive		13 past subjunctive	
venda	**vendiamo**	**àbbia venduto**	**abbiamo venduto**
venda	**vendiate**	**àbbia venduto**	**abbiate venduto**
venda	**véndano**	**àbbia venduto**	**àbbiano venduto**
7 imperfect subjunctive		14 past perfect subjunctive	
vendessi	**vendéssimo**	**avessi venduto**	**avéssimo venduto**
vendessi	**vendeste**	**avessi venduto**	**aveste venduto**
vendesse	**vendéssero**	**avesse venduto**	**avéssero venduto**

	imperative	
—	**vendiamo**
vendi (non **vendere**)	**vendete**
venda	**vèndano**

Words related to this verb
Abbiamo venduto tutto.   We are sold out.
vendere a buon mercato   to sell cheaply
vendere all'ingrosso   to sell wholesale

to come

The Seven Simple Tenses		The Seven Compound Tenses	
Singular	Plural	Singular	Plural
1 present indicative		8 present perfect	
vèngo	veniamo	sono venuto	siamo venuti
vièni	venite	sèi venuto	siète venuti
viène	vèngono	è venuto	sono venuti
2 imperfect indicative		9 past perfect	
venivo	venivamo	èro venuto	eravamo venuti
venivi	venivate	èri venuto	eravate venuti
veniva	venívano	èra venuto	èrano venuti
3 past absolute		10 past anterior	
venni	venimmo	fui venuto	fummo venuti
venisti	veniste	fosti venuto	foste venuti
venne	vénnero	fu venuto	fúrono venuti
4 future indicative		11 future perfect	
verrò	verremo	sarò venuto	saremo venuti
verrai	verrete	sarai venuto	sarete venuti
verrà	verranno	sarà venuto	saranno venuti
5 present conditional		12 past conditional	
verrèi	verremmo	sarèi venuto	saremmo venuti
verresti	verreste	saresti venuto	sareste venuti
verrèbbe	verrèbbero	sarèbbe venuto	sarèbbero venuti
6 present subjunctive		13 past subjunctive	
vènga	veniamo	sia venuto	siamo venuti
vènga	veniate	sia venuto	siate venuti
vènga	vèngano	sia venuto	síano venuti
7 imperfect subjunctive		14 past perfect subjunctive	
venissi	veníssimo	fossi venuto	fóssimo venuti
venissi	veniste	fossi venuto	foste venuti
venisse	veníssero	fosse venuto	fóssero venuti

	imperative	
—		veniamo
	vièni (non venire)	venite
	vènga	vèngano

* Like *venire* are *avvenire, convenire, divenire, intervenire, prevenire, provenire, sopravvenire, sovvenire, etc.* In some meanings *prevenire* and *sovvenire* are conjugated with *avere*.

Words related to this verb
Io vengo a casa sempre alle otto.   I always come home at eight.
Verrò a casa tua domani.   I will come to your house tomorrow.

to dress oneself

The Seven Simple Tenses		The Seven Compound Tenses	
Singular	Plural	Singular	Plural
1 present indicative		8 present perfect	
mi vèsto	ci vestiamo	mi sono vestito	ci siamo vestiti
ti vèsti	vi vestite	ti sei vestito	vi siete vestiti
si vèste	si vestono	si è vestito	si sono vestiti
2 imperfect indicative		9 past perfect	
mi vestivo	ci vestivamo	mi èro vestito	ci eravamo vestiti
ti vestivi	vi vestivate	ti èri vestito	vi eravate vestiti
si vestiva	si vestívano	si èra vestito	si èrano vestiti
3 past absolute		10 past anterior	
mi vestii	ci vestimmo	mi fui vestito	ci fummo vestiti
ti vestisti	vi vestiste	ti fosti vestito	vi foste vestiti
si vestì	si vestírono	si fu vestito	si furono vestiti
4 future indicative		11 future perfect	
mi vestirò	ci vestiremo	mi sarò vestito	ci saremo vestiti
ti vestirai	vi vestirete	ti sarai vestito	vi sarete vestiti
si vestirà	si vestiranno	si sarà vestito	si sàranno vestiti
5 present conditional		12 past conditional	
mi vestirèi	ci vestiremmo	mi sarèi vestito	ci saremmo vestiti
ti vestiresti	vi vestireste	ti saresti vestito	vi sareste vestiti
si vestirèbbe	si vestirèbbero	si sarèbbe vestito	si sarèbbero vestiti
6 present subjunctive		13 past subjunctive	
mi vèsta	ci vestiamo	mi sia vestito	ci siamo vestiti
ti vèsta	vi vestiate	ti sia vestito	vi siate vestiti
si vèsta	si vèstano	si sia vestito	si síano vestiti
7 imperfect subjunctive		14 past perfect subjunctive	
mi vestissi	ci vestíssimo	mi fossi vestito	ci fóssimo vestiti
ti vestissi	vi vestiste	ti fossi vestito	vi foste vestiti
si vestisse	si vestíssero	si fosse vestito	si fóssero vestiti

	imperative	
—		vestiamoci
vèstiti (non ti vestire)		vestitevi
si vèsta		si vèstano

Words related to this verb
Mi vesto presto la mattina. I get dressed early in the morning.
Lei si veste bene. She dresses well.

to win, to conquer

The Seven Simple Tenses		The Seven Compound Tenses	
Singular	Plural	Singular	Plural
1 present indicative		8 present perfect	
vinco	vinciamo	ho vinto	abbiamo vinto
vinci	vincete	hai vinto	avete vinto
vince	víncono	ha vinto	hanno vinto
2 imperfect indicative		9 past perfect	
vincevo	vincevamo	avevo vinto	avevamo vinto
vincevi	vincevate	avevi vinto	avevate vinto
vinceva	vincévano	aveva vinto	avévano vinto
3 past absolute		10 past anterior	
vinsi	vincemmo	èbbi vinto	avemmo vinto
vincesti	vinceste	avesti vinto	aveste vinto
vinse	vínsero	èbbe vinto	èbbero vinto
4 future indicative		11 future perfect	
vincerò	vinceremo	avrò vinto	avremo vinto
vincerai	vincerete	avrai vinto	avrete vinto
vincerà	vinceranno	avrà vinto	avranno vinto
5 present conditional		12 past conditional	
vincerèi	vinceremmo	avrèi vinto	avremmo vinto
vinceresti	vincereste	avresti vinto	avreste vinto
vincerèbbe	vincerèbbero	avrèbbe vinto	avrèbbero vinto
6 present subjunctive		13 past subjunctive	
vinca	vinciamo	àbbia vinto	abbiamo vinto
vinca	vinciate	àbbia vinto	abbiate vinto
vinca	víncano	àbbia vinto	àbbiano vinto
7 imperfect subjunctive		14 past perfect subjunctive	
vincessi	vincéssimo	avessi vinto	avéssimo vinto
vincessi	vinceste	avessi vinto	aveste vinto
vincesse	vincéssero	avesse vinto	avéssero vinto

imperative

—	vinciamo
vinci (non víncere)	vincete
vinca	víncano

* Like *víncere* are *avvíncere*, *convíncere*, and *rivíncere*.

Words related to this verb
Io ho vinto la partita.   I won the game.
Il cavallo nero vinse la corsa.   The black horse won the race.

visitare Ger. **visitando** Past Part. **visitato**

to visit; to examine (medical)

The Seven Simple Tenses		The Seven Compound Tenses	
Singular	Plural	Singular	Plural
1 present indicative		8 present perfect	
vìsito	visitiamo	ho visitato	abbiamo visitato
vìsiti	visitate	hai visitato	avete visitato
vìsita	visitano	ha visitato	hanno visitato
2 imperfect indicative		9 past perfect	
visitavo	visitavamo	avevo visitato	avevamo visitato
visitavi	visitavate	avevi visitato	avevate visitato
visitava	visitàvano	aveva visitato	avévano visitato
3 past absolute		10 past anterior	
visitai	visitammo	èbbi visitato	avemmo visitato
visitasti	visitaste	avesti visitato	aveste visitato
visitò	visitàrono	èbbe visitato	èbbero visitato
4 future indicative		11 future perfect	
visiterò	visiteremo	avrò visitato	avremo visitato
visiterai	visiterete	avrai visitato	avrete visitato
visiterà	visiteranno	avrà visitato	avranno visitato
5 present conditional		12 past conditional	
visiterèi	visiteremmo	avrèi visitato	avremmo visitato
visiteresti	visitereste	avresti visitato	avreste visitato
visiterèbbe	visiterèbbero	avrèbbe visitato	avrèbbero visitato
6 present subjunctive		13 past subjunctive	
vìsiti	visitiamo	àbbia visitato	abbiamo visitato
vìsiti	visitiate	àbbia visitato	abbiate visitato
vìsiti	vìsitino	àbbia visitato	àbbiano visitato
7 imperfect subjunctive		14 past perfect subjunctive	
visitassi	visitàssimo	avessi visitato	avéssimo visitato
visitassi	visitaste	avessi visitato	aveste visitato
visitasse	visitàssero	avesse visitato	avéssero visitato

imperative	
—	visitiamo
vìsita (non visitare)	visitate
vìsiti	vìsitino

Words related to this verb
Ho visitato l'Italia. I have visited Italy.
Il dottore mi ha visitato. The doctor examined me.

The Seven Simple Tenses		The Seven Compound Tenses	
Singular	Plural	Singular	Plural
1 present indicative		8 present perfect	
vivo	viviamo	ho vissuto	abbiamo vissuto
vivi	vivete	hai vissuto	avete vissuto
vive	vívono	ha vissuto	hanno vissuto
2 imperfect indicative		9 past perfect	
vivevo	vivevamo	avevo vissuto	avevamo vissuto
vivevi	vivevate	avevi vissuto	avevate vissuto
viveva	vivévano	aveva vissuto	avévano vissuto
3 past absolute		10 past anterior	
vissi	vivemmo	èbbi vissuto	avemmo vissuto
vivesti	viveste	avesti vissuto	aveste vissuto
visse	víssero	èbbe vissuto	èbbero vissuto
4 future indicative		11 future perfect	
vivrò	vivremo	avrò vissuto	avremo vissuto
vivrai	vivrete	avrai vissuto	avrete vissuto
vivrà	vivranno	avrà vissuto	avranno vissuto
5 present conditional		12 past conditional	
vivrèi	vivremmo	avrèi vissuto	avremmo vissuto
vivresti	vivreste	avresti vissuto	avreste vissuto
vivrèbbe	vivrèbbero	avrèbbe vissuto	avrèbbero vissuto
6 present subjunctive		13 past subjunctive	
viva	viviamo	àbbia vissuto	abbiamo vissuto
viva	viviate	àbbia vissuto	abbiate vissuto
viva	vívano	àbbia vissuto	àbbiano vissuto
7 imperfect subjunctive		14 past perfect subjunctive	
vivessi	vivéssimo	avessi vissuto	avéssimo vissuto
vivessi	viveste	avessi vissuto	aveste vissuto
vivesse	vivéssero	avesse vissuto	avéssero vissuto

	imperative
—	viviamo
vivi (non vívere)	vivete
viva	vívano

* Like *vívere* are *convívere* and *rivívere*. See *Introduction*.

Words related to this verb
Io vivo bene in America.   I live well in America.
Quella scrittrice vive ancora.   That writer is still living.

volare   Ger. **volando**   Past Part. **volato**

to fly

The Seven Simple Tenses		The Seven Compound Tenses	
Singular	Plural	Singular	Plural
1 present indicative		8 present perfect	
vòlo	voliamo	ho volato	abbiamo volato
vòli	volate	hai volato	avete volato
vòla	vòlano	ha volato	hanno volato
2 imperfect indicative		9 past perfect	
volavo	volavamo	avevo volato	avevamo volato
volavi	volavate	avevi volato	avevate volato
volava	volàvano	aveva volato	avévano volato
3 past absolute		10 past anterior	
volai	volammo	èbbi volato	avemmo volato
volasti	volaste	avesti volato	aveste volato
volò	volàrono	èbbe volato	èbbero volato
4 future indicative		11 future perfect	
volerò	voleremo	avrò volato	avremo volato
volerai	volerete	avrai volato	avrete volato
volerà	voleranno	avrà volato	avranno volato
5 present conditional		12 past conditional	
volerèi	voleremmo	avrèi volato	avremmo volato
voleresti	volereste	avresti volato	avreste volato
volerèbbe	volerèbbero	avrèbbe volato	avrèbbero volato
6 present subjunctive		13 past subjunctive	
vòli	voliamo	àbbia volato	abbiamo volato
vòli	voliate	àbbia volato	abbiate volato
vòli	vòlino	àbbia volato	àbbiano volato
7 imperfect subjunctive		14 past perfect subjunctive	
volassi	volàssimo	avessi volato	avéssimo volato
volassi	volaste	avessi volato	aveste volato
volasse	volàssero	avesse volato	avéssero volato
	imperative		
	—	voliamo	
	vòla (non volare)	volate	
	vòli	vòlino	

Words related to this verb
Le aquile volano alte.   Eagles fly high.
Il tempo vola.   Time flies.

Ger. volèndo   Past Part. voluto   **volere**

to want

The Seven Simple Tenses		The Seven Compound Tenses	
Singular	Plural	Singular	Plural
1 present indicative		**8 present perfect**	
vòglio	vogliamo	ho* voluto	abbiamo voluto
vuòi	volete	hai voluto	avete voluto
vuòle	vògliono	ha voluto	hanno voluto
2 imperfect indicative		**9 past perfect**	
volevo	volevamo	avevo voluto	avevamo voluto
volevi	volevate	avevi voluto	avevate voluto
voleva	volévano	aveva voluto	avévano voluto
3 past absolute		**10 past anterior**	
vòlli	volemmo	èbbi voluto	avemmo voluto
volesti	voleste	avesti voluto	aveste voluto
vòlle	vòllero	èbbe voluto	èbbero voluto
4 future indicative		**11 future perfect**	
vorrò	vorremo	avrò voluto	avremo voluto
vorrai	vorrete	avrai voluto	avrete voluto
vorrà	vorranno	avrà voluto	avranno voluto
5 present conditional		**12 past conditional**	
vorrèi	vorremmo	avrèi voluto	avremmo voluto
vorresti	vorreste	avresti voluto	avreste voluto
vorrèbbe	vorrèbbero	avrèbbe voluto	avrèbbero voluto
6 present subjunctive		**13 past subjunctive**	
vòglia	vogliamo	àbbia voluto	abbiamo voluto
vòglia	voliate	àbbia voluto	abbiate voluto
vòglia	vògliano	àbbia voluto	àbbiano voluto
7 imperfect subjunctive		**14 past perfect subjunctive**	
volessi	voléssimo	avessi voluto	avéssimo voluto
volessi	voleste	avessi voluto	aveste voluto
volesse	voléssero	avesse voluto	avéssero voluto

imperative

	vogliamo
(*in the sense of* please) vògli (non volere)	vogliate
vòglia	vògliano

* *Volere* takes *èssere* when the following infinitive requires it.

Words related to this verb
Voglio mangiare perchè ho fame. I want to eat because I am hungry.
Cosa vuole Lei? What do you want?

vòlgere*

Ger. volgèndo   Past Part. vòlto

to turn, to direct

The Seven Simple Tenses		The Seven Compound Tenses	
Singular	Plural	Singular	Plural
1 present indicative		8 present perfect	
vòlgo	volgiamo	ho vòlto	abbiamo vòlto
vòlgi	volgete	hai vòlto	avete vòlto
vòlge	vòlgono	ha vòlto	hanno vòlto
2 imperfect indicative		9 past perfect	
volgevo	volgevamo	avevo vòlto	avevamo vòlto
volgevi	volgevate	avevi vòlto	avevate vòlto
volgeva	volgévano	aveva vòlto	avévano vòlto
3 past absolute		10 past anterior	
vòlsi	volgemmo	èbbi vòlto	avemmo vòlto
volgesti	volgeste	avesti vòlto	aveste vòlto
vòlse	vòlsero	èbbe vòlto	èbbero vòlto
4 future indicative		11 future perfect	
volgerò	volgeremo	avrò vòlto	avremo vòlto
volgerai	volgerete	avrai vòlto	avrete vòlto
volgerà	volgeranno	avrà vòlto	avranno vòlto
5 present conditional		12 past conditional	
volgerèi	volgeremmo	avrèi vòlto	avremmo vòlto
volgeresti	volgereste	avresti vòlto	avreste vòlto
volgerèbbe	volgerèbbero	avrèbbe vòlto	avrèbbero vòlto
6 present subjunctive		13 past subjunctive	
vòlga	volgiamo	àbbia vòlto	abbiamo vòlto
vòlga	volgiate	àbbia vòlto	abbiate vòlto
vòlga	vòlgano	àbbia vòlto	àbbiano vòlto
7 imperfect subjunctive		14 past perfect subjunctive	
volgessi	volgéssimo	avessi vòlto	avéssimo vòlto
volgessi	volgeste	avessi vòlto	aveste vòlto
volgesse	volgéssero	avesse vòlto	avéssero vòlto

	imperative	
—		volgiamo
	vòlgi (non vòlgere)	volgete
	vòlga	vòlgano

* Like *vòlgere* are *avvòlgere*, *capovòlgere*, *coinvòlgere*, *ravvòlgere*, *rivòlgersi*, *sconvòlgere*, *svòlgere*, etc.

Words related to this verb
Mi volsi a lui.   I turned toward him.
Lui si volge verso casa.   He turns homeward.

to limp

The Seven Simple Tenses		The Seven Compound Tenses	
Singular	Plural	Singular	Plural
1 present indicative		8 present perfect	
zòppico	zoppichiamo	ho zoppicato	abbiamo zoppicato
zòppichi	zoppicate	hai zoppicato	avete zoppicato
zòppica	zòppicano	ha zoppicato	hanno zoppicato
2 imperfect indicative		9 past perfect	
zoppicavo	zoppicavamo	avevo zoppicato	avevamo zoppicato
zoppicavi	zoppicavate	avevi zoppicato	avevate zoppicato
zoppicava	zoppicàvano	aveva zoppicato	avévano zoppicato
3 past absolute		10 past anterior	
zoppicai	zoppicammo	èbbi zoppicato	avemmo zoppicato
zoppicasti	zoppicaste	avesti zoppicato	aveste zoppicato
zoppicò	zoppicàrono	èbbe zoppicato	èbbero zoppicato
4 future indicative		11 future perfect	
zoppicherò	zoppicheremo	avrò zoppicato	avremo zoppicato
zoppicherai	zoppicherete	avrai zoppicato	avrete zoppicato
zoppicherà	zoppicheranno	avrà zoppicato	avranno zoppicato
5 present conditional		12 past conditional	
zoppicherèi	zoppicheremmo	avrèi zoppicato	avremmo zoppicato
zoppicheresti	zoppichereste	avresti zoppicato	avreste zoppicato
zoppicherèbbe	zoppicherèbbero	avrèbbe zoppicato	avrèbbero zoppicato
6 present subjunctive		13 past subjunctive	
zòppichi	zoppichiamo	àbbia zoppicato	abbiamo zoppicato
zòppichi	zoppichiate	àbbia zoppicato	abbiate zoppicato
zòppichi	zòppichino	àbbia zoppicato	àbbiano zoppicato
7 imperfect subjunctive		14 past perfect subjunctive	
zoppicassi	zoppicàssimo	avessi zoppicato	avéssimo zoppicato
zoppicassi	zoppicaste	avessi zoppicato	aveste zoppicato
zoppicasse	zoppicàssero	avesse zoppicato	avéssero zoppicato

	imperative	
—		zoppichiamo
zòppica (non zoppicare)		zoppicate
zòppichi		zòppichino

Words related to this verb
L'uomo zoppica. The man limps.
un ragionamento che zoppica a weak argument

The *to* of the English infinitive is omitted. Italian verbs are given in their normal form, without accents.

confuse **confondere**, 59
conquer **vincere**, 295
consist **consistere**, 61
construct **costruire**, 74
contain **contenere**, 63
contend **contendere**, 62;
  pretendere, 195
contract **contrarre**, 65
contradict **contraddire**, 64
convince **convincere**, 66
cook **cuocere**, 77
correct **correggere**, 68
correspond **corrispondere**, 71
corrupt **corrompere**, 70
cover **coprire**, 67
cross out **cancellare**, 42
crush **premere**, 190
cry **piangere**, 182
curse **maledire**, 149
cut a fine figure **comparire**, 51
cut a sorry figure **scomparire**,
  239

D

deceive **illudere**, 126
decide **decidere**, 79
deduce **inferire**, 134
defeat **sconfiggere**, 240
defend **difendere**, 82
delude **illudere**, 126
demand **domandare**, 104;
  pretendere, 195
depend **dipendere**, 85
depict **dipingere**, 86
descend **discendere**, 89; **scendere**,
  238
describe **descrivere**, 80
destroy **distruggere**, 98
detain **ritenere**, 227; **trattenere**,
  284
develop **svolgere**, 275
die **morire**, 156
diffuse **diffondere**, 83
direct **dirigere**, 88; **volgere**, 300
desire **desiderare**, 81
disappear **scomparire**, 239
discover **scoprire**, 241
discuss **discutere**, 92
displease **dispiacere**, 94
dispose **disporre**, 95
dispute **contendere**, 62
disappear **svanire**, 273
dissolve **dissolvere**, 91

distinguish **distinguere**, 96
distract **distrarre**, 97
distress **affliggere**, 9
divide **dividere**, 102
do **fare**, 113
do again **rifare**, 219
draw **trarre**, 283
draw up **redigere**, 211; **stendere**,
  267
dream **sognare**, 250
dress oneself **vestirsi**, 294
drink **bere (bevere)**, 37
dye **tingere**, 279

E

eat **mangiare**, 152
edit **redigere**, 211
elect **eleggere**, 107
emerge **emergere**, 108
endure **soffrire**, 249
enjoy **godere**, 124
enjoy oneself **divertirsi**, 101
entertain **trattenere**, 284
envelop **involgere**, 143
establish **stabilire**, 265
examine (*medical*) **visitare**, 296
excuse **scusare**, 244
exist **esistere**, 109
explain **spiegare**, 262
express **esprimere**, 110
extend **estendere**, 112; **stendere**,
  267
extinguish **spegnere (spengere)**,
  260

F

faint **svenire**, 274
fall **cadere**, 40
fall asleep **addormentarsi**, 7
fasten **figgere**, 115
feign **fingere**, 116
find **trovare**, 285
finish **finire**, 117
fix **figgere**, 115
fly **volare**, 298
follow **seguire**, 246
force **costringere**, 73
foresee **prevedere**, 197
forget **dimenticare**, 84
fry **friggere**, 119
fuse **fondere**, 118

live **abitare**, 2; **vivere**, 297
look **apparire**, 22
look at **guardare**, 125
look for **cercare**, 44
lose **perdere**, 178
lower **abbassare**, 1

M

maintain **mantenere**, 153
make **fare**, 113
make again **rifare**, 219
marry **sposare**, 264
may **potere**, 188
mean **intendere**, 137
meet **conoscere**, 60; **incontrare**, 132
melt **fondere**, 118
mistreat **maltrattare**, 150
mount **salire**, 234
move **commuovere**, 50; **muovere**, 158
must **bisognare**, 38; **dovere**, 106

N

notice **accorgersi (di)**, 6; **avvedersi**, 34

O

observe **osservare**, 168
obtain **ottenere**, 169
occupy **occupare**, 162
occur **accadere**, 3; **avvenire**, 35; **succedere**, 270
offend **offendere**, 163
offer **offrire**, 164; **porgere**, 184
omit **omettere**, 165
open **aprire**, 25
oppose **opporre**, 166
oppress **opprimere**, 167
ought **dovere**, 106
overwhelm **opprimere**, 167
owe **dovere**, 106

P

paint **dipingere**, 86
pass over in silence **tacere**, 276
pay **pagare**, 170
permit **permettere**, 179

perceive **avvedersi**, 34
persuade **persuadere**, 180
pick **cogliere**, 47
pinch **pungere**, 207
place **mettere**, 154; **porre**, 185
play **giocare**, 121; **suonare (sonare)**, 271
please **compiacere**, 52; **piacere**, 181
plunge **immergere**, 127
point at **indicare**, 133
portray **ritrarre**, 229
possess **possedere**, 187
pour out **spandere**, 258
precede **prevenire**, 198
predict **predire**, 189
prepare **apparecchiare**, 21; **preparare**, 192
present **presentare**, 193
preserve **mantenere**, 153
press **premere**, 190; **stringere**, 268
pretend **fingere**, 116
prevail **prevalere**, 196
prick **pungere**, 207
print **imprimere**, 130
produce **produrre**, 199
promise **promettere**, 200
promote **promuovere**, 201
pronounce **pronunziare**, 202
propose **proporre**, 203
protect **proteggere**, 204
provide **provvedere**, 205
pull **trarre**, 283
pull down **abbassare**, 1
push **spingere**, 263
put **mettere**, 154; **porre**, 185
put out **spegnere (spengere)**, 260

R

rain **piovere**, 183
raise **alzare**, 14
raze **radere**, 209
reach **raggiungere**, 210
read **leggere**, 148
receive **accogliere**, 5
recommend **raccomandare**, 208
reduce **ridurre**, 218
refer **alludere**, 13
reflect **reflettere**, 220
regret **rincrescere**, 222
rehire **riassumere**, 215
remain **rimanere**, 221
remove **togliere**, 280

unfold **svolgere,** 275
uphold **sostenere,** 255

V

vanish **svanire,** 273
visit **visitare,** 296

W

wait for **attendere,** 31
want **desiderare,** 81; **volere,** 299
walk **camminare,** 41; **passeggiare,**
174

warm up **riscaldere,** 224
wash **lavare,** 146
wash oneself **lavarsi,** 147
waste **perdere,** 178
watch **osservare,** 168
wear **portare,** 186
weep **piangere,** 183
weigh down **opprimere,** 167
welcome **accogliere,** 5
win **vincere,** 295
wish **desiderare,** 81
withdraw **ritrarre,** 229; **sottrarre,**
257
wrap up **involgere,** 143
wring **torcere,** 281
write **scrivere,** 242

Index of Irregular Verb Forms

Italian reflexive verbs are listed alphabetically under the first letter of the verb
itself and not under the reflexive pronouns.

A

abbi, *etc.* 18
àbbia, *etc.* 18
accesi, accese, accésero
4
acceso 4
accòlsi, accòlse,
accòlsero 5
accòlto 5
mi accòrsi, si accòrse,
si accòrsero 6
accòrtosi 6
afflissi, afflisse,
afflíssero 9
afflitto 9
aggiunsi, aggiunse,
aggiúnsero 11
aggiunto 11
ammesso 16
ammisi, ammise,
ammísero 16
andrèi, *etc.* 17
andrò, *etc.* 17
me ne andrèi, *etc.* 18
me ne andrò, *etc.* 18
apèrsi, apèrse, apèrsero
12
apèrto 25
appaia, appàiano 22

appaia, appàiano
(*Imperative*) 22
apparso 22
appartènga,
appartèngano 23
appartèngo, appartièni,
appartiène,
appartèngono 23
appartenni, appartenne,
apparténnero 23
apparterrèi, *etc.* 23
apparterrò, *etc.* 23
appartièni, appartènga,
appartèngano
(*Imperative*) 23
apparvi, apparve,
appàrvero 22
apprèsi, apprese,
apprésero 24
appreso 24
arsi, arse, àrsero 26
arso 26
assalga, assàlgano 29
assalga, assàlgano
(*Imperative*) 29
assalgo, assàlgono
29
assistito 30
assunsi, assunse,
assúnsero 31
assunto 31

attesi, attese, attésero
32
atteso 32
avrèi, *etc.* 33
avrò, *etc.* 33
avvènga, avvengano
35
avvenne, avvénnero
35
avverrà, avverranno
35
avverrèbbe,
avverrèbbero 35
avvenuto 35
avviène, avvèngono
35

B

benedetto 36
benedica, *etc.* 36
benedicèndo 36
benedicessi, *etc.* 36
benedicevo, *etc.* 36
benedici, benedica,
benediciamo,
benedícano
(*Imperative*) 36
benedico, benedici,
benedice,

D

da', dia, díano
(*Imperative*) 78
dai, dà, danno 78
darèi, *etc.* 78
darò, *etc.* 78
decisi, decise, decísero
79
deciso 79
descrissi, descrisse,
descríssero 80
descritto 80
dessi, *etc.* 78
detto 87
deva (debba), *etc.*
106
devo (debbo), devi,
deve, dobbiamo,
dévono (débbono)
106
di', dica, diciamo,
dícano (*Imperative*)
87
dia, díano 78
dica, *etc.* 87
dicèndo 87
dicessi, *etc.* 87
dicevo, *etc.* 87
dico, dici, dice,
diciamo, dícono
87
dièdi (dètti), *etc.* 78
difesi, difese, difésero
82
difeso 82
diffusi, diffuse,
diffúsero 83
diffuso 83
dipesi, dipese, dipésero
85
dipeso 85
dipinsi, dipinse,
dipínsero 86
dipinto 86
dirèssi, dirèsse,
dirèssero 88
dirètto 88
discorsi, discorse,
discórsero 90
discorso 90
discussi, discusse,
discússero 92

discusso 92
disfa', disfaccia,
disfacciamo,
disfàcciano
(*Imperative*) 93
disfaccia, *etc.* 93
disfaccio (disfò), disfai,
disfà, disfacciamo,
disfanno 93
disfacèndo 93
disfacessi, *etc.* 93
disfacevo, *etc.* 93
disfatto 93
disfeci, *etc.* 93
dispiaccia, *etc.* 94
dispiaccia,
dispiacciamo,
dispiàcciano
(*Imperative*) 94
dispiaccio
dispiacciamo,
dispiàcciono 94
dispiacqui, dispiacque,
dispiàcquero 94
disponèndo 95
disponessi, *etc.* 95
disponevo, *etc.* 95
disponga, *etc.* 95
dispongo, *etc.* 95
disponi, *etc.*
(*Imperative*) 95
disposi, *etc.* 95
disposto 95
dissi, *etc.* 87
distinsi, distinse,
distínsero 96
distinto 96
distraèndo 97
distraessi, *etc.* 97
distraevo, *etc.* 97
distragga, *etc.* 97
distraggo, *etc.* 97
distrai, *etc.* (*Imperative*)
97
distrassi, *etc.* 97
distratto 97
distrussi, distrusse,
distrússero 98
distrutto 98
divènga, divèngano
99
divèngo, divièni,
divIène, divèngono
99

divenni, divenne,
divénnero 99
divenuto 99
diverrèi, *etc.* 99
diverrò, *etc.* 99
divièni, divènga,
divèngano
(*Imperative*) 99
divisi, divise, divísero
102
diviso 102
dòlga, dòlgano 103
dòlgo, duòli, duòle,
dogliamo, dòlgono
103
dòlsi, dòlse, dòlsero
103
dorrèi, *etc.* 103
dorrò, *etc.* 103
dovrèi, *etc.* 106
dovrò, *etc.* 106
duòli, dòlga, dogliamo,
dòlgano (*Imperative*)
103

E

èbbi, èbbe, èbbero 33
elèssi, elèsse, elèssero
107
elètto 107
emèrsi, emèrse,
emèrsero 108
emèrso 108
èro, *etc.* 111
èsca, èscano 289
èsci, èsca, èscano
(*Imperative*) 289
èsco, èsci, èsce, èscono
289
esprèssi, esprèsse,
esprèssero 110
esprèsso 110
estesi, estese, estésero
112
esteso 112

F

fa', faccia, facciamo,
fàcciano (*Imperative*)
113

Index of Over 1,000 Italian Verbs Conjugated Like the Model Verbs

The number after each verb is the page number in this book where a model verb is shown fully conjugated.